My Life with Janáček
THE MEMOIRS OF
ZDENKA JANÁČKOVÁ

My Life with Janáček

THE MEMOIRS OF
ZDENKA JANÁČKOVÁ

edited and translated by

John Tyrrell

faber and faber
LONDON · BOSTON

First published in 1998
by Faber and Faber Limited
3 Queen Square London WC1N 3AU

Photoset by Parker Typesetting Service, Leicester
Printed in England by Clays Ltd, St Ives plc

A CIP record for this book
is available from the British Library
ISBN 0–571–17540–6

2 4 6 8 10 9 7 5 3 1

TO
JIM FRIEDMAN
ROSEMARY WILLIAMSON
AND PHILIP WELLER

Contents

List of plates

Introduction

There are not many instances of a composer's wife writing her memoirs. Cosima Wagner's diaries are the best-known contender for a document of this sort, but it must be remembered that her years with Wagner formed only part of Wagner's creative life – Cosima was his second wife. The case of the Czech composer Leoš Janáček and his wife Zdenka is thus all the more remarkable in that Zdenka knew her future husband from the very beginning of his career, when she was twelve and he was twenty-three, and, despite all the difficulties in their relationship, they lived together until his death over fifty years later. Unlike Cosima's hero-worshipping account of her husband, Zdenka had few illusions about hers; there is no intent to gloss over Janáček's less attractive features. Quite the reverse. One might have imagined that such a frank memoir, written just a few years after Janáček died and running to over 120,000 words, would be a key source, familiar to all those interested in Janáček.

This, however, is not the case. It is clear that portions of Vladimír Helfert's unfinished Janáček biography of 1939 – he completed one volume out of a projected four or five – and the standard one-volume life and works by Jaroslav Vogel (issued first in German in 1958) rely to some extent on Mrs Janáčková's memoirs. Occasionally they are cited in the footnotes of both books, and the title finds its way into Vogel's bibliography. But, at least until recently, any researcher attempting to consult the manuscript at the Janáček archive in Brno would have received the same discouraging answers that I did twenty years ago. The manuscript, if it was there then, was not available for study.

A few years ago I had a surprising enquiry from an English antiquarian dealer in books on music. Could I tell them anything about Mrs Janáčková's memoirs? They had a copy. The 236-page typescript was in my possession a few weeks later. It was a carbon copy, and thus not necessarily the only one, written in Czech and entitled 'Zdenka Janáčková: Můj život' [My life]. It was bound as a book and contained ten titled chapters and an epilogue, all in Mrs Janáčková's first-person narrative. This was topped and tailed with an introduction and an afterword dated January 1939 and signed by 'Marie Trkanová'.

Marie Trkanová (1893–1974) was born in Vienna but educated in Brno, where she lived for the rest of her life. Her first husband died in 1914, and in 1920 she married Josef Trkan (1897–1941), violist of the Moravian Quartet. From 1920 to 1923 she served as secretary at the Brno Conservatory, where she came into contact with both Janáček and his wife since their home had been built in the grounds of the conservatory. Janáček died in 1928 at the age of seventy-four; his widow Zdenka continued to live on in the house. In her introduction, Mrs Trkanová described how Zdenka's memoirs had come about. Offering Zdenka her condolences, Trkanová realized that Janáček's widow needed help with all the correspondence that now came her way in her dealings with Janáček's estate and with the considerable interest his music was now arousing. She offered her services as an unpaid, unofficial secretary and for several years she visited Mrs Janáčková several times a week for this purpose. Some matters needed more detailed explanations and Trkanová was struck by the depth of Mrs Janáčková's knowledge of her husband's life and works. The more she learnt, the more sympathetic she found herself to Mrs Janáčková's situation.

Janáček's career as a composer took off only in the final decade of his life, when he was well into his sixties. This period overlapped with his fervent, though platonic, affair with Mrs Kamila Stösslová, thirty-seven years his junior and the wife of an antiques dealer in Bohemia. As Trkanová explains in her introduction, the Czech musical world was divided into those who condemned Janáček's uninhibited enthusiasm for the wife of another man and those who applauded his zest for life at an advanced age, something which seemed to tie in with his astonishing late artistic flowering. For the latter group the figure of Zdenka, limited by background and character in her understanding of what her husband was achieving, was simply a foolish and jealous old woman, whose views were of no interest. But there were those who, like Trkanová, saw her as a much maligned and loyal wife who, despite extraordinary provocation, provided Janáček with regular meals and a stable, well-run home environment and the security from which he could devote himself entirely to composition. As she relates, Trkanová felt that Zdenka Janáčková's story needed to be heard and thus suggested that she write her memoirs.

Zdenka was reluctant. Memoirs were only for important people, she contended, but Trkanová was persistent and Zdenka began telling her about her childhood. After a few sessions, however, she sent a message that she did not wish to continue, since it would mean 'speaking the truth' about Janáček. Trkanová did not entirely abandon the project. She continued to visit in her capacity as secretary and would occasionally ask questions designed to elicit more information. Thus Zdenka would start talking, and Trkanová would take down what she said. Zdenka apparently looked on all this with some scepticism but nevertheless co-operated. In this way, during the four years up to the end of 1932, Trkanová assembled a large collection of random notes.

Then, as she relates, on 1 January 1933 she was visited unexpectedly by Zdenka in great excitement. Upset by memories from five years earlier, the last New Year's Day of Janáček's life, in which the Kamila Stösslová affair was coming to a head, Zdenka had taken a decision. She and Trkanová would write her memoirs and she would hold nothing back, so that those who came after would be able to make up their own minds. From then on the two women had regular sessions, and Zdenka began systematically talking about her life with the composer.

Many hours were spent in this way and, after almost two and a half years, in May 1935 and on the eve of Zdenka's seventieth birthday, the memoirs were complete. A year later, in the summer of 1936, Trkanová read through them and slightly revised them with the thought that she might be able to publish some of them. She gave the manuscript to Zdenka to read again. And, as she reports, Zdenka would say after each chapter: 'Yes, it was like that' or 'How well you understand me!' In the autumn of that year, Zdenka's health deteriorated and she died of cancer of the liver on 17 February 1937.

At the end of Trkanová's introduction she writes the following:

Finally I'd like to point out that from the beginning both of us were aware that because of their intimate character the memoirs would perhaps never appear as a book, that they would remain simply as study material for those dealing in detail with Janáček.

Fittingly the typescript soon found itself in the hands of Professor Vladimír Helfert, the leading Janáček scholar of his day, who was then engaged in writing a biography. He published one volume (Janáček's life up to 1887) in 1939 with a dedication to the memory of Zdenka Janáčková. Then the war intervened and Helfert, as a prominent Czech intellectual, was interned. He died in 1945 shortly after his release from concentration camp, with no further volumes written.

Even a cursory reading of the manuscript made me realize that it was the source of much attributed, and sometimes unattributed, information in Helfert's and Vogel's biographies. I made a copy for my own research, intending to give the original to the Janáček archive in Brno. But when I announced this plan I was told the archive did have a copy after all, two in fact. I now had access to them and found that one (A)[1] was the top copy of my carbon copy although, unlike my copy, it had many pages missing. The other (B)[2] had been retyped, the page breaks falling in different places. The contents of B were identical with those of A apart from minor editorial interventions (usually cuts), some of which had been indicated in pencil in A. In other words A (and my carbon copy of it) was the original; B was a tightened-up revision. Although the copies in the Janáček archive had apparently been acquired with the condition that they should not be published, this did not apply to the copy I owned, and I made it available to the Brno musical periodical *Opus musicum*, which serialized an abridged version.

Not all of the many facts and insights contained in Mrs Janáčková's memoirs are new. Some information had already appeared in Helfert, Vogel and in Svatava Přibáňová's short biography (1984). Furthermore, some material had also appeared in the memoirs of the Janáčeks' maid, Marie Stejskalová. This remarkable woman joined the Janáček household in 1894 and remained with Janáčková until her death in 1937. Her memoirs appeared in Prague in 1959 (revised edition 1964) under the following title: Marie Trkanová: *U Janáčků: podle vyprávění Marie Stejskalové* [At the Janáčeks: as told by Marie Stejskalová]. So in fact the same Mrs Marie Trkanová who in the 1930s worked with Janáčková on her memoirs had, twenty years later, worked with the Janáčeks' servant to compile her memoirs, now published under Trkanová's name. From a comparison of the two sources it is clear that Trkanová had access to her earlier venture with Janáčková when she drafted the maid's memoirs.

As is clear from the extracts opposite, Stejskalová adds her own gloss, or her own detail, but much of the time it looks suspiciously like Janáčková's memoirs recycled, with 'I' turned into 'the mistress' and 'Leoš' turned into 'the master'. There was some justification in this since Stejskalová and Janáčková were thrown together a great deal,

1 BmJA, D 450 LJ; there is a museum acquisition date of 15.11.1982.
2 BmJA, D 455 LJ. According to the front cover this version belonged to Professor Bohumír Štědroň. The title is in his handwriting and is dated '10.7.76'.

Zdenka Janáčková: *Můj život* [My Life] (*c*1935), Chapter 5

In the afternoon we all sat by her. My husband had then just finished *Jenůfa*. During the whole time he was composing it, Olga took a huge interest in it. And my husband also used to say later that his basic model for *Jenůfa* was his sick daughter. Now Olga asked him: 'Daddy, play me *Jenůfa*, I won't live to hear it.'

Leoš sat down at the piano and played . . . I couldn't bear it and ran off again to the kitchen.

A terrible night again. . . .

Things were bad there, very bad. Olga screamed: 'Daddy, Daddy, go off again to that miracle doctor. Let him give me something to bear this torment.'

So my husband went off again bringing this person with him at once. I don't know what they said together, what he again advised us, I wasn't capable of taking it in, I knew that this mountebank wouldn't help where God didn't want to.

In the afternoon Olga became a little quieter. She asked me and my husband: 'Daddy, Mamička, can I do what I want with my things?'

Of course she could. When my husband had to go off to school, she called Mářa and me to her. She said that she wanted to make her will. She ordered Mářa to write, I couldn't do so for crying.

Marie Trkanová: *U Janáčků: podle vyprávění Marie Stejskalové* [At the Janáčeks: as told by Marie Stejskalová] (Prague, 1959), Chapter 3

In the afternoon [Olga] was quite well. We all sat at her bed. During that time the master was just finishing *Jenůfa*. The whole time he was composing it he had to tell Oluška about it, she knew it well. Now she asked:

'Daddy, play me *Jenůfa*, I won't live to hear your opera in the theatre.'

The master sat and played. If Oluška had asked him to have his hand cut off, so that it would relieve her for a moment, he would have done so at once. When the mistress heard the beginning of *Jenůfa*, she clasped her head and ran out into the kitchen so as not to burst out crying in front of Oluška. The latter lay there peacefully, and without moving listened through the whole opera. The master's hands were trembling, he was deathly pale, but he kept going until the end. When he got up from the piano, Oluška said to him:

'It's beautiful, what a pity I won't see it.'

We sat by her long into the night. And in the morning she was very bad again. She cried out with pain: 'Daddy, Daddy, go off again for that miracle doctor. Let him give me something to bear this.'

The master went off and brought the doctor, the latter gave Miss Olga some pills.

They worked so well that she calmed down after midday. She asked:

'Daddy, Mamuška, can I do what I want with my things?'

They told her she could.

'Mářa, have you got a moment? Take some paper and write what I'm giving to whom.'

and the maid took the part of the mistress in any dispute. The areas of overlap are, however, limited to certain chapters. In terms of the ten chapters of Janáčková's memoirs, Stejskalová arrived as servant to the Janáček household near the beginning of Chapter 5. Thus the first four chapters of Janáčková's memoirs (concerning her upbringing, her first acquaintance with Janáček as his piano pupil, their courtship,

marriage, birth of first child and temporary separation), all took place
before Stejskalová arrived and could not form any directly reported
part of her narrative.

One of the remarkable features of Janáčková's account is her
frankness in sexual matters. She is open about Janáček's lady-friends
and mistresses and about her own sexual relations with Janáček.
Although it is clear that Janáčková shared many of her secrets with her
maid, such material could not appear quite so easily in the maid's
account, and was certainly not deemed suitable for publication in the
straitlaced Communist 1950s. Thus the maid's account is a far more
humdrum and sanitized version which omits, for instance, all the
events recounted in one of Janáčková's longest chapters – Chapter 7,
some 18,000 words devoted to Janáček's torrid affair with the singer
Gabriela Horvátová, Janáčková's subsequent suicide attempt and the
Janáčeks' informal divorce settlement after which they lived in the
same house, but which left Janáček free to pursue his own amatory
affairs.

The typescript is entitled 'Zdenka Janáčková: My Life' but Mrs
Janáčková's part is not authenticated by any handwritten signature, at
least in any of the typescripts I have examined. Although Trkanová
asserts that it was read by Janáčková at least twice, and had her
approval, we have only Trkanová's word for this.

There is, however, no case for doubting its authenticity. Trkanová's
connections with Janáčková were well known in Brno society. The
memoir was clearly regarded as authentic by Professor Helfert, who
knew all three players: Janáček, his wife and Trkanová. Helfert was a
fine and scrupulous scholar and he had no qualms in quoting this
source and acknowledging it. We are dealing then, with an attested
collaboration, though the extent of Janáčková's part in it is unclear.
From her introduction we know that Trkanová was unimpressed by
Janáčková's powers of expression. Trkanová's account of how she
worked with Janáčková is revealing:

I typed out her narration immediately and then reworked it into coherent
chapters. At first I thought that this would be the most authentic and thus also the
best way simply to write down what she dictated. But soon I saw that it wasn't
possible. Mrs Janáčková had been educated in German and this was often very
evident in her Czech [. . .] She tried to speak properly but perhaps for this very
reason it had the effect that much in her speech was flat, cold, uninvolved. [. . .]
Often she didn't find an adequate Czech expression.

In the end Trkanová hit on the method of trying to put herself in

Janáčková's place and then narrating her story in her own words. This is much more dangerous territory. It is not clear how much was added or lost when Trkanová attempted to retell Janáčková's story.

There are few independent examples of Janáčková's narrative style. Most of her surviving letters are brief greetings with little personality showing through and none of them deal with the dramatic events depicted so vividly in her purported memoirs. The only exception is the late flowering of her correspondence with Joža Janáčková, the widow of a cousin of Leoš Janáček. Zdenka wrote to Joža in German and her prose is much more fluent and uninhibited. Most of the events depicted in Chapter 10 are corroborated in her regular bulletins to Joža in Prague. And so is the personal voice. In these letters Janáčková's anger over the Stösslová affair boils over; in her memoirs her attitude to the Stössels has clearly been somewhat toned down for the purposes of a more permanent document. But on the basis of a comparison of these letters with Trkanová's version it is the same voice that comes through.

The quality of any such collaboration will depend upon the amount of access the writer has to the memoirist, their rapport, and the extent of their acquaintance. Here Trkanová was in an exceptionally strong position, doing business with Janáčková on a regular basis for several years before embarking on the project. The period of serious writing itself took over two and a half years. Again, we have mainly Trkanová's word for it, but the timescale is plausible and her account convincing.[3]

Although the book did not appear in Janáčková's lifetime, when its publication would have constituted a type of authentication, one could argue that the fact of its publication at second hand during the lifetime of the loyal servant Marie Stejskalová provides a more limited type of authentication, confirming Zdenka's own information or amplifying it in some way.

And there are other, more objective tests which one can apply to the narrative. Much of the factual information provided can be precisely dated by reference to Janáček's correspondence. This correspondence would not have been accessible to Trkanová and thus provides an independent corroboration of Janáčková's involvement and the veracity of her account. Some of it is of course uncontroversial, but in

3 We have also Stejskalová's word, copied from her diary: writing the memoirs began on 27 December 1932 and ended on 28 December 1934 (Trkanová 1964, 169, fn.27). These dates are slightly different from the ones that Trkanová herself supplied; see above.

the case of Janáček's affair with Gabriela Horvátová, the events described provide a convincing context for the surviving correspondence between Janáček and the predatory singer.

Many of the specific facts that Janáčková mentions concerning Janáček, herself and Kamila Stösslová can be verified in this way – a particularly persuasive source since Janáček's letters to Stösslová remained inaccessible to everyone except the Stössel family until November 1939: that is, two years after Janáčková's death and almost a year after Trkanová dated her epilogue. Even after the acquisition of the letters by Masaryk University in Brno these letters remained closed to scholars until Svatava Přibáňová's complete edition in Czech (*Hádanka života*, 1990), and my English edition (*Intimate Letters*, 1994).

There is yet another source of verification. At virtually the same time that Trkanová was working with Janáčková on her memoirs, Janáčková was visited by Robert Smetana, whom she knew from their trip to Hukvaldy to collect Janáček's manuscripts (see p.240). In 1933, the first year of Janáčková's regular sessions with Trkanová, Smetana published several substantial articles based on Janáčková's reminiscences 'which she had willingly described during several visits' (Smetana 1948, 132).[4] Unlike Trkanová's redaction, these reminiscences appeared during Janáčková's lifetime and were later absorbed into his book *Vyprávění o Leoši Janáčkovi* [Stories about Janáček] (1948). A final source of verification of one crucial incident should be mentioned, a handwritten note by Professor Helfert, dated 27 September 1935,[5] in which he described a visit to Janáčková, during which she divulged to him details of her separation from Janáček in 1883 (see Chapter 3). Helfert's account is essentially a précis of the much fuller account given in these memoirs.

The present book represents Zdenka Janáčková's memoirs drawn from the two principal sources, those compiled by Trkanová and those compiled by Smetana. They have been amplified by reference to Trkanová's edition of Stejskalová's memoirs, of which Trkanová's excellent and detailed notes have been an exceptionally useful source of information in identifying personalia and places. Janáček's correspondence and other sources in the Music History Division of the Moravian Regional Museum have been drawn on to provide

4 According to Stejskalová (Trkanová 1964, 125), she also took part in these sessions.
5 BmJA, D 78.

corroboration or correction and, in particular, dating. I have kept to the shape and to the chapter division and headings used by Trkanová, with Smetana's version or my own commentary interleaved. Today we have a fuller picture of some events than was available to Trkanová and I have not hesitated occasionally to interrupt the narrative and provide more context and explanation. Similarly Chapter 6 is much expanded, since Janáčková seems to have said little to Trkanová about the holiday trip to Croatia, a topic on which, on the other hand, she was particularly forthcoming to Smetana. I have used his account to flesh out this episode.

Mrs Janáčková's memoirs provide a fascinating insider's account of Janáček's domestic life over a very long period. It is a compelling document in its own right, written unashamedly to tell her side of the story, and it is startlingly frank. It paints a fascinating picture of the changing times during which the composer lived with its woman-in-the street's perspective of the First World War and the break-up of the Austro-Hungarian Empire. Although I have not included Trkanová's introduction and epilogue, or indeed Janáčková's account of her life in the years after Janáček's death, I have presented the memoirs almost complete. In the later part of the book (Chapters 8–10), when Janáček's fame led to a more public profile and foreign travel for them both, Janáčková's comments shade into more generalized travelogue descriptions which I have cut where they seemed of less interest. The same goes for a few overlong reflections on life. I have also cut repetitive passages, over-detailed comments about Janáčková's furniture and so on. All cuts are signalled thus: [. . .].

Since Janáčková's style has been refracted through its stylization by Trkanová I have not felt it necessary always to preserve the sentence and paragraph construction. I have also not preserved Janáčková's formal way of referring to some of her friends and acquaintances. She uses, for instance, the familiar contemporary Austrian and Czech style of referring to married women by their husbands' professions. Her friend Mrs Váchová is usually referred to as 'paní radová Váchová', a styling that emphasizes that Váchová is the wife of Judge Vácha and that the latter has achieved the rank of 'rada'. I have occasionally left in 'the judge's wife' to help place the lady, but have avoided unidiomatic formulations such as Mrs Judge Vácha or Mrs Law Councillor Vácha. Modern Czech prefers to spell Mrs Janáčková's first name as 'Zdeňka'. I have, however, retained the form 'Zdenka', with which she signed her letters, and which Janáček and everyone else called her.

I have tried to identify all the people and places mentioned in the narrative. Those that occur more frequently are gathered up into a Glossary; others are dealt with in the footnotes. When dating events I have made use without special comment of Bohumír Štědroň's calendar (1939) of Janáček's stays in Luhačovice, of my own 'Diary of Meetings' (*IL*) and of dates that can be inferred from Janáček's published correspondence with Kamila Stösslová. For other dates I provide evidence as appropriate. Since this is a document more about Janáček's life than about his music I have generally not thought it necessary to fill out references to Janáček's compositions in the same way. I have, however, identified works by references to the catalogue numbers used in *Janáček's Works* (Simeone, Tyrrell and Němcová, 1997).

Acknowledgements

The early stages of work on the book were completed during my period as a British Academy Research Reader in the Humanities and I acknowledge the Academy's help with gratitude. Jitka Bajgarová, head of the Music History Division of the Moravian Regional Museum, allowed me access to the Janáček Archive in Brno on many visits and, with her staff, made these visits both productive and pleasurable. References to unpublished letters and other sources in the archive are shown with the sigillum BmJA. All the photographic material used in the book is from the fine picture collection assembled in the Museum and is reprinted with its kind permission. The typescript of Zdenka Janáčková's memoirs, however, comes from a different source: without John May (of May and May) this book would not have been possible.

It is my pleasure to thank the following friends and colleagues for their help: Svatava Přibáňová and Jarmila Procházková, Brno, for their specialist knowledge of Janáček; Eva Drlíková, Brno, for help on local Brno history and many other matters; Vojtěch Kyas, Brno, for advice on nineteenth-century Brno; Nigel Simeone, Cambridge and Nottingham, for wide-ranging expertise; Brad Robinson, Munich, for checking my translations from the German; Heinz Stolba, Vienna, for help on local Viennese vocabulary. Richard Klos, Prague, advised me on legal matters. Milena Flodrová, Brno, put her unrivalled knowledge of Brno local history at my disposal; her help is evident in many footnotes. Stephen Lock, formerly Editor of *The British Medical Journal*, read the manuscript and made many comments and suggestions which I have gratefully incorporated in the text and footnotes; his view of Olga's final illness provides the first appendix. Once again Jana Kuchtová, Brno, checked my translation from the Czech and contributed most ably and imaginatively to the final English version. Ruth Thackeray and Ingrid Grimes helped put the manuscript into a final form. Audrey Twine read the proofs.

Without the interest and continued support of three friends, Jim Friedman, Rosemary Williamson and Philip Weller, I would never have begun or completed this project. They read through the entire manuscript and made countless suggestions for its improvement. It is to them that the book is affectionately dedicated.

John Tyrrell
Nottingham, 17 November 1997

I
Childhood

Painfully, I have to admit to myself that only my childhood was a time of brightness and well-being in my life.

I was born in Olomouc on 30 July 1865. My father, Emilian Schulz [1836–1923], was a teacher at the upper Realschule[1] there. In 1871 he was transferred to the German Realschule in Kroměříž. Although I was then only six years old, I have pleasant memories of that stay. In my thoughts the archbishop's park,[2] with its poultry farm, pheasantry, goldfish in greenish basins with garlands of flowering water-lilies, retains the charm of a lost paradise. I think that my parents, too, remembered the cheerful social life of Kroměříž with pleasure. But the very next year my father became director of the 'Imperial and Royal Czech Institute for the Education of Teachers', at the time the official title of the Men Teachers' Institute in Brno. I was the only child of young parents. As a family we had a happy life together at home even though Father was a Czech – the son of the doctor to the gentry in Obříství near Mělník – and Mama[3] was of German origin: her father, Gustav Kaluschka, was the private secretary of the Archbishop of Breslau.[4] Papa was uncommonly good-natured and cheerful. From the early morning he'd sing or whistle Czech folksongs to himself. All that was needed for his contentment was a pipe, a visit to the café and occasionally a hunt. He was very popular with his students.

Zdenka's account to Robert Smetana[5] of her father, while not neglecting to mention his smoking (a cigar here rather than a pipe) and his drinking, emphasizes his good-hearted nature even more. She describes him attending each morning to his collection of creatures, including an owl and a squirrel, before going up to the

---

1 A type of secondary school which, instead of the Classical languages taught at a Gymnasium, concentrated on science. As at almost all of the schools in Bohemia and Moravia at that time, the language of instruction at the Olomouc Realschule was in German.
2 Olomouc was the seat of the Archbishop of Moravia, in Beethoven's time still a Prince-Bishopric. His estates included a palace in Kroměříž. Together with the capital Brno, Olomouc and Kroměříž were the largest and culturally most important towns in Moravia until overtaken by the industrial complex of Ostrava. See also Glossary: 'archbishop's estate'.
3 Anna Schulzová, née Kaluschka (1840–1918).
4 Now Wrocław in Poland.
5 See Introduction.

office, and mentions his good relations with his students. 'To the whole institute of which he was director, he was a kind and benevolent father, helping people on first acquaintance and if necessary even paying for students' accommodation. He used to have his name-day on 11 October. This used to be a holiday at his institutes.'[6]

Mama was stricter. I know that she loved me very much, but she didn't allow me to get away with anything. Beautiful, slim, elegant, with strict moral principles, she lived only for her household which she ran simply and frugally. She brought me up in this way too.

According to family traditions the Kaluschkas were originally Poles who had emigrated to France (though how they then got to Silesia was not stated). Anna Kaluschka spent her childhood in Johannisberk (now Janský Vrch) near Javorník in Silesia, developing into a type of 'strict, energetic and frugal townswoman who always cared about the social position of her husband.'[7] From Olomouc she knew some Czech but disliked speaking it, and her daughter Zdenka was brought up in German. Zdenka's emphasis on the linguistic differences between her parents was an important one for the unfolding of her story. It should be remembered that at the time, more German was spoken in Moravian towns such as Olomouc, Kroměříž and Brno than was the case in Prague.[8] Nevertheless, as Zdenka maintained to Smetana, Schulz got on 'splendidly with his strict and frugal wife', taking life lightly, letting her have her way without being under her thumb.[9]

I remember clearly what it was like in our first Brno flat in Pekařská ulice no.37, on the second floor. At the time there was no tied accommodation for the director of the Teachers' Institute because the school didn't have its own building and was housed partly in the Minorite monastery, partly in hired rooms in the neighbouring houses. Only later [1878] was the present Teachers' Institute erected in Old Brno.[10] In Pekařská ulice we had a four-room flat with a view on to the Špilberk.[11] I liked looking at how the hillside changed colour according to the time of day and year; with curiosity I'd watch the mysterious, gloomy fortress which crowned it, grey and heavy; I was intrigued by the activity in the street below. But I was allowed to see this only through closed windows. For our windows didn't open out, the lower half merely moved up and down – something most unusual[12]

6 Smetana 1948, 1, 20–2.
7 Smetana 1948, 22.
8 In 1880, for instance, 65% of Olomouc's population spoke German in contrast to 18% in Prague (*Ottův slovník naučný*: 'Olomouc', 'Praha: statistika').
9 Smetana 1948, 22–3.
10 Staré Brno, a district of Brno. It was a predominantly Czech-speaking part of the city.
11 Or Spielberg (German): a hill in Brno with a fortified castle at the top. The medieval royal castle was a notorious Habsburg prison from 1621 until 1862, when the buildings were turned into barracks and the slopes beneath made into a public park.
12 Sash windows are uncommon in the region.

– and the shifted frame was held on springs. For some reason, however, the springs worked badly: when we raised the window so as to let fresh air into the room, it fell down every now and then with a bang. How many times Mother chased me away fearing that I'd be guillotined by the heavy frame! But I was drawn to the windows again and again because for me it was almost my only contact with the outside world. I didn't have any friends with whom I could have played; in my free time I was almost always alone. Most of all I liked to sit in the big room which was called the 'Klavierzimmer' because a piano[13] stood between the windows. There were several cabinets there, a chest of drawers – called a 'Schubladkasten'[14] – and a bookshelf. Beneath it I had my toys. But as early as my tenth year the books on the shelf began to interest me more than the dolls beneath it. And because Mama strictly forbade me to take books from the shelf, I did it like this: I sat down to the toys, I dressed the dolls, I clinked the toy kitchen-set, I tidied the toy furniture – but only as long as Mama was on the horizon. No sooner had she gone out of the door than I pulled out one of the books. It was a real treasure-trove for my taste at the time: Marlitt, Carlén, Schwartz,[15] authors whom I devoured, curled up in the corner with the toys all around me. The books were in German. My whole upbringing was German. I spoke Czech only with the servant. It seemed a matter of course to Mama that she should bring me up in her native German (besides which she spoke Czech very poorly), and Papa gave way to her. At the time this wasn't anything unusual in Brno. And so something happened that today everyone would think very strange: the director of an institute for the education of Czech teachers would teach his daughter in German, and even his Czech colleagues would teach her in German. For I didn't go to school, I had lessons at home.[16] For the time and for my age I had a very painstaking education: Papa taught me history, geography, physics and German grammar. I didn't get on well with the last and Father got angry with me so many times that he decided to hand over this unfortunate subject to the teacher Mr Lhotský[17] from the institute's

13 The Schulz family had a 'nice Bachmann' piano (Smetana 1948, 24).
14 An Austrian expression; the normal German word is Kommode.
15 All three were popular novelists of the time: E. Marlitt was the pseudonym of Eugenie John (1825–87), a German. Emilie Carlén (1807–92) and Marie Sophie Schwartz (1819–94) were both Swedish. Zdenka would have read the last two in German translations, of which many were made.
16 According to Smetana (1948, 22), Zdenka's education at home was on account of her health, though there is no indication that she was at all sickly as a child.
17 Josef Lhotský (1839–1924).

practice school,[18] who was already teaching me arithmetic and writing. He didn't complain about me, he was pleased with me, as was Father Ruprecht[19] in religion. For needlework, my favourite subject, I went as an external pupil to the teacher Miss Waltrová[20] in the Women Teachers' Institute. I played the piano from about my eighth year. I was taught by Professor Vorel[21] from the institute. I loved practising and made rapid progress.

Even in the holidays I always had something to do. We didn't go away anywhere in summer. Only once when I had whooping cough and the doctor recommended a change of air, Father took me off for the holidays to my grandfather[22] in Obříství. I was about eleven at the time. On the way we stopped in Prague. I saw it for the first time and it seemed to me like an enchanted mirage.

When I was at home I got up at six in the morning, I said my prayers and got dressed. Last thing every night I'd carefully fold all my clothes near the bed. Mama was particularly concerned that I should be careful with my things. Then I saw to the canaries and helped with the cleaning and the cooking. At home we cooked simply: beef with sauce and dumplings, plenty of vegetables especially carrots, pulses, *buchty*[23] on Friday. We hardly ever had fancy pastries. And, sticking to this diet, both my parents reached a very great age. In our family there was a similar plainness in dress too. Mama dressed me in particular very simply. At home I always had to protect my clothes with an apron. Once I wanted very much to have a black velvet dress. It seemed to me then the height of beauty. How I used to long for it in vain! Until it was eventually given to me for Christmas, lined with muskrat and a cap of the same material to go with it. These were the only fancy clothes I ever had during my entire childhood.

At our house there was an atmosphere of love and peace, without

18 A type of single-grade school attached to teacher-training institutes at the time to provide teaching practice for the trainees.
19 See Glossary.
20 Antonie Waltrová (1844–1908), needlework teacher at the Women Teachers' Institute in Brno, an expert on and collector of folk embroidery.
21 Antonín Vorel (1843–1925), lecturer at the Men's Institute, later a school inspector. He edited several collections of folksongs for use in schools.
22 According to Smetana, Dr Josef Schulz was 'a popular doctor in the services of Count Trautmannsdorf'. He came from a peasant family settled in Mělník in Bohemia, and although he had to study in German at the medical faculty in Prague, throughout his life he retained a strong awareness of his Czech nationality (Smetana 1948, 20).
23 *buchta* (plural *buchty*), a traditional yeast-raised cake, usually with a sweet filling (curd cheese, poppy seed or jam).

excitement, without any great events. Apart from going to church and for walks, I hardly ever went anywhere, only sometimes my parents took me with them in the evening to a restaurant for beer, usually to 'U Sehnalů' in Dvorecká ulice.[24] They visited almost nobody and visitors very seldom came to us – and even then, mostly only someone from the family, two of Mama's old aunts, Fanny and Marie, who adored me. They were poor rather than rich but they never forgot to bring me poppy-seed *buchty* from the confectioner's because they knew how I enjoyed them. Then there was Grandmother, my mother's mother. She stayed in turn with her three children, especially after the marriage of my uncle Julius [Kaluschka], for whom she had previously kept house. Sometimes she stayed with us for as long as three months. She was hospitable and kind. Mama used to say that she spoilt me. But I wouldn't say so. Grandmother sometimes managed more effectively than Mama to instil the notion of what was proper and what wasn't. For instance as a little girl I very much liked looking at myself in the mirror. They tried vainly to get me out of the habit, until Grandmother arrived. She began to tell me that the 'Krampus mit der roten Zunge'[25] would appear there. And she did it so suggestively that up to this day I cannot look into a mirror at twilight: I have an unpleasant physical feeling and have to turn away.

Professor Blažek[26] lived in our street and I was allowed to play with his two children, Mařenka and Milan. They were both much younger than me, but I didn't mind, at least I could be among children. I almost ached for the company of other children, for someone who would be like me. But I didn't have a friend in my entire childhood, perhaps for the reason that I didn't go to school, or that I was somehow always more grown-up and more sensible than girls of my own age. Gusta Horníčková,[27] the sister-in-law of another teacher we knew, also lived in Old Brno. She was four years older than me, I adored her and longed ardently to be friends with her. But Mama wouldn't hear of it. Perhaps she seemed too grown-up for me, perhaps there was

---

24 The inn at Dvorecká [now Slovákova] ulice no.10 had been owned from 1867 by Johann Zehnal and continued to be run by his heirs after his death in 1877. It was popularly known as 'U Sehnalů'.

25 The devil with the red tongue. In Austrian culture a 'Krampus' was the traditional companion of St Nicholas. While St Nicholas (i.e. Santa Claus) rewarded virtuous children, the 'Krampus' punished the naughty ones. In the English-speaking world Zdenka might have been threatened with the 'bogeyman'.

26 Matyáš Blažek (1844–96), writer on Czech grammar and literary history; from 1875 professor at the Teachers' Institute in Brno.

27 Augusta Horníčková [Hornitschková]. She was born on 21 August 1862 and was thus only three years older than Zdenka.

something she didn't like about the girl who was later to be bridesmaid at my wedding and afterwards became an actress.

Although I didn't have a girlfriend, I had a friend: our little dog Žoli.[28] He was a wise, long-suffering brown terrier. I dressed him in my clothes, I brushed his hair, I fed him like a small child, he put up with everything. But then he grew old, he got sick, my parents had him put down so I wouldn't know about it. I cried for him, but my joyful childhood soon overcame my missing him. Yes, my childhood was joyful. Sometimes I almost felt the brightness and happiness glowing from me – and most of all love. I loved the whole world at that time, all people, all creation, and above all, to be sure, God himself. Passionately I prayed to him to give joy to the whole world, not to let anyone suffer. For me then, heaven was close, within reach of hands clasped [in prayer].

When I was twelve years old, my uncle Julius, who was a railway inspector in Feldkirch in Vorarlberg, was due to get married. My parents went to visit him in the [summer] holidays and took me with them. We travelled via Salzburg, we viewed that delightful town and its surroundings. In Feldkirch they welcomed us very kindly. The brother of my uncle's bride-to-be, a sixteen-year-old student called Karl,[29] was my companion in games and on outings. We became very friendly and found it hard to say goodbye. He especially. He knew how to carve wood beautifully and as a memento he made me a miniature Swiss cottage for [keeping] a clock [in]. When we said goodbye at the station before leaving, the adults told us that as future relatives we should also kiss one another. Feeling embarrassed by this, we touched each other's lips, red with shame.

We returned home to Brno by way of a detour through Munich because my parents wanted me to get to know that highly cultured city. With amazement I saw the Glaspalast[30] and the Glyptothek.[31] Everything there left an unforgettable mark on my childish impressionable nature. Most of all there lodged in my mind the enormous picture entitled *The Death of Wallenstein*. I wasn't grown-up enough then to remember the name of the painter,[32] but even today I still see

---

28 A name derived from the French *joli* [pretty].
29 Karl Klement, see p.14.
30 The Crystal Palace, erected in 1854 opposite the Botanical Gardens and used for exhibitions.
31 The Sculpture Gallery, built 1816–30.
32 It was perhaps the German painter Karl Piloty (1826–86), whose *Seni before the Corpse of Wallenstein* (1855) was famous at the time for its highly realistic depiction of costumes and metals. At the time it was displayed in the Munich Neue Pinakothek.

how the diamond painted on Wallenstein's finger sparkled. From Munich we travelled to Vienna. There in turn my most striking memory is that of Wildtová[33] in Donizetti's opera *Lucrezia Borgia*. She wasn't pretty to look at, she was very fat, but she acted and sang so magically that one forgot about her figure. For the first time in my life, then, I saw an opera; in Brno I'd been only to some sort of operetta in the German Theatre[34] in Lažanského náměstí. It was an indescribable enchantment for me.

This journey opened out my spiritual horizon more than all those years of reading and learning at home. When we returned, everything in Brno seemed small to me, narrow, colourless. Lessons began again and humdrum work at home; my life as a much-loved but quite lonely child continued at its peaceful tempo.

33 Marie Wilt (1833–91), Austrian soprano. She was engaged at the Vienna Hofoper from 1867 to 1877 in a wide range of parts such as Norma, Lucrezia, Aida, Donna Anna, and Elisabeth in *Tannhäuser*.
34 The Interimstheater, in use for eleven years until the Stadttheater was opened in 1882. The layout of the former Lažanského náměstí changed after the destruction of the Deutsches Haus at the end of the Second World War. The area falls into what is now the Moravské náměstí [Moravian Square].

2

Betrothal

As a twelve-year-old girl [i.e. in 1877] I could already play so much on the piano that Professor Vorel advised Father to entrust my further musical education to Janáček, then twenty-three years old but already outstanding, who had gained the favour of the whole of Czech Brno with his performance at chamber concerts and as conductor of the Beseda Philharmonic. My father knew him very well: when he became director of the Brno institute, Janáček was just graduating. His attention drawn to Janáček's outstanding musical talents, Father recognized that this young artist could sink without trace in some village school, and so he did everything possible to have Janáček appointed supernumerary teacher at the institute, where he later taught music and other subjects at the practice school.

Janáček went to Brno as an eleven-year-old schoolboy in 1865, the year in which Zdenka was born, and qualified at the Teachers' Institute in 1872. He soon made his mark on Brno's musical life, becoming choirmaster of the Svatopluk choral society in 1873 and, in 1876, choirmaster of the Philharmonic Society of the Brno Beseda, the most important musical institution in Czech Brno at the time. His earliest compositions date from this period, mostly male-voice choruses for use by Svatopluk and liturgical music composed during a study year (1874–5) at the Prague Organ School.

I was very frightened of my teacher. I knew him a little from the institute and heard from his pupils that he was very strict. Even his appearance had something dark for me. He was slim then,[1] a figure smaller rather than larger, his pale face made a strong contrast with his hard, curly full beard, thick black curly locks and very striking brown eyes. Already at that time I was particularly taken with his small, full white hand, which when he touched the keyboard became an independent being with a soul of its own. My fears were groundless; Janáček didn't indulge me, he didn't speak unnecessarily, he demanded that I learn my lesson perfectly as a matter of course, yet I couldn't say that he used to be particularly strict let alone ill-natured, as was

1 In fact Zdenka describes him in her account to Smetana as 'very thin' and that, although his frame was firm and healthy with no signs of consumption, he appeared undernourished (Smetana 1948, 24).

frequently said of him. I did my best so he should be pleased with me: for one thing, I really liked playing the piano very much, for another I was proud of the fact that everybody told me what an excellent piano teacher I had. For about a year Janáček came to give lessons at our old apartment in Pekařská ulice: then [in 1878] we moved into the director's apartment in the new institute building in Old Brno.

At that time I suddenly matured so that even at the age of thirteen I had the appearance of a young woman. In the new apartment I had lessons in the dining-room. Two French windows led into the garden, the piano had its keyboard turned towards them, on the opposite wall a large mirror hung in an oldfashioned black frame. In this mirror I observed for the first time that the behaviour of my teacher towards me was changing. It was during the lesson: I was playing and my glance happened to slide down to the mirror opposite. And there I glimpsed that the man who until now had been always completely indifferent to my little person was sitting somewhat behind me and observing with approval the long golden plaits which fell on my back. Out of artful curiosity I'd then catch such glances more and more often. And I noticed other attentions too. Before, he spoke to me only of things which directly concerned my piano playing, now he initiated conversation on other topics; he recommended my visiting this or that concert, he invited me to organ recitals in the Old Brno monastery, trifles from which I got twofold pleasure: both as a pupil who had been singled out, and as a girl within whom a woman was awakening. I had three piano lessons a week. Janáček told me that we were being held back too much in them by [practising] playing four hands; that in future we'd have a separate lesson on this. He said that he'd come to us on Sunday mornings and that he didn't want any fee for it. And the height of his attentiveness towards me was that at the end of the winter, during one of the musical evenings that he got up with his pupils at the institute, he did me the honour of playing with me Dvořák's *Slavonic Dances* for four hands.[2]

Besides being attracted to the young Zdenka, Janáček was probably taken with his first experience of a middle-class home. Sent away from home at the age of eleven, he had from then known only institutional life at the Old Brno monastery choir school or been isolated in private lodgings, so, as Zdenka speculated to Smetana,[3] the Schulzes' protective care for their daughter in a well-ordered household must have been something of a revelation for him.

2 They played *Slavonic Dances* (unspecified) on 2 March 1879 and *Slavonic Dance* no.5 on 18 May 1879 (Trkanová 1964, 139, fn.38).
3 Smetana 1948, 24.

At Easter [1879] Janáček conducted Beethoven's *Missa solemnis* at the concert of the Beseda Philharmonic.[4] It was a grand occasion, he had a great success and received a silver baton and an embroidered music-case. I was also at the concert but didn't speak with my teacher; I simply observed his success joyfully from the sidelines. In the next lesson, however, Janáček himself began to tell me about it, and said that he'd bring the presents to show me. And indeed he came – it was on Wednesday [9 April], the day before Maundy Thursday. Mama was a little poorly, so he was greeted by Grandmother, who knew how to be very sweet and hospitable. She invited Janáček to coffee. She loved music, in a while they were chatting about it in a friendly fashion, and he soon felt at home. He quite forgot that at four o'clock he had the Holy Week Office[5] at the Old Brno monastery. Only when a breathless chorister, who had been looking for him all over Old Brno, came running in did he jump up and rush off to the church.

On Easter Monday my parents invited several teachers from the institute to supper. From the time we moved to the institute we received many more visitors altogether, especially Father's friends and colleagues. My teacher was also invited on that occasion, and made it clear that he came to our home frequently and liked doing so. We played the piano together, then he played solo; the atmosphere was exhilarating. I was helping to serve the guests and when I went into the room next door for wine, Janáček slipped in there behind me and kissed my hand. Now I was no longer in any doubt that he was courting me. From that time he came to us more and more frequently, he accompanied us on family walks, he danced attendance on Mama and Grandmother so engagingly that both of them soon fell in love with him as their own son. Father, although he valued Janáček's talents and was helpful to him in everything, wasn't so keen, especially when he began to observe that something was going on between the two of us. But he was far too good-natured to intervene in any way. Only once did he reproach me for paying attention in company only to Janáček, and not to the others as well. But I thought to myself: 'It's all very well for you to say that, but I don't care for the others and don't enjoy being with them.'

The 'others' were mostly older, rather serious colleagues of my father, who saw me as a little girl. They were people towards whom I felt indifferent, who didn't mean anything to me, who gave me nothing. But Janáček brought so many new things into my former way

4 The performance took place on Wednesday 2 April 1879.
5 *Tenebrae*, the combined Offices of Matins and Lauds sung in Holy Week, which includes the Lamentations of Jeremiah.

of life which, after my trip abroad, now ceased to satisfy me – he brought something uplifting, artistic, so that he became the pivot around which all my thoughts turned.

On one occasion we were alone together in the room. We were talking calmly about something when suddenly he threw himself on his knees before me, he clasped me by the waist and, trembling all over with excitement, told me that he loved me and wanted to marry me. I was so taken aback by this unexpected outburst that I couldn't say a word. I simply nodded my head. Passionately he seized me and kissed me. The feeling which I felt at the time wasn't at all pleasant: I was scared out of my wits. Only now do I know how to explain it: although I was already a young woman and drawn to my teacher as if by magic, in heart and soul I was nevertheless still a child not yet ripe for love. At the time, however, neither of us realized this. Instead of his former 'Fräulein' my teacher began to call me 'Zdenčička', 'Zdenčinka'.[6] I was embarrassed to address him at all intimately and, as before, continued to make life easy for myself with a simple 'Sie'.[7] We used to speak a lot about music, he'd tell me of his plans for the future, that he was preparing to leave in the autumn to study at the Leipzig Conservatory. Within him he had an insatiable longing for higher music education. He used to be closest to me when he ran round the garden with me after our big guard dog Vořech.[8]

My parents observed everything, but they said nothing. Mama was too fond of Janáček; Papa maybe didn't want to say anything too definite about it because of my youth. And perhaps he was also hoping that Janáček's departure for Leipzig would snap the tender, just emerging threads of our relationship. Only Grandmother often made a joke of the fact that my teacher and I were 'friends'.

It was May [1880] already, and Janáček's departure for Leipzig had to be fixed. On the advice of my father he asked for paid leave since otherwise he wouldn't have had anything to live on abroad. His colleagues at the practice school were so noble-minded that each promised to take on one of his lessons without pay so that the state wouldn't have any outlay and would accede to his request without difficulty. He then went in person to the ministry in Vienna and was granted study-leave in Leipzig. I bowed to the necessity that we'd have to part and I didn't think any further about it. Somehow things were continuing to evolve without my participation.

6 With 'Zdenči' diminutive forms of 'Zdenka'.
7 You (formal) in German.
8 Literally 'mongrel'.

On one occasion in August my teacher said to me that he wouldn't be coming to us that evening because he was engaged elsewhere. I was sorry that I'd be alone for the whole afternoon and evening. I wept because of this into the evening. Then through the window on to the garden I saw that Janáček was nevertheless on his way to see us. I was confused. I didn't want him to see that I'd been crying. I hid from him, but he soon found me. He was surprised by my tear-stained face and burst out: 'I'll ask for your hand at once.'

I didn't want him to. But before we could agree on anything Mama came after us. It was getting dark. We sat down on the settee, he in the middle, we on either side of him. While he chatted with Mama about this and that, I fell asleep. I don't know how it could have happened: perhaps weariness from crying in the afternoon. It had already got very dark when I woke up and began to take in the voice of Mama: 'But she's just a child, she's not ready for marriage. She must go on learning. And she also doesn't know yet how to run a house.'

And I heard her saying also that I wouldn't be rich, although I'd get a dowry and my parents would help with everything after the wedding and beyond, but that I didn't have any wealth to speak of.

Then Janáček replied. He retorted passionately that he didn't want anything, only me. That there'd be no need for me to look after the household and to work in it; he wouldn't even allow me to do so. Mama quietly laughed at this. She knew his financial position, she knew he was poor and that he was supporting his widowed mother and that his wife consequently wouldn't be able to expect a lavish style of living. Then they fell silent. I forced myself to keep my eyes closed because I was ashamed of what I'd overheard. But I had to move at some stage. They both turned to me. Mama said to me: 'So you want to leave me already, Zdenči?'

How was I to answer her? I kept quiet. Janáček replied for me: 'We won't be leaving you, will we? And besides a daughter, in me you'll also have a son.'

Mama promised us that she'd tell it all to Father herself. I think that she had quite a hard time before she managed to stop him making objections. Publicly, however, we were engaged only after a year, although it was known in Brno circles that Janáček was courting me.

The timing of this incident is either 'August' (as above) or 'early September' (as in Smetana).[9] Either way it should be remembered that on 30 July 1879, a month or two earlier, Zdenka had celebrated her fourteenth birthday.

9 Smetana 1948, 25.

On 1 October 1879 Janáček went to Leipzig. As a parting present I gave him a purse with 20 ducats which I'd received as a child from a lady we knew. He wept, he told me the whole time that he was afraid that I'd forget him. I had to promise him that I'd write to him as often as possible; he said that I'd be getting a letter from him every day. I was very lonely after his departure, but even at that time I was able to find relief from pain in work: I threw myself into my lessons, and in addition Mama began to get me doing housework even more. Besides, every day had some joy for me too: the letter from Leipzig. My fiancé wrote to tell me how he was getting on, what his teachers at the conservatory were like, that he was very homesick. He complained frequently about the food, which he didn't care for. Not surprising, since, coming from Brno, he was used to the celebrated kitchen of the Old Brno monastery from which, as their choirmaster, they sent him lunches and suppers in lieu of pay. Mama was sorry for him and so every week a little hamper from our kitchen made its way to Leipzig.

Janáček's time in Leipzig is well documented by his letters to Zdenka (none of hers to him has survived). He wrote daily, sometimes several times a day, recording his impressions of Leipzig and those he met there, and in particular of his unremitting efforts to perfect his technique as a composer. He was too poor to take advantage of the city's musical life.

Originally he said that he wouldn't come home for a whole year. But before Christmas he began to get unbearably homesick. He wrote that he'd come at once if only he had money for the journey. My parents took pity on him. They told me to invite him to our house for Christmas, saying that they'd pay for the journey. Joyfully I informed him of this. Then for two days I didn't get a letter. I thought that he was angry because previously he'd written to me saying that he wanted to transfer from Leipzig to Paris, and I'd tried in a letter to talk him out of it.

Janáček's first reference to this possibility was in his letter of 25 November 1879,[10] where he suggested that by Easter, once he had finished his 'Symphony' (in the end he hardly began it), he would move on to Paris, to study with Saint-Saëns, whose F major Piano Trio and Second Piano Concerto he had performed in Brno the previous year. He suggested this as a plan that they could discuss at Christmas and asked her to tell him what she and her parents thought of it. From this Zdenka deduced that Janáček now wished to be a 'travelling virtuoso' and hotly opposed the plan, as is clear from Janáček's letter of 29 November,[11] in which he tried to explain that he only wanted to learn more. The topic recurred in their

10 *IB*, 102–3.
11 *IB*, 107–9.

correspondence until 2 December,[12] when Janáček wrote of his sadness about the contretemps.

But on the Sunday before Christmas,[13] just when I was writing to him again, a carriage rolled up in front of our apartment and out of it jumped my fiancé. For me that was the most beautiful Christmas present. And he just beamed. He stayed with us, upstairs in Father's office. For meals he was our guest. In those joyful days we got even closer, we began to say *Ty*[14] to one another and I got used to calling him 'Leoš', as his mother called him. It was indeed a happy and merry Christmas. But by the end a shadow was cast over it for me, as over everything I experienced thereafter, leaving me with not a single unclouded joy. At New Year, Mama got a letter from the Klements, the parents of that student whom I'd met in Feldkirch. And at the same time I too received a card from them with New Year greetings. It was unheard of that someone would write separately to Mama and to me. Mama didn't give me her letter to read. Immediately I worked out that there was something wrong. For some time now, something was being concealed in our family. Mama used to be sad, often upset; she and Papa had sharp exchanges which suddenly subsided when I came in sight. I couldn't make out what it was. Except that I had a suspicion that it had nothing to do with either me or my fiancé. When that letter had come for Mama, I felt that it was connected with everything that was being hidden from me. I began to cry and wanted to know what was going on. Mama was taken aback, then she sat me down on her lap like a little child and said: 'You see, Zdenči, you are already a bride now so I can tell you. You will have a little brother or sister. It was very awkward for me that I had to hide it from you for so long. I'm glad that you know now.'

From her tone I felt she was ashamed and that she was asking my pardon. I clasped her round the neck and cried on her shoulder. She comforted me, saying that she and Father would love me just as much as before. But it didn't worry me that I wouldn't be the only child any more, on the whole it made no difference to me. It was something else that I was afraid of: what my fiancé would say about it. I suspected that he wouldn't like it. In fact, when we met again and he saw me

12 *IB*, 112.
13 *Zlatá neděle* ['golden Sunday'], the last Sunday before Christmas Eve. Janáček's letters to Zdenka continued daily until 11 December. There is thus a ten-day gap between then and Zdenka's *zlatá neděle*, which in 1879 fell on 21 December. It seems more likely that Janáček's return to Brno was in fact a week earlier, Sunday 14 December, since at the end of his letter of 11 December (*IB*, 124) he signed off with the thought of seeing Zdenka 'very soon'.
14 See Glossary: 'Ty and Vy'.

---

tearful, he asked me what had happened to me. I told him what we could look forward to. Unpleasantly surprised, he pulled a face and he said only: 'Well, I'm amazed they weren't more sensible.'

From that moment onwards it was as if he had grown cold towards me. Soon after the New Year he left again for Leipzig,[15] again he wrote to me frequently, he came to us for Easter too, but it seemed to me as though there was none of his earlier ardour. After Easter he didn't return again to Leipzig, but left for the conservatory in Vienna.[16] I don't remember now for certain what reasons he had for it. But the most probable would be that Vienna in its turn now seemed even better to his unquiet spirit. From there he came to us for the Whitsun holidays as well.[17] The night after Whit Monday, just when Leoš was getting ready to go again, my little brother was born. It was a terrible night, everyone was awake in the flat. With alarm I listened to Mama's cries and I literally trembled with fear when I realized that this could be my lot too when I got married. Then a child's cry rang out: it was so hateful to me that I fled to my own room and lay down still dressed on the bed and cried for a long time. They came for me, Mother was calling for me. I didn't want to go, I didn't want to see anyone, the young child in particular. They dragged me forcibly to my mother's bed. With pain I looked at her sunken face, but when they foisted the boy on me, I covered my eyes with my hands and ran away again. But as soon as I began crying again in my bedroom, I suddenly felt such an access of love towards that small thing there in the baby quilt that I then no longer knew whether I was crying out of pity for Mother, or out of sisterly love, hitherto unrecognized. I fell asleep, confused by my own feelings. First thing in the morning I ran to Mama, I held the little boy and kissed him and my parents were pleased that I'd accepted him. My fiancé also came down from Father's office and put on a more or less welcoming face at the baby. That very day he left for Vienna, but he soon returned again for the christening, to represent my absent uncle from Kolín[18] as a godfather.[19] The ceremony took place in our flat and we laughed a lot at the fact that my fiancé was holding his

15 Janáček's letters to Zdenka began again from Leipzig on 8 January 1880 (*IB*, 125).
16 Easter Day fell on 28 March 1880. Janáček left Leipzig on 24 February (having written a final letter to Zdenka that day) and went to Vienna on 31 March (*IB*, 196–7).
17 Whit Sunday fell on 16 May 1880. Janáček left Vienna for Brno probably on 14 May (his last letter was on 13 May; *IB*, 232).
18 Uncle Julius Kaluschka, a railway inspector, had presumably by now been transferred from Feldkirch (in southern Austria) to Kolín (in Bohemia).
19 According to Zdenka's account above, Janáček left for Vienna on the Tuesday after Whitsun, 18 May. He did not write again until Monday 24 May when, at 3.30 p.m., he wrote that he had 'just arrived' in Vienna (*IB*, 232). This suggests that he returned to Brno

future brother-in-law during the christening and making promises for him. And we also laughed at the coincidence that three Leoš's were gathered together here: the stand-in godfather, the christened child, and christening priest.[20]

It was now almost the end of the school year and my husband-to-be remained in Brno. He'd moved out from his mother, who had then taken in students, and found himself a room with the Freyschlags opposite 'U modrého lva'[21] and again took up the post of choir director at the monastery. There were the holidays: it seemed that it would now be granted us to continue with the happy idyll of a betrothed couple. But that's not how it was. Above all there was a young child here and much worry and work with him. My little brother would often be ill, and I nursed him and watched over him for whole nights; I learnt how to bath him and care for him just like Mama, who all the time was still weak. But it tired me out, there was no peace at our place, the work mushroomed continually, it wasn't the right atmosphere for a young engaged couple and my fiancé took it badly.

And something else was beginning which was afterwards the reason for so much bitterness and which wasn't there before. Up till now Leoš spoke Czech only with Father, German with the rest of us; he taught me in German, he asked for my hand in German and wrote letters to me in German. The way I'd been brought up, this seemed quite natural to me. But after his return from Vienna he began to urge me to speak Czech with him. Why shouldn't I do that for him when I loved him more and more? I knew a fair amount of Czech, but only from our servants, with whom I had to make myself understood in their native language because none of them knew German. Mama always picked only Czech servants; she said that they were more hardworking and loyal than German girls. I was afraid that I might have learnt to speak somewhat incorrectly from them and that Leoš would laugh at me. But he replied to me in a serious tone: 'This is something we Czechs don't do, we're glad when someone wants to learn our language.'

And so we began. From that time we always spoke Czech when we were alone or with Father. Also in company I began to be less tongue-

for the christening (presumably the weekend after Whitsun) and did not bother to write to Zdenka during the intervening days in Vienna. This was uncharacteristic but perhaps explained by his ill temper over the birth of Zdenka's brother.

20 In Zdenka's account to Smetana (1948, 25–6) this is no coincidence: her brother was specifically named after the officiating priest and the stand-in godfather.

21 'At the Blue Lion', a well-known inn, dating from the thirteenth century (but demolished in 1934) at the intersection of what are now Václavská ulice and Křížová ulice.

tied in Czech. The sort of society at our place used to be an absolute Babel. Because Mama and Grandmother scarcely knew any Czech, guests spoke German with them, Czech with Father. Now they drew me into it too and because they were continually praising me and I saw myself that it wasn't so difficult I began to get the taste and the nerve for it. But it didn't suit Grandmother, who from the birth of my little brother stayed with us permanently. By birth and upbringing she was *echt deutsch*, her maiden name was Axmann, the daughter of a teacher at the Olomouc Normalschule[22] near St Mořic church with some sort of dark tradition of aristocratic origins. When one said 'Czechs' to her she imagined servants and a few of the most wretched paupers. According to her, anyone who didn't speak German wasn't an educated person. And now I, her little darling, her pride and joy, was beginning to speak the language of these despised creatures! And what's more, in company! And at the instigation of her fiancé! From the beginning she was enchanted by Leoš, she loved him as a son, but this she couldn't forgive. She continually badgered Mama who, perhaps under the influence of her marriage, was very tolerant in matters of nationality. First thing in the morning I'd hear sharp and uncompromising words in the kitchen: 'Aber Anna, wie kannst Du das erlauben, dass das Kind fort mit ihm böhmisch spricht!'[23] And Mother replying casually: 'Aber, Mutter, gib mir Ruh', was liegt dran?'[24]

But when people continually goad, something of their speech nevertheless remains in the person being got at. The little bit of fire began to smoulder and Leoš also did nothing to put it out. Provocatively, almost tactlessly, he made a show of his Czechness. He completely stopped speaking German. If it was necessary to come to an agreement about something with Mama or with Grandmother he turned to Father or to me and we translated it for him. It was embarrassing and made no sense when after all he knew perfectly well that Mama and Grandmother really couldn't speak Czech; and they in turn had vivid memories of how, not so long ago, he'd conversed pleasantly with them in German. Once it became too much even for Mama and she said gently, just *en passant* – that it wasn't good manners for someone to speak a language in front of others who don't understand it while at the same time knowing their language. Leoš was furious although he made out as though he didn't understand what

22 Formerly a type of primary school introduced in 1774 by Maria Theresa's educational reforms in the larger towns throughout the empire.
23 'But Anna, how can you allow the child to be speaking Czech with him all the time!'
24 'But mother, let me be, what harm is there in it?'

Mama was saying. During such crossfire I'd be as if on the spit. Whose side should I take? My understanding was with my family, my heart with him.

It went on like this into winter. All the while the trousseau was being made and I went to the Old Brno monastery to learn how to cook. That was a jolly apprenticeship! There were twelve of us girls, all brides-to-be, and with us one soldier. He was also learning to cook. They gave him the toughest kitchen tasks to do. Everything was funny for us: the soldier, the thin woman pastrycook, *frajle* [Fräulein] Máli,[25] and the chef, who cooked to line his pocket, so we soon observed. I remember it with pleasure.

It was agreed that the wedding would take place when I was sixteen. Leoš demanded this at the beginning of our engagement, although at first my parents wouldn't agree to it. Now, when there was a baby here, and everything was so tense, we all wished it over and done with. I looked forward to it most of all because Leoš and I got on well together and he continually reassured me that after the wedding it would be as nice again as in the first days of our engagement.

Only once could we not agree among ourselves and it almost came to a breach between us. Leoš began again to speak unkindly about my parents. He made it clear that he didn't like them. This hurt me very much. I thought very hard about it. When in the afternoon he went to teach and dropped by at our flat, as was his wont, I went out with him into the lobby and there I told him that I found his dislike of my parents hard to take. That it would perhaps be better for us to part if it was going to go on like this. He didn't say anything in response and flew through the door like a shot. I returned to the big room where they were cutting out linen for my trousseau on the table. 'Stop', I said, 'there'll be no wedding.'

Alarm. Mama began asking me what had happened. I told her. She didn't agree with me. It seemed to her that in doing this I'd wanted to sacrifice my love for the sake of my parents, she feared that one day I'd reproach her for it. She herself wrote a letter to Leoš – I don't know what – and he came again after teaching as if nothing had happened. And now the wedding was already fast approaching. Father found a beautiful four-room flat for us not far from the institute on the first floor of the corner house in Měšťanská ulice [now Křížová ulice]. But when I joyfully announced this to Leoš, he scowled and said that he didn't want it. It was hard work getting out of him what he didn't like

25 A diminutive of Amálie.

about it. Eventually he said to me in Czech in front of Mama and Grandmother: 'It's very near your family.'

It was embarrassing for me and made me feel sorry when I had to repeat this to Mama. But it was never in my nature to lie about something. My parents swallowed that too. Father simply proclaimed that he wouldn't look for another flat for us. And because Leoš himself didn't do anything about it at all, we nevertheless took that flat in the end. My parents bought furniture for me, most of which I still have today: the bedroom suite, the dining-room suite, some of the pieces of which I now have in the salon.[26] Grandmother gave me a beautiful glazed china cabinet which she'd been given as part of her dowry. [. . .] In my trousseau I also received a new piano, an Ehrbahr, which Leoš chose himself.[27] Later he wrote many of his compositions on it. When everything was ready, Leoš moved into the flat immediately so that he wouldn't pay rent unnecessarily.

Originally the wedding was to have been after the summer holidays, but the continual misunderstandings hurried it forward to 13 July [1881]. We had to think about the banns. Leoš kept silent about that, as if nothing was happening. And then suddenly one afternoon Mama began to ask in what language we wanted them to be in, adding the wish that they should be in German out of regard for our relatives. The two of us went silent and then Mama began to press me to say what I thought about it. Leoš suddenly jumped up, grabbed his hat and rushed out without saying goodbye. I took fright but I saw from my parents' faces that it hadn't upset them at all. I now think that they deliberately provoked this scene so that the two of us would part. Father had never been keen on my choice and recently Mama had now also looked on it differently. She kept on saying to me: 'Child, you won't be happy with him.'

And I, half from the depths of my love, half out of childish wilfulness, said in reply: 'I'd rather be unhappy with him than happy with someone else.'

In this way then, ignorant girl that I was, I determined my own fate. [. . .] How many times I remembered these words afterwards when life had become particularly bitter for me!

When Leoš rushed away from us like this I was left powerless. My

---

26 Part of the furniture was made by a cabinet-maker in Rájec, part bought in a Brno furniture shop (Smetana 1948, 26).
27 The Ehrbahr baby grand, which Janáček picked out at Gregor's piano shop, was specifically thought of as being for Zdenka's future husband, and replaced a borrowed instrument (Smetana 1948, 26).

parents showed no desire to help me. I comforted myself with the thought that Leoš and I would come to an agreement when I went the next day to cook in the monastery. He always used to wait for me. He didn't come. I didn't see him either for the next few days. Then I realized what he'd become to me. During those few days I suffered more than during my whole life before. Then I couldn't bear it any longer. Without my parents' knowing I wrote to him asking him to come to the school garden. He came. Scowling, angry, at once he began to dictate the conditions for a reconciliation. That if the wedding was to happen at all, it would have to be in Czech, and if we had children they'd have to be brought up in Czech.

'Well of course', I said in surprise. For it hadn't even occurred to me that it would be otherwise and I didn't understand why he'd got so angry on this account with me, who was at one with him. If he hadn't run away we'd have calmly told my parents what we both wished and it would have been fine. It vexed me that I had now to concern myself with making peace between him and my parents, I who wasn't to blame for anything. But that, I suppose, was just a part of his character: many times afterwards he forced me in a similar fashion to sort out for him the things that he ruined through his impetuousness.

I then went home and, weeping, I begged my parents not to be angry any more and for the wedding to take place just as Leoš wanted it.

Smetana provided a few more details: 'A month before the wedding Zdenka Schulzová was confirmed by Father Ruprecht, the professor of religion at the Teachers' Institute. Later, the engaged couple both attended catechism and Leoš Janáček also attended confession. For this, apparently, he had to prepare himself from Zdenka's catechism book as he said he had forgotten the regulations. In the final days [before the wedding], the couple had themselves photographed (the bride-to-be in a simple black dress).'[28] Zdenka recalled the black dress in Chapter 3 of her memoirs: 'This photograph [see jacket] was our substitute for a wedding photograph in which, because of the state of photography in those days, the bride almost always appeared as a large white unshaded blob.'

And then there was the wedding day, 13 July 1881. Leoš was then twenty-seven years old, I was a few days short of sixteen. The wedding ceremony was due to take place late afternoon.[29] In the morning we took holy communion,[30] then there arrived the best man, Professor

28 Smetana 1948, 26–7.
29 At five o'clock in the church of the Augustinian monastery in Old Brno (Smetana 1948, 27).
30 In Zdenka's account to Smetana (1948, 27), this took place the day before, on Tuesday 12 July.

Dlouhý,[31] and the wedding witness and a friend of Leoš, the painter Šichan,[32] 'to pay a visit' as was necessary according to the *bon ton* of the time. After their departure – it was already getting on for noon – Leoš told me to come with him at about two in the afternoon to see his mother, who lived in Klášterní (Mendlovo) náměstí. I was surprised at this, because she'd promised us, when we invited her to the wedding, that she'd come to us before the ceremony. It was even rather awkward for me: I now had my hair in curlers – at that time we women did our hair at home ourselves without a hairdresser, even for special occasions – and after two o'clock it was time for me to begin to get ready. I knew also that every curious person in the street would gape at where we were hurrying off to now just before the wedding. But since Leoš was urging me so inflexibly I promised him that I'd go. When he left I told this to Mama and she was most surprised; she said something must surely lie behind it. That frightened me. And so when Leoš came for me in the afternoon, I told him that I wasn't going anywhere, that it wasn't right for me to be running down the street before the wedding, since, after all, his mother was coming to us. He replied: 'No, my mother won't cross this threshold. She won't be going to the church either because she hasn't got the right clothes. She'll go only to the Besední dům for the reception.'

I remained puzzled at what had happened to his mother. But then I proclaimed again that I wasn't going out. Angrily he turned away from me and ran off. What now? I knew him well enough already to know that he was capable of spoiling the whole wedding. In my fear I burst into tears. My uncle Julius came to me in the room, he comforted me and advised me all the same to go to Leoš's mother. He took me there himself. My bridegroom was there already. I asked why his mother didn't want to come to us. And she said to me then that she didn't know [the reason] but that Leoš had forbidden her to go to us and to the church. Then we parted on good terms. Leoš and I didn't exchange a single word and my uncle took me home.

Zdenka's account to Smetana is at odds with the above description in that Janáček's mother and sister seem to have attended the wedding, though not the

31 František Dlouhý (1852–1912), a teacher (1874) and later professor (1892) at the Brno Teachers' Institute. He was well known as a writer (including two books on Czech dances) and as an editor of various Moravian journals.
32 Josef Ladislav Šichan (1847–1918), painter and photographer. Although he also painted portraits (including oil paintings of Zdenka and Leoš given as a wedding present), he specialized in religious paintings, many of which can be found in churches throughout Moravia.

gathering beforehand at the Schulz home.[33] This is perhaps understandable;
'linguistic reasons' (offered in Smetana) would explain why Janáček's mother did
not go to the German-speaking Schulz family though neither this nor 'no suitable
clothes' could explain their absence at the church yet their presence at the
reception afterwards. Wherever the truth lies, the difficulty over Janáček's mother
underlines that the difference in class and culture between Janáček's mother and
the Schulz family was an embarrassment to him. It is significant that while Janáček
knew Zdenka's family well over several years, she has nothing to say about her
future husband's, and this is the only occasion that Zdenka reports meeting
Amálie Janáčková. It seems that Janáček kept his mother out of the way and did
not encourage contacts with his future wife.

I was perturbed, my head spun. It was time for me to get dressed. So I
went to Father's office where my wedding gown was prepared. Made
of pale-rose satin with a long train, richly decorated with fresh myrtle.
Rose satin shoes. A veil of white illusion with a crown of myrtle and
orange flowers covering the face and the whole figure. According to
custom the bride should have been in white, but I wanted it this way.
For quite recently, an English princess had had a wedding and it had
been reported that she'd worn a rose-coloured gown,[34] and I liked the
idea so much that I wanted to have one too. Mama and I had thought
everything through so carefully, chosen everything and prepared it,
and now I had the feeling that I was getting ready for the grave. I saw it
clearly as never before that I'd never be happy with Leoš because of his
nature. Professor Dlouhý came to me with a most beautiful bouquet of
myrtle, red roses and orange blossom – he made it a condition that
he'd give me the bridal bouquet himself, not the bridegroom as was the
custom – my bridesmaid, Gusta Horníčková, looked so radiant, all
around was full of hustle and bustle, only I thought the whole time
about how the two of us would live together. I said to myself: 'Either
he's bad or he doesn't love me. Wouldn't it be better if even at this
stage I were to say that I didn't want him?'

But it wasn't in my power to stop the course of events which were
already in motion. I was too weak for that. There wasn't the time to
think out the consequences. My wedding dress was ready, I parted
from Mama and the best man led me down into the salon where the
guests were waiting. The bridegroom beamed when he saw me. He

33 Smetana 1948, 27.
34 This is a mystifying detail. The most recent English princess to be married before
Zdenka's marriage in July 1881 was Victoria's daughter Louise (married 1871). Even if the
search is broadened to include Louisa Margaret of Prussia (who married Victoria's son
Arthur, Duke of Connaught, in 1879) or even Frederike, daughter of George V of Hanover
(who was married at Windsor Castle in 1880), both brides, according to reports in *The
Times*, kept conservatively to white satin.

bounded up to me as if nothing had happened. I scrutinized him coolly, I wanted to tell him what was going on inside me but all that came out was: 'What do you want, I'm not going with you, am I?'

Someone told him to go upstairs to Mama, to ask for a blessing. He went alone. Meanwhile I said farewell to Father and sat in the carriage with the best man. The sun was shining, the church could hardly take the onlookers, the organ played festively. It seemed as if I was in a daze and simply did everything that was required of me. The ceremony was conducted by Father Ruprecht, assisted by the priest at Old Brno, Father Anselm.[35]

Zdenka's account to Smetana[36] gives a greater sense of occasion: the wedding party, including some twenty guests, departed in cabs from the Teachers' Institute, and the procession to the church was followed with great interest by passers-by. Many of Janáček's pupils returned during their holidays to sing at their teacher's wedding, and to see him off from the station on his honeymoon the next day. While Zdenka describes her rose-coloured gown, only in her account to Smetana did she mention that her husband was sporting his *čamara*, a braided black coat, worn on ceremonial occasions as a kind of patriotic manifestation.

After the ceremony we drove off to the Besední dům where the reception was prepared in the Small Hall. My husband's mother came to that. The orchestra of the German Theatre, which provided extras at concerts of the Beseda Philharmonic, played in the rooms next door the whole night – that was its wedding surprise for my husband – and of course we danced to their music.

Janáček himself did not dance (he did not know how to; it was only later that he learnt the *beseda*, see pp.31 and 46). He also drank very abstemiously, but nevertheless glowed with happiness. Father Anselm made a witty speech. The festivities continued until three in the morning.[37]

We all grew merry, especially with the champagne, Leoš drank a toast to calling my parents *Ty*.[38] But the next day, when we then went from the new flat to my parents for lunch, he was again cool as ice and surprised my parents by calling them *Vy*.

35 Father Anselm Rambousek (1824–1901). He was abbot at the Augustinian monastery from 1884 (he succeeded the famous geneticist Johann Gregor Mendel) until his death.
36 Smetana 1948, 27–8.
37 Smetana 1948, 28.
38 See Glossary: 'Ty and Vy'.

3

Marriage. A child. Separation

The day after the wedding we went off on honeymoon. We made a stop at my grandfather's in Obřístvi. After the death of my grandmother he had set up house with an unmarried daughter. He was a typical *staročech*.[1] My father, when he reached old age, became strikingly like him. We didn't spend much time at Grandfather's because we made many trips into the countryside round about. However, I remember distinctly only the trip to Mělník. And also how surprised we both were by the wealth and intelligence of the local farmers, compared with our own Moravian ones. From there we went for a week to Prague.[2] It was a really beautiful stay. Leoš introduced me to several excellent people: Father Lehner,[3] who lived at the rectory in Karlín, and most of all Antonín Dvořák,[4] whom he knew already from earlier times and about whom he talked enthusiastically to me. My first encounter with Dvořák was quite comic. Leoš and I were travelling somewhere by carriage when Dvořák came walking along the pavement in the opposite direction. Leoš let out a cry of joy, gave orders to stop and called out to the Maestro, saying he wanted to introduce me. Dvořák came up to the carriage, stuck his head inside, opened his eyes wide at me and exclaimed: 'What have you been doing marrying a child!'

After that he was with us very often and appeared to me to be a

1 'Old Czech', a member of the Národní strana [National Party], the original Czech political party founded in the 1860s. The name arose when the *mladočech* [Young Czech] wing split off from it in 1874. It was perceived, e.g. by Smetana and other artists and men of letters, as the feudal and clerical party, attracting those with money and property.
2 The Prague musical periodical *Dalibor* recorded in its issue of 10 August 1881 that 'the composer Lev Janáček from Brno spent several days in Prague' (*Dalibor*, iii (1881), 183).
3 Ferdinand Lehner (1837–1914). Lehner was a fervent advocate of Witt's Cecilian reforms of church music, running a choir school for this purpose at Karlín, Prague, where he served as chaplain from 1865, and founding the Czech music journal *Cecilia* (later *Cyril*) as a platform for these views. Janáček knew Lehner from his student days in Prague in 1874–5; later Janáček wrote occasional articles for *Cyril*. His setting (1881) for organ of ten Czech hymns from Lehner's hymnbook (*JW*, II/10) seems to have arisen from their meeting during his honeymoon trip to Prague.
4 Antonín Dvořák (1841–1904), the leading Czech composer of his generation. Janáček may have met Dvořák during his studies in Prague in 1874–5. Janáček was an enthusiastic performer of Dvořák's works in Brno Beseda concerts from April 1877 onwards and was instrumental in Dvořák's visiting Brno for a concert in December 1878.

simple, dear person with ridiculous ideas. My husband and I laughed for a long time afterwards at one of these. Dvořák went with us to Karlštejn,[5] taking a great interest there in everything and listening most carefully when in the tower the guide told us about the call of the castle guard. On the way back afterwards he continually repeated it to himself but in a caricatured form: 'Away from the castle, five minutes away.'[6] And it wasn't possible at all to see from his face whether he took it seriously or was making a joke.

We had pleasant company the whole time. Professor Dlouhý – whose parents lived in Prague, where he stayed for the holidays – was often with us. We went many times to the Provisional Theatre.[7] There we got to know the famous baritone Lev and struck up friendly relations with him.[8] He showed us round the newly completed National Theatre[9] and delighted in our enthusiasm. Not in a million years would it have occurred to any of us that we'd never again see all that beauty in that form. For we'd already returned to Brno when the National Theatre burnt down on 12 August [1881]. On the day after, I was getting breakfast when Leoš took up the newspaper and suddenly exclaimed: 'The National Theatre has burnt down!' He was in despair, I cried my eyes out for several days, it was as if our dearest friend had died. And then a wave of enthusiastic self-sacrifice swept over Czech Brno: each gave what he could, we didn't talk about anything other than the collections for building a new theatre.[10]

But all that was still in the future and meanwhile we spent happy days in Prague. I'd so liked to have shared these beautiful impressions with my parents, at least in writing. But my husband didn't want me to write to them. He said that I must get weaned from them. He wanted me only for himself. Once we were sitting together in Petzold's restaurant[11] when I suddenly saw my Grandmother there.

5 Gothic castle built by Bohemia's most celebrated monarch, the Emperor Charles IV, in 1348–58. It is 33 km from Prague.
6 A standard formula, not necessarily implying imminent danger.
7 The Provisional Theatre was the first exclusive and, despite its name, permanent theatre for Czech opera and drama from 1862 until its replacement by the Prague National Theatre in 1883.
8 Josef Lev (1832–98), the leading baritone at the Provisional Theatre, and creator of all the important baritone roles in Smetana's operas. Lev sang at a concert in Brno on 15 March 1874 at Janáček's invitation (Helfert 1939, 198).
9 The National Theatre was opened, still not quite finished, for twelve performances between 11 June and 23 July 1881.
10 The self-sacrifice was not limited to Brno; collections proved so successful that the theatre was rebuilt within two years.
11 A well-known restaurant in what is now Celetná ulice, between the Powder Tower and the Old Town Square.

She'd come by chance from Kolín, where she was visiting my uncle Gustav. I wanted to rush over to her, but my husband looked so disapproving that I didn't dare. We greeted each other only perfunctorily and I made an excuse that we had to leave because we were invited elsewhere. I was sorry for Grandmother and it was embarrassing for me. I became frightened that it would be like this when we got home. Confirming my fears, Leoš behaved with similar stiffness towards uncle Gustav, at whose house we broke our journey on the way home. It didn't help that my uncle was hospitable and did all we could have wished: he was a German and Mama's brother and that was unforgivable. Only my little cousin, who didn't know any German at all, found favour; Leoš chatted the whole day with him. This visit of ours turned out cold-hearted, it was uneasy. I was glad when we got away to take a look at Kutná Hora[12] and then finally departed. Home wasn't much better. Papa came to the station for us, he took us home for a meal, then he accompanied us to our own flat. There were plenty of signs there that during our absence he and Mama had lovingly taken the trouble to make everything as cosy as possible for our return. The salon, the bedroom, the dining-room, Leoš's study, everything had been carefully cleaned and tidied, but my husband didn't even thank Father, didn't even show that he took pleasure in all this.

After a week we got ready for a new journey. First to Vnorovy[13] u Veselí in Slovácko,[14] where Leoš's uncle Jan Janáček[15] was parish priest. I realized that I'd have preferred to have stayed at home with Mama and left Leoš on his own. I began to find it hard to be with him. It wasn't the life he'd promised me before the wedding, he wasn't the attentive young man in love from the first period of our engagement. He stopped calling me 'Zdenči', 'Zdenčinko', and began to call me 'Zdenko' in his clipped manner.[16] I didn't like this address, it sounded harsh to me, sometimes almost tyrannical. I didn't know how to say it, and so just countered it with the remark that one calls boys this, and

12 A town in central Bohemia. Its silver mines led to the minting of money there from the second half of the thirteenth century, its resultant prosperity to a distinctive Gothic architecture.
13 Zdenka uses an old form, Znorov.
14 See Glossary.
15 Jan Janáček (1810–89), the older brother of Janáček's father Jiří. After Jiří's death in 1865, Jan Janáček supported his nephew financially and looked after him during the school holidays. Janáček's earliest surviving letters were written to his uncle, who served as parish priest in Vnorovy from 1870 until 1888.
16 'Zdenko' is the standard vocative form of 'Zdenka'; the other forms are affectionate diminutives.

not girls.[17] He took no notice. He got angry with me at every little thing – no, this was not as it used to be at my parents' home.

Of course I nevertheless went to Vnorovy, and didn't regret it. Leoš's uncle was a very nice, affable gentleman, we got on famously together. We went on many trips. In Strážnice, where there was some folk celebration, I wore a borrowed Vnorovy costume. I was pleased with myself when I saw people turning their heads at my sleeves[18] and flowing plaits.

From Vnorovy we went to Velehrad, Buchlov and to Hukvaldy, since Leoš wanted to show me his birthplace. I liked it very much there. The beauty of the countryside was complemented by the pleasant company of teachers and estate officials with whom we mixed at the Stará hospoda [Old inn].[19] My sister-in-law Josefka,[20] who was a domestic-science teacher, was still unmarried then and, although she was getting on for forty, she was great fun. She smoked, and they also taught me to smoke then. But I didn't get into the habit although afterwards I sometimes smoked for fun in company. My husband also remained all his life only a special-occasions smoker.

On the return journey we stopped off in Olomouc. I also wanted to see my birthplace, which I didn't remember at all. Leoš in turn was looking forward to seeing Father Křížkovský again, who was choirmaster at the cathedral.[21] Then a ridiculous incident took place. At the time I still didn't know Leoš's financial side. It didn't even occur to me to follow what he was doing with the money. At home things of this sort had been in perfect order and I took it for granted that it would be like that with us too. Up to now, therefore, I'd not asked my husband at all how much we'd spent and how much we still had. At that time, he was the type who didn't think about it until things were bad. So it happened that on the way from Hukvaldy to Olomouc he was going through and counting his money and became very gloomy. But he didn't say anything to me. It was time for lunch, I was hungry and asked where we were going to eat. To my amazement I was told 'nowhere', that we weren't going to eat today because the journey to

17 The male form of the name is Zdeněk, with its vocative form 'Zdeňku', but a Germanized version also exists, Zdenko. In this form the vocative would also be 'Zdenko'.
18 In the folk costume these would have been wide and elaborately embroidered.
19 i.e. the original inn 'U Uhlářů' as opposed to the later hotel Mičaník.
20 See Glossary: 'Dohnalová, Josefa (Adolfína)'.
21 Pavel Křížkovský (1820–85), composer and choirmaster. In 1848 he was ordained priest and became choirmaster of the Augustinian monastery in Old Brno and head of the choir school, where he taught Janáček as a chorister. From 1874 to 1883 he was choirmaster at Olomouc Cathedral.

Brno was costing a huge amount of money. I didn't see that this should be a reason for fasting when, after all, we'd known from the beginning of the journey that we'd have to return to Brno. Only after much coaxing did Leoš admit to me that we didn't have enough money even for the train journey, let alone for food. For the first time in my life I heard that we didn't have money and it was terrible. Later, unfortunately, I had to get used to it. Staggered, I held out until Olomouc. But there I got terribly hungry. I begged for a snack at least, but I wasn't allowed even that. My husband comforted me with the thought that he himself had also often gone hungry during his student years. He did indeed endure the fasting more easily than I did. Of course he wasn't plagued by a sixteen-year-old's bottomless appetite. In a desperate mood we went to visit Father Křížkovský. And he – good soul – lent us 5 zl. without any fuss when Leoš confided his troubles in him. We returned happy to the hotel. I at once ordered a full-blown dinner after which I was immediately sick, although it seemed that I'd never eaten anything so good in my life. Then the next day we found out at the station that the tickets didn't cost nearly so much as Leoš had calculated, and that we could have got home comfortably even without the help of Father Křížkovský.

Our honeymoon ended with the return to Brno and I began to run my own household. There was plenty of work. I had to carry water from the pump in the courtyard because piped water had not yet been laid on. We didn't have enough to employ a servant, so the worst work was done for me by a daily help. But with the cooking I had much less to do. My husband continued to get his lunches and suppers from the monastery (in addition to an extra 15 zl. a month wage after marriage) and when I'd cooked some small thing to add to this it was enough for us both. We didn't get visitors, so at the beginning I should have had a fair amount of spare time to continue with my education, something my parents would have been very glad to see. But somehow it didn't work out. Leoš had neither the time nor the inclination to guide me or to instruct me. All he did was emphatically to forbid my reading any German books at all. And I didn't know enough Czech at the time to read instructive things. He borrowed light novels from the library for me, usually translations. He simply said to me: 'Read!' and I slaved away without a teacher, without a dictionary. At the beginning I sometimes didn't understand perhaps half of it. But I put two and two together, I guessed a good deal, so that within a year I was already getting on quite nicely.

But there was something for which linguistic knowledge wasn't necessary and which gave me so much pleasure: my piano. After the wedding Leoš taught me for a little while longer, but he soon left off. I'm not surprised: he was so busy. In the morning, teaching at the institute, every day at noon a rehearsal with the choristers at the monastery, in the afternoon teaching again, often rehearsals with the Beseda Philharmonic and lots of other occasional work. Where would he have found the urge to occupy himself with me? He had things to learn himself. He longed passionately to go still higher and at that time didn't know what to decide on. Things were continually fermenting and seething within him. He was then as if at a crossroads, he didn't know whether he was a pianist, a conductor or a composer.[22] Only later did he leave the conducting, explaining to me that a conductor cannot be a great composer because he's influenced too strongly by the works which he performs.

But at the time of which I'm speaking he suddenly threw himself furiously into playing the piano. Before he went off to Leipzig he'd studied with Mrs Amalie Wickenhauser, a Brno German and an excellent pianist with whom he also used to play in chamber concerts in the Besední dům.[23] This tall, thin brunette came to like Leoš more than was permissible for a married woman. As far as I know from what he told me, he didn't give any cause for this. So long as she didn't suspect that he loved me, she was said to praise me and to praise even my piano playing, which she heard at performances at the institute. But when she discovered that he was engaged to me, she began to get jealous and to dissuade Leoš from marrying me, so that he stopped going to her for lessons. Left to his own devices, after our marriage he practised in the way he'd learnt in Leipzig and Vienna. As I've already mentioned, he practised furiously and didn't know where to stop. Every free moment was devoted to the piano.[24] If he was free, he was able to sit at it for ten hours daily. Naturally I withdrew if he wanted to play and I also didn't disturb him if he got up in the morning tired, complaining of back pains and wanting peace and quiet. So sometimes I didn't get to the piano for several days. I saw that I was regressing, I

22 In his letters from Leipzig, however, he was much clearer in his aims: 'I must master the piano to the point where they would at least respect me; I think that my real calling will be to compose, and then playing the piano will matter less to me' (29 November 1879; *IB*, 108).
23 Amalie Neruda (1834–90) was a member of a celebrated Brno family of musicians (her sister, the violinist Wilma Neruda, became Lady Hallé). After taking part in family European concert tours, she married the music teacher Arnošt Wickenhauser and settled down in her native Brno, where she became a leading figure in its musical life.
24 Rather than to composition; in the first three years after marriage Janáček virtually stopped composing.

regretted it and I stopped enjoying it. And later, when the children came, there was no longer even the time for it.

Through my husband I got to know Czech Brno society. I joined the Czech Ladies' Committee for Charitable Works which looked after children in Czech children's homes, chiefly their Christmas presents. We went around collecting gifts of money, we made clothes at home for the children. Up till Christmas there was plenty of work. In the autumn Pištěk's company[25] played for three months in the Besední dům, so I went every day to the theatre. Very often we also used to go to the Readers' Club in the Besední dům, where Czech intelligentsia gathered.[26] We felt at home here, as if on a firm island in the middle of the German sea around us. Over a glass of beer we'd sit in pleasant conversation there with Father Ruprecht or the painter Šichan. The doctors' wives Mrs Kusá and Mrs Tučková[27] introduced me to the ladies, Leoš introduced me to the leaders of Czech Brno at the time: the doctors Šrom, Kusý, Tuček, Wurm and Klenka.[28] It was like being in a family whose members liked one another and knew how to forgive and understand one another: the wife of Dr Šrom, for instance, was German and everybody here spoke cheerfully with her in her native tongue and nobody reproached her for it. Sometimes I thought regretfully how sharp Leoš was with Mama and Grandmother: I began to realize that this intolerance wasn't a characteristic of all Czechs but only of my husband.

At the time I also danced a lot. We probably didn't miss a single Czech ball. Participation was then virtually a national duty. No wonder, our little circle was only small: the ladies always anxiously counted those taking part and were overjoyed if thirty pairs of us danced in the Great Hall of the Besední dům. They certainly banked on my being there. They put me into the leading pair although I was

25 Jan Pištěk (1847–1907) founded a travelling theatrical company in 1877 which visited Brno in 1879, 1880 and 1881.
26 The Czech Readers' Club was founded in 1861 (as the Slavonic Readers' Club). It was the leading Czech cultural club in Brno, the model for many other cultural societies, and attracted the Czech-speaking élite of Brno as its members. Janáček was a member from 1874. Although very young at the time and from a German-orientated family, it seems Zdenka had started going there even before Janáček went to Leipzig since there are frequent references in his letters to evenings when he imagines her there.
27 Julie Kusá (1858–1908) and Olga Tučková (1855–1919). After her husband's death Kusá married the architect Josef Fanta, and later became known as Julie Kusá-Fantová. The Janáčeks lived in a block of flats owned by the Fantas (see p.103).
28 František Alois Šrom (1825–99), Wolfgang Kusý (1842–86), Josef Tuček (1845–1900) and Josef Wurm (1817–88) were all leading Moravian politicians, their doctorates in law. Eduard Klenka (1844–81), a doctor at the General Hospital in Brno, was a patriot and prominent figure in the Vlastimil choral society. His wife Paulina and Julie Kusá were sisters.

always embarrassed and went pale with stage-fright. It surely wasn't that I wouldn't have known how to dance: I was confident about that, even though no one had ever taught me how to. But I found it very difficult when the attention of everyone was turned on me. Leoš seldom danced with me. He knew only the *beseda*²⁹ and – something that surprised me about him as a musician – he couldn't dance in time. He was impossible at round dances. But he enjoyed going with me to the balls and glowed with pleasure when he saw my success.

My first ball was the *šibřinky*³⁰ of the Readers' Club. That was still before my marriage. Not long before, I'd seen *Faust* in the theatre³¹ and I was so taken with Marguerite that I wanted to be her for at least one evening. Leoš had a Faust costume, while his friend and colleague from the institute, [Berthold] Žalud, the brother of the late professor of the Brno Conservatory Theo Žalud, was Mephistopheles.³² Leoš wore a black velvet coat which suited his pale face, his black beard and curly hair, and his dark eyes very well. At his side he had a sword. I had a blue dress just like all Marguerites have in the theatre, and on my breast and at the end of my loose plaits, I'd fastened posies of yellow daisies – marguerites. And today, after all those years, I must say that we really made a handsome couple.

I also have a very nice memory of a student celebration in the Lužánky hall³³ soon after our return from honeymoon. It was a concert linked to a dance party. I seem to remember that Ondříček played and his first wife sang.³⁴ After the concert I was a little put out for a while because I wasn't able to dance. For I'd put on my black silk

29 A Czech social dance, invented in the early 1860s, it was inspired by the quadrille but incorporated steps based on Czech folk dances and (unlike the quadrille), involved alternations of duple- and triple-time dances. See also Glossary: 'Besední dům'. Janáček's mastery of the *beseda* may have come some years later (see p.46).
30 Derived from the German *Schabernack* (prank, practical joke), the term *šibřinky* was used to denote the masked ball given in the Prague Sokol Hall in 1865 and thereafter became a synonym for a masked, fancy-dress ball, usually at carnival time.
31 This may have been Gounod's opera since it was in the Pištěk company's repertory in 1880, when it visited Brno.
32 Berthold Žalud (1856–86) was a friend of Janáček from his days in Brno as a chorister at the Augustinian monastery and later at the Teachers' Institute. His brother Theodor (1862–1932) sang bass in German theatres and later became the first teacher of solo singing at the Brno Conservatory (1920–7).
33 See Glossary: 'Lužánky'.
34 Janáčková's memory may have played tricks here. The Czech violinist František Ondříček (1857–1922) played for the first time in Brno on 5 October 1882 at the Besední dům, and in company with the harpist Karel Kovařovic (later chief conductor at the Prague National Theatre) and the singer Leopold Stropnický (Kyas 1995, 52–3). The singer Anna Hlaváčková (1860–1918) studied and sang mostly abroad until marrying Ondříček in 1885. Their first appearance together in Brno was on 29 October 1891.

dress – the one in which I'd been photographed with Leoš shortly before the wedding. [. . .][35] Since the dress had a train, I was frightened of ruining it during dancing. I thought that without dancing I was going to get bored, whereas in fact I had a wonderful time. I particularly remember the editor Hübner,[36] then still a student, and what a nice-looking and delightful companion he was.

I also became a member of Vesna[37] and diligently attended the lectures which it arranged each week in the corner room on the ground floor of the Besední dům (at the time Vesna didn't have its own building). It was only later that we joyfully saw its first school set up in the house 'U Hurschů', which stood next to the Institute for the Blind in Raduitovo náměstí [now Žerotínovo náměstí]. I got to know more closely all those noble-minded ladies who ran Vesna so successfully at the time: the chairwoman Mrs Kusá, the gentle Miss Koudelová,[38] the fiery secretary Miss Machová.[39] I admired them so much and would have liked to be like them too. But it wasn't given to me to be a leading figure: nothing on earth would have induced me to speak publicly or give my opinion aloud; I'd rather have crawled into a mouse hole. Helping great work quietly and in secret – that's what I liked to do.

My life at home unfortunately wasn't so nice as my social life. Not everything went as I'd have wished and as I'd imagined. Above all the eternal lack of money weighed heavily upon me, although our income was quite decent and, in addition to a monthly contribution of 25 zl. from my parents, I also used to get all our fuel from them. But my husband didn't know how to apportion money sensibly so that it wouldn't get frittered away. And he didn't want to entrust this to me. Before the wedding we agreed that we'd keep a joint kitty, from which each would take what he needed. But it turned out unhappily in the very first month: by the twentieth the kitty was empty and I had nothing to keep house with. So I urged Leoš to divide the money and from that time he gave me a certain sum for housekeeping and kept the rest for himself. I came out well on my share, but he could never properly work his out. And indeed, he had many expenses: he supported his mother and his brother,[40] he was paying off some

35 See p.20, to which one sentence about the dress has been transferred.
36 Janáčková writes 'Hýbner', but she is probably referring to Václav Hübner (1857–1920), editor of *Moravská orlice* from 1886.
37 See Glossary.
38 Perhaps the daughter of Adéla Koudelová (see Glossary).
39 See Glossary.
40 He gave help to his youngest brother Josef (*b* 1858) on an occasional basis (see Přibáňová 1984a, 135).

smaller debts that he'd incurred before his wedding, he bought many books and pieces of music. But all that could have been put right nicely if he'd entrusted it to me, or had at least consulted me, for I always had much more financial sense than he did. But he never let me in on anything important, he preferred to do stupid things. He also never gave me more than he'd allocated me for the household. Once, when I wanted to take a tiny amount from the money which I used to get from my parents to buy some small and necessary toiletry item, he flew into a terrible rage. He hid the money and gave me none.

A second, very painful thing for me was Leoš's unfriendly attitude towards my parents. They weren't allowed to visit us at all. I needed so much to consult my mother about the household, I'd so have liked to tell my parents how I was getting on, but my husband virtually forbade me to go home. Only secretly, when he was at the school, did I drop in there. He got angry and used to say that I spoke German with Mama there. But I think that the real reason was different: perhaps he was a little jealous of my fondness for my parents, perhaps his mother was unwittingly to blame. As far as I could tell from our rare meetings with her, she wasn't a bad person. She got on very nicely with me and with my parents. Soon after our wedding she moved in with her daughter Eleonora[41] in Švábenice near Vyškov. After about two years there she fell ill with stomach cancer. She went off to Josefka in Hukvaldy, where she died in 1884.[42] I might perhaps even have loved her if I'd known her better. But Leoš stood between us, always speaking of her as though she didn't like me and wasn't satisfied with me. In the end I was frightened of her because of this. Among Leoš's papers [after he died] I found her letters from the first year of our marriage; nowhere there did she come across as unfriendly towards me, reproaching Leoš only with the fact that he'd promised that she'd live with us after the wedding and that he then didn't keep his promise.[43] To me it seemed odd: even before the wedding Leoš had come to an agreement with my parents that we young people would remain on our own. Leoš never showed me these letters from his mother, but I think that they preyed on his mind. Perhaps, since he didn't have his mother around, he thought that I shouldn't have

41 See Glossary: 'Janáčková, Eleonora'.
42 The deterioration in Amálie Janáčková's health was clear by May 1884. She was taken to Hukvaldy in the summer, where she died on 16 November 1884 (Přibáňová 1985, 86).
43 Sixteen of Amálie Janáčková's letters to her son have survived, all but one dating from December 1881 to 1884 (printed in Přibáňová 1985). Zdenka's description of their contents is accurate.

contact with my parents: he always had such childish ideas. This
grudge against my parents certainly had no rational basis.

And another thing: apart from violent outbursts of my husband's
passion there was no tenderness and warmth between us such as I was
used to at home. We had too much of a social life, but no family life at
all. There were never warm intimate conversations between us, my
husband was always working or was hurrying off somewhere. He
never had time for me. Today I don't wonder at him. From his tenth
year he was at his studies, snatched away from his family. His father
died when he was eleven and his mother had her work cut out with
eight children.[44] He was thrown too much on his own devices. Life
among strangers certainly didn't teach him tenderness. Perhaps the
thought didn't even occur to him that it ought to be different in our
house, but I, who at home was used to love and tender concern,
suffered from the coldness of the new home the more it went on. And I
didn't know how to help myself: I was too young and inexperienced
even to sort out for myself what I was really missing here. I just knew
one thing: that at home with my parents there was warmth and I felt
good there. Like a thief I used to steal off more and more often to my
parents and I used to cry a lot at mother's. She was also unhappy at
this but she couldn't help me.

In October the first signs of pregnancy began to show on me.
Mama observed me for some time and when it was certain that she
wasn't mistaken she advised me to tell Leoš. She hoped that
everything would now improve between us. But she was wrong. My
husband heard it out, not showing any pleasure, and didn't change in
any respect. There would be more frequent scenes now, and anger at
every little thing. And then Mama decided on a course of action
which, with her proud and delicate nature, must have been very hard.
She came to us – something which had never happened before – and
wanted to talk to Leoš. But she didn't stay even five minutes in the
study with him and left in a state of agitation. Later I learnt that she'd
begun begging that he'd now be kinder to me and he showed her the
door.[45] And my dear Mama bore this humiliation for my sake. More
and more I began to realize what I'd lost in my parents and what I
had instead.

---

44 Janáček was sent away to school in Brno in the autumn of 1865. His father died on 8
April 1866. Of the thirteen children born to Jiří Janáček and Amálie Janáčková, nine
survived childhood.
45 This incident is briefly described in Zdenka's account to Helfert (BmJA, D 78; see
Introduction).

Christmas came. I wasn't even allowed home for Christmas Eve.[46] My husband invited his friend Šichan to dinner, they talked together in the room while I, sad and filled with a sense of loneliness, prepared my first Christmas Eve dinner in the kitchen. It was little comfort that beforehand I'd secretly nipped back home for Christmas recipes and that I'd managed everything so successfully that all was just how we used to have it at home. But then again, when I thought that we could all have been pleasantly together, my tears began to fall into the food. This was not the joyful Christmas Eve of my years as a girl.

At Carnival I still went to the balls and continued to dance a lot, but after moments of merriment I started getting depressed. Life began to seem unbearable to me. Home, I longed to go home again, and only the thought of the child kept me where I was. I don't think these were the moods of a pregnant woman: I coped with my approaching motherhood very easily, after all I was young, strong and healthy. But this continual coolness and fear of what unpleasantness the next moment might bring disturbed me from morning till night. Among other things my husband suddenly got it into his head that he'd leave his post at the institute and support himself on private teaching alone. A post which anyone else would have considered a prize! I never got out of Leoš why he wanted to do such a stupid thing, I just assumed that he didn't want to be my father's subordinate. I suffered much anxiety at the time. Even with regular monthly employment he said to me there wasn't enough money, what would there be with the insecure income from private teaching? How a child would be taken care of under such circumstances was something he hadn't considered. Not only I but my parents were plagued by this. My father thought a lot about how he could safeguard me against hard times. Eventually he wrote to my husband that the 25 zl. monthly contribution which he'd paid us so far would be increased from now on and from it he would take out an insurance policy at Slavia[47] so that in the event of my father's death, the capital would be paid out. He wanted to protect me in this way in case we should be in need and he could no longer help. Leoš agreed to this and I was immensely grateful to Father. He then paid the insurance premiums for me all of twenty years up to his death:[48] I got a very

46 See Glossary.
47 A Czech-orientated 'mutual insurance bank', founded in the 1860s and operative until the Second World War.
48 Zdenka's father died in 1923, forty years after this incident. Twenty years would have been up to his retirement.

decent lump sum. It would have been a magnificent one if the war hadn't eroded the value of money.

Leoš hardened his heart towards me more and more. For every offence, for every misunderstanding, he had a punishment ready and waiting. For example in July [*recte* 8 August 1882] his friend Žalud got married. Both we and my parents were invited to the wedding, but only Papa and Leoš went: my advanced pregnancy was the complication for me, Mama in turn couldn't leave my brother. I was frightened of remaining in the flat alone through the night in case I should suddenly go into labour. So I asked my husband to come home for sure by ten o'clock, otherwise I'd rather go and sleep over at Mama's. He promised me quite definitely that he'd come. I waited vainly for him until 10.30 then, alone in the night, I hurried off to Mama. My father returned from the wedding at one o'clock and told me that my husband had already left long ago. I saw that things were in a bad way. I didn't sleep any more the whole night and in terrible fear the next morning I rushed out before five to our flat. The door was bolted so I couldn't get in with the key. I rang, I knocked, I cried, I banged on the door, but he didn't open up for me. And he wasn't sleeping. He was walking to and fro behind the door whistling a song. There was nothing for it but to go home to my parents again. And then on the way I decided that I'd rather not return to my husband again. But when I came out with this at home my parents gently and earnestly talked me out of it and so towards about eight I set out on the journey again. The door was no longer bolted, I went in and reproached my husband with what he was doing to me. He said roughly: 'You should have stayed at home, after all nothing would have happened to you.'

I began to fear him. When I simply heard him returning home, fear came over me. We became more and more estranged from one another.

Regardless of my state he looked out for a new flat. He rented one in Klášterní náměstí[49] and arranged that we'd move on 14 August [1882]. All without my knowledge. So we moved. Or rather I moved. He had no notion of domestic work, he simply didn't care about it, only requiring everything to be in good order. It didn't even occur to him to make an exception for the move. I had to worry about everything myself. Although the caretaker at the institute and our daily woman helped me, I really had to put my back into it, to run around and climb up and down stepladders. I hurried as if I had a presentiment of what was awaiting me. Everything was finished the

49 Klášterní náměstí no.2 (see p.57).

very same day so that in the evening I could even hang the curtains. In the night the first signs of labour appeared. Already long before I'd agreed with my parents and my husband that I'd go to them when the child was due to be born. In Brno at the time there were no nursing homes for this purpose and no decent lady would have gone into a maternity hospital. It was prejudice of course, but I was far from reforming the times. My husband himself recognized that the best arrangement would be if I went to my parents. But when on the morning of 15 August 1882 I got up with labour pains and told him that it was already beginning and that the time had come for me to go, he got very angry. He turned violently from me, he stopped answering me and let me leave without saying goodbye. I dragged myself home on my own and there began immediately a difficult and prolonged labour. In my agony I called continually for Leoš. When it had already got towards noon, my parents sent for him. They knew that he was in the monastery: that day, the Feast of the Assumption of the Virgin Mary, there was a banquet there to which my husband was usually invited. He heard the message, but he didn't come. At two o'clock I gave birth to a little girl. My parents sent to the monastery again. Later I learnt that my husband was just lighting up a cigar when the messenger sought him out. He calmly began smoking and didn't show the slightest excitement or even inclination to have a look at the child. Only at the urging of one of the priests, Father Augustin,[50] did he finally consent and got up from the table. He came to my parents' place; he didn't greet them, it was as if he didn't see them. He scarcely glanced at the child, he kissed me coldly and then at once went away again. Perhaps it upset him that it wasn't a boy – during my pregnancy he often repeated to me: 'It must be a boy.' And yet Oluška[51] was such a dear, beautiful child.

I remained with my parents for a fortnight. I felt so good there and I got quite a bit better. Fearfully, I then returned to my husband. Meanwhile his mother was keeping house there. No sooner had I arrived than he welcomed me with the news that there was no money, even though it was just after the first of the month and though my parents had settled all the expenses for the confinement and the christening and had not accepted anything from us for my stay with them. Father even gave me a little money when he said goodbye so I could buy beer with it; in those days it was much recommended that

50 Father Augustin Krátký (1829–1927), Augustinian monk and teacher of religion.
51 Olga, especially as a child, was known by the diminutives 'Oluška', 'Olinka', 'Olguška' etc.

nursing mothers drank beer. When I now saw that my husband didn't
have anything I gave him this money on condition that he'd buy beer
for me himself. He took the money but when sometimes I asked him to
give me something for beer he shrugged his shoulders: 'I haven't got
any.'

And so it went on from bad to worse. I looked terrible, the child was
ill the whole time. She needed a doctor but my husband wouldn't
allow one to be called. There was no money for it, he said. But when
Oluška used to cry at night, he flew into a rage, saying that he needed
peace and quiet, that he must sleep. I doubt if he ever nursed the child,
or ever played with her. Though my parents again showed so much
goodness, the bad feeling between them and him got worse the longer
it went on. I was allowed to visit them with the child only once a week.
Out of fear I kept to this rule strictly. But he continued to get angry
about everything. Arguments broke out over every little trifle. Once
during such a scene he struck me in anger. I was holding Olinka in my
arms and we'd both have fallen if I hadn't held on to something. That
was too much for me. I can't bear to be physically hurt. Only one more
incident was needed as the final straw for our marriage to collapse. It
was found very soon. In the very next argument my husband
threatened me: 'I'll bring my mother here. She'll sort you out.'

I've mentioned that I feared his mother. So I really took fright at this
threat. And although I countered it immediately with the objection
that according to the agreement before our wedding we were to stay
on our own, he saw my fear and proclaimed resolutely: 'I'll take her
in.'

I looked at him and was convinced that he'd do so. 'So I'll go home',
I decided suddenly.

Nonchalantly, he started to leave for school. Once again I asked
him:

'Is that your last word? Do you really want to take in your mother?'
'I'll take her.'

And off he went. I packed the most essential items, I got both myself
and the child dressed, I told the servant – since the birth of Oluška
we'd had a servant – to bring the other things to my parents and left
the house. They took me in, suspecting it would turn out like this. My
husband didn't come for me, he didn't ask after me, he didn't write to
me. It was a strange separation. Neither from my side nor from his was
there any longing for someone else. Why he gave me and Oluška up so
easily I never learnt. For my own part I can say that I kept loving him,
but I couldn't take his hard, sharp dealings with me. At the time, I was

still too young, I hadn't enough strength within me. Later I'd never have done it. I learnt to suffer without hope, without retreating, without a way out. But then, just on the threshold of life, I knew only one way out of suffering – flight. Home, back to my parents.

4

Return

Once again, then, the quiet, kind atmosphere of my old home surrounded me. I must admit that I was almost happy. My parents weren't too pleased, but they accepted me without reproach, without complaint. I depended on them completely, [knowing] that they would see to my future. My father didn't want me to have the stigma of being a woman who had run away from her husband. He wanted the matter to be settled legally and so we went together to our old friend, the lawyer Dr Hoppe.[1] He advised a voluntary divorce without a trial so that I and my husband could possibly return to one another. He also called Leoš in to see him. Perhaps as a result of this conversation – I can't say for certain, however – the Old Brno parish priest, Father Anselm,[2] came to see us some days later. After Mama and I had welcomed him as a respected friend, he intimated to us delicately that he'd been sent by Leoš to ask me if I wanted to return. I told him openly about our married life and begged him to advise me. He thought for a moment and said: 'If that's the way it is I can only advise you to stay where you are.' If I was perhaps still wavering a little, this advice from an experienced priest completely strengthened me in my resolve. From Leoš's side it was the first and last step towards reconciliation.

How completely different was my life at home from what it had been with him. My parents immediately called a children's doctor for Olinka. He discovered that the child was digesting her food very badly and prescribed raw meat for her. She visibly began to recover. And an absolute miracle happened to me. Within a short while I positively blossomed. Life was so carefree under Father's protection and such fun with the two young children, my brother and daughter, who appeared like siblings and who so liked one another too. Not to mention Mama, who was clearly glad to have me home. At that time Grandmother was no longer with us, she'd gone off to Uncle Gustav in Kolín and Mama and I most happily shared the housework and caring for the children. I

1 Dr Bedřich Hoppe (1838–84), lawyer and Czech patriot who instigated the first private Czech school in Brno. He worked as a solicitor in Brno for the latter part of his life.
2 Father Anselm Rambousek (see p.23).

felt that I'd found my niche and this cheered me up. I worked willingly and at everything: in this way I tried at least a little to repay my parents for the unpleasantness which I'd caused them. Father in particular had many worries on account of my divorce: it distressed him more than he let on to me. Only once was he unable to control himself. It was when the court allowed me to take my furniture and dowry from my husband's flat. With the caretaker of the institute I went to pack up the china so it wouldn't get broken while being transported. My father went with me. My husband greeted us in a most unfriendly fashion and he snapped at Father, saying that he had no business there. And then something boiled over in my usually kindly father. 'You ungrateful boy!', he shouted and ran up to Leoš, who didn't expect anything like that. Leoš fled and started calling to the police for help. The caretaker and I rushed up to Father, held him back, and I pacified him and pleaded with him until he agreed to go home. The next day he didn't come with me. I saw to it myself that my things were taken away in good order. Leoš was again at home. Mama told me to leave him his bed from my furniture in the flat, but he refused it when I suggested it to him. He returned the wedding ring to me. I took it; I told him that I'd wear mine because I thought that we should continue to be faithful. With that we parted.

We met again only at the court hearing for the divorce. It went smoothly. Father acted for me because I was not of age. He didn't want to have my husband paying alimony. When, however, the lawyer tried to persuade him that the father should pay something for the child, he accepted 25 zl. monthly for Olinka. Leoš wanted to be allowed to see the child once a week. And I in turn stipulated that I wanted to be present. For I had fears – no doubt foolish and romantic – that he might abduct Olinka. So it was arranged in writing that we'd meet for this purpose at our mutual friends, the Žaluds.[3] With this the formalities of the divorce were out of the way and we were free again. On Leoš's side this changed virtually nothing. He went on living in our flat, now almost empty since I'd taken the furniture away. Even from the outside it made a sad impression: a lace curtain remained on one window only, the rest stared emptily into the street. He borrowed a piano. The thing that he'd threatened me with, and the reason for my going, he didn't carry out: he didn't invite his mother to live with him.[4]

3 See p.31 and Glossary: 'Žaludová, Cyrilla'.
4 In an undated letter, probably written in December 1882, Amálie Janáčková reproached her son for suddenly changing his mind: he had said once she was well that he would take her in and the 'small living-room' would be her dwelling (Přibáňová 1985, 91).

Mrs Žaludová cleaned for him – they lived in the same building – he continued to get his meals from the monastery. Almost every day I used to meet him when I went shopping. We walked past one another as if we didn't know one other. He'd see Olinka almost always when he went to the school; she'd be playing with my brother in the garden. She was adorable: she was beginning to stand up and to babble. He never even glanced at her. Olinka didn't miss him either, she was too young. She called my Papa 'Daddy', hearing it from my brother. It was easy to keep my promise that she'd be brought up only in Czech since at home we didn't speak anything else with the children. As soon as my brother began to speak, Mama decided that he'd go to Czech schools and that he must therefore speak Czech from the beginning. At first she spoke German with him. The little boy got confused when he heard his father speaking one way, his mother another. Whereupon Mother heroically launched into Czech, which was so hard for her, and made herself understood with her little son as best she could.

We lived in peace and quiet until the [summer] holidays. I didn't go out anywhere, I devoted myself entirely to Olinka and the household in the way I saw Mama doing. Father, however, wanted me to continue my education, and to move about in society. [. . .] [Once] Father took me to an exhibition in Vienna. He liked taking me with him, saying that I was observant and noticed everything. In Vienna we happened to meet a friend of my husband, Professor Horvát, who introduced us to a young lawyer from a prominent Brno Czech family. He was a very gentle and courteous person. He accompanied us every day for the whole of our stay in Vienna. When afterwards he completed his studies and went to Dr Šrom[5] in Brno as an articled clerk, we frequently used to see each other at balls. He was always very attentive to me, kind, absolutely correct. Never did he overstep the bounds of propriety by so much as a single word. In this way we were acquainted with one other for very many years. Only when he died did one of the ladies from Brno society tell me that he had loved me. He'd confided in her. I'm told he used to describe me gallantly as 'that rose of mine, that unapproachable rose of mine'.

And I never noticed anything of this about him. I had no feeling for flirtation, coquettishness or even playing at sweethearts. To enjoy myself, to dance, yes, but nothing more. Leoš was the first and only man in my life, and after we parted I'd remained absolutely faithful to him, although people told me tales that he wasn't paying me back in

5 See p.30.

kind. It didn't worry me, although I didn't stop loving him even after our separation. Fear of him, however, was greater than the desire to be with him. I had Olinka, I had the calm and careful love of my parents – this was quite enough for me. Life seemed to me exquisite now that I'd passed through that gloomy intermezzo of a marriage torn apart by conflicts. At home everything was now so peaceful, so harmonious, there were no misunderstandings, there were no arguments, there were no financial difficulties, the children were healthy. In this happiness I bloomed in such a way that people began to call me an 'Old Brno rose'.

It was after the holidays.[6] Once I was walking through Měšťanská ulice by the café 'U Simonů'.[7] My husband was sitting there inside, by the window, and when by chance I looked at him, he made a deep bow to me. I remained paralysed. At home I then debated with Mama for a long time what it might mean. Soon afterwards he met me in the street, again a deep bow. I thanked him as is right and proper and, completely confused, I told Mama without delay. Shortly afterwards I got a letter: 'Madam, I'd like to see the child', signed Leoš Janáček. He had a right to this of course. But it was odd that he was making use of it only now. So I got Olinka dressed up – she was already walking and had exquisite curly hair – and went with her to the Žaluds in accordance with the divorce settlement. They sent for Leoš. He came after a while, we greeted one another and I went on chatting with my hostess. My husband went up to Olinka and stood helplessly over her. She didn't know him and he didn't know what to say to her. Then our hostess got up, took Olinka in her arms, and went outside. We remained on our own. Immediately he got up his confidence: 'Did you go away for the holidays, Madam?'

I answered very briefly, but this didn't deter him. He went on asking me things, and according to the questions I saw that he was well informed about my every step. He showed pleasure in the fact that after our divorce I went on mixing only with Czech society. And suddenly he blurted out jealously: 'And have you been having a good time?'

That was too much for me. I fell silent, but since he was evidently waiting for an answer, I said defiantly: 'Yes, I've enjoyed myself.'

This didn't put him off, on the contrary he even went a step further.

6 i.e. in the autumn of 1883.
7 The café on what is now Křížová ulice no.16 was acquired by Václav Simon in 1881 and remained in the hands of the Simon family until 1906, but even afterwards continued to be known as 'U Simonů'.

He complimented me that I was simply blooming and asked if he could see Olinka again in a week's time.

I came home all agitated from this meeting. From that time he wanted to see his little daughter every week. But it soon dawned on me that Olinka was just a pretext for speaking with me. He always just caressed the little girl and thereafter didn't take any notice of her. But he hovered around me, he entertained me, he was delightful – and he knew how to be when he wanted: once again it was the same charming Leoš from the time before our wedding. I was reserved at first, but I soon melted; repressed love flared up within me once more. Again I longed to see him, to hear his voice, his expressive clipped speech. My parents had a subscription to the German theatre (there was no permanent Czech stage at the time).[8] We had a permanent seat: one could go to the theatre every day. My father went very seldom, in fact just my mother and I took turns. And once, when it was again my turn and I was walking to the theatre,[9] Leoš was waiting for me at the end of Pekařská ulice and asked if he might accompany me. I didn't refuse. How surprised I was when I saw him again after the performance in front of the theatre. Strange: we, who during our marriage had had nothing to say to one another apart from our arguments, suddenly had in common so many topics for conversation that Leoš asked me if he could wait for me again next time. It became a matter of course that we'd walk together to and from the theatre. In a short while he asked me to return to him, to forgive him, saying that he knew that he'd behaved badly towards me. But I didn't want this. I was happy that he was near me and that he was so nice to me, but living with him was something that I still continued to fear. Some things were too deeply imprinted on my soul. He pleaded with me, he made promises, he acknowledged that he'd been unkind to my parents and he assured me that he wouldn't be so any more. He sent a letter of apology to Mama and when she accepted it in a conciliatory spirit, he even came personally to be forgiven. He behaved splendidly: even Mama allowed herself to be charmed again. She forgave him everything, and they agreed that he'd speak Czech and she German.

From then on Mother and I seriously began to think about my returning to my husband. It was clear that we still loved one another and that although our present relationship was good, it couldn't stay

8 From 14 November 1882 the Schulzes would have attended the newly opened Stadttheater in Brno; see Glossary: 'Brno Theatre'.
9 It would have been a good half-hour walk from Old Brno to the theatre on the far side of the centre of town.

like this indefinitely. To be a divorced couple in Brno then incurred a great social stigma. Though no one had ever treated me inconsiderately on that account, Mama would have been glad to see me properly married again. But mainly we thought of Olinka. I continually dreaded that my husband might take her away from me when she was seven, for he had a legal right to this.[10] And Mama in turn emphasized that a child could be brought up properly only in a normal family circle. For all these reasons, but mostly through Leoš's continual pleas and attentions, my resistance weakened and so it was, at the beginning of spring [1884], that I resolved to return to him. But when we told Father, he wouldn't hear of it. He didn't understand why I wanted to return to what I'd been so glad to run away from. Mama and I had quite a job to persuade him at least not to stand in my way even if he couldn't agree with it. On Holy Saturday [12 April 1884] we began inviting Leoš to supper once again. Papa did indeed control himself: he welcomed him; he was cool but he was courteous, even if he spoke as little as possible. Then we made an application for annulling the divorce. Within a week it was approved. But all the while I still couldn't screw up my courage to go back. I put it off almost until the beginning of the summer holidays. Then Leoš got a bad cough, and not long afterwards I did too. The doctor diagnosed inflammation of the bronchial tubes in us both and recommended a stay in Gleichenberg.[11] This speeded up my decision. We moved my dowry[12] back into my husband's flat again, we got everything straight, we engaged a servant, my parents gave us money for a stay at the spa, and off we went. We left Olinka at home with the servant. Gleichenberg did us both good, in three weeks we were well again.

When we returned to Brno, everything was very nice to begin with. My parents would have done anything for us, my husband was very kind to them and to me, we visited each other regularly. But this state of well-being didn't last long. My brother fell ill with scarlet fever, Olinka kept on getting a temperature and so our contacts with my parents stopped for a while. We spent Christmas Eve with them, but

10 This was a myth. In Austrian law at the time the father had no right to 'take away' a child at the age of seven. This misunderstanding could perhaps be based on the fact that the period of childhood, when the child was absolutely dependent on the mother, was deemed to end at seven, after which more favourable arrangements to the father could be considered. But there was no established right even to this.
11 An ancient spa in Styria, Austria, its waters were considered particularly effective for treating catarrh in the mucous membranes. Janáček's trip was mentioned in *Moravská orlice* (17 August 1884).
12 i.e. furniture in addition to furnishings and personal 'bottom drawer' items.

after the new year 1884 [*recte* 1885] my husband's mother died at Josefka's in Hukvaldy.[13] We couldn't even get to the funeral: Leoš was again coughing badly, and I too wasn't well. All we could do was to send money for the funeral. After the death of his mother Leoš was very sad for a long time. I asked him if I should go into mourning, but he didn't want me to. From that time he clearly avoided visiting my parents. I saw from his face that it even upset him if I took Olga with me. In the end it settled into the pattern that she'd go with me only on Sunday morning. However, he didn't stop me from visiting my parents by myself when I wanted to. Vainly my parents and I racked our brains as to what had happened. There was no obvious reason why Leoš had become estranged again. I didn't dare ask him outright, I was frightened of maybe disturbing the peace in which we were now living.

Are far as our finances were concerned everything was now in order with us. Our income hadn't increased, but I came out well on what I got each month, and Leoš also stopped complaining about the lack of money. My parents didn't stop supporting me: they clothed me, they gave us all our fuel and Father continued to pay insurance for me in the event of his death.

Once again the busy social life that we'd lived before the divorce resumed: theatre outings, concerts, entertainments, balls. My husband wanted me never to be missing from Czech society, and people already counted on my being there. Director Havlíček, 'der böhmische Trompeter', as the Brno Germans nicknamed him,[14] used to say to me: 'When you're not there, that's no ball at all. Not one of the ladies keeps going as long as you in the dancing.' It was true, I could go on dancing till dawn. Leoš liked it. He learnt the *beseda*[15] and used to partner me in it.

In the holidays [e.g. summer 1885] he'd go off to convalesce because he was continually in poor health. After an attack of bronchitis, he then got nerve pains in the back for a change; later he had trouble with his throat. Once he went to Gleichenberg, another time to Cukmantl,[16]

---

13 In fact Amálie Janáčková died on 16 November 1884.
14 Jan Havlíček (1850–1937), a leading light at the Brno Beseda, holding many functions. By then a head-teacher (hence Zdenka's title), in his youth he had become notorious in the German press for demonstrating his Czech allegiance although a junior teacher at the main German school in Old Brno. In 1872 he had joined the Sokol (a patriotic Czech organization) and was seen playing the trumpet at the head of Sokol processions. This earned him the derogatory nickname of 'der pémiše Trompetr', an ironic Czech transcription of 'der böhmischer Trompeter' [Czech trumpeter]. See Havlíček's memoirs of Brno life printed in Moravian newspapers 1922–3 (collection in BmJA).
15 See p.31, fn.29.
16 Now Zlaté Hory, Silesia.

finally he took a fancy to Luhačovice, to which he remained faithful until his death. I never went with him, remaining at home with Olinka. On the one hand our income was hardly enough for Leoš's trip, so for that period I had to scrimp and save at home as much as possible, on the other hand I felt that my husband wanted to be alone. There was always some unpleasantness if I went with him or went to join him. When he was first in Luhačovice (1886) my parents also happened to be there and I went with Olinka to pay a visit to them all. I hardly saw my family because my brother had a cough and I was frightened that Olinka might get it from him. Also I didn't enjoy much of my husband. He was in the midst of an amusing company, which meant he couldn't devote himself to us. And when Olinka kept on going up to him and got in his way he was very, very unkind to her. She cried so much then, and, saddened, I left for home earlier than I'd intended. We remained out of sorts with one another so that he didn't even write and tell me when he was returning. I was on a visit to my friend Mrs Žaludová in Královka beyond Komárov[17] at the very time he arrived home. I was most surprised when on my return I saw that he'd already been back from Luhačovice a long time. I reproached him for not even sending me a message via the servant. 'You know', he said to me, 'I was in such high spirits from that company that I had first to go and calm down on my own.'

On his own. I regretted it. I felt that something stood between us. But when everything continued in its old tracks I forgot about it. Early one morning – it was already well into the autumn (the heating in the stoves was on) – my husband was getting ready for school. I was brushing his suit. I was taking everything out of his pockets so that it wouldn't get in my way during the work, when suddenly I caught sight of a letter without an envelope with the greeting 'Geliebter Leo'. Who could have been writing to my husband in this way? I looked at the signature 'Ihre Sie liebende Marie'.[18] I didn't see any more. Leoš rushed up, tore the letter from my hand and threw it into the stove. In a trice I realized the connection between this *billet-doux* and my husband's desire to be alone; it dawned on me whose was the crumpled lady's handkerchief which he'd brought in his luggage from Luhačovice and of which he swore that he didn't know how he'd come by it. And I'd actually believed him then! I had the handkerchief washed and kept it carefully. I got terribly angry that I'd been deceived in this way. I

17 i.e. 'Královský mlýn' [The Royal Mill], just beyond what was then the village of Komárov, to the south of Brno.
18 'Your loving Marie' (but note that the writer is using the formal 'Ihre' and 'Sie').

rushed to get the handkerchief, I tore it to pieces and threw them at my husband's feet. And I told him my opinion about it all in no uncertain terms. He was contrite, he begged me not to get angry, saying that there had been nothing bad in it. I never learnt anything more from him. But when I complained about it to Mama, she let slip that they already knew about that affair of Leoš's in Luhačovice. They'd kept quiet about it so as not to provoke him any further. I soon calmed down when I didn't notice anything else suspicious. Once again my husband threw himself completely into his work. In his spare time he composed *Šárka* to Zeyer's text. Only when he was finished did he ask Zeyer for his permission and was infuriated when the famous poet replied in the negative.[19] It was not a happy time for him then in his composition. He was very dissatisfied with himself and tore up many things.

It was at that time that I became friendly with Leoš's eldest sister, Eleonora. We called her 'Lorka'. She was a needlework teacher in Švábenice near Brno. We soon hit it off together despite the considerable difference in age – she was older than my mama.[20] Gentle, kind and attentive, for me she was always a welcome guest. She came to us frequently and always brought something: fruit, eggs, poultry – she kept chickens – and this attention to our household pleased me. But I was equally pleased to see her even when she came empty-handed – if only for Olinka's sake, who was very fond of her aunt Lorka. Leoš behaved coldly towards her: she often complained that he didn't like her. It was clear that they didn't get on.

In the year 1887 [*recte* 1886] we suffered a very painful loss. Our friend Žalud died of tuberculosis. His wife, with whom I'd struck up a friendship like that of a sister, moved to Komárov to her brother, who was renting a mill there. I often visited her there because I missed her very much. On one occasion I was with her the whole holidays while Leoš was somewhere at a spa.

In February 1888 Olinka fell seriously ill with an infection of the joints and around the heart. It was the result of frequent sore throats, but at the time we didn't know about the harmful after-effects of seemingly trivial complaints; the illness came without warning and alarmed us. Although I was expecting a second child, I nursed Olga

19 Janáček wrote his first opera, *Šárka* I/1, in the first half of 1887. He then sent the score to Dvořák for his opinion and applied to the writer Julius Zeyer for permission to set a text originally intended for Dvořák. On Dvořák's advice Janáček completed a second version, despite Zeyer's categorical refusal to let him use the text.
20 They were in fact both born in 1840.

day and night. After all, I couldn't entrust her to someone else when she was in danger. After two anxious months, she began to mend, but I was completely exhausted and the little boy, who was born on 16 May 1888, was very weak. This didn't stop us from welcoming him like a prince. Leoš especially. Here at last was the longed-for heir to his name. He was happy, he was proud of the little fellow, he held him in his arms, he played with him – how different he'd been with Olga and only because she wasn't a boy. He even put up with the fact, although with evident distaste, that for the puerperium, Mama was with us in order to look after me. The christening was the most lavish imaginable. Papa was the godfather, the godmother Lorka. We called the boy Vladimír to have a counterpart to Olga. My husband and I liked these Russian names very much,[21] I especially liked 'Olga'. I always regretted that my parents hadn't christened me that. But there again 'Zdenka' was my mother's desire when she was young: maybe she also didn't care for her own name 'Anna'.

Our little one, despite all the care and love, didn't thrive. I had little milk – I was weakened by Olga's illness. It took a lot of work before I could force my husband to call a doctor. He said that only a wet-nurse could save the child. And Leoš, for all his fondness for Vladíček, shrugged his shoulders and said: 'I'm not a baron who can afford a wet-nurse'.

It was true that a wet-nurse didn't come cheap. Apart from full board – and it had to be very good – a wet-nurse would get 12 zl. a month. But it was our duty to provide one, to find the money at any cost. I was convinced that it could be done, I suggested it to my husband, but he was firm as a rock. And the child cried whole nights from hunger, he was fading away in my arms whatever I did. I was desperate, I couldn't understand what the matter was with my husband. To my weeping and pleading his answer was always the same: 'I've got no money.'

And so in this misery I was left again with just those two people on whom I could always rely – my parents. It wasn't easy, I was already ashamed of going continually with requests. And this wasn't a small one. But for Vladíček I would have embarked on anything. My father thought about it when I went sobbing to tell him everything and then he said to me: 'So then, we'll give you money for a wet-nurse, but your husband must pay for her food.'

21 Both names were considered 'Slavonic' and became fashionable among Russophile Czechs in the nineteenth century. The two names were brought together in a widely read Russian classic: Olga and her lover Vladimir Lensky in Pushkin's *Eugene Onegin*.

Leoš consented to this. Or rather in his own way: he said, well then, I should get a wet-nurse but he didn't add a penny for her food. I didn't attempt to remind him in case he made another scene. I had to see to paying it myself out of the little that he gave me. To economize on food wasn't possible, on the contrary, one had to cook better so that the wet-nurse had nourishing food. So I did it like this: I cooked well, but less. I gave the wet-nurse my lunch and pretended that I didn't feel like food. Afterwards in the kitchen I secretly ate what remained, or potatoes or bread. And when hunger for something more substantial came over me, I went to my parents and they fed me. My husband didn't notice anything: he never cared how I lived and whether I needed anything.

It was worth economizing. At first I was afraid that it would all be for nothing, that the little boy was too weakened: instead of drinking he fell asleep at the breast. But little by little he improved, he slept at night, he rallied and put on weight. Within a fortnight no one would have recognized him. Also the wet-nurse Cilka was a nice girl, she soon got used to us, and we to her. Her child had died and she fell in love with Vladíček as her own. When after six months we weaned him, she couldn't part with him and stayed on with us as a servant. So thanks to my parents, peace returned to us again, even happiness. For me at least it was my happiest time, when I could experience motherhood without fear, proudly and to the full. There was work, there were worries, but it was joyful and holy.

My sister-in-law Josefka brought a little ill humour to our Christmas [1888] when she came on a visit from Hukvaldy. She began to give me advice about weaning Vladíček and I told her that as an unmarried woman without experience this was something she simply didn't understand. Josefka got very angry, she even flew into a rage. She had such a violent nature. I saw with amazement what a difference there was between her and the gentle Lorka. Leoš rushed to Josefka's defence. Those two always supported one another. Even when one of them saw that the other wasn't in the right he or she would swear that black was white. But at the time I didn't know this, I wanted to convince Leoš that I was right. The cross-fire began and in the thick of it of course I succumbed. It was clear that Josefka and I wouldn't get on. And indeed despite all attempts at friendship our mutual dislike extended throughout our lives until her death. It upset Leoš, he wanted to bring us together. But he was always a bad psychologist and a bad diplomat: his attempts at reconciliation drove us even further apart. For instance, he set his heart on our going for the holidays [summer

1889] to Josefka in Hukvaldy. It suddenly became important for him that we should spend the holidays all together although for so many years before he'd wanted to be on his own. How gladly I'd have gone with him to any other place. But the memory of the ruined Christmas took away my appetite for a stay with my sister-in-law. My husband, however, insisted on Hukvaldy, and only Hukvaldy. And here I rebelled: I sent Oluška off with him and for my part remained at home with the little boy. It didn't pay off. Leoš was so angry with me that he didn't send me a single line throughout the summer. And later I found out that he'd taken his revenge on me through something far worse.

Christmas 1889 was bad. Flu was raging in Brno – as far as I can remember, for the first time. It reached us too. Christmas Day we still celebrated cheerfully. My parents were invited to our place, everything went beautifully, only Olinka was coughing a little. The next day she got measles. My brother and Vladíček caught the infection from her. Then Cilka had to go to bed: she had flu. Immediately afterwards Leoš fell ill. It was like a field hospital at our place. Neither of my parents came to us because they didn't want to spread the infection from my brother, we couldn't send anyone to them because people were frightened of the new illness and didn't want to go anywhere where somebody was ill. I rushed from bed to bed in an unhappy daze until one day I caught it as well. My whole body ached, I had a temperature, I was staggering with weakness. I couldn't lie down of course, I dragged myself from one to the other and anxiously waited to see what would happen next. No one came to us, elsewhere whole families also fell ill, day and night the streets rumbled with the sounds of doctors' carriages. But as far as I know nobody died of flu then and at Carnival people were already dancing again merrily.

At the beginning of spring [1890] Leoš again began speaking of holidays at Hukvaldy. Because he taught me such a harsh lesson with his silence the previous year I resolved that I'd go too. At first I didn't regret it. Any misgivings about my sister-in-law were groundless; she was kind to me, we kept house together and got on well. And Hukvaldy was really beautiful – the castle, the deep forests, the mountains; in a short while I fell in love with everything. The people were welcoming, kind, one fitted in among them like in a family. At first Leoš spent a lot of time with the children and me. He took us for walks, he showed us the herds of fallow deer in the park, he taught us how we could get almost right up to them. I was interested most of all in the herd of black Spanish horses. I'd loved horses from childhood and had longed to be able to ride one. For me it was a delight to see so many beautiful animals here together, to be able to stroke them, speak to them, give them sugar, look into their beautiful fiery eyes, and observe how their arched nostrils flared proudly. At six in the evening the horn was sounded on the Hukvaldy stud-farm and then the whole herd galloped home. It was dangerous to get in their path at that moment, but the magnificent wild ride was splendid to watch from the sidelines.

I got to know two nice ladies: Mrs Jandová, the wife of the leaseholder of the Vyškov brewery, and her mother from the Hukvaldy brewery.[22] I felt happy in their company and we soon became good friends.

I was happy, nothing worried me, I lacked for nothing. And here again of course the inevitable shadow had to fall. Once my husband and I were walking from the park. As we were approaching the brewery, a carriage in which a lady was sitting was just going into the gates. Leoš entirely brightened up, he took off his hat and waved it in greeting. The lady returned the greeting in a friendly fashion. 'You know, that's Mrs Rakowitschová',[23] he said to me.

I already knew that it was the sister of Mrs Jandová, the daughter of the old lady from the Hukvaldy brewery, and that she was married to a forestry official and that she was coming with her children for the holidays. I soon got to know her personally: a chestnut brunette with wide lips, slow-witted, she got bored in women's company, she enjoyed being with men, she smoked a cigar and had no interest in art. Otherwise I didn't notice anything remarkable about her. But my husband changed in a trice. We no longer meant anything to him, he was now in the service of this lady. On excursions, in the inn, at chance meetings, everywhere he saw only her. The next Sunday there was a firemen's expedition to the Matulov wood. The whole of Hukvaldy was there and all the local dignitaries. Mrs Rakowitschová came too. Here my eyes were opened when I saw how my husband hovered around her. And what I didn't see people filled in with hints and knowing smiles. I learnt that my husband had already had a good time with Mrs Rakowitschová the previous holidays. And now it got worse and worse. We all slept together with Vladíček in one room, my

22 Janáček's friend and a prominent Hukvaldy personality, Josef Jung (1836–1912), leased the Hukvaldy brewery from 1870. His wife was Marie née Adamková (1839–1926). Their eldest child Marie (1863–1952) married Arnold Janda (becoming thus Mrs Jandová – Janáčková wrote 'Janová'), an engineer in Kroměříž and a then brewer in Vyškov (Procházková and Volný 1994, 41–3).
23 Janáčková writes a Czech transliteration: 'Rakovičová'; see Glossary: 'Rakowitschová, Mrs Františka'.

husband alone in the kitchen. When we were all already in bed I'd hear him sneaking out quietly and returning late. He began to make it clear to me that he didn't want me to go walking with him, later he even behaved as if I wasn't there at all. After a short moment of complete happiness I regretted his behaviour twice over.

Why on earth was he doing this to me? I hadn't harmed him in any way. I was twenty-five years old, Mrs Rakowitschová was a little older. She wasn't any more beautiful than I was, any more refined or more intelligent, she wasn't even more nationally aware (a few years later Leoš mislaid a postcard from her: 'Wie unangenehm dass jetzt Deine Frau hier ist',[24] from which I gathered that she was even allowed to write in German). There grew in me a feeling unknown so far – jealousy. And also of shame that my husband was going out with a married woman, the mother of two children. It was intolerable. Something had to explode. One day I told Leoš what I thought of his contacts with Mrs Rakowitschová. He ignored it. I felt that I was powerless and looked around for someone to help me. Who else could it be other than Josefka? I hoped that she'd understand me, that she'd stand up for me, that she wouldn't be indifferent to what was being said about her brother. But when I confided in her, she made fun of me in a bitchy female way. What I saw was nothing at all, she said. Men must have their fun and games, mustn't they, it's their prerogative.

Everything at Hukvaldy began to make me uneasy. When Vladíček got a cold sore from the damp, I made it my excuse for going home with him. My husband was clearly glad. When after the holidays he returned with Olinka we didn't discuss Hukvaldy, but the tension between us remained. Here in Brno I bore it calmly. I got even more closely attached to the children. They were my surest support, they were now my everything. On them and with them I built my future life.

---

24 'How unpleasant that your wife is here now!' Unlike Janáček's Luhačovice admirer, Mrs Rakowitschová addressed him with the informal 'Du'.

5
Our children

[. . .] When my husband and I returned to one another, Olinka was two years old. A beautiful blonde child, clever, cheerful and healthy. But even when she was little she had her father's stubbornness. Sometimes she was terribly naughty, so that she had to be spanked if I wanted to bring her up properly. Despite all my great love for her I didn't over-indulge her. She would have spotted this sort of weakness at once and made use of it. When she was about four, she became obsessed by a mania for cutting up things. She went around the whole time with a pair of scissors – we couldn't keep track of her. Once she cut out a square for her dolls from the beautiful bedspread I got in my dowry and of which I was so proud. I remember how I buried my head in my hands because it wasn't possible to repair the damage.

Even at that time she learnt very easily. She knew lots of little poems and songs and recited them to everyone with a delightfully childish charm. Her first and favourite playmate was my brother. They grew up as brother and sister and loved each other as brother and sister too. It was odd, but nice. I, at least, got used to it and into my loving relationship with Mama our simultaneous motherhood brought even more understanding and affection. It was a pity that my husband didn't see all this. Altogether, he had little feeling for the beauty of family life. Today it doesn't surprise me. [. . .] As a poor boy he had to fight hard to make his way, his talent, his impulsive sometimes almost ferocious character forced him into daring deeds, into intensive public activity, whereas it should have been enough for him to warm himself in the bosom of his family. But to understand this I needed great experience of life and perhaps the distance of years, so that at that time, when we'd been together only for a short while, his lack of consideration and his coolness towards both Olga and myself used to cause me much pain. In particular his severity and, at times, even harshness towards Olinka was very hard to take. I'm not saying that he didn't like her, on the contrary he loved her very much in his own way, which knew the rod rather than the caress. But he was able to get on quite well without her. He didn't cling to her. For me, however, Oluška was everything. In her was my hope and joy, it was for her that

I counted my pennies and economized, I thought about her even during the liveliest of entertainments.

Then when Vladíček came along and all the initial worries about him were sorted out, I felt that I was really beginning to live and to fulfil my role in life, that I was like a tree which only now had put down deep roots in new soil, blossoming and bearing fruit. My longing for the old home vanished, I don't even know how. Through his behaviour my husband put himself in second place, after the children, though this wasn't a matter of indifference to me. His occasional flirtations were painful to me and my only cure for this was by [finding] escape in the children. The trusting, cheerful eyes of my little ones gave me strength, calm and the certainty that nothing more serious could happen. The children were the strongest link between me and my husband, especially Vladíček, the pride of his father.

As we watched him grow up, we took greater and greater pleasure in him. Dark eyes after Leoš, golden-haired, dark eyebrows, lovely white skin – an exquisite child. He was always high-spirited, he laughed and sang the whole day long. For his age he was uncommonly clever: already at two and a half he spoke entirely correctly. He wore a broad hat and carried a little stick when he went for walks. He greeted the ladies and gentlemen whom he knew; he'd say 'rukulíbám'[1] and with charming politeness raised his broad hat at the same time. And he was a good child. When he was given some little treat, he didn't put the morsel into his mouth without first sharing it out with all of us. He liked his former wet-nurse Cilka best of all. When 'Nána', as he called her, was with him, I could go about my social duties without anxiety: the little boy didn't miss me. Cilka also doted on him and found it difficult to part with him when she left after two years in service with us.

Leoš avidly registered the first signs of musical ability in his young son: his little songs, well in tune, and his interest in the piano. When Leoš worked, Vladíček sat down next to him, observing him fixedly, and listened. And when Leoš went off, the little boy climbed on to the piano stool and began to 'play', and with a pencil scrawled in the music as if he were writing. His Daddy would take him up in his arms and say happily: 'My lad, you'll be a musician.'

In October 1890 Olga got scarlet fever and after five weeks, when she was already peeling, Vladíček caught it from her. The illness took its course with him very violently. It was accompanied by an infection

1 'I kiss your hand', a greeting to ladies in polite society, even then somewhat antiquated.

of the brain membranes[2] and our hope and pride was gone in two days. He became ill on Friday evening, he got convulsions in the night between Saturday and Sunday, he sank into unconsciousness and never came round, although the doctor arrived immediately. He died in convulsions on Sunday 9 November 1890 at 11 a.m.

It was the very worst thing that could have happened to us. And since Mrs Rakowitschová still stood between us each of us was alone in our pain. For some time now, Leoš and I had not lived as man and wife. There were no intimacies between us, not even affectionate words. As long as Vladíček was around, it was bearable. It was my consolation that at least my husband loved the boy, but now it was terrible. Next to one another, mutual unhappiness, mutual pain, and yet each one so alone.

After a while this terrible blow produced a strange reaction within me: an enormous desire to be a mother again. Everywhere I went I thought only about having Vladíček again, albeit in a different form. It was so strong that it overcame my self-control and forced me to something which in normal circumstances I'd never have done: I went to Leoš and begged him to give me a child.

I'll never be able to forget what happened next. With a grimace, he looked at me and said harshly: 'Hm, that's what you would want, but I don't.'

With a feeling of terrible shame and humiliation I endured this cruel blow. Only now, after many years, can I understand why he hurt me in this way. After Vladíček's death I mattered less to my husband than I'd suspected. Leoš thought of the other woman with all his violent passionate being, so that there remained no more room for me; with my request I appeared to him like an interloper. It's said that there are women who can take such refusals and after a while are able to implore again, or get what they want through some stratagem. I'm not one of those. Those few words and that glance froze in me for ever not only any desire for a child, but also for my husband. I say 'desire for my husband', not love for him. That seemed as if it welled up within me from a quite different source, having nothing to do with mutual physical contact. It was stifled somehow, it was painful, but it lasted: it could appear any time should my husband give me occasion for it. But he remained cold and remote for years.

Only Olga was left to me and I transferred all my faith, hope and love on to her. After her illness she began to go to school again. She

2 Streptococcal meningitis. This is rarer today because of antibiotics.

was blooming, talented, quick-witted; she got excellent school results. Until the fifth form we sent her to the school in our building at Klášterní náměstí no.2. Then she transferred to the Women Teachers' Institute, where she attended the council school.[3] And there too she was one of the most talented pupils. She had an amazing memory. The history teacher did experiments on her; without pausing the teacher said everything that she wanted the pupils to learn for the next class and then called on Olga to repeat it. Olga knew it all almost word for word. But then she relied too much on her memory. I'd say to her:

'Olga, you aren't doing any homework, are you?' and she'd reply:

'Don't worry, Mamička, I know it already.'

And she did.

It was a disappointment for my husband that she didn't have any great musical talent. She liked music very much, she learnt the piano with Mrs Kuhlová[4] but neither that excellent teacher nor my husband were satisfied with her. It was strange, for she had the same exquisite plump hands, the same proud, temperamental, defiant and at the same time sensitive soul as her father. Perhaps it was caused by the fact that she didn't know how to practise patiently and tenaciously. Her artistic tendencies found another path: from childhood she showed great dramatic talent. She passionately loved reciting and acting in plays, and she was one of the foremost in all school performances. My husband and I didn't want to make an actress out of her although I wouldn't have stopped her if she'd seen her happiness in it. Our plans for her were more modest: we wanted her to study and to become a teacher. But fate had its own terrible plan.

When she was coming up to her twelfth year – she was then going to the first class of the council school – in February [1894] she fell ill, again with rheumatic fever affecting her joints and the outer covering of the heart.[5] It was an almost fatal illness, lasting several months. Although Olga pulled through, it left its mark on her for the rest of her life with a heart defect and physical weakness. From now on I never had complete joy in her, it was always overshadowed by anxiety about her frail health. My task in life was now to keep watch over her and to nurse her continually. How painful it was when I constantly had to forbid her all childish delights: running, skating, swimming. Longingly

3 *měšťanská škola*: a type of school, lasting three years, with a general mandatory curriculum, following on from the fifth grade of the junior school.
4 Marie Kuhlová (1862–1951) taught piano at the Organ School in Brno from 1891 to 1909 in addition to running her own school.
5 Zdenka described this as 'rheumatism of the joints and inflammation around the heart'.

she'd look on at her companions happily romping around. She didn't understand what threatened her all the time since on the whole she had no trouble, only a faster heartbeat and a high temperature after any more vigorous activity. She'd be thoroughly grumpy and miserable from the endless prohibitions and reminders. It was then that I got out of the habit of laughing; I lost it for the rest of my life and afterwards no longer even knew how to laugh, even when my husband demanded it of me as a condition for our continuing to live together.[6] Olga was now going to school again, where she forgot that she wasn't well; my husband, who looked on her illness optimistically and believed that all would be well again, worked on *Jenůfa*;[7] it was only I who was plagued by the weight of fear. Hour after hour in the darkness of the night I listened to Olga's breathing, or jumped up from my sleep with the terrifying thought that Olga's heart had stopped beating; it was only I who didn't forget that death prowled round about us. And I lived like this for ten years.

We went on going to Hukvaldy for holidays. The doctor wasn't very keen on it, saying that there were many hills there and it wasn't good for Olga to climb them, but my husband wouldn't have it any other way. By then Josefka had already married the teacher [Jindřich] Dohnal[8] and they lived in Hulváky near Ostrava.[9] We'd hired a room at the Sládeks[10] on the main road to Místek. There the road was level, and with continual vigilance I managed to ensure that Olga didn't walk up hills, and even that she always got a lot better at Hukvaldy.

In August 1894 a new servant came to us, Marie Stejskalová, my devoted, kind Máŕa. She was then twenty-one. She'd had a pretty hard life so far. Her father, who had at first been a merchant in Jamné near Německý Brod [now Havlíčkův Brod] had moved with his family to Brno, where he set up a workers' eating-place on Křenová ulice, a 'soup kitchen' or *Auskocherei* as it was called in Brno slang. He died soon afterwards and her mother married again – unhappily. Máŕa's [step-]father soon used up everything – even what was meant to belong to the orphans (apart from several half-brothers and half-sisters, Máŕa had two blood brothers). When hard times came, the older of the brothers[11] had to abandon his studies at the Gymnasium, and Máŕa,

6 A reference to the 'divorce' settlement of January 1917 (see pp.257–8).
7 Janáček's third opera, I/4.
8 See Glossary: 'Dohnalová, Josefa (Adolfína)'.
9 Now a suburb of Ostrava.
10 See Glossary.
11 Hubert Stejskal (*d* 1941).

who had wanted to be a domestic-science teacher, had to leave the Vesna school. She was then trained to sew white linen with a seamstress, who went on employing her after her apprenticeship. There she had to sew six men's shirts every day. Her health suffered as a result so that she preferred to go into service. A friend of hers happened to recommend her to me. We both like recalling how embarrassed she got at our place at the very beginning. When before the holidays she came to introduce herself to us, Olga and I were just getting ready to go for a walk. Máŕa noticed that I was wearing a dress made from the same material as she had for her Sunday best. It made her thoroughly wretched because it appeared as if she wanted to put herself on a par with me. When after the summer holidays she entered our service she was ashamed of wearing this dress. She continually wore her everyday one because she didn't have a third. I noticed this and after long inquiries Máŕa told me, much troubled, that she really couldn't go around dressed like her mistress. So I had to order her expressly to wear the dress, saying that it didn't bother me at all.

I soon got to like Máŕa. With her intelligence she easily got the hang of everything although she'd never been in service before. Even my husband noticed her honesty and diligence. And to Olga she became her dearest companion and confidante. Soon one couldn't be without the other. Hardly had Olga jumped out of bed in the morning than she ran to the kitchen to see Máŕa. They took breakfast together on the coal-box.[12] They whispered to one another and laughed the whole day long. And as Olga grew up their friendship became stronger and stronger. Olga thought up a whimsical nickname for Máŕa: 'Féfka'.[13] Máŕa called her 'sleči' ['missy']. I didn't have any objections to this friendship, after all Máŕa was gentle, sensible, self-sacrificing. She didn't gad about like other girls in service, she never had a lover: she says that there wasn't time for it. The very first year that she was with us, her mother died and out of her tiny pay – at the beginning she got 6 zl. a month and 2 zl. for suppers – she supported her younger brother Karel[14] in his studies at the Teachers' Institute. She'd have done anything on earth for Olga. Her greatest joy was to comb Olga's exquisite, long, strawberry-blonde hair. When she was older and had

12 This is not to be confused with the painted peasant chest whose origins as a coal-box are described on p.107. No longer used for keeping coal but for Janáček's manuscripts, the chest stood in Janáček's study, the coal-box in the kitchen.
13 In her notes Trkanová suggested that the word derived from the Christian name Jenovéfa (cf. Jenůfa) and meant, in Brno slang, 'crazy girl' (Trkanová 1964, 144).
14 Karel Stejskal (d 1951).

an adult hairstyle, Olga would frequently let down her elaborately piled-up coiffure either out of high spirits or because she didn't like it. Máŕa simply said: 'Just wait, Missy, wait, would Missy prefer it like this?' And patiently and lovingly she'd begin all over again.

Máŕa and I were in agreement about wanting to have Olga as beautiful as possible. From me she inherited the sense for always being neat and tidy; she also liked jewellery. What a job I had and how I had to rack my brains for my daughter to be nicely turned out from what little money I had. My husband didn't want to contribute even a penny towards Olga's clothes. Only when she grew up did he realize that she couldn't be completely without money and gave her 5 zl. pocket money. It wasn't possible to get much with that, because she had to pay all her expenses herself. So I dressed her from what my parents still continued to give me for my own clothes. There was nothing left over for me after that, but it didn't worry me as long as Olga was pretty. I used to say to myself: 'Make the best of it, poor thing, who knows how long it will be granted you.' And so again I pondered, counted my pennies, and with a cheap private dressmaker refashioned my old wardrobe into a modern one.

The year 1895 was eventful for us. Preparations were being made for the opening of the Ethnographic Exhibition[15] and my husband had lots of work to do. With Mrs Bakešová[16] he was in charge of the Moravian Days.[17] For a whole year before, he travelled throughout the Moravian countryside and to Prague; he oversaw the practising of dances and above all supervised their musical performance. It was so lovely when he headed the whole procession through Prague from Žofín[18] to Stromovka,[19] where they performed the dances in the exhibition-site arena. He was wearing a *čamara*.[20] Originally he wanted to wear Valachian[21] folk costume but at the last moment he

---

15 Národpisná výstava česko-slovanská [The Czecho-Slavonic Ethnographic Exhibition] was held in Prague from mid-April to the end of August and demonstrated all aspects of Czech indigenous culture.

16 Lucie Bakešová (1853–1935), collector of folksongs and dances in Moravia and with Janáček and others one of the editors of the three-volume *Národní tance na Moravě* [Folk dances in Moravia] VIII/10.

17 Four days were devoted to performances of Moravian folk music. The procession that Zdenka mentions from Žofín to the exhibition site took place at 10 a.m. on 15 August 1895; that day and on the following three days there were afternoon or evening concerts. The printed programme is reprinted in Janáček 1955, 527–9.

18 Now called Slovanský ostrov [Slavonic Island], one of the three islands in the river Vltava as it runs through Prague.

19 A large park on the left bank in Prague.

20 See p.23.

21 See Glossary: 'Lachian/Valachian'.

found something wrong with it.[22] Olga and I stood on the Žofín bridge and were very proud of her Daddy. Olga was then in Prague for the first time – what happiness and enthusiasm she showed! At home afterwards we kept on reminiscing about it all until, in the November after the exhibition, a new blow struck. Olga got acute rheumatic fever affecting the joints again.[23] She was in bed almost the whole winter and was very poorly. We thought then that it was the end. But in the spring, amazingly, she began to recover quickly, she grew stronger and her delicate childlike appearance began to change into a young girl's charm. When in June [1896] we went off together to Hukvaldy, she began visibly to blossom both physically and mentally. She was cheerful, witty, kind, sociable. When I saw her like this, there grew even in me a shy joy and hope that perhaps after all it was my husband who was right and that Olga would recover. I looked on with delight at how my girl was enjoying herself in the company of young people. She even had an admirer. She was courted by an under-huntsman on the archbishop's estate,[24] a young man who also was still hardly more than a boy, a German. However, on Olga's account, he spoke a wretched Czech. Olga was delighted that she had an escort: she accepted it as an entertaining new game. I wished her this from the bottom of my heart because I saw that it wouldn't harm her in any way, in fact that she'd develop more and more. When my husband arrived to join us in July, he took great pleasure in Olga. He didn't stay long with us, he went off to St Petersburg to his brother František, who was director of a machine-factory there.[25]

When he returned from Russia he began to take a dim view of Olga's beau. He didn't like the fact that the lad was a German and Olga still a child. One couldn't convince him that the whole thing was just a shimmering bubble which would soon dissolve of its own accord. He forbade Olga to go out into company where she might see the young German. Even when the two of us went out somewhere in the evening, Olga had to stay at home. She'd weep. Not perhaps out of longing for her huntsman but because she got bored alone at home and her Daddy's prohibition seemed unfair to her. Only towards the

22 Stejskalová reported (Trkanová 1964, 45) that he had not tried on the costume in advance, and when he put it on found that the trousers were too small.
23 Zdenka wrote: 'rheumatoid arthritis', but this is a different disease from the rheumatic fever which Olga had earlier.
24 See Glossary: 'archbishop's estate'.
25 Janáček went to Russia to visit his brother (see Glossary: 'Janáček, František') and to see the All-Russian Industrial and Artistic Exhibition in Nizhny Novgorod; he also went to Moscow and the Gulf of Finland. He was away from about 18 July to 2 August 1896.

end of the holidays did my husband recognize that Olga had been
enjoying herself harmlessly and let her be. We were already making
preparations for our departure. Then Olga got chickenpox. It wasn't
possible to leave. My husband had to, because teaching was
beginning; I remained with Olga a few more weeks until she was
quite well again. When the first fears about her had passed, Olga and I
weren't too cross at having to stay. The weather still continued so
beautiful, every other moment Olga's beau came to ask after her
health, and this gave her pleasure. When we finally left for Brno, he
came with us as far as Suchdol and wept when he said farewell. Even
in Brno he visited us once, and he and Olga wrote to one another.[26]
However they soon got bored with it and during the next holidays
they passed one another merely as good friends now, hardly even
remembering last year's little fling. I, however, didn't forget it even
after many years and to this day I'm grateful to Mr Reinoch for giving
Olga so many pleasant moments and no pain.

When Olga was completely well and was about to go to school
again our doctor urgently recommended that she continue her
education privately. I would have followed this advice, especially
since my father himself offered to teach Olga, of whom he was terribly
fond. But my husband didn't want this. He made up his mind that
Olga must finish studying properly, come what may. So she continued
to go to the council school at the [Women Teachers'] Institute, being let
off only needlework, drawing and physical education. When she
finished at the council school, she was sixteen years old. She couldn't
become a schoolmistress[27] because of her chronic heart disease.[28] She
had, however, a great liking and aptitude for studying languages, so
my husband and I decided that she could take the state examination
and teach foreign languages. So she began to attend the Russian
Circle[29] and later learnt Russian with Professor Tacl[30] from the Old
Brno Gymnasium.

She grew into a beautiful girl: slender, quite tall, with exquisite small
hands and feet, so tiny that she wore a child-size shoe. She had a

26 No correspondence survives in BmJA.
27 *literní učitelka*, i.e. a teacher of all school subjects at a middle school, apart from
needlework, as opposed to *industriální učitelka* (i.e. a domestic-science teacher), as was
Janáček's sister Josefka.
28 Zdenka described this as 'heart defect', but today a defect is usually considered
congenital.
29 See Glossary.
30 František Tacl (1843–1913) taught at the Slavonic Gymnasium 1881–6. He had
previously lived in Kharkov, Ukraine, where his three children were born.

delicate complexion, a smooth skin with a hint of peach, her father's chin with a dimple. Remarkable and touching was the look from her blue eyes. Even when she laughed there was sorrow at its depth, something like a sad foreboding. Everyone liked her; everyone brightened up when they saw her. Among the neighbours in our house we called her 'naše slečinka' ['our little miss']. She won people over without particularly trying to, merely by the fact that she was kind, natural and cheerful. Her dramatic talent showed itself more and more. She played puppet theatre, she took part in presentations and amateur performances. Everywhere her deeply felt delivery achieved success, as did her melodious, resonant contralto. It was truly amazing where it came from in that slender little body. She knew that people liked her. Sometimes she'd go up to the mirror and look at herself for a long time. Then she'd say: 'What do these people see in me? I don't see anything beautiful in myself.'

While she was still going to school, she often smiled roguishly when out on walks with me. She wouldn't tell me why. Once we were walking again to Lužánky:[31] she with a friend of hers, I behind them with my husband. The girls kept on laughing. At home I asked Olga again, and now she confessed that whenever she went out, she had a gentleman in tow. Then she showed him to me on Česká ulice.[32] A small, fair-haired man, he wasn't good-looking, but with his eyes absolutely riveted on Olga. Then at the Readers' Club he had himself introduced to us by some mutual friends of ours. He was a doctor of law, very bright, a brilliant career before him.[33] He asked my husband whether he might be allowed to accompany us on walks. My husband gave him permission. Olga only laughed at all this: the young lawyer wasn't to her taste. I liked him very much. He told me straight out that he loved Olga, I pointed out that she wasn't healthy, but he already knew this from my husband's cousin, Dr Dressler.[34] It didn't worry him, he was willing to wait for Olga as long as we wanted. At first my husband laughed at this. But then people began to talk about it; they began to say that Olga was engaged. It reached the school, so that my husband decided firmly to put an end to all this talk, telling the young lawyer not to come with us in future. Olga couldn't have cared less. It was I who regretted it the most, especially later, when Olga's fate took

31 See Glossary.
32 Still called Rudolfská ulice at the time.
33 He is identified in Stejskalová's account (Trkanová 1964, 47 and 145) as Dr Hugo Minářík (1874–1938), later deputy procurator general in Brno.
34 See Glossary: 'Dressler family'.

a more and more gloomy turn, and when – many years after Olga's death – I met that young lawyer again, by then holding down a very high position, and found out that he still continued to think lovingly of her.

The relationship between my husband and Mrs Rakowitschová[35] also didn't escape Olga's keen eye, though I did my best to hide it from her. For a long time I was convinced that she didn't know anything, though all the while she and Máŕa chatted about it in the kitchen and felt sorry for me. But I learnt this from Máŕa only after Olga's death. Thus, she said, once during lunch a photograph of Mrs Rakowitschová fell from my husband's pocket. None of us noticed it apart from Olga. Deftly she purloined the photograph and took it into the kitchen to 'Féfka'. And there behind the glass doors they watched maliciously to see what my husband would do. They saw how he looked everywhere for the picture, how unhappy and uncertain he was when he didn't find it. The two of them both disapproved of my husband's relationship and vowed that they'd get their own back at least on the photograph if not on the original. And so when both my husband and I had gone off, the two of them took the picture, pricked out the eyes and finally burnt it. Not a word in front of me, I hadn't the faintest idea about it.

We began to introduce Olga into society. Opposite us at the time, in the Fanta house on Klášterní náměstí, stood the Old Brno Beseda, a Czech readers' club which was meant to counterbalance the Germanism in Old Brno.[36] Czech intellectuals met there from the entire surrounding district: teachers from the two teaching institutes,[37] from the lower Gymnasium, which was then housed in the Men Teachers' Institute, doctors from the St Anna hospital, priests from the Augustinian monastery. My husband and I had attended for a long time; now we took Olga with us. There was a St Catherine's Day dance.[38] All the girls were dancing, only Olga sat next to us, observing excitedly and with regret. Poor little thing, she was forbidden to dance. It was so painful when I saw that something which had given me such

35 See Glossary.
36 The Starobrněnská beseda was founded in 1888. It had its own library, and organized lectures, various entertainments and patriotic evenings. The society met in hired rooms, from 1891 in the house of the Janáčeks' neighbours Josef Fanta and his wife Julie Kusá-Fantová (see p.30, fn.27).
37 i.e. the Men Teachers' Institute and the Women Teachers' Institute.
38 This suggests that the date was 25 November [1896] (the feast of Catherine of Alexandria, patron saint of the Holy Roman Emperor and King of Bohemia Charles IV), a date confirmed by Olga in a long letter (30 November 1896, quoted in Trkanová 1964, 146–7) to her friend Josefa Jungová about the event.

pleasure was denied her. A young doctor from the hospital came up to ask her to dance. Sadly she refused. He asked her again, whereupon she told him that she had a heart defect[39] and that she wasn't allowed to dance. He turned to me and told me that he was a doctor,[40] that he'd pay attention to Olga and that nothing would happen to her. Olga fixed me with a look of passionate entreaty – I couldn't refuse her.

She danced for the first time in her life, not badly, and was happy. It was well worth my moment of anxiety, which, as it happened, was groundless because the dance didn't do Olga any harm at all. From then on I allowed her to dance occasionally. She soon knew how to dance excellently, although she'd never learnt properly.

A French Circle was founded in the [Old Brno] Beseda. Olga and I thought that it would be good for her to go there too. But my husband wouldn't hear of it. He maintained that Olga would get mixed up if she learnt two foreign languages at once. It was a thoroughly ridiculous objection, which undeservedly belittled our talented and intelligent Olga but it was useless trying to prove my husband wrong. I very much wanted Olga to speak French, I also thought that she'd find there a suitable group of young people yearning for education. Consequently I took great exception to my husband's intransigence. And since it was to do with Olga I found enough courage within me to stand up to him as inflexibly as he opposed me. We had a big argument about it at the time, we then didn't speak to each other for ages, but Olga did attend the circle. I was glad that I could successfully fight for a good cause on her behalf, although at the price of her Daddy's annoyance.

She developed more and more. The dark shades of illness retreated from her, she glowed with health and cheerfulness. She was enchanting in her Valachian folk costume and at the fancy-dress evening and *šibřinky*[41] at the beginning of 1898. It was love that she bloomed with! She was attracted by the young doctor who took her for a dance for the first time in her life and who now also attended the French Circle. Among all those young men who evidently found her appealing she saw only him. But he didn't have any of the spontaneous feeling for her which she expected. He paid attention to her, he danced with her, sometimes as if burning with love, at other times cold and negative. She suffered a great deal because of this, though out of pride she didn't

39 See fn.28.
40 The doctor is identified by Stejskalová (Trkanová 1964, 47 and 145) as Dr Jan Bílý, who in 1896–9 was a houseman at the St Anna hospital.
41 See p.31, fn.30.

talk about it and masked her pain with a carefree cheerfulness. In this way she took in everyone, but not me. I suffered with her when that doctor had to go off for a while to the country in order to stand in for a colleague. I experienced with her the joy of resurrection when he returned at Easter and his love for her flared up again. Vesna then was holding a *pomlázka*[42] and Olga was [serving] in the buffet. She didn't realize that the man she loved had returned to Brno. When she suddenly caught sight of him at the *pomlázka* she grew so beautiful and joyful that she enchanted everyone. Both of them then were radiant with love.

Another young doctor, who also liked Olga, was evidently plagued by jealousy because of this, and that fair-haired lawyer who used to go for walks with us came to me and asked me reproachfully why we hadn't allowed him to go out with Olga. I was sorry for him, but there again I was pleased that Olga had such successes. Even my husband noticed the charm which glowed from her, he brightened up and was happy and cheerful. But soon afterwards the doctor left Brno for good. He left 'not having spoken', as we used to say then. I think that he truly loved Olga, but that he feared her illness. She probably thought that too. She suffered greatly but was silent, not mentioning a word of it even to me: through my maternal instinct I just had to guess everything from the odd remark, from the expression of the face, the colouring of the voice. Owing to her suffering she got into a strange state which I didn't like. She began somehow to play fast and loose with all the young men who gathered round her. She drove them mad and then jilted them; often she played around with them quite cruelly. I observed this especially during the holidays in Hukvaldy. Most of all it struck me that this game clearly didn't amuse her. Behind her laughter was well-masked pain; boredom and emptiness behind her cheerfulness. I couldn't help her: it was impossible to speak with her about it, it would have caused her too much hurt. I also didn't have any reason to intervene because during all this Olga never overstepped the limits of propriety, on the contrary she began to behave like a real lady even though she was so young. And so nothing remained for me but to observe her, to suffer silently with her and for her, and to pray that

---

42 A *pomlázka* is the wand made of willow branches used by Czech youths to 'beat' young girls as part of the Easter Monday rituals (the girls then have to give the boys presents such as coloured eggs for beating them). Stejskalová (Trkanová 1964, 48) describes this event as an Easter Fair, put on by Vesna in the Besední dům as a fund-raising exercise with stalls selling traditional Easter goods and food. Zdenka herself used to serve on the stalls, but in 1898 (when Easter Monday would have fallen on 11 April), she sent Olga in her stead.

with her temperament and youth she'd get over it as soon as possible. My husband knew nothing of this. Olga knew how to fool him and after that argument about the French Circle we were still not talking to one another. And here in Hukvaldy he had an interest other than caring about the emotional life of Olga, who continued to seem no more than a child to him.

I was glad when we returned again to Brno. Olga began to attend the sewing classes at Vesna – to save her father, so she said, at least the cost of a dressmaker. Again there was a touch of her pride in this: she found it hard to accept the fact that it was only unwillingly and after long begging that my husband gave us money for bare necessities. I was glad that Olga was going to Vesna, which I so loved myself; I wished that my daughter would get equally fond of it. I looked forward to the fact that there'd be distractions at school and that she'd forget.

Straight after our return, Eliška Machová founded the Útulna [shelter].[43] I was elected to the committee and naturally Olga also took part in the work and all the activities which they organized to raise funds. She gave recitations at the gala musical evening in the theatre, she shared every detail with me when we passed a resolution that, at Carnival time, we'd organize a ball under the title of 'Slovanská Beseda' where they'd dance the dances of the Slavonic nations: Russian, Polish, a Serbian reel, a Valachian *požehnaný*[44] and a Czech polka, to be performed by several chosen costumed pairs.[45] The ladies asked my husband to arrange the dances for orchestra,[46] I had to rehearse the *požehnaný*, which I knew well, and to see about the costumes. I threw myself into it with enthusiasm. Drilling them in the dance went nicely; it was worse with the costumes. Four pairs always danced, dressed in the appropriate folk costume. The mothers of the dancers each had their own ideas about the costume and I had to call on all my energy and sense of diplomacy to make them conform to a single idea. And even afterwards I had my head full of worries at what would come of it since each girl acquired her costume at her own expense and each had a different dressmaker. But it all turned out well and to this day I remember how pleased I was at the praise of Director

---

43 See Glossary.
44 A 'Blessed' dance. Despite Zdenka's epithet it was Lachian in its origins (see Glossary: 'Lachian/Valachian').
45 The 'Slovanská Beseda' took place on 11 January 1900 in the Besední dům.
46 This request resulted in Janáček's three orchestral dances written in 1899, the *Požehnaný* VI/11, the *Cossack Dance* VI/12 and the *Serbian Reel* VI/13.

Mareš,[47] that through my own energy I'd achieved such good results. I had worries with the dancers only at the ball. Director Šubrt[48] had lent costumes for them from the Prague National Theatre[49] for which I had to take responsibility. How fearful I was! Hardly had they finished dancing their solo than I forced them to change into their own clothes, though many of them were reluctant to take off the costumes which suited them so well. I heaved a sigh of relief only when everything was packed up neatly again in crates.

Olga shared all these concerns with me. Before the ball, while I was travelling around with Miss Machová to invite women sponsors – of which there were a good many, all of Olga's friends assembled at our place and wrote addresses for the invitations. It was so jolly when I returned and saw all that gathering of young girls looking forward to the event. It seemed to me as if the frosty clouds were destined to fly away from us, as if a sunny and carefree spring was about to come to us. And indeed, things also began to brighten up between my husband and myself. We still got cross with one another but we had to speak to one another, we had to confer since my husband was conducting the dances we'd rehearsed. I don't even know how it happened that at the ball we made it up with one another.

But, as always in my life, the next unhappiness germinated in the brightness and joy of that beautiful evening, when I least expected it. It began the very next day first thing in the morning. As if it were yesterday, I can see Olga sitting blooming and happy on the coal-chest drinking coffee and telling Máŕa what it was like the evening before, how she liked dancing the polka, the *požehnaný* and the polonaise. And suddenly she said to me: 'Well now, Mama, you ought to know that yesterday someone declared his love for me.'

In all that bustle I'd noticed that at the ball one of our acquaintances, the son of my first piano teacher,[50] had been hovering round her rather too much. A medical student, but he'd already been studying for a very long time. Tall, thin, with a sensuous expression of the face and the beginnings of a bald patch. I didn't find him congenial. I didn't know myself what put me off him – it was something

47 See Glossary.
48 František Adolf Šubrt (1849–1915), administrative director of the Prague National Theatre (1883–1900).
49 i.e. for the dances from the other Slavonic nations; Zdenka had supervised the making of the costumes only for the *požehnaný*.
50 Antonín Vorel (see p.4). The youngest of Antonín Vorel's five children, his son Vladimír (1880–?), would appear to be the best candidate for Olga's admirer. His two older brothers both trained and practised as medical doctors.

instinctive. I definitely couldn't and didn't want to imagine my Olga
next to him. To make certain I asked her:

'Surely not, Olga, that Vorel?'

'Yes.'

'For God's sake, I beg you, just don't start up anything with him.'

She was silent.

'You don't like him, do you?'

'Yes.'

From her tone I recognized that she'd already taken a bite into this
new friendship. It was best not to oppose it too harshly. And also in
this she took after her father: resistance didn't frighten her off as it did
me, but spurred her on. So I simply made it known that I didn't agree
with her choice. She took no notice. I looked forward to the fact that it
would stop of its own accord when Vorel went off again to Vienna for
his studies. I miscalculated. He went off, but he wrote to Olga. At first
only postcards, then letters, which made Olga blissfully happy. He
even came to another ball which we attended, and the next day Olga
told me that they'd come to a serious understanding there and that
he'd marry her as soon as he'd finished studying.

'For God's sake, Olga, what on earth are you doing!'

'Mamička, I love him.'

What now? So far my husband knew nothing about it; Olga's trivial
affairs didn't interest him. But now he had to be told everything. I sent
Olga to him in the study to tell him about it herself. At first he
launched into her brusquely: 'It's immoral of you to be in love at
seventeen.' But Olga clashed with him just as sharply: 'I ask you,
Daddy! After all, you married Maminka when she was sixteen.'

And so it went on no less acrimoniously. My husband knew the
medical student well and was against him just as I was. He knew how
to say everything to Olga sternly and cogently. But she didn't give way,
she fought with him so long for her love that in the end he said to her:
'Well, do what you want. I don't agree and I don't want to know
anything about it.'

That was in fact a half-permission. My husband didn't speak about
the matter with me. But the next day – I remember it was 1 February
1900 – he ran in impetuously from school. His hat was pulled down
right to the back – a sure sign of great indignation. Seeing him like this,
I stood there bewildered, but he ran past me into the study and on the
way simply retorted: 'Have Olga come to see me.'

I went into the kitchen to pass on the message to her. I was
trembling, Máťa turned green. Although Olga also took fright, she

bravely went straight to see her Daddy. After a while she returned crushed and in tears. My husband had ordered her to break off all acquaintance with Vorel immediately. The reason was really very serious, and even Olga herself acknowledged this. Someone whom we could all completely trust had disclosed to my husband that Vorel had done something dishonourable concerning money. I couldn't help Olga, my husband had no option but to forbid Olga any further contact with such a person. But I was terribly sorry for her. Máŕa and I comforted her the whole day, in the night none of us women slept and by the morning Olga was like a shadow. She was due to have a date with Vorel; she didn't go. That very afternoon her girlfriend came with a message from him. Through her, Olga told him what had happened at our house. The next day there was a new message from Vorel saying that what he was accused of wasn't true, that she should go and meet him, that he'd explain everything to her. But I didn't allow Olga to go. I feared that on the one hand she'd get over-excited, on the other that she'd let herself be easily talked round. I went to see Vorel myself.

It really ought to have been my husband who went, but he'd already said his say and thereby considered the matter closed. He was used to his will being done at home without objection. He never bothered about how it was carried out. The journey was abhorrent to me, but it was for Olga's sake. In Ugartova ulice [now Václavská], where we met, I told Vorel straight out what he was accused of. He couldn't deny it outright, but he explained to me that it was quite different, that it had happened in jest. He didn't convince me. I asked him to leave Brno and to maintain no further contact with Olga. He obeyed me only in part: he went off, but he wrote to Olga. She didn't have the strength to send his letters back, and she read them through carefully, avidly. She didn't hide them from me, her anguish brought us still closer together. Only to my husband we said nothing, we were too frightened. But Vorel sent a letter to him too. He promised that he'd stop writing to Olga until he'd finished his studies and up till then he'd entrust her to his fatherly care. At the time we both took exception to the claims he continued to make on Olga, but on the other hand we were relieved that there'd be peace now. From that time he did indeed stop writing to Olga, but she loved him too much. And in this she was too much her father's daughter: come what may, she had to achieve what she longed for. At first she suffered. She was broken spiritually, and physically she was literally fading away. The anxieties which had ceased when I saw her cheerful and blooming returned again. Once again there were nights awake with worry about her sick heart. I was willing to do anything simply for her to recover. And so I was glad in fact when one day another letter came from Vorel. I think that Olga herself had somehow got him to write when she could no longer bear his silence. The correspondence began again behind my husband's back. I myself was in two minds about it: I was in agreement with Leoš – this friendship perhaps disgusted me even more than it did him – and there again I couldn't bear Olga to be anxious and waste away before my very eyes. So against my own conviction and against my husband's prohibition I continued to be Olga's confidante, and shielded her.

The worst thing was when Vorel returned again to Brno at the end of the semester. Already long ago in his letters he'd convinced Olga that everyone had wronged him. She now had to meet him even if the whole world stood against it. She didn't care if people slandered her, providing she could see Vorel somewhere alone. However I couldn't allow anyone to say unpleasant things to her, and therefore I always preferred to leave off everything at home and went with her. These weren't the joyful walks of a mother, taking pride in the happiness of her daughter. Even though after a while I overcame my distaste for Vorel, I never overcame the terrible fear that my husband might happen to meet us. I didn't even want to imagine this catastrophe. And again Mářa was a loyal helper. Like me she knew about everything, she too didn't approve of this friendship, but when sometimes I couldn't go with Olga, she patiently walked behind so that 'Missy' wouldn't be unaccompanied. Before the master she was silent as the grave.

This relationship lasted one and half years and did no one any good. During this time evidence accumulated that my husband and I were not wrong in our judgement of Vorel. We got wind of how he expressed himself cynically about Olga and about me, we learnt that he didn't take being faithful to her very seriously, and there were still worse things. At first Olga didn't believe it, then she forgave him, but her impetuous feelings cooled. Eventually she wrote to Vorel saying that she was breaking off relations with him. He replied that he'd shoot her when he met her in the street. I took fright at this, believing that he was capable of carrying out this threat. Instead of relief that Olga had at last grown wiser, a new burden of fear and anxiety weighed me down even further. Olga herself didn't shed any tears over it. She already had a new plan for life and followed it, paying no heed to anything else. Essentially it was the same that my husband and I wished for her. She set her heart on taking the state examination in the Russian language and she set to work passionately, studying for days on end. My husband took great pleasure in this. He began to be kinder to both of us, and, feeling bolder, I told him that it was only now that Olga had definitively broken off her unfortunate relationship. This pleased him even more. The whole of our family life brightened up. There was just one thing that both of us feared: Vorel's return from Vienna.

Even my husband took exception to his threat. He thought about it and decided that it would be best if Olga left Brno for a while. During our last holidays in Hukvaldy, my brother-in-law František[51] came to visit us and invited Olga to go and stay with him in St Petersburg. My husband decided to send Olga to him for about five months. During this time she was to improve her Russian. At first I considered it an excellent idea for Olga to get away like this from her former suitor. Olga was highly delighted and began to make preparations at once. She made her outfit herself, she prepared everything carefully and at the same time eagerly continued studying.

In the early spring she began to cough so alarmingly that I took fright. I asked the doctor who was treating her what he thought about a stay in St Petersburg. He shrugged. Then I began to fear her departure, suddenly I couldn't imagine how we could live for five months so far from one another. I was dominated by a sort of presentiment which told me that the devil you know is a lesser evil than whatever awaits you in an unknown foreign country. Perhaps Olga caught it from me, perhaps she also felt something similar, but clearly she'd have preferred now to remain at home. I mentioned this to my husband. He thought it was ridiculous. I began to ask him more and more urgently to leave Olga at home for me. But he was an enthusiastic Russophile and had fallen in love with the idea that Olga at any rate would be where he himself wanted to be. However he didn't say this to me, only objecting, quite correctly: didn't I myself want Olga to be as far away from Vorel as possible? How was I to explain this dark fear of mine to him? He thought it was ridiculous, my fears sounded like feminine over-sensitivity, something to be discounted. He now got angry when I went on and on begging him. Olga said to me: 'Mamička, it's all useless. You know, don't you, that when Daddy's got the idea into his head, I must go off, come what may.'

But there was nothing else I could do. On the last day, in utter desperation, I begged him to leave Olga to me, to wait until she was well.

51 See Glossary: 'Janáček, František'.

'No,' he said, in his clipped manner, 'everything is prepared, she must go.'

'But you'll answer to me for it if something happens to her there, then you'll answer to me for it', I cried out at him. He got angry.

The next day she lay in my arms for the last time. In a grey bodice lined with grey fur with matching muff and cap. Her golden hair gleamed for me for the last time, her blue eyes glanced up to me for the last time. Without speaking we huddled together as closely as possible. My husband had to pull her out of my arms when it was time to leave. I didn't have the strength to go with them to the station. It seemed to me that the world was falling apart.

From that day, 13 March,[52] I didn't have a happy moment. It was all the worse because my parents were no longer in Brno. After my father's retirement and my brother's school-leaving examination at the Czech Gymnasium at Schmerlingova ulice [now třída kpt. Jaroše], they'd moved in 1899 to Vienna, where my brother began his law studies. So I was completely isolated. I walked around like a body without a soul. I suspected the worst. Mářa behind me like a shadow. Shared pain at that time brought us closer.

My husband travelled with Olga all the way to St Petersburg and returned after a few days. Nothing happened, everything was absolutely fine. I was slightly relieved. And my husband was very attentive and gentle towards me when he saw my grief. He suggested that we make a trip together to Vranov u Brna.[53] I liked the idea, I told myself that I'd pray there to the miraculous Madonna for Olga's happiness. When we arrived at the church, a funeral procession was coming towards us: they were taking a young girl to her grave. We both stood as if transfixed and returned home dejected. The next day we got the news that Olga had fallen ill with typhoid fever,[54] that she was in hospital and that we should go to see

---

52 Zdenka's date is nine days too early. Olga's last letter from Brno to her uncle František was written on 20 March 1902 (BmJA, A 5397) and two days later she began her journey with her father, documented by a succession of postcards sent to Zdenka from various stops along the way.

53 A favourite place of pilgrimage, 10 km from Brno, with a well-known statue of the Madonna.

54 Zdenka uses the ambiguous term *tyf* [typhus]. There was confusion between typhoid and typhus fever in the nineteenth century and the terms were used loosely. The former is due to a bacillus carried in food or water; the latter is due to a rickettsia transmitted by lice. Relapses (see p.74) can occur in both but is more likely in typhoid, usually seven to fourteen days after the initial recovery. It is probable that Olga contracted typhoid fever, which was very common in St Petersburg.

her there at once.[55] That was some time towards the end of April or the beginning of May.[56] I didn't have a passport. All the formalities which I had to go through before I got one seemed to me unbearably long and agonizing. But before they were completed, my brother-in-law wrote to us again saying that Olga was better already, that they had taken her from hospital to the flat again and that he'd give us news of her every day. Slowly, slowly the terrible anxieties faded as each new comforting letter followed. Eventually Olga wrote to us herself.[57] She wrote that she was now well again, that she liked St Petersburg, that she didn't want to return home for the time being because she wanted to finish her studies at all costs. Later she wrote that she was already allowed out of the house. It seemed that everything would be well after all and we all calmed down. Then in June a telegram[58] came saying that Olga had a recurrence of the typhoid fever and that this time she was in bed in my brother-in-law's flat. We both left immediately.[59] Originally my husband wanted to accompany me only as far as Warsaw, but on the journey he decided that he'd travel all the way to St Petersburg.[60] The endlessness of those two and a half days when I had to sit idly in a train while I was hounded by the agonizing thought that I'd never see Olga alive again.

'Is she alive?', I exclaimed to my brother-in-law when I spotted him at the station. She was living. In fact she was already better again. She didn't know that we were coming. Only then did my brother-in-law go and break the news to her.

And so I saw her again, my beloved, my only child. She'd lost weight, grown weak, but she was breathing, she smiled and with that melancholy look of hers she said something that she often repeated

55 Zdenka was not averse to making a good story out of the incident by juggling with the dates. The Vranov expedition is attested by a dated postcard of 30 May 1902 (BmJA, A 5571), exactly a month after the receipt of the first extant telegram from František about Olga's illness (see fn.56).
56 According to the Brno date stamp, František's first extant telegram was received on 30 April 1902 (BmJA, D 1281). But since it states that Olga was better, it must have been preceded by at least one more saying that she was ill. So the news of her illness must be somewhat before this date.
57 15 May 1902 (BmJA, A 3506); the Russian postmark is 2 May 1902 (old style), the letter was date-stamped in Brno on 17 May 1902.
58 This has not survived.
59 Not quite so immediately. On 4 June (BmJA, A 3564) Janáček wrote saying that they had had a (second?) letter from František and that they were making preparations to leave, either the next day (if they received a telegram to do so) or on Saturday 7 June.
60 This is not the impression given by his letters on his way home, but it would be an odd detail for Zdenka to get wrong (she goes on to mention when he left St Petersburg).

afterwards: 'Mamička, it was the most beautiful day in St Petersburg when I had you again.'

My husband travelled home the next day; I remained. Seven weeks[61] of pleasure at having her again, seven weeks of anxiety that I might nevertheless lose her, seven weeks in a strange city which didn't get dark at night so that up to midnight I could sit at the window and watch over the sleeping Olga. I didn't go out much, but she forced me out, she wanted me to look at all that magnificence of churches, the bustle of the splendid *prospekty* [avenues], the mightiness of the Neva. So I walked through St Petersburg but my soul was with Olga. Most often I stopped by the Neva, I looked into its waters and said to myself that I'd jump in if Olga didn't get over her relapse. But she recovered from this too. She began to walk around the room, she began to get dressed. Although she was terribly thin, her dresses were too small around her waist. That was her liver swelling from her heart failure. We both had the same one desire: to get home as soon as possible. Eventually, after seven weeks, the doctor gave us permission. We were glad to leave this beautiful city which had brought us only pain.

Leoš was waiting for us in Warsaw, where we arrived the evening of the next day. Olga was well, she was happy; through her Daddy a little bit of home welcomed her. We travelled on further. Late that evening her feet began to swell and hurt. In the train the next day she could hardly change out of her slippers into her shoes; during the customs inspection in Hranice[62] we almost carried her from the train and in Studénka, when we changed trains for Příbor, we really did carry her. Máňa was waiting there at the station. When she saw her 'Missy' being carried from the train to the carriage, she broke into noisy sobbing. 'Don't cry, Féfka, it's not as bad as all that', Olga bravely comforted her.

No sooner had we got to Hukvaldy than we called in the local doctor, Dr Strébl.[63] He detected that the rheumatism of the joints had returned again. He devoted so much care to Olga that she was soon walking again. But only around the house: thin, very pale, her hair fell

61 Zdenka's calculation appears to be correct. She probably set off on Saturday 7 June (arriving on Monday 9 June). The dating of the end of the trip is less clear, but on 30 July Olga wrote to her uncle, thanking him for the trip. Allowing two days for the journey and one day's rest before writing would suggest a departure date of 27 July. Monday 28 July would be exactly seven weeks from Zdenka's arrival in St Petersburg.
62 Zdenka writes 'Granice'. From its location as a crossing point on the Warsaw–Studénka line, she probably meant 'Hranice', then a small town with a customs office on the border with Silesia (*Ottův slovník naučný*, xi, 1897, 756), today absorbed into Karviná.
63 Dr Augustin Strébl (1870–1916), doctor to the archbishop and general practitioner specializing in homeopathic medicine.

from her head like leaves from the white birches in autumn. Her heart
didn't improve, albumin appeared in her water, her kidneys started to
fail. At night she had high temperatures, she could neither breathe nor
sleep. My hope that Hukvaldy would perk her up once again, as so
many times before, faded in those nocturnal vigils, where in a single
rented room Mářa and I took turns watching over her. My instincts
told me that this time Olga wouldn't pull through. After such watchful
nights my nerves were so shattered that I didn't even know what I was
doing. My husband didn't live through this with us. He slept in the
school, in the little room of the under-teacher, who was on holiday. He
persisted in not taking Olga's illness tragically, he didn't believe that it
could be hopeless. He still went visiting his friends and was the
constant companion of Mrs Rakowitschová. Olga saw it just as I did
and also found it hard to bear. She'd clasp me round the neck and say:
'Mamička, let Daddy do what he wants. After all you have me.'

Once, my sister-in-law Josefka came to visit us: her husband
meanwhile, through my husband's influence, had become head-teacher
in Hukvaldy. While we were talking, Olga couldn't contain herself and
let slip something about her Dad and Mrs Rakowitschová, I also
began to complain that he ought not to be doing this when Olga was
so ill. Josefka sympathized with us and chimed in with our comments
so sincerely that we told her everything openly and were convinced
that she truly felt for us. Soon afterwards we had a very bad night
again, Olga was feeling very poorly. In the morning my husband came
into our room without having had a proper sleep, with his clothes
stinking of tobacco fumes and beer. You could see that he was
returning home only now. The contrast between his night and ours
vexed me. I began telling him off. He got angry and retorted that I'd
better keep quiet, that anyway I'd already told tales about it to Pepka
(as he called Josefka) and went straight on to tell me everything that
I'd supposedly made my sister-in-law believe about him. In essence it
was what Olga and I had said, but everything coloured, distorted and
biassed against me. Normally I'd have been able to bear it like so much
else, but now it upset me dreadfully. No sooner had my husband gone
than I got dressed and went to see her at the school to find out what
she'd really told Leoš. She came out to meet me in the hall. By chance
she was carrying a large kitchen knife. Hardly had I told her why I was
there than she gripped the knife and lashed out at me: 'I'd have given
you a thrashing there and then for being like that.'

I completely lost my mental balance. I guessed from those words
that she had indeed only been pretending in front of Olga and me and

that she'd then gone and told my husband what he'd reported to me. And as I saw her enraged, with a knife in her hand, the thought flashed through my mind: 'She'll kill you now.'

Straight after that I struck her in the face without thinking. She started screaming and her husband rushed in and began reproaching me. But I'd already come to my senses and was appalled by what I'd done. I ran back to Olga, red with shame. To this very day I don't understand how I could have done it, I regret it and am deeply ashamed of it. I told Olga what had happened. From that time she didn't want to see either of the Dohnals. We stopped seeing them. My husband of course continued to go there, he didn't do anything differently after these scenes. We, however, cut ourselves off from virtually the whole of Hukvaldy society.

At the end of the holidays Olga got congestion of the lungs.[64] After several visits, Dr Štrébl called me out of the room. My husband was already standing in the hall, pale, shattered; behind him Máňa was sobbing quietly but desperately. The doctor had just told them that things were very serious with Olga and that he'd like us to call a doctor from Brno. He didn't have to tell me that: already long before I'd guessed that it was hopeless. But my husband was so devastated that I forgave him everything that I'd recently held against him. I saw that only now did he realize how it really was with Olga. She herself suspected nothing. We all controlled our feelings, we concealed everything from her. Even with the doctor from Brno we managed to arrange things discreetly. Just then, Máňa was due to leave for home to put the house in order. We gave her the task of sending Leoš's cousin Dressler to us at once. He came the next day but one, as if on a visit. Olga meanwhile was more comfortable and Leoš's cousin consoled us, saying that it wasn't so bad, that congestion of the lungs was simply difficult to treat in people with a weak heart. On his advice we put only poultices on Olga's back instead of bandages and she soon felt better.

Teaching was starting, my husband had to leave, we [i.e. Olga and Zdenka] remained.[65] It was already quite chilly when he suddenly arrived to take us [home]. We weren't prepared, I packed quickly, he ordered Olga to say goodbye in writing to her uncle and aunt Dohnal. After what had happened, she didn't want to do that. Everything in

64 Zdenka described this as 'bronchial catarrh'. See Appendix 1 for a general comment on the course of Olga's final illness.
65 Janáček must have been gone by 15 September since Olga wrote to him on that day (BmJA, A 3488).

her always rebelled when her Daddy used to force her to do something
she didn't want. She'd say defiantly that he was bullying her. But in the
end, she obeyed, either out of love for him or because I talked her into
it. She rebelled this time too, nevertheless she then wrote a letter to the
Dohnals and sent it. By now she was again no longer confined to bed
and moved slowly about the house. Because she didn't tell anyone that
she'd written the letter, my husband thought that she hadn't obeyed
him. He was angry with her. Throughout the journey to Brno he didn't
say a word to her. She saw it clearly, even drawing my attention to it.

'So tell him that you sent the letter', I asked her.

'I won't tell him and beg you not to do so either.'

With defiant pride she bore my husband's anger. Only when we were
home, when she'd again caressed everything she loved, she turned to
my husband: 'Well, Daddy, you think I didn't write, but I did.'

My husband beamed, in no time at all he was all kindness and
tenderness towards her and she repaid him in kind. And I looked on
them half smiling, half in pain, and thought to myself: 'Same blood,
same blood.'

I didn't understand why they tormented each other so unnecessarily.

Dr Dressler was now treating Olga. It seemed that her condition was
improving. Although she wasn't able to get out, we did everything so
she wouldn't get bored at home. She was given a beautiful canary from
Hukvaldy, she called him 'Valašek';[66] he sang the whole day and in the
evenings and he kept her amused. We bought her a little poodle, a
puppy. He was all black with white spots only on the chest and on one
paw. He kept on putting out his little tongue, and that's perhaps
why Olga christened him 'Čert' ['devil'].[67] They were so merry
together. When she could no longer bend down to him and chase
about with him she'd tease him with her tiny foot. Once he got over-
excited and chewed right through her slipper. She laughed so much at
it then. Like me she loved flowers: I took great care to see that she
always had plenty of them about her. She read a great deal: she'd
brought back many books from Russia and now she read Gogol,
Pushkin, Tolstoy, Dostoyevsky and other authors in the original. She
made extracts, she translated from Russian, and the newspapers
published her translations. She kept a diary, but later she burnt it. It
now came in handy that she'd learnt fancy needlework in Vesna. She
embroidered a beautiful pillow in *petit point* for me – it's now on our

66 i.e. Little Valach. Properly speaking, if he came from Hukvaldy in Lašsko he should have
been named 'Lašek' [Little Lach] (see Glossary: 'Lachian/Valachian').
67 Czech folk representations of devils often have long tongues hanging out.

divan in the salon. She made herself a morning coat, *ranoška*[68] she called it, and was very fond of it. Her body swelled up more and more so that everything was too small for her. Her beautiful slim figure became distorted. So she made large aprons for herself which covered up everything. She asked me not to let her friends in: 'They all look at me so strangely.'

One last time we went for a walk together. It was a beautiful October day, sunny and warm. Olga longed to take a walk. I was overjoyed seeing her outside again. Neither she nor I suspected that we were walking together in the sun for the last time. Olga had on her beautiful grey-blue costume. But how she looked in it now! A shadow of her former beauty. Slowly we crossed the Klášterní náměstí and went past the brewery towards Bauer's Ramp.[69] And here she said to me crestfallen: 'Mamička, I can't walk any more.'

A slow, sad return.

She had one great wish: to see my parents again. She talked about it all the time. But we both feared my husband's outbursts if we so much as mentioned it to him. For over the years my husband's distaste for them had deepened into hate. There was no evident cause and my parents often asked me sorrowfully: 'What have we done to him?'

I feared talking to him about it directly – an argument would certainly have broken out – but I think that his dislike of them was for patriotic reasons: that he held their half-hearted nationalism against them. But wasn't that inevitable in a marriage of mixed nationality? As it was, my mother and father had made huge concessions one to the other.

Where I would have been left with a simply unrealizable desire, Olga got her own way. She thought out the whole plan and thought it out well. We invited my parents and put them up in a hotel. We arranged that they came to us when my husband was at school. He never learnt about this ruse. Olga was happy and it seemed as if a weight had been taken from her, so that my parents left again for Vienna with the hope that she'd nevertheless recover.

That was in October. Up to Christmas we struggled along. Long nights, grey days, glimmers of hope, a worsening of the illness – it dragged on like this in an endless gloomy chain. Things were bad at Christmas. We got the presents ready as usual, Olga even gave me a little help when I baked the sweet biscuits, but I already knew that it

68 From *ráno* = morning.
69 Bauerova rampa, the site of the present Brno Exhibition Grounds. Bauer's former sugar-refinery, from which the name is taken, is today known as the Zámeček [Little castle].

was the last Christmas Day that we'd spend together. She herself decorated the Christmas tree. Often she stopped and said sadly: 'Who knows if it isn't the last.'

Christmas Eve was sad although the presents were lavish. From us Olga received a reproduction of the picture *Old and Young Love*, from my parents in Vienna a diamond ring with a pearl. She took great pleasure in it, she slipped it on her finger and never took it off. That evening Leoš was very solemn, calm and loving. He was preparing to leave for Hukvaldy. He wanted a break. 'I must get away', he'd said to me earlier.

And we were waiting for it, because it was only then that Olga's greatest joy could happen. My parents had promised us that they'd come and see Olga again when my husband was away. They indeed came on a visit on St Stephen's Day and this time stayed with us, so that we had them with us the whole time. But only the first day was joyful. Then Olga's condition deteriorated, her legs began to swell. She didn't allow us to call the doctor, only after my parents left, she said. Parting was sad, my parents realized that they'd never see Olga walk on the grass again. After their departure I called Dr Vašíček,[70] who had once treated Olga. 'It's the beginning of the end', he told me.

Only Máŕa saw my pain; to Olga I went with the calm reassurance that it would all be well again. Máŕa also learnt to be carefree and laugh in front of 'Missy'. My husband returned only after the New Year, when teaching was due to begin again. He couldn't even believe or understand that things could be so bad. We called in Professor Maixner[71] from Prague. He comforted Olga, he encouraged her to spare herself so that in the summer she could go again to the country, but he didn't hide from us that it was now completely hopeless.

Her kidneys were beginning to stop functioning. She continually took medicine just to make them work a little. But it didn't help very much. Dropsy set in. So that Olga could have more air, she and I moved from our little room into my husband's study, where she then lay on his bed and at night I slept on the divan, if I can call sleep that strange, tortured unconsciousness out of which I pulled myself at Olga's every sigh. She suffered more and more. She could neither lie down nor sit, everything hurt her in every position. Máŕa and I laboriously turned her over every so often because she wished it. She was heavier and heavier as everything in her filled up with water which couldn't escape.

---

70 Dr Ervín Vašíček (1851–1918), chief district medical officer in Brno.
71 Dr Emerich Maixner (1847–1920), a Prague specialist in internal diseases.

It was Carnival time again, in the Besední dům there was the Zora ball[72] and *šibřinky*,[73] the merry creaking of carriages resounded through the quiet of the night and Olga lamented: 'People are dancing, they're having a good time, and I have to suffer here so.'

During the whole time she broke her silence about her former love just once. That day in the afternoon Vorel came to see us. My husband wasn't at home, Máŕa was in the laundry, and Olga and I were dozing because we hadn't slept again that night. He knocked in vain and went away. But our neighbour, Mrs Bartošová, the doctor's wife,[74] saw him and told Máŕa. I told Olga[75] about it carefully. I wanted her to decide for herself whether to say goodbye to him. Her face darkened: 'Don't let him come to see me', she said almost venomously, 'I curse him. I have to die because of him. I should, Mamuška, have taken your advice, I could have been well and happy today. That was a dear person.'

She was thinking of that fair-haired lawyer with whom we'd broken off relations because of people's talk. Poor thing, she was convinced – besides the doctors had also confirmed it for me – that she'd have remained relatively well if there hadn't been that unfortunate journey to St Petersburg. And the blame for having to undertake it she put down to the threat of her former admirer.

It was as if a flash of lightning struck me in the eyes. I remembered how unwillingly she went off and how I resisted it; I remembered whose will it was that she left. At once I suppressed this terrible thought, energetically I drove it away on the sensible grounds that no one was guilty for this cluster of unfortunate coincidences. But the thought was implanted in me without my will, it etched itself secretly into my soul without my being aware.

Vorel never came to us again but people said that he kept on asking Olga's friends about her.

She didn't want to die, she had moments when she felt sorry for herself, at other times she defied death with all her stubborn nature. Even now she still took care – as far as was possible – to maintain her neat appearance, she still liked Máŕa doing her hair. Once, not long before the end, she was cleaning her exquisite teeth. Máŕa handed her

72 The Academic Readers' Club Zora (the word 'Zora' is the Slavonic equivalent of Aurora, or dawn) was founded in the 1860s at the Technical University in Brno. It aimed not only to guide Czech students in their technical education at what was then a German institution but to raise national awareness through lectures, concerts and other entertainments.
73 See p.31, fn.30.
74 In fact the widow of the physician, Dr Josef Bartoš, Mrs Josefa Bartošová.
75 'Máŕa' in manuscript in error.

the necessary things. Olga went over her teeth with the brush and her hand dropped.

'You see, I can't do it any more, I haven't the strength.'

'Don't worry about it Missy, you've got your little teeth white even so.'

'Oh yes, it's a pity about them going into that black earth', Olga sighed.

At times she began to scream: 'I don't want to die! Help me, help me, don't let me go into that cold earth.'

I thought I'd go mad, it tore my heart so. And in fear she went on crying: 'Help, help! I'm so young, I don't want the worms to eat me.'

I had nothing for her other than my powerless terrible pain. All comfort and delusions were now futile. She wouldn't have believed them. She no longer even believed the doctors, she didn't want them to come to us. The only thing she still waited for was a miracle. Someone told my husband about a miracle doctor in some village or other near Brno. When he mentioned it at home, Olga passionately pinned her faith on the thought that he might be able to help her. How could we have deprived her of a single relieving moment of hope? My husband set off at once to see this charlatan, who of course promised that he'd cure Olga. He sent her various kinds of tea without having even seen her. She took them all with joyful trust. Her condition worsened, perhaps because of the amount of fluid that she drank. But she didn't lose faith in that person. She asked her Daddy to bring him to her. He went off at once. The miracle doctor arrived, examined Olga and ordered her to drink strong wine – sherry, I think. Everything in me rebelled against this senseless treatment, but I sent for the wine. After all it was again a few moments of relief for her, at least spiritual, if not physical. Of course she couldn't drink the wine, she swallowed just a few drops.

And again a new torment. She fought for breath. Anxieties came upon her. The fluid pressed unbearably on her poor insides. In the dining-room next to the study the window was open the whole time because the coolness relieved the patient. For her heart she even had a special cooling device in which cold water always circulated. It was February, it was impossibly cold in the study, Máŕa and I shook even in our overcoats, but Olga lay only in her batiste morning coat and no longer felt the cold. Slowly all this began to get the better of me. I was already like a shadow. During those endless nights I couldn't bear her cries. I'd flee to the kitchen and there I'd scream with pain like an animal. But again I'd be hounded back, I was jealous of every moment that I could still experience with Olga. She turned her eyes to me when I returned and would say:

'Mamuška, have you been crying again?'

'No, no', I tried to smile.

But she continued, inspecting me through and through with her deep eyes: 'Mamička, I know that you're the one in greatest need. Daddy will recover from this, but you'll remain abandoned.'

On Sunday 22 February, the morning after a night of great suffering, Olga called me to the bed and said: 'Maminka, I'm a Christian, I know what my duty is. Call a priest to me.' I began sobbing. 'Don't cry, you know well and I know well too that I shall die.'

I went to consult my husband. He frowned and didn't say anything when I told him that Olga wanted a priest. But afterwards he went to Olga, and Mářa heard him saying to her: 'That's the right way. It would have upset me that you're saying goodbye to your friends and not to God.'

I got dressed and went to the monastery to Father Augustin Krátký.[76] He was a teacher at the Realschule, sensitive and educated. Up to his death he was my confessor. He came almost at once. Mářa meanwhile prepared everything at home for the last rites. When Olga was making her confession I went into the room next door and there I saw that my husband had locked himself into the little room where we used to sleep before. He didn't come out at all. Again each of us experienced our grief separately. After confession I went to Olga. She was due to receive communion. Mářa and I wanted to light the candles around the crucifix on the little table. But Father Augustin wouldn't allow it. 'Don't light them, she'd find it difficult to breathe.'

God reward him eternally for this attentive tenderness towards my Olga.

When the ceremony was over, Olga looked at me with a particular look, not of this world, and breathed a sigh of relief: 'Mamuška, I feel relieved.'

She was relieved physically too. And I, who had lived through everything with her, also wanted to experience with her this state of spiritual cleansing. I asked Father Augustin to hear my confession too the next day, saying that I'd go to him early next morning in the monastery. The rest of the day was sad like the last smile while saying

76 See p.37, fn.50.

farewell. Olga got an appetite for food. She wanted chicken and Mářa rushed off at once to the Dominican market.[77] At the time things were still for sale everywhere on a Sunday morning. She carefully cooked the chicken, but Olga took only two mouthfuls and said mournfully: 'I can't eat any more.'

In the afternoon we all sat by her. My husband had then just finished *Jenůfa*. During the whole time he was composing it, Olga took a huge interest in it. And my husband also used to say later that his basic model for Jenůfa was his sick daughter. Now Olga asked him: 'Daddy, play me *Jenůfa*, I won't live to hear it.'

Leoš sat down at the piano and played . . . I couldn't bear it and ran off again to the kitchen.

A terrible night again. In that suffering I remembered what was said about holy communion, that what is asked for with one's first thought after receiving the body of Our Lord comes true. By the morning, out of the depths of my pain a resolution grew within me that I'd implore God for Olga. I raced through the grey winter morning to the monastery for a miracle. I so believed in it, I so hoped, I begged so passionately . . . I went home almost certain that Olga would be left to me.

Things were bad there, very bad. Olga screamed: 'Daddy, Daddy, go off again to that miracle doctor. Let him give me something to bear this torment.'

So my husband went off again bringing this person with him at once. I don't know what they said together, what he again advised us, I wasn't capable of taking it in, I knew that this mountebank wouldn't help where God didn't want to.

In the afternoon Olga became a little quieter. She asked me and my husband: 'Daddy, Mamička, can I do what I want with my things?'

Of course she could. When my husband had to go off to school, she called Mářa and me to her. She said that she wanted to make her will. She ordered Mářa to write, I couldn't do so for crying.

She remembered everyone. When she was still small, my husband had her insured so that as an eighteen-year-old she got 2000 zl. from the insurance company. With it we bought bonds for her. Now she left some of them to the children of our landlord in Hukvaldy [Vincenc Sládek], some to her aunt Lorka. She remembered my parents, my brother. To her girlfriends she gave away her jewellery and clothes. She

77 i.e. the Dominikánské náměstí, where until 1935 there was a market for the sale of poultry, eggs, butter etc.

forgot only one girl, Bedřiška Nahodilová,[78] now head-teacher of a school. And as in the folksong about the father and his three daughters of whom the one to whom nothing was given remembers him the most, so it was this friend who has been the most faithful of all. She never forgets to send a beautiful bouquet to Olga's grave at All Souls.

When she got to Máňa Olga stopped: 'What do you want? You deserve the most. I'll give you my diamond earrings.' Máňa didn't take them. She said she didn't want anything, that she didn't deserve it, and that it wasn't right for her to wear diamond earrings. Olga acknowledged the last reason. So she gave Máňa her golden watch with a short chain. After a long hesitation Máňa took this in memory of her. Olga had brought back from Russia some special black material for a blouse. She also presented Máňa with this now: 'Take it so you can wear mourning for me.'

In the end all that remained to her was the ring which she'd received from my parents at Christmas. For a long time she turned it on her thin little finger and then she asked slowly: 'And to whom should I give this?'

I saw clearly that she couldn't bring herself to part with it and said to her: 'Oluška, leave that ring for yourself.' Joyfully she agreed: 'Yes, Mamuška.' And the ring then went with her into her grave.

She even thought of Čert. She begged me earnestly: 'Mamička, don't give Čert away, keep him in my memory.'

At the end she remembered herself too.

'I want to have a nice funeral. I have money for it' (she had a savings book). 'Let the procession go from the church right to the institute. I was born there. I'd like lots of flowers and, Mamuška, always put plenty of flowers on my grave. Dress me up nicely for the grave. Do my hair as I used to wear it: curls around my forehead. And don't put white flowers into the coffin. If I can't be a living bride, I don't want to be a dead one either.'

Even now she knew how to strike a defiant note against her fate. But immediately sorrow blew it away again: 'Put violets around me, I liked them best of all the flowers.'

My God, my God! This child who so burningly loved life, beauty, joy, saw herself in her coffin, surrounded by a wreath of fading violets. Weeping aloud I took her in my arms. She lay in them quietly for a moment as if she were thinking. And suddenly: 'Féfka, promise me that you won't leave Mamuška unto death.'

---

78 Bedřiška Nahodilová (1882–?) qualified as a teacher in 1910 and was later head-teacher of a school in Brno-Židenice.

In August 1934 it was forty years since Máǎa first came to us, forty years that she has served me faithfully. In moments both of joy (there weren't many of these) and of sorrow, in the terrors of the World War, despite the modest pay, hounded by Leoš because of her faithfulness to me, Máǎa remained with me because she promised Missy this. When it seemed to me that everyone had deserted me and perhaps even the heavens, my Máǎa stood faithfully by me. If God grants it, she will serve me unto death, she will shut my eyes and fulfil my last wish as she fulfilled that of her Missy. And even if everyone forgets Olga and me, Máǎa will certainly not forget, that most faithful of the faithful.

When the will was ready I had to promise Olga that everything would happen as she wished. She asked me that very emphatically and several times. In that moment I didn't realize why, it didn't occur to me that the child was gazing beyond her death.

Towards evening when again she had a fit of anxiety, she said to me sadly: 'I'd so like to see Granny and Grandad again. But it can't be. So write to them at least.'

At the corner of the piano in my anguish I scribbled: 'Olga is dying. I'm to send you her last greeting.'

Again for a while she fought her hard battle. Then she started lamenting: 'I can't hold out! Have them take this water from me. It's unbearable!'

My husband rushed off to the hospital with a request for help. They told him there that it wasn't possible to do what Olga wanted, that she'd die at once. Now – after thirty years – it's said that doctors take off water and relieve the sick. This is a great boon. When I hear about it, I think with pity of my poor Olga. Science then didn't know how to relieve her suffering. When my husband returned then, she complained desperately: 'They are unfeeling people! Why do they let me suffer so much!'

Towards eight o'clock she couldn't stay in bed. We sat her in the armchair. It's the one which is now in the museum with the heart-shaped cushion with the legend 'Z lásky' [From love], a present from one of my nieces some time after the death of my husband. Olga sat there quietly for a moment, then she asked that the doctor's wife, Mrs Bartošová, and her daughters, Olga's girlfriends Dana and Fedora,[79]

79 Daniela (Dana) and Fedora Bartošová both became teachers. Daniela drowned in 1926 on a school outing trying to rescue children when their boat capsized. Fedora (1884–1941) was the librettist of Janáček's fourth opera, *Fate I/5*, which she began at his invitation a few months after the death of Olga.

be called. This surprised me because recently she hadn't wanted to see anyone, she didn't even want a nurse, which the doctor recommended when he saw how tired I was. Then I guessed that Olga wanted to say goodbye. The Bartoš women came at once. Two girls knelt beside her and, crying, kissed her hands. My heart burst when I saw them so healthy and beautiful beside my poor suffering girl. And when she said to them in her weakening alto: 'You see, girls, I have to go now . . .'

I came round when they resuscitated me and were calling me. For the first time in my life I'd fainted. Because what was now happening was the hardest thing that I'd lived through so far.

When the Bartoš women went off, a difficult, endless night awaited us again. This time not even my husband slept and from time to time he came through from his room into Olga's. A new day. She wanted to see two other friends of hers, Mařenka and Eliška Kalusová. Lamenting, they took their leave of her. Hardly had they gone – it was getting on for ten in the morning: 'Call Mrs Dresslerová and the children to me.'

Mářa's younger half-sister was at our place to help us with all these comings and goings. She virtually flew so that we could fulfil each of Olga's wishes. There was no more cooking, we didn't do any housework, everything stopped, all was irrelevant, pointless. No one ate, the beginning and end of all our thoughts was Olga, we devoted ourselves only to her. In these last days my husband took time off from school.

When Olga wanted to see the Dresslers, he ordered a carriage and went to collect them. In a moment Ida and the children Věra and Aťka were here. The children were then still small.[80] They sat next to Olga and looked at her fearfully. Olga was in the armchair again, more lying than sitting and looked at the cuckoo clock in front of her. 'Vladíček died at eleven, I'll go at the same time. Mamička, farewell.' She became quiet as if she really was going. A quiet moment of terror. Then she moved: 'Mamička, I want to lie down.'

I knew why. They say that when a patient with dropsy like this lies down carelessly, the water pours over the heart and the patient dies. Olga wanted that. She now wanted to make an end of it. In vain I asked her to remain sitting; we had to lay her down. Again she lay quiet for a moment and then moaned: 'Even that doesn't help.'

---

80 The Dresslers' girls were Věra (*b* 1897), Naděžda (*b* 1899) and Ljuba (*b* 1902). Aťka is the diminutive of Amálie, not Naděžda, so Zdenka seems to have muddled her name.

After a while Dr Dressler came too. She clasped him round the neck and begged: 'Dressler, I know you can't help me, but at least give me something to relieve me.'

My tears welled up. He gave her some drops. He ordered us to open all the windows – outside it was a beautiful sunny day – and fan her with fans. We took turns in this work, dressed in our winter coats, but Olga wasn't cold. In a while a fainting fit came over her and we held a sponge wetted in vinegar to her mouth to help her breathe better.

In the afternoon she began to cry: 'Grandad, Granny, do come!'

I and my husband didn't even look at one another. Now it seemed that her crying would fall on deaf ears. And then Máŕa plucked up her courage. Energetically she turned to my husband and in front of everyone she said to him: 'Sir, this is where all hatred stops. Everything must be granted to the dying. You must send a telegram for them to come from Vienna. Missy wouldn't be able to die.'

Leoš got up. He wrote the telegram himself. My family was here by return. At the time it was easy: one could get from Vienna to Brno in two and a half hours. When, weeping, I greeted them and let them into the room to Olga, my husband stood at the window of the dining-room. They greeted him, he didn't respond. So he didn't permit even a hair more than the most essential. Olga was overjoyed. After the medicine which Dr Dressler gave her she recovered a bit, even the blood started coursing through her. But it was as if she'd become childish. She spoke like a small child. She called to Mama: 'Granny, I won't die now, I've got little warm hands now.'

They sat by her for a long time. Eventually Mama tore herself away from the patient and said that they were going now. She didn't want to stay when she saw my husband's enmity. And now I in turn got up my courage. I went to my husband – he was again in Olga's room – and said to him resolutely in a way that I'd seldom spoken with him: 'Listen, put hate aside now. Now something higher has taken over. They want to leave because of you, and Olga would like to have them here. You must control yourself. It's your duty.'

He didn't answer me, he didn't move. I left. I thought that I'd spoken to him in vain. But after a while he went out and began talking with my brother, who was sitting in the dining-room. And slowly even my parents joined in the conversation. The tension eased. We sat the whole night through and chatted. Olga was happy.

On Wednesday morning she began to be delirious. My husband leant over her and she said softly: 'Daddy, it's so beautiful there, there are just angels there.' And he said to her fervently: 'And you're the most beautiful angel of all.'

'Just say that to them there, they'd laugh at you.'

Again after a little while: 'And there's Vladíček there. He's waiting for me.'

Then as if she came to her senses. She fixed her anxious gaze on my husband: 'It would be horrible, if there was nothing there.'

And Leoš gathered together all his eloquence and assured her convincingly that heaven and God existed.

Towards eleven she began to be restless again: 'Something will be lost and can't be found, and that will be such a pity.'

And then: 'It's already eleven, so I must go now.'

After a while: 'They still won't let me inside there.'

Then intermittently: 'Kuk. Tak. Tak. Tak. Pryč, pryč. Jeje.'[81]

Then came the death-struggle. She stopped talking, she breathed irregularly and in fits and starts, she lay motionless. Mama didn't move from her and put the damp sponge to her lips. When towards noon my family left, Olga didn't react to anything. We sat there and waited for the end. It wasn't necessary to do anything else. People continually dropped in on us, friends came, Olga's friends, no one looked after them, no one greeted them, no one spoke to them. They came, they went, my husband and I, Mářa and the Dressler women sat there the whole time and looked at Olga. After his surgery hours, Dressler came and was surprised: 'Is she still alive? What lungs she's got!'

And nevertheless after Olga's death people maintained that she died of tuberculosis.

Night again. Each lay down where he could and slept. They put me on the divan too. I didn't sleep, I listened constantly to Olga's irregular breathing. And again I jumped up and went out from the room somewhere, without sense, without purpose. I also wandered into the dining-room. The window wide open. I positioned myself in front of it and as the icy air was fanning me, I began to think. I imagined how life would go on without Olga. A conception so desperate that at the thought I wanted to run and jump out of the window so that I wouldn't have to go on living in this way. I'd already clutched the window-sill when I remembered my promise to Olga.

---

81 'Kuk' and 'tak' could relate to Olga's preoccupation with the cuckoo clock, though 'tak' also means 'so'. 'Pryč' = 'away'; 'jeje' is a sigh or expression of pain or surprise. Janáček also recorded Olga's last words, some with speech melodies. The two accounts have a few phrases in common, with slightly different wordings.

That I'd see that everything was done as she wanted in her will. I wasn't allowed to go then, I had to stay. When I remembered this later, I realized that this sharp-witted girl had foreseen earlier than I had how I'd feel after her departure, and that for this reason she had so urgently bound me with a promise so that I couldn't leave until I'd carried it out. And that it would take quite a long time, so that I'd learn again how to bear my unhappiness.

Terribly agitated, I staggered back to her again. At that moment only Leoš and our neighbour, Mrs Vencálková,[82] were with her. I bent over Olga. She had her eyes shut, her face drawn and yellowed: when I stroked her forehead, it was damp and cold. A strange smell came from her body. Now the blood was decomposing. A new wave of despair caught me up in a maelstrom. The end, the inevitable end. And she could be living if she hadn't got that typhoid fever. [. . .] Who caused Olga's death? Whose will was it that she went off to St Petersburg? [. . .] Everything changed within me into wild hate for Leoš. He sat at the bed without moving, his head bent. I rushed up to him, shook him and cried like a madwoman: 'Return my child to me, return Olga to me, look where you've taken her. It's your work. It's your fault.'

He began crying. He was experiencing his unhappiness in a different way from me, how could he have understood what was going on within me.

'Look what she's doing to me', he cried out to Mrs Vencálková.

She perhaps understood me better. Gently she began to pacify me. But the outburst had already passed. I fell on to the divan devoid of feeling, exhausted. I thought no more about anything, only something in me paid attention to Olga's breathing. For hours and hours now it had the same tempo: a few fast breaths and then a pause.

The night dragged on. And then suddenly – it was already growing light – the rhythm of the breath changed. I jumped up. I knew infallibly that this was the end. Everyone who was with us in the flat came, we knelt before Olga's bed and in complete silence we waited . . .

The breath stopped. It was 6.30 a.m. on Thursday 26 February 1903.

It's terrible when a person has to do things after the death of a loved one. To think of the thousands of senseless trifles concerning the

---

82 Karolina Vencálková (1864–?), wife of Vincenc Vencálek, a soda-water manufacturer. From 1902 they lived in Brno in Klášterní náměstí no.2, i.e. in the same block as the Janáčeks.

funeral when one hasn't a moment for one's pain. And perhaps that's good. It began with my saying 'the end', standing up, kissing the corpse and pressing her eyes shut. And immediately Máňa and I began to do everything according to Olga's will. My husband didn't help. He gave himself over entirely to his grief. He tore out his hair, crying: 'My soul, my soul!'

It wasn't possible to talk with him about anything, he was indifferent to everything, he was more in the way [than of any help]. But many other willing hands were found. Eliška Kalusová helped me to tidy Olga's room. We decorated it entirely with Moravian embroidery, of which I had plenty. Olga had asked me not to leave her in those black funeral sheets. Máňa meanwhile combed little Missy's hair for the last time and – also according to her wishes – curled her beautiful hair for the last time. Then we put her into the coffin. Abbot Bařina[83] sent us a message that he'd have the entire room where Olga would be lying decorated with flowers from the monastery greenhouse. They were brought over that very day and Olga lay in a grove of palms. Her friend, a daughter of Mrs Vencálková,[84] sewed a shroud of white satin, Ida Dresslerová put a wreath of artificial violets round Olga's head and Máňa and I strewed her with posies of fresh violets, which we changed each day until the funeral. In her coffin she was as beautiful as when she was alive, with a calm smile.

Hundreds and hundreds of people came to us as if going on Good Friday to God's tomb. We no longer even closed the door. Students came to ask if they could carry Olga to the grave. That pleased us: before her death she'd said, 'I don't want those black crows[85] to carry me.'

We had to send Čert away to one of our friends. He howled until our hair stood on end and he didn't want to stir from Olga.

I slept that night. When I lay down, absolutely worn out, I realized that for ten months now I hadn't gone to bed undressed, I'd always just dozed in my clothes, curled up at the edge of the pillow. So now I could sleep, without worries, peacefully, there was nothing any more that would wake me; all dead, desolate in the flat, in my head and in my heart. To be able to sleep without waking.

But the day came and again I was drawn into the stream of worries

83 Father František Bařina (1863–1943), the first Czech abbot of the Augustinian monastery in Brno and an enthusiastic Czech patriot.
84 Karola Vencálková (1885–?), the oldest of Mrs Vencálková's four children.
85 i.e. the undertaker's assistants.

about the funeral. It was as well that good people helped so compassionately. Our friends even did the shopping for me, they sent a telegram to Vienna, Mrs Vencálková cooked lunch and forced us each to eat something. The doctor pointed out that we should shut the coffin that very day, saying that decomposition would occur and that it would be terrible. But my husband didn't wish it. He wanted the people from Hukvaldy, who were coming for the funeral, to see Olga once more. So the coffin remained open, although towards evening Olga began to change; there was a hissing coming from her and blood flowed from her mouth.

Saturday, the day of the funeral. I got up very early in order to make the most of the sight of my beloved girl. I bent down over the coffin. Terrible, terrible what I saw. That thing was Olga now, my beautiful child! I cried out in horror, I don't know how it was that I didn't go mad. Máŕa ran up. She too saw it. I found a thick veil, with it we covered the face of the dead, we heaped up many posies on her, no one was allowed to see her any more now. Just her father perhaps. I went to see him. He was still sleeping.

'Go and have a look. It's terrible. Why didn't we listen to the doctor!'

He didn't go, he remained spared of the sight which I'll see in tormenting clarity to my dying day.

At eleven they took her away from me to the Old Brno church. I didn't even say farewell to her. Under some pretext they called me from Olga's room and quietly carried her off. They told me only afterwards, and I got only a glimpse from the window of the black carriage slowly driving away and behind it a young girl walking all on her own, Maŕenka Kalusová. Olga was right to say it before her death: she really left us for ever and ever at eleven o'clock.

The funeral. Perhaps the whole of Brno was at the Old Brno monastery that warm, almost spring-like afternoon. Olga's coffin lay on a high catafalque deluged with greenery and lights. More I don't know. Without tears, without feeling I walked behind the carriage up to the institute, where we got seated in the carriages and drove to the Central Cemetery and then afterwards behind the students who carried the coffin. Leoš walked beside me like a stranger. We didn't go arm in arm. Again, each on his own. Around Vladíček's grave, further, further, right up to the cemetery wall I went to give the earth that last thing which remained to me as a mother. Hymns, the thudding of frozen clods of earth; it was all over, all over. Máŕa and Dressler pulled me from the grave. At the cemetery gate stood Director Mareš. There was great sympathy in his gentle, all-seeing and all-understanding gaze. I flew to him. 'Mr Director, my Olga . . . .'

I don't know what he said to me but his quiet voice brought me to my senses, as if bringing me back to life.

We were home again. The guests from Hukvaldy didn't stay, they went off by train immediately, Mama and my brother had to wait for a train at our house. Father didn't come for the funeral, already such exertion was too tiring for him. My husband shut himself again in Olga's room. I heard him sobbing there. We let him be. Then he came out and joined us in the dining-room and we were all together until the departure of my family. The two of us remained in the dining-room on our own. Deserted, not speaking. I gazed at Leoš. He sat before me, devastated, grown thin, greying. I thought to myself that now I have only him. Suddenly I saw how little I had been able to devote myself to him while the children were here, that we'd really been strangers to each other all the time. Clearly, my present duty stood before me: to care for and live only for him. All bitterness towards him dissolved, there remained only sympathy and love. I went to him, for a long while, for a very long while, I clasped him again around the neck. Perhaps he felt what was going on inside me, perhaps he was experiencing something similar; he didn't push me away, but said gently: 'So we will go on living this life alone now.'

A warm little spark of rapprochement began to smoulder between us while frozen earth was settling on Olga's grave.

6

New home. The World War

One day followed another and each was full of work. The pain, awareness of the futility of everything here on earth? This had to be put aside. Above all it was necessary to do everything as Olga had wished. Then there was her grave and, in caring for it, a little relief. As if one was saying to oneself: you see, I don't forget. I'm doing for you what's still within my power.

We had the Racek firm[1] construct the tombstone. It was a piece of sandstone into which was set a relief made of Carrara marble depicting Olga's profile covered with a veil fastened with a bunch of roses in the corner [see Plate 12]. The relief was the work of Professor Vávra from the Brno Industrial School, the brother of Professor Vávra from the Brno Conservatory.[2] Under it, on a black marble plaque, was engraved a verse by the Brno poet Jaroslav Tichý-Rypáček[3] ('Young and quiet, gentle and good, she fell asleep like a white rose, the beautiful pale flower of spring') together with an inscription in Russian, by Olga's teacher Naděžda Veverica,[4] of which the translation went as follows: 'Her spirit is where there is love and rest.'

People called and with them came business and social duties; one had to talk, to think about things other than the main one, so painful. The whole of Brno showed a warm sympathy for us. It was only then that I realized how large the turnout at Olga's funeral had been, that there had been such crowds of people in the church that they could hardly make room for us to pass, that there were so many wreaths and bouquets of white flowers. Among them, a single posy of violets. I had a nice black cloak from days gone by and wore this for Olga's funeral. Ladies told me now how much they had pitied me when they saw from

1 K.F. Racek, stonemason, Wawrova [now Hybešova] no.14.
2 Miloslav Vávra, from the Brno Industrial School, was the brother of the violist Oldřich Vávra (1879–1957).
3 František Rypáček (1853–1917), a schoolteacher and the librettist of Janáček's second opera, *The Beginning of a Romance* I/3, wrote under the pseudonym of Jaroslav Tichý.
4 Maria Nikolayevna Veveritsa, a native Russian living in Brno, taught Russian to Olga in the Brno Russian Circle. She later wrote the words which inspired Janáček to write his *Elegy on the Death of my Daughter Olga* IV/30. Zdenka gives her surname in a common Czech transliteration and seems to have muddled her first name.

the way it hung on me how much weight I'd lost. The very Sunday after the funeral a resident of Old Brno, Mr Beer, paid a visit. He was a German, but he spoke Czech. On behalf of the residents of Old Brno he expressed sympathy at our having lost 'that dear creature'. This thought pleased both my husband and myself. Mr Klíč, the owner of the largest Brno photographic studio 'Rafael',[5] displayed Olga's photograph [Plate 11] adorned with a mourning band. The school wanted to give Leoš leave. But he refused. He always went to the cemetery on Sunday mornings. Alone. We went to Olga's grave together just once, on the Sunday after her funeral. From that time on he never offered to accompany me to the cemetery nor did he ever ask me to go with him. I understood from this that he didn't want to have anyone witness his grief and I didn't intrude.

In addition, housework called. Suddenly it could be seen how neglected and untidy everything was. Mářa and I got down to it. And the hard physical work was a good cure for me. I worked from dawn till dusk until I dropped, falling into a dreamless sleep the moment I lay down on the bed. On Olga's bed, which I couldn't bring myself to take out of the child's room. Hungrily I seized the last traces of all that was left of my only child. When, straight after the funeral, Leoš suggested that once again I slept with him in the bedroom – we'd slept apart for many years now – I declined with thanks and spent the night in the child's room, where everything was just as it was from the funeral. Among the scent of flowers and burnt-out candles I caught something here which was uncommonly precious to me and which was vanishing irrevocably: the odour of Olga's corpse. She was there in that too, the last thing that emanated from her body – I couldn't give up that. When later we rearranged the child's room as it had been during her lifetime, I slept on her bed. At least it was warmed by the heat of my body if not by Olga's. And also I thought that I'd be better able to call her to me there. I wished with all my being that she'd materialize, coming to me in the night as a spirit. She promised me this before she died. But she never came.

When the flat was in order again, I became restless at home. I'd go out often and would wander aimlessly God knows where. I'd flee from my friends, avoiding people altogether. It was unpleasant for me if they took even a fleeting glance at me, so I'd wear my thickest veil. I could bear to have only Čertíček near me: Olga's faithful friend would accompany me everywhere. But apart from making me tired, my

5 Otakar and Jaroslav Klíč's studio 'Rafael' was at Neugasse [now Lidická] no.4.

wanderings would bring me nothing, neither calm nor refreshment.
Eventually I agreed with my husband that I'd go to my parents in
Vienna for about a fortnight's rest. And what I'd longed for so much in
vain at home came to me at my mother's house: I saw Olga in a dream.
Radiant and beautiful, she came and said to me: 'Mamuška, I'm fine.'
It relieved me in a trice. I could live again, I could return home to my
duties. Olga came and is with me.

Even Leoš found relief. In his work as a composer. He was much
taken up then with *Jenůfa*. In hope and fear he took it to Kovařovic[6] in
Prague. He said to Leoš that he'd send him news once he'd finished
studying the opera. We were both excited but didn't let on to one
another. After many long weeks Leoš wrote to Kovařovic.[7] The answer
came immediately.[8] My husband didn't have the courage to open the
letter. He asked me to read it.[9] I trembled like a leaf and lost all hope
when I saw that the whole communication consisted only of about
three lines. Its sense was that *Jenůfa* was being sent back to my
husband 'for [his] own good'. It happened in the room where Olga
died. My husband sat at the desk. He buried his head in his hands and
broke into terrible sobbing. In a sharp fit of depression he blamed
himself that he didn't know anything. I couldn't bear that. However
he'd behaved to me, although he'd not always been a model husband,
I'd always believed in his mission as an artist, I also believed in the
beauty and the greatness of *Jenůfa*. So I embraced his head
passionately and, in tears myself, comforted him. Only a great faith
in his work could have given me all those words of comfort and
encouragement. They must have been convincing because they calmed
him. And thereafter I was always on the lookout so that such an attack
shouldn't be repeated. I'd wait for the post so that the returned score
should come into my own hands. As it happened, my husband wasn't
even at home when it came. I hid it so that he shouldn't see it. He
remembered it only some time later.[10] I saw that there was nothing to
fear and I told him that they'd already returned it from Prague. He
took it quite calmly.

6 Head of opera at the National Theatre in Prague; see Glossary.
7 On 27 April 1903 (*JODA*, JP14).
8 From Gustav Schmoranz, administrative director of the Prague National Theatre (28 April
1903; *JODA*, JP15).
9 Stejskalová's recollection of this incident is different, reporting that 'the master read the
letter in the study' (*JODA*, JP16).
10 According to Stejskalová, the fact that the score appeared not to have arrived raised
Janáček's hopes that the National Theatre had perhaps changed its mind, thus forcing
Zdenka to disclose that it had been returned (*JODA*, JP16).

Sometime in the summer [of 1903] I was walking down Rudolfská ulice [now Česká ulice] and met the surveyor Kallus.[11] He was on the committee of the Družstvo [i.e. managing consortium] of the Brno Theatre. He began a conversation with me about *Jenůfa*. In Brno they were all up in arms that the score had been returned to my husband from Prague. They would like to see the opera given in Brno. But my husband wouldn't hear of it. Mr Kallus now began to persuade me to work on my husband. I promised him I would. It took a lot of doing, my husband was too wounded by the failure. But nevertheless I succeeded. Straight after the summer holidays the conductor Hrazdira[12] began to rehearse *Jenůfa* in the Old Theatre.[13]

In the holidays we all went off, Leoš to Hukvaldy, I to Vienna,[14] Máňa to her relatives in the Českomoravská vysočina.[15] Although Leoš and I were now living at peace with one another we each went to a different place: from experience I knew now that a temporary separation like this has a good effect. We parted on good terms and looked forward to seeing one another again. It seemed as if our relationship was constantly rejuvenated. I loved the joyful look with which he always greeted me at the station. This time he decided to take Čert with him to Hukvaldy. But he soon regretted it. The dog couldn't stand geese and hens. Whenever he caught one he'd seize it by the head and worry it until it expired. Leoš couldn't keep up paying for the damage. He soon had enough of it and took Čert back to Brno.[16] He wrote to me about it. I had to return from Vienna, I entrusted the dog to our caretaker and off we went again, Leoš to Luhačovice,[17] I again to my parents. After a short while I got a letter from him in which he told me that he'd 'found an angel just like the one that we'd buried'. And that she also had a heart defect.[18] I thought that the 'angel' was

11 Rudolf Kallus (1872–?1917); Zdenka writes 'Kalus'.
12 Cyril Metoděj Hrazdira (1868–1926), conductor at the Brno theatre 1903–7. He conducted the première of *Jenůfa* on 21 January 1904.
13 i.e. the Czech theatre on Veveří ulice (see Glossary: 'Brno Theatre'). Rehearsals could not have started straight after the summer holidays since it was only on 9 October 1903 that the theatre collected the score from Janáček (*JODA*, JP20). Parts still need to be copied (Janáček reported that it took 'another fortnight'). Around Christmas Janáček wrote to Kamila Urválková that the soloists knew their parts, but that the orchestra had not started rehearsing (*JODA*, JP22).
14 From Frenštát (the nearest railway station to Hukvaldy) Janáček wrote to Zdenka in Vienna that he had arrived safely and had Čert with him (?17 July 1903; BmJA, A 3868).
15 Trkanová 1964, 64: 'to Matějov'.
16 Stejskalová reported (Trkanová 1964, 64) that later the master would take Čert to Hukvaldy only in the winter, when the geese and chickens were shut up in the courtyards.
17 Janáček arrived in Luhačovice on 11 or 12 August 1903.
18 None of Janáček's letters written to Zdenka from Luhačovice in 1903 survive.

some young girl and wrote back accordingly. But when he returned after the holidays and began telling me about this angel, it turned out that it was the young and beautiful Mrs Kamila Urválková, the wife of a forest ranger from Dolní Královice.[19] Apparently she couldn't bear to see Leoš so sad and isolated in Luhačovice. She sent him a bunch of red roses to his table. They then got acquainted. He told me also that they'd be writing to one another, but I shouldn't worry because he'd give me all the letters to read. I went along with this, it really seemed to me that Leoš was now more cheerful. But that was perhaps because the rehearsals for *Jenůfa* had started. Certainly, however, he was very sweet and attentive to me. One evening he came to me in my bedroom and suggested to me that we should get together now we were so alone: that I should be his wife again. I felt bad in the child's room where everything reminded me of Olga's death – but he was my husband and I loved him. From that time we lived together again as man and wife. Later he suggested that I should go out into society with him. And I didn't deny him that either, although earlier I'd refused to go to the theatre again. He kept on corresponding with Mrs Kamila [Urválková]. I read the letters, there was nothing improper in them, nothing that would have made me anxious: she used to write to him about her illness, and he to her about *Jenůfa*, and about his new opera, *Fate*, which she inspired through her account of her love for the conductor Čelanský. Originally the opera was to have been called 'Red Roses', an allusion to the bunch of flowers which she sent to my husband in Luhačovice. Fedora Bartošová, a friend of my Olga, wrote the libretto for my husband.[20] Those were the main things which I read in those letters.

There was indeed nothing 'improper' in the letters which have survived. Those of Janáček's, mostly from October 1903,[21] provide a fascinating insight into Janáček's earliest ideas about his new opera, *Fate*, which, unlikely as it seems, had as its starting point the brief love-affair between Mrs Urválková and the conductor and composer Ludvík Čelanský (1870–1931). Zdenka Janáčková would also have needed some patience to decipher Mrs Urválková's long letters and would probably have found, like subsequent readers, that the result hardly repaid the effort.

But suddenly a suspicion emerged, I don't know where it came from.

19 The 'angel' motif was clearly in Janáček's mind when he wrote on Mrs Urválková's fan 'Your angelic appearance brings back to life someone who in his boundless grief was in despair' (quoted in Štědroň 1959, 160).
20 Fedora Bartošová was sent Janáček's scenario in instalments and in return fashioned a libretto in verse (see *JODA*, 114–28; see also p.86, fn.79).
21 Printed in Štědroň 1959; in English in *JODA*, OS3, OS7.

And it kept warning me for such a long time that I began to be on my guard. I realized that in the letters there was much that wasn't said in full, that they were written for me [to read]. And something else struck me. Leoš, who was so careless and disorganized in everything, suddenly took to locking his writing-desk carefully and carrying the keys about with him the whole time. I became ever more suspicious but I said nothing to him. I was frightened of spoiling our good rapport and also I already knew from experience that he wouldn't tell me the truth if I asked directly. One morning – now in the winter [of 1903–4] – he nevertheless forgot the keys and went to get dressed in my little room. Quickly I opened his writing-desk. In the front I saw letters which I'd read with him, further back I suddenly caught sight of a pile of other letters with the same handwriting. So my suspicion about a double correspondence was correct. Quickly I took the bundle, locked the desk, and put the keys where my husband left them. Where to put the letters now? It was cold in the flat, I wasn't dressed, he was in my bedroom – I hid the letters in the pantry in the corridor. I wanted to read them when he went off to school. But when he returned to the study and saw that he'd left the keys lying around, he unlocked the desk. He ran to me angrily:

'Where are my letters?'

'I've hidden them.'

'Give them back to me at once.'

'Certainly, when I've read them.'

'No, no, give them to me at once, or I'd have to kill myself.'

He begged, he threatened, eventually he promised me that we'd read them together. I believed him and brought the letters. He tore them out of my hand and hid them. I got angry. I told him that he was unfaithful and asked why should he come to me when he then wanted to deceive me. He didn't defend himself, he didn't make excuses, he was clearly very frightened. I never learnt why, since surely there couldn't have been anything so terrible in those letters.

Then for a few days we didn't speak to one another. He went on corresponding with Mrs Urválková, but didn't give me letters to read any more. I began to worry about things again, again I felt myself isolated, neglected.

Christmas 1903 we didn't even celebrate at home.[22] He went to Hukvaldy, I to Vienna, because mother got an infection of the middle

22 But they clearly exchanged presents; Janáček wrote to Kamila Urválková before leaving for Hukvaldy that he had received from Zdenka a medallion of Olga and an embroidered cushion (undated letter around Christmas 1903; *JODA*, JP22).

ear and had to have an operation. Leoš returned to Brno earlier than me: he had to be at the *Jenůfa* rehearsals. Máŕa remembers to this day how he got into a rage with her then. One day he gave orders for her to fry doughnuts and to bring them and his case to the station because he had to travel to Prague. Máŕa did everything as she was told to the very last detail and started off for the station in good time. She was already well on her way when she remembered that she'd left the travelling rug at home. And she said to herself, there's plenty of time, and the master might catch cold in the train. So she turned back for home, took the shawl and got to the station just as the train was pulling out. The master ran along the platform and greeted her angrily.

'What's this? What are you trying to do to me here?'

He wanted to go to Mrs Urválková and Máŕa spoilt it for him. He didn't go home; in a bad mood, he went off to the theatre, where they were rehearsing *Jenůfa*. As it happened, he was much needed there, so that finally he had to concede that it was good that he hadn't gone to Prague. For all his shouting, he not only forgave Máŕa, but almost praised her into the bargain.

On 27 [*recte* 21] January 1904 there was the grand première of *Jenůfa*. Given the conditions in Brno, it was very fine [. . .]. My husband was pleased. I was very excited, and, still in mourning, I couldn't stop myself crying when, in the second act, Jenůfa sang 'Tož umřel'.[23]

I remembered how my husband had composed it already after [*recte* before] Olga's death, how he'd played *Jenůfa* to her as she lay dying.

Leoš also invited Mrs Urválková but she refused to come. After the première when we returned home, he came to me and in my joy at the fine success of the work, which I adored, I made my peace with him. Despite this he continued to correspond with Mrs Urválková. And it all ended quite suddenly: her husband wrote to Leoš saying that he didn't want him to go on corresponding with his wife because he'd received an anonymous letter from Brno. This intervention by a decisive man achieved what I'd been vainly striving for all these months: Leoš immediately broke off correspondence with Mrs Urválková.

Janáček's last substantial letter to Mrs Urválková (28 January 1904)[24] reported on the première of *Jenůfa*. Soon after that he seems to have visited Mrs Urválková at her home at Zaháj u Dolních Královic (roughly midway between Brno and Prague) and, judging by the absence of further letters, the husband's intervention

23 'So he died'; Jenůfa's lament on hearing about the death of her baby boy.
24 *JODA*, JP33.

took place shortly thereafter. Janáček's last recorded contact with Mrs Urválková was a postcard from Warsaw, postmarked 20 April 1904 and with the revealingly terse message: 'A greeting'.[25]

And now there was a time of peace and contentment for me. My husband retired so that he could compose in peace; in the autumn of 1903 he got a year's leave and in 1904 he was granted permanent retirement. But only from the Teachers' Institute:[26] he carried on running the Organ School; that was his creation, he loved it and couldn't leave it. The school moved several times after 1881, when it was founded by the Society for the Promotion of Church Music in Moravia. My father, who was on the committee of the society, managed at first to get them rooms at the Teachers' Institute. Then they taught in Starobrněnská ulice, and still later in the Tachovský house in Rudolfská ulice – now Česká ulice. My husband didn't like these rooms. Then a villa of the firm Haas & Kordina[27] came up for sale on the corner of Kounicova ulice and today's Smetanova ulice, the present conservatory.[28] It wasn't expensive. It occurred to Leoš that it could be easily converted for the use of the Organ School. So the society bought the villa, letting part of it and teaching in the remaining rooms. When afterwards the school was a success, all rooms were taken up by teaching.

The 'time of peace and contentment' evidently lasted several years; Zdenka Janáčková did not recall any specific events between the end of the Urválková episode in 1904 and the move to the new Organ School in 1908. Although Janáček had retired from the Teachers' Institute in order to compose, there was not noticeably more activity on this front after 1904. *Fate* I/5, with its various revisions and its dispiriting history at the Vinohrady Theatre in Prague, continued to occupy Janáček until 1913, when hopes for its performance in Prague were finally laid to rest. This is perhaps one reason why he found it difficult to settle on any further operatic project. When he finally decided on *The Excursion of Mr*

25 Štědroň 1959, 183.
26 Janáček's 'retirement' from the Teachers' Institute began as sick leave. He was ill at the beginning of November 1903 and stopped teaching there from 9 November. To Mrs Urválková, however, he described it (on 13 November 1903) as a year's leave in which he would work on his new opera *Fate*. He even wrote, mystifyingly, that he had her to thank for it. The leave was confirmed only on 4 January 1904; permanent early retirement was approved on 14 September 1904 (Štědroň 1959, 179, fn.28).
27 Its builder, the solicitor Ctibor Chleborád, was an enthusiastic Czech Russophile, and intended it for the Russian consulate, or so it was said. Afterwards it served as a town house for the owners of the parquet firm Haas & Kordina (Smetana 1948, 35).
28 The building served as the Brno Conservatory until 1947. Since 1956 it has housed the music section of the Moravian Museum. After the ownership of the building was assigned to the Catholic Church, an institute for the training of church musicians was established on the top floor in 1995, thus bringing part of the building back to its function under Janáček.

Brouček to the Moon I/6 in 1908, that had its own problems. Much of Janáček's energies were in fact taken up by folksong. In 1905 he was appointed chairman of the Moravian and Silesian working party in charge of collecting folk music for a government-sponsored collection *Das Volkslied in Österreich*. This was not a topic that Zdenka found interesting and her references to Janáček's work in this field are sparse.

The year 1909, Zdenka reported, brought them 'bad holidays' with Janáček going off to Tišnov, a well-known spa town 30 km from Brno to cure his overwrought nerves. 'He wasn't ill – on the contrary – he appeared very well – but he was very tired. [. . .] as soon as his affairs at the Organ School permitted he went off to Tišnov, part summer retreat, part some sort of convalescence in Dr Kuthan's sanatorium, to which he'd been attracted not only by the imposing architecture, but also perhaps because the woods and hills surrounding Tišnov resembled the magnificent Hukvaldy scenery. The plan he drew up for his recuperation was very good, but he carried it out differently from the way he'd intended it. Instead of giving himself a rest in the quiet of the Tišnov forests, he let himself be drawn by the slopes of the Tišnov hills and climbed them so relentlessly and determinedly that during the three weeks of his Tišnov stay he lost at least ten kilos in weight.'[29] Smetana adds that Janáček's sudden loss of weight had severe medical complications for the rest of the year. After Tišnov, Janáček then went to Hukvaldy, as a letter to Zdenka confirms,[30] to continue his holiday. Zdenka herself had gone in early June to Bad Ischl,[31] a popular spa near Salzburg, while Janáček continued his teaching at the Organ School. In early July she moved to Vienna to stay with her family.[32]

There I got a terrible attack of gallstones, with which I'd suffered for about fourteen years. But it had never been so bad as in these holidays. Despite the fact that I had the doctor immediately, the attack wouldn't let up. I had to have an operation. According to the law we had to have the permission of my husband for it. We sent him a telegram. Meanwhile they took me into a sanatorium, where I was to be operated on the next day. Leoš came at once.[33] He was broken-hearted when he failed to catch me at home at my parents' house and he cried inconsolably there. When I was safely over the operation, he behaved very tenderly towards me. He remained another four days in the hotel, having meals with my parents and going round Vienna with my brother. Only when he saw that I was out of danger did he leave for

29 Smetana 1948, 34.
30 14 August 1909; BmJA, D 1210.
31 In a card, confirming her safe arrival in Vienna (5 June 1909; BmJA, A 2459), Zdenka wrote that she was leaving for Ischl.
32 From July 1909 Janáček addressed his cards and letters to Zdenka to Vienna.
33 At about that time Janáček had gone from Hukvaldy on a two-day folksong-collecting expedition (19–20 August 1909), sending Zdenka a card from Rožnov on 20 August 1909 (BmJA, A 3869). The telegram (no longer extant) presumably awaited his return that evening.

Hukvaldy.[34] There he had some heart problems, perhaps as a result of losing weight so suddenly. He went off to Teplice for treatment, but they wouldn't take him there. So he returned to Brno and entrusted himself to his cousin Dressler.

Janáček's perambulations were in fact more complicated. The Teplice trip happened not at the end of the holidays, but at the beginning. There they discovered he had an irregular heartbeat[35] and made it clear that Teplice was not the best place to treat a heart condition. Janáček informed Zdenka about it in a letter of 7 July 1909[36] and came up with an alternative: Tišnov. Within a week he was there,[37] after a short stay in Hukvaldy. He returned to Hukvaldy after Tišnov (by 30 August)[38] and from there went on his annual, but this time much curtailed visit to Luhačovice (4–12 September).[39] It was only shortly before the new school year began (15 September) that he was in Brno.[40] Despite his heart condition, he considered going to Vienna to collect Zdenka,[41] but in the end left her brother to do that, and she returned in late September, having been away continuously for more than three months.

Mářa was quite taken aback when she saw me; well, both my husband and I looked a fine sight. All the doctors advised him that he shouldn't walk too much, and generally that he should spend the whole time in the fresh air. There wasn't too much of that in our old flat. I'd not been happy there for ages. The house belonged to Mrs Fantová-Kusá.[42] The rooms there were nice, but the flat lacked modern, hygienic conveniences. Although it had four rooms, our flat didn't have a bathroom, or even a tap. For water one had to go to the pump in the courtyard. Lighting was by means of a petrol lamp. The biggest problem was with the lavatories. The outflow was made of wood and sewer rats had chewed through it. We women especially used to go in fear and trembling to the w.c. and banged on it when we heard noises and squeaking underneath. Sometimes it happened that a sewer rat got into the house. Once, during the time of my pregnancy with little

34 On his way home, he sent a card from Brno on 25 August 1909 (BmJA, A 3776).
35 What may be meant here is 'paroxysmal tachycardia', an unusually rapid heartbeat which occurs without heart disease in association with too much alcohol, caffeine or tobacco, giving rise to palpitations and disappearing when these are stopped.
36 BmJA, A 3888.
37 Janáček to Zdenka, 13 July 1909 (BmJA, A 4592).
38 He wrote to Zdenka from Hukvaldy on 30 August 1909 (BmJA, A 4955).
39 Janáček wrote to Zdenka on 2 September 1909 (BmJA, A 4956), announcing that he was leaving for Luhačovice.
40 In a letter to Zdenka dated Brno 12 September 1909 (BmJA, A 4985) Janáček described his heart condition (an intermittent pulse of 120) and explained that he needed absolute calm, which he did not find in Luhačovice.
41 He mentioned the possibility in his letter from Hukvaldy of 2 September 1909 (BmJA, A 4956).
42 See p.30, fn.27.

Vladíček, I was carrying bread from lunch into Olga's room. The thing is we didn't have a larder, just a cupboard outside on the corridor: Olga's room was very cool and so I kept food there in summer. Three steps led down from the door. As I stepped down, a sewer rat ran between my feet. I screamed, threw down the bread on the ground, leapt over all three steps and bolted the door behind me. I couldn't get over it, I screamed the whole time with all my strength. Leoš ran in, the servant, the neighbours and then even the owner of the house who lived across the way, and all the time I still wouldn't be pacified. They were afraid that I'd have a miscarriage, but nothing happened to me. They opened the room carefully, but the sewer rat had already gone. [. . .]⁴³

I looked several times for a new flat, but when I came to Leoš with it, he wouldn't hear of it. Now, when the doctors prescribed living in the fresh air he began to weaken. We even considered buying a little villa somewhere in Královo Pole.

The problem, too, was that Janáček, after his health problems during the summer, was far less able to get around. The walk from Old Brno to the new building of the Organ School took at least half an hour. Janáček was then boycotting the trams which, under German ownership, carried only German names. Nothing was left for him but to hire a cab or to move house.⁴⁴ Stejskalová reports that Janáček himself found somewhere to live in Údolní ulice (a ten-minute walk from the Organ School) though in the event this came to nothing. The plan to buy a small single-storey house with a garden in Královo Pole (still then an independent town) seems to have been more realistic, and in her recollection to Smetana, Zdenka even gave a location (Jungmannova ulice). According to Stejskalová, the plan fell through for lack of money.⁴⁵

But suddenly Leoš had a better idea. In the grounds of the newly acquired building of the Organ School there were stables. They were now completely redundant. Leoš came up with the idea that it would be good to demolish them and in their place build a garden house in which the director of the school would live, paying rent for the house.⁴⁶ The committee of the society approved Leoš's suggestion and construction began at once.

Stejskalová remembered more of these events: 'They left the master a free hand to suggest how he saw the house. They wanted only the front to be in Giskrova ulice [now Kounicova ulice]'. This would have meant the house being on a main road,

43 Account of an 'evil neighbour' omitted, another factor for leaving.
44 Smetana 1948, 34–5.
45 Trkanová 1964, 66.
46 Thereby gradually paying off the mortgage on the house (Smetana 1948, 36).

wedged in between the Organ School and the Engelmannová villa (which stood in what is now a small park, Janáčkovo náměstí [Janáček Square], until suffering a hit in the war). 'But when the master wanted the garden house to be as far as possible from the street so that he would have peace for composing, they agreed to this too.' Thus the house was set back considerably from the road, with its entrance from the quiet courtyard of the Organ School. 'The master wanted above all a warm, light and quiet study, the mistress wanted a salon with a bay-window and a veranda at the entrance of the house, and I spoke up for a comfortable kitchen through which outside visitors wouldn't come. And to the plan the master and the mistress added a little room behind the kitchen that would be mine. All three of us looked forward to the electric light and to a bathroom. [. . .] The master could even choose the builder himself: it was Alois Horák[47] from Kamenomlýnská ulice, already well on in years, honest, he knew how to advise the master and meet his requirements, and for this reason he chose him. The master and the mistress took great care before all was done.'[48] After several weeks of negotiations, building began before the end of November 1909. In the end the budget went up from the agreed K 14,000 to K 20,000.[49]

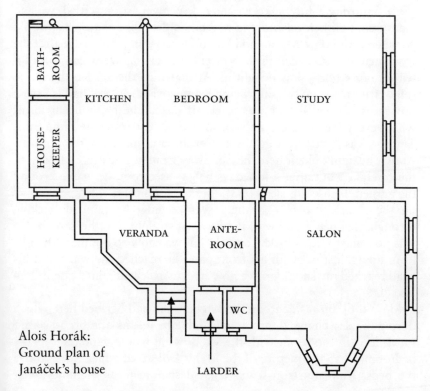

Alois Horák:
Ground plan of
Janáček's house

47 An otherwise unknown builder (see notes to Trkanová 1964, 152, fn.10).
48 Trkanová 1964, 67.
49 Smetana 1948, 36.

I was happy; lovingly I thought out everything, ran around, cared for everything, and Leoš and Mářa and I kept consulting one another on how best to organize everything, we also continually promised Čertík what wonderful times he would have soon. Every evening I went to get my husband from the school, we looked to see how the building was coming on and went for a walk. And now we had topics for conversation that we didn't exhaust even by the time we got back. We didn't have much money, we had to count our pennies all the time. But our happiness wasn't bought by money, it was within us, in what each brought the other with his joy and happy anticipation of the new nest. Although we now had a whole house to live in, we hardly had to buy anything extra to furnish it, in fact I had my worries how to fit the furniture of a four-roomed flat into our new three-roomed house. We simply had everything newly painted and we bought chandeliers for the electric light.

On Saturday 2 July 1910 we moved. We were soon settled, we had measured it all beforehand and had taken decisions as to what would go where. And once Mářa and I had put everything into order after the workmen, our *domeček* [little house; cottage] – as we began to call it within our circle – was delightful. At that time the garden there was full of fruit trees; on the side facing Kounicova ulice Leoš had fourteen box trees planted – that was after his taste. The magnificent ferns, which everyone admires, we've also had almost from the same time. The rest was done by the gardener. Čert became master of the veranda. At first he didn't like it here, he ran away from us back to Old Brno to the caretaker. But after a few days he got used to it, he walked round the garden, he used to sleep on the veranda in his little den or sat here on the chairs. When a stranger was coming, he jumped barking through the open window of the veranda straight into the garden. He was no longer Olga's little Čertíček, but was now so big that when he leant up against me with his front paws he reached my waist and his head reached my shoulder. We now had an excellent guard dog in him [see Plate 13].

Mářa took up residence in the kitchen: she had her bed here which during the day changed into a work table by means of a broad slab.[50] Next door in the room with the window on to the veranda was the bedroom: I had the picture of the *Mater Dolorosa*, which hung above the beds, from my trousseau. What desperate pleas of mine, what

---

50 It seems that Stejskalová did not sleep in the 'little room behind the kitchen that would be [hers]' (see p.105).

hopeless sighs, what cries that Mother of God heard! The room next door with the windows into the garden and on to Kounicova ulice became Leoš's study. His bed stood there for a long time since just as in the old flat he wanted to be able to sleep in his study. This room is now in the museum.[51] The book cabinet we had made only after we moved. We bought the painted chest for 1 zl. or so from the coalman in Old Brno, he kept coal in it. We had it cleaned and repaired. Then a beautiful woman painter from Slovácko[52] came into the Útulna[53] for her education – the wife of Jožka Úprka.[54] Leoš knew Úprka very well so his wife often stayed with us. [. . .] She stayed with us for whole days and I asked her[55] if she could renew the painting for us on our chest. She advised me to have it painted light blue and brown and then she filled it in with a Slovácko pattern. It went well together with the paintings on glass which Máŕa brought from her home. Olga's photograph is from Mr Klíč's studio ('Rafael').[56] Even before her departure for Russia he asked Olga to have her photograph taken in his studio as an advertisement. He then made one large photograph of her for the shop window and another one to give her as a present. It was according to the photograph that Professor Vávra then also did the relief on the monument. The piano, the writing-desk and the chairs are from my trousseau. The bay-window room next to Leoš's study was designated a dining-room for guests. [. . .]

Zdenka's detailed account of the furniture includes the story of a cupboard, which originally came from her grandmother in Silesia, where it was rescued from a fire. Later Máŕa's stepfather painted it black and fitted it with dark glass as a cabinet for Janáček's office in the Organ School, where it remained until his death. Another family heirloom was a distaff and, from Zdenka's grandmother, a sewing-table on which she put Olga's fan and 'her unbelievably tiny shoes'. There was also a column, 'a concession to the fashion of the time: there was a custom to put a vase or a statue on this sort of artificial fragment of an antique column'.

Finally we further decorated the whole house with old pieces of folk embroidery, of which we had a great number. Women from Slovácko wore them then and at that time they used to have really old, valuable

---

51 i.e. the room was re-created in the main building of the Moravian Museum; after Zdenka's death the house itself became a museum.
52 See Glossary.
53 See Glossary.
54 Anežka Úprková (1875–1959) lived in the Útulna from 1904. She must have painted the chest by early 1906 since Janáček captured speech melodies of her comments on the colours in his article 'Rozhraní mluvy a zpěvu' [The border between speech and song] XV/185, published in the spring of 1906. She was married to the painter Joža Úprka (1861–1940).
55 Stejskalová (Trkanová 1964, 69) claimed that this was Janáček's idea.
56 See p.95.

pieces. Leoš had a feel for it and knew how to select beautiful, oldfashioned patterns. I learnt this from him and soon I fell prey to collector's passion. It didn't cost me much money: for example a beautiful corner-piece cost just 10 zl. But I lost almost everything during the war: I had to exchange our magnificent pieces of embroidery for food. And I also gave lots away. Máňa and I had beautiful aprons, my husband nagged us until we gave them to the leading interpreters of *Jenůfa*: Horvátová, Jeritzová and Weidtová.[57]

When we'd put everything into order we went off for our holidays [summer 1910]. My husband to Teplice for more treatment,[58] I to Hukvaldy to my sister-in-law Marie. I should explain that my brother-in-law František had returned from Russia and bought an old Valašsko cottage in Hukvaldy.[59] He did it up but didn't enjoy it for long: he died of cancer of the stomach.[60] His wife, a German, a very good woman,[61] went on living in the cottage in Hukvaldy.[62] So I lived with her and after a while Leoš joined me there. It wasn't too happy for us then. Not only did Marie have her grief, but troubles came also for Josefka. She was in the process of leaving her husband, the head-teacher Dohnal. He was twenty-five years her junior, he married her because she'd looked after him when he was ill and afterwards he wasn't faithful to her – it wasn't a happy marriage. I found the atmosphere hard to take and went off instead to my parents in Vienna.

Stejskalová meanwhile was left in charge of the house: 'In the ground floor of the Organ School, lived the Simandls, the caretakers. They had two boys and a one-year-old girl Milenka;[63] she had something wrong with her leg, and the doctor said she would be lame. On the holiday of 15 August [i.e. the Assumption of the Virgin Mary] Simandl had gone off with the older son to Střílky, leaving the younger one and his wife at the Organ School. Simandlová took advantage of the fact that there was no one in the school and, in the first-floor classroom behind the choir-rehearsal room, she poisoned Milenka with gas. It was already evening, I was just writing a letter to [my relations in] Matějov when she came to me and told me about it. I called one of my friends from the neighbourhood and rushed off for the

57 Gabriela Horvátová played the Kostelnička in the Prague 1916 production of *Jenůfa*, Maria Jeritza and Lucie Weidt (Zdenka wrote Veithová) were respectively Jenůfa and the Kostelnička in the 1918 Vienna production (see Chapter 7).
58 Janáček got there between 15 July 1910, when the term ended, and 18 July, when he wrote to Zdenka about his treatment (BmJA, A 3893).
59 Hukvaldy is in Lašsko, rather than Valašsko: see Glossary 'Lachian/Valachian'.
60 See Glossary: Janáček, František (Josef); he died on 20 December 1908.
61 Stejskalová (Trkanová 1964, 71) explains that Marie Janáčková thought of Olga as her own daughter (after Olga's long stay with them in 1902) and so Zdenka felt at home there.
62 Later the cottage passed into Janáček's possession (see p.188).
63 Karel Simandl (1880–?) and his wife Emilie Simandlová (1882–1948) had two sons, Karel (*b* 1906) and Jaroslav (*b* 1907), and a daughter Emilie [Milenka] (1909–10).

police. They took Milenka to the mortuary in the hospital for an autopsy, Simandlová and her son were arrested and taken off to Cejl.[64] The next day Simandl arrived back and took the boy home, his wife remaining in jail. I'm usually fearless, but this time I was frightened to be in the house on my own. Suddenly on 17 August for no reason the master arrived back. He said he had become restless in Hukvaldy, something was telling him that he was needed at the Organ School. I told him everything immediately and the fear fell from me. He hadn't trusted Simandlová before and had dealt sharply with her, but when he heard what she'd done, he didn't say a single word against her. Then at the trial Dr Bulín[65] defended her so well that she was released.'[66]

Mářa and I took it as a sign that we wouldn't be happy in the new house. But just the opposite was true: a peaceful time full of contentment came. Financially we weren't too well off, the pension was small,[67] the pay from the Organ School wasn't large and from it we had to pay for the house – we had to scrimp and save. Mářa and I dug the garden ourselves, we made our own underwear, and we knitted everything ourselves. Leoš also created lots of work: he always insisted on food being prepared in an exemplary fashion and on its careful presentation. We stopped going out, only occasionally going to Bellevue or to Slavia,[68] where we had a few good friends: the senate resident Vácha and his wife,[69] Dr Veselý and his wife – the writer Calma-Veselá,[70] the director of village schools J. Němec[71] and Miss Illnerová, a music teacher.[72] But we didn't usually talk about music. My husband used to say that he went out to get away from music. He knew lots of people well, but a friend, a real friend whom he loved as a brother and to whom he could tell everything, that was something he never had.

Few people came to the new house to see us.[73] Most were simply my

64 There was a prison in Cejl no.71 from 1786 (still in use in the 1950s for political prisoners). Court hearings took place there from the nineteenth century, today the building is used as administrative offices for the courts.
65 Dr Hynek Bulín (1869–1950), lawyer (see also p.170).
66 Trkanová 1964, 71.
67 Because Janáček had taken early retirement.
68 Bellevue, a café on the corner of Joštova ulice and Kounicova ulice, opened in 1913. The hotel Slavia, on Silníční ulice, was one of four hotels in Brno at the end of the century. It billed itself as 'the only Czech hotel' in Brno, equipped with a 'Národní kavárna' [national café].
69 See Glossary: 'Váchová, Vítězslava'.
70 See Glossary.
71 Josef Němec (1866–1943), director of Vesna town and commercial schools.
72 Zdeňka Illnerová (1877–1962), piano teacher. She studied at Janáček's Organ School 1894–6.
73 Stejskalová (Trkanová 1964, 72) gives the chief visitors as Miss Illnerová, the composer Jan Kunc (see Glossary) and his wife; and the conductor of the Moravian Teachers' Choral Society, Ferdinand Vach and his wife.

husband's pupils coming for consultations and then the poorest came to lunch. Evenings were the nicest at our place. We used to read or I'd settle down to sewing and other handiwork, Leoš would pace up and down the bedroom and we'd chat.[74] Mostly about his work. He was always full of ideas about what could be done to raise the standard of musical life in Brno. He founded the Organ School concerts in the Lužánky hall,[75] he organized concerts in the Besední dům,[76] he served on the folksong committee, he talked to me about his compositions, about school, about what he was reading. At the time he had long been studying Wundt's *Psychology of Nations*; he said that it helped him a great deal in his study of phonetics.[77] Sometimes he gave whole lectures on music theory. When I didn't understand something, I asked him and he explained it with pleasure. He had moments when he actually bubbled over with the desire to talk about his own work. He initiated me into everything in which he was involved. I found it strange that he was telling me everything, and I worried that he might take his desire to communicate elsewhere, somewhere where it might be abused. I was proud of this myself and knew how to be silent when it was necessary to be attentive in the presence of someone else. However, one thing I understood about Leoš was that he didn't have the gift of really knowing people: he saw them quite differently from what they were in real life. He was careless in his actions and in his speech: he blurted everything straight out to everyone and didn't care what results it would have. Often I drew his attention to it, but he just shook his beautiful head and said: 'Oh you see everything so blackly!'

I had to be spiritually ready all the time to keep up with him, flexible enough to adapt myself immediately to his mood and to his ideas. I was

74 This account omits Stejskalová from the circle, but she was there too. She writes (Trkanová 1964, 72) that they would all sit outside in the garden in front of the house on the white painted furniture (see Plate 20): a table, two chairs and the master's favourite armchair, until it was dark – in summer up to 9.30. And Zdenka contributed to the conversations too, with accounts of what she had been reading (after Olga's death she had more time for reading), or what she had heard from friends. Stejskalová added items of local gossip. In the winter, or when the weather was bad, they would sit in the bedroom.

75 See Glossary: 'Lužánky'. The Sunday morning concerts, four or five in a series, were given for three winter seasons from 1911 to 1914 and included a mixture of chamber and orchestral works (including all of Beethoven's symphonies except no.9).

76 Mrs Janáčková is perhaps thinking back to a much earlier period; Janáček parted company with the Brno Beseda in 1889.

77 Zdenka's reference is to Wilhelm Wundt's *Völkerpsychologie* (Stuttgart, 1900), but it was Wundt's *Grundzüge der physiologischen Psychologie* (Leipzig, 1874) that Janáček studied so systematically. In his autobiography (Veselý 1924, 47), Janáček provided details of his reading of the three volumes of the 1910 edition, providing dates which span 12 December to 25 August 1915. Janáček included references to this work in the 1920 edition of his harmony manual XV/202.

aware of it, it pleased me, through it I grew. I used to remember what my mother had taught me: the wife must always take an interest in her husband's work and in his profession, otherwise she does great harm to herself. She herself had long conversations with my father about all sorts of things in his field. I still remember from childhood days how father would read her his reports to the ministry. Now I felt so happy in her footsteps, it was so beautiful when Leoš walked around the table where I was working and went on speaking and speaking, overflowing with new ideas, sparkling with fresh insights, entrusting me with new corners of his rich spirit. I looked forward to those evenings as if to the most beautiful thing which the day could bring, they became something I couldn't do without. And yet my fear of my husband didn't quite disappear even at that time. It appeared always when he was working at home, especially when he was composing. Mářa and I were like mice. God forbid that we should dare to do some noisier work: he would get very angry.[78] I'd guard the doors like Cerberus to turn away visitors who wanted to go and see him at that time. I'd really get into trouble [if I didn't]. A beautiful, beautiful time.

For a long while I'd had a great desire: to see the sea. But it was never really possible. Eventually in the [summer] holidays of 1911 [*recte* 1912], when I'd been begging my husband for a whole year, we went to Crikvenica. [. . .]

Janáčková not only got the year wrong, but was unforthcoming about the nature of the 'begging'. In 1899 she had 'entered the circle of Brno women around Eliška Machová who founded the so-called Útulna. It became an important social institution which gave refuge not only to abandoned and orphaned children, but also supported women in need'.[79] Smetana reports how, with the deaths of both children, Zdenka's work as a committee member for the Útulna increased. At this time the Brno Útulna had founded a special children's home in the Croatian coastal resort of Crikvenica, near Rijeka (then part of the Austro-Hungarian Empire). Through her contacts with the Útulna Zdenka discovered that a trip there would cost little more than Janáček's usual trip to Luhačovice. The director of the Brno Útulna, Marie Steyskalová (no relation to the Janáčeks' servant), found them a 'cosy room with a balcony in a beautiful villa on the seafront with a view of the beach and the sea, and in particular worked out a travel itinerary for the couple'. The route went south via Vienna through the Semmering Pass into Styria, through Slovenia (then a province of the Austro-Hungarian Empire), to Sv. Peter where the railway line divided, the Janáčeks continuing south to Rijeka and

---

78 A fact confirmed years later by one of Janáček's letters to Mrs Stösslová (14 February 1921, *Hž/IL*, no.170: 'she [Zdenka] knows more than anyone else that both she and Mářa are frightened to enter my room while I'm working. When I'm at work, I have to stop immediately at the entrance of any person whomsoever, at any incident whatsoever.'
79 Smetana 1948, 43, see also Glossary: 'Útulna'.

finally along the Croatian coast to Crikvenica. Thus, for the first time in many
years (apart from family gatherings at Hukvaldy) the Janáčeks went off on holiday
together.

   Smetana, who provides a whole chapter devoted in considerable detail to the
Crikvenica trip, reports that the Janáčeks left by the afternoon express for Vienna
soon after 15 July (the end of the Organ School term) and the same evening
continued on their journey from Vienna. The next morning they changed trains in
Sv. Peter for Rijeka. They travelled comfortably, sending on their cases ahead, so
that they could look round Rijeka before the afternoon departure of the steamer
for Crikvenica. At Crikvenica they were met off the pier and taken to their
accommodation.[80]

In Rijeka and Crikvenica I used to sit for whole hours on the rocks and
look at the sea. Leoš was taken with it possibly even more than me. In
Venice[81] we sat together in the Giardino pubblico or on the Lido, we
didn't speak, and just gazed the whole time at that magnificence before
us. The great expanse of water itself was not a novelty, we already
knew the sea from St Petersburg: at the time when Olga began to feel
better again I was once with my brother- and sister-in-law on Yelagin
island.[82] But the north sea is like lead, the southern sea is a rainbow
glow. [. . .] Leoš couldn't have enough of the sea. Whereas I looked at
it more, he seemed as if he wanted to become one with the sea. He was
in the water the whole time. Twice a day he was in the Útulna
swimming-pool.

However, Smetana reports that while Zdenka bathed in the Útulna pool
somewhat further off, Janáček, in order not to waste time, used the pool
opposite their accommodation. Neither of the Janáčeks could swim and
therefore both were somewhat restricted. Once he went out too far and almost
got out of his depth when the high tide came in faster than he had expected.
Originally Janáček had expected to spend only a week in Crikvenica, planning
to go on further to Kupari,[83] but after his first dip he announced to his wife that
they would be staying put. So the couple had three weeks in the area, bathing
and going for walks in the coastal forest Vinodol surrounding Crikvenica, and
taking a trip to the island of Krk in small fishing vessels (in his autobiography,
Janáček remembered the 'women worn out with work; the comfortable
fishermen').[84] They also took a few longer excursions by steamer, to Pula, then

80 Smetana 1948, 44.
81 This single reference to Venice is a slip. It is not supported by Smetana's very detailed
account, and from Zdenka's description of their trip to Venice in 1925 for the International
Society for Contemporary Music (ISCM) Festival (see Chapter 9), it is clear that the couple
were there for the first time.
82 The northernmost island in the mouth of the Neva, looking out on the Gulf of Finland.
However, Zdenka makes no mention of this expedition in Chapter 5.
83 A small coastal resort south-east of Dubrovnik.
84 Veselý 1924, 70.

an Austro-Hungarian naval base, where they saw the Roman amphitheatre, and another trip round the island of Krk (this time by steamer). On this journey they experienced rough weather, though neither of the Janáčeks succumbed to seasickness like the rest of the passengers. In Krk they got off and inspected the town of Veglia.[85] On the way back the weather worsened and the ship was caught in a severe storm which it had to sit out at sea since it was too dangerous to try and dock on the rocky shore. Wet through on his return, Janáček could not be restrained from standing and listening to the sound of folksongs from an inn, to the fury of his equally drenched wife. On a final excursion by the steamer they visited Baška, another town on the island of Krk, eating in the Czech inn 'U Geistlichů'.

Zdenka proposed a different trip back to Brno via the Alpine pass into Austria in the Karawanken mountains (taking the western rather than the eastern fork at Ljubljana), but Janáček's fear of new places prevailed so that at first his only concession was to travel to Opatija by steamer. In Opatija they had a meal, looked at several churches and parks, and then went on to Rijeka by train. But on the train to Sv. Peter they met a Czech-speaking couple who, as rather more experienced travellers, recommended a stop in Trieste, and offered their services as guides there. Their new friends found them accommodation, ordered them a complicated fish meal in an *osteria* with the appropriate wine and took them to coffee and ice cream in a café, and then for a walk to the harbour before retiring. 'It was midnight when the Janáčeks returned to the hotel with their companions and at five in the morning Janáček impatiently woke up his wife again and looked round Trieste tirelessly the whole morning.[86] It was 15 August and in one of the churches Mrs Janáčková remembered the birthday of her late daughter Olga some thirty years earlier.'[87] Somewhat emboldened by the success of the Trieste expedition, Janáček consented to stop further in Bled where 'they found a lovely room in one of the villas next to the station' and made a half-day trip to Vintgar gorge with its waterfalls and visited the tiny shrine on an island in the lake at Bled. Since Bled is the last town before the border on the Karawanken mountains, it sounds as though Mrs Janáčková's original return plan (the western route) prevailed.[88] The return trip also included a two-day stop in Ljubljana – 'white Ljubljana' as Janáček described it,[89] 'the castle and its guard, a Czech pensioner' – before taking the train to Vienna, where Zdenka remained visiting her parents, and Janáček went on further to

85 The Italian word for Krk. Krk/Veglia is the chief town of the island.
86 Ten years later, Janáček's only recollection of Trieste in a letter to Kamila Stösslová (10 August 1918; *Hž*, no.80) was that the sea water was not clean since the town sewerage went straight into the sea.
87 This and further quotations and paraphrases in this section all from Smetana 1948, 44–9.
88 However, Smetana also reports that the two-day stop in Ljubljana occurred 'after Bled' – which would mean the Janáčeks' retracing their steps and then taking the eastern route. It is possible, however, that this route through unfamiliar terrain got muddled in the telling. Janáček's own terse account in his 1924 autobiography places Ljubljana before Bled and adds a view of the mountain Triglav, visible from Bled.
89 Veselý 1924, 71.

Brno. He could only have been there for a day or so: on 21 August 1912 he registered at the Augustinian House at Luhačovice for a week's stay.[90]

But some time after returning (it was already winter), Leoš fell sick with a strange illness[91] which we put down to the excessive bathing in the sea. His feet and his hands swelled up,[92] he couldn't even move, he didn't sleep from November to March. Mářa and I had to turn him continually on the sheets, he was in such pain.[93] Taking aspirin gave him some relief, otherwise nothing else was any use. At the same time he was active, he wanted to work, his pupils from the Organ School had to come to our house for lessons. They sat round his bed in the study[94] and he taught them. Sometimes after their departure the place looked a real mess; and still worse after the masseuse.[95] The floor was covered with stains from her ointments. Leoš loved being massaged right to the end of his life. At that time during his illness he was very keen on an old lame woman and greatly praised her expertise.

The masseuse, according to Stejskalová, was named Koláčná[96] and she had 'golden hands'. 'To my dying day I won't forget how she once came to help me while we still lived at Klášterní náměstí; now the master in his turn couldn't praise her enough. He got so used to her that she came afterwards for many years. When the master needed her he wrote her a postcard asking her to come again for tea. She would keep these invitations and after the master's death it's said that she sold them for lots of money because it was his manuscript.'[97] Another treatment that seemed to have helped at this time was 'Hukvaldy honey' – bandages soaked in honey (sent by the Sládeks in Hukvaldy).

According to Smetana, however, Janáček's improvement was due to Dr Stix of Panská ulice, who treated Janáček, encased in cotton wool 'with some sort of electrified magnetic implements' after which he slept well for the first time.[98] After more cotton wool and keeping to a strict diet, the swelling reduced, but his entire skin peeled off. Other doctors that Janáček consulted at the time included Dr Hora from Francouzská ulice, who prescribed compresses, Dr Jan Hnátek from Prague

90 Štědroň 1939.

91 Stejskalová (Trkanová 1964, 72) described it as 'terrible rheumatism', Smetana (1948, 51) as 'rheumatism or gout'. Today it might be described as 'reactive arthritis' occasioned by an intestinal infection but it is hard to say what this could have been.

92 According to Smetana (1948, 51) his 'whole body and neck' was swollen.

93 He also had to be fed, being unable to move his arms (Smetana 1948, 51).

94 Janáček was propped up against 'an ingenious construction of pillows' (Smetana 1948, 51).

95 Janáček had the ministrations of a masseuse in the summer of 1909; see his reference in a letter to Zdenka (15 September 1909, BmJA, A 4960).

96 Antonie Koláčná (1877–?). In 1923 she married one František Koláčný and thus retained her original surname. The couple lived near the Janáčeks, in Dvorecká (now Slovakova) ulice.

97 Trkanová 1964, 73.

98 Smetana 1948, 51–2.

(see p.143), consulted by post, who recommended the drug piperazine[99] (of which Janáček consumed several bottles), Dr Dressler (Janáček's cousin) and Dr Jaroslav Elgart from Kroměříž. The last two paid particular attention to his diet, especially the avoidance of salt. In addition Dr Dressler tried to cure him by means of warm air and massages.

It was already spring [1913] when he recovered, but we still didn't trust it too much. On St John's Day [24 June] we went to Prague, my husband looked in on the doctor,[100] who sent him to Karlovy Vary[101] for the summer holidays. He went alone, I myself got an infection of the nerves in my left hand. When it got better, I went again to my parents in Vienna. There I got a letter from Leoš saying that he was leaving for Mšeno[102] to complete the treatment. But hardly had he arrived there the next day than he got erysipelas[103] over his whole body.[104] They took him in to the hospital in Roudnice. I wasn't allowed to go and see him because erysipelas is infectious and I waited in Vienna anxious as to what would happen next.

'When afterwards he was better', Stejskalová recollects, 'he wrote to me to prepare a good lunch because he was arriving with the Roudnice doctor, since the hospital didn't want to let him out on his own. So to welcome him I baked pigeons, we kept two pairs in the loft of the Organ School.'[105] Stejskalová also wrote to Zdenka asking her to return from Vienna. Zdenka's first sight of her husband caused her much distress. 'She saw him sitting in the garden house, sad, miserable, thin and completely yellow, and when the couple met, Leoš Janáček broke down at the memory of what he'd been through during his illness.'[106] 'From that unhappy journey [Stejskalová reported] the master brought each of us an expensive present: a golden tie-pin for Simandl, and for Simandl's wife and me, golden brooches with the first letters of our Christian names.'[107] Zdenka remembered them as 'garnet

---

99 Used normally for the treatment of roundworm and threadworm infestation.
100 Dr Hnátek (see Smetana 1948, 52).
101 Janáček went off to Karlovy Vary about a month after he had seen the doctor, some time between 17 July 1913, when he wrote to Rektorys (JA iv, 158) that he was going, 'unwillingly', and 25 July, when he wrote to Zdenka (BmJA, A 3861), evidently after a few days there. Smetana (1948, 52–3) reports that there he was treated with various water and mud cures. He was still there by 6 August (letter to Zdenka, BmJA, A 3920).
102 On the recommendation of Dr Malý at the Organ School (Trkanová 1964, 73).
103 Or 'Saint Anthony's fire', an infectious skin disease, characterized by purplish raised lesions especially on the face (Zdenka uses the graphic Czech word *růže*, which also means a 'rose'). It is accompanied by fever, headache and vomiting.
104 Janáček must have set off for Mšeno straight after writing to Zdenka from Karlovy Vary on 6 August since on 8 August he wrote a brief note to Dr Veselý from Mšeno (JA viii, 33) saying that on his third day there he had caught a fever. A further letter to Dr Veselý (26 August 1913, JA viii, 34) thanks him for his intervention: as Stejskalová reports (Trkanová 1964, 73) Dr Veselý kept in touch with the Roudnice doctors throughout Janáček's stay there.
105 Trkanová 1964, 73.
106 Smetana 1948, 53.
107 Trkanová 1964, 73.

brooches in the form of the letter with which these women's names began – M and E'. She herself received a golden medallion decorated with garnets.[108]

Although he was weakened, Leoš didn't let up and soon began to go about. From that he got spasms in his leg, he had to lie or at most sit. And as if on purpose I tore a ligament in my leg, it was caused somehow by wearing high heels. The doctor ordered peace and ice packs. So we sat opposite one another for whole days like two invalids, but we felt good together and were cheerful. I remember how we laughed when Headmaster Bílý,[109] my husband's colleague from his schooldays, came to visit us, and we neither of us could move.

'From the time of that illness, the master began to fear for himself and take more care. Not that he would have kept to a diet; he still insisted on good food. But he began to go for lots of walks, he invited the masseuse ever more frequently and feared every ache and pain. He suffered with his teeth a lot at that time. Also he began to lose his hair. At once he went to consult Dr Dressler. He advised some sort of water and the master thereafter always moistened his hair with it. It helped; his hair seemed to thicken even more and took on that lovely white colour admired by everyone and about which so much was written. It shone around the master's head like white fire. Dr Dressler now had the master under constant observation and we also began to take care of him like a precious ointment. For food we chose the very best; when the temperature fell a little we made a fire for him in the study, when he sweated we immediately got him a dry, warmed shirt.'[110]

And then came the year 1914. The political pall that was in the air occasionally blew even in our direction from the newspapers and from what my husband had to say. We felt that d'Este[111] was the villain who was provoking it. But everything was put into the shade by the preparations for the Brno Sokol Rally.

It is significant that for Zdenka Janáčková 1914 meant basically the beginning of the First World War and the Brno Sokol Rally. In her memoirs she ignored her husband's sixtieth birthday on 3 July, as he attempted to do himself. Only Smetana provides any account of how unwillingly Janáček celebrated this birthday, and how, when he got to hear of preparations at the Organ School, he strictly forbade any festivities. In the end he relented to the extent of allowing delegations of staff and students from the Organ School and from the Russian Circle to bring their

108 Smetana 1948, 54.
109 František Bílý (1854–1920), a schoolfriend of Janáček's from 1866, became a headmaster of a school in Prague and a distinguished literary historian.
110 Trkanová 1964, 74. Smetana reports (1948, 51) that Janáček sweated profusely at the least exertion; from his thirties onwards a warm, dry shirt, which he had to change into at once, always awaited his return.
111 i.e. Archduke Franz Ferdinand (1863–1914), the heir to the Austrian throne, represented rather unfairly as a warmonger in the Czech press.

gifts and good wishes. In response he took the Organ School teachers and their wives to a simple dinner at the Lužánky restaurant, bringing them back afterwards to his garden to enjoy wine and biscuits with him until late into the balmy summer evening. Smetana puts Janáček's reluctance down in part to a feeling of embitteredness at a lack of more general recognition.[112] The fact that his birthday came less than a week after the débâcle of the Brno Sokol Rally was perhaps another reason for his attitude.

The Czech Sokol movement was founded in 1862 by Czech patriots. Ostensibly a physical-training movement, with regular rallies centred on mass gymnastic displays, the Sokol movement contained within it powerful nation-building elements. It was essentially a Czech movement (the Germans had their Turnverein, on which the Sokol movement had been modelled) and it was this national aspect which particularly attracted Janáček. One of his more curious occasional pieces was the *Music for Club Swinging* VIII/13, written for the 1893 rally; even the much more famous Sinfonietta has connections with the Eighth National Rally of 1926. The Brno 1914 Sokol Rally, held at the Královo Pole stadium, celebrated over fifty years of the movement in Brno and featured the 'Moravský rok' [Moravian Year], demonstrating 'the habits and customs' of the Moravian people'.[113]

Although my husband no longer took an active part, he followed everything passionately: he was a Sokol member from the beginnings of its existence in Brno.[114] The Dresslers' daughters did their drill in the Sokol and in their company we caught something of the atmosphere of the rehearsals. We made preparations that we would go to Crikvenica again after the rally. This time my husband's Prague niece Věra Janáčková[115] was to have travelled with us. Additionally in the spring we had unpleasant work on the house [. . .].[116]

At last the rally came. A storm of joy waved from the red and white flags, it wafted to us in cheers from the street, it was written in every Czech face. Naturally all three of us wanted to see as much of the rally

112 Smetana 1948, 58–9.
113 Trkanová 1964, 75.
114 An exaggeration: Janáček joined in 1876, more than a decade after the movement was established in Brno.
115 See Glossary. Věra had been invited two years before but wrote belatedly on 17 July 1912 that her doctor had advised against it (BmJA, A 5712). Two years later Janáček certainly counted on her company. They were leaving on 5 August, he wrote on 12 July 1914 (BmJA, B 2321) and in a further letter on the subject (18 July 1914; BmJA, A 6282) announced that they were staying in the Villa Josefina, with Věra in a separate room for K 120. They had plans to go on to Montenegro or to Venice.
116 Stejskalová's account is fuller: 'Right at the beginning of spring an unpleasant thing came upon us: the bad side of our little house was that during the building they had not reckoned with the dampness and a mushroom appeared in the house. More and more grew, so that in the end there was nothing for it, but to dig up the floors, tear out the door and the window frames – three months it lasted before everything was in order again' (Trkanová 1964, 75).

as possible. But we were frightened to leave our little house unattended. The caretaker and his family went to the rally, there wasn't anyone to guard it. So we divided it up among ourselves like this: on the first day my husband and Máŕa would go to the Moravian Year, the second day I would go with him.

It was Sunday 28 June. When my husband and Máŕa went off, I sat with Čert in the garden. It was a beautiful day, quiet, the street was clear of people, all life had flowed into the stadium in Královo Pole, I too was there in my thoughts.

Máŕa was of course there in person and described how it began with the men's gymnastics and the enthusiasm which greeted their display. When they had finished, they went off and people waited for the next event 'but nothing, only a strange silence. We looked at one another – there was something wrong. No one would explain why the women were not already beginning their display. And then they announced to us that the heir to the Austrian throne and his wife had been killed in Sarajevo and that the display was being halted. It came like a bolt from the blue. We dispersed, shocked, friends talking quietly among themselves. I rushed home to tell the mistress what had happened. But she already knew.'[117]

Suddenly I heard a cry somewhere in the street. It didn't stop, but on the contrary it got stronger. I ran to the gate, I wanted to have a look, but I was locked in. The caretaker's family had locked up when they went. In vain I tried to catch sight of something through the bars. A woman went running by. I asked her what was happening.

'Jézus, in Sarajevo they've murdered the trónfolgr and his frau!'[118]

I stood at the bars as if I'd been struck. Then a policeman came up saying that we should immediately fly a black flag. I told him that I was alone at home, that he must be patient. After a while silent pedestrians began to trickle back from Královo Pole. The authorities forbade the rally from continuing. My husband came with Máŕa. None of us spoke, we felt the storm. Only my husband thought aloud for a moment:

'Well, everyone likes living, they surely ought not to murder.'

And again it was quiet at our place.

The Moravian Year on [the feast of] SS Peter and Paul[119] didn't take place. We heard that the Serbs who were at the rally were sent home immediately by the police. The atmosphere was as stiflingly oppressive but nevertheless we believed that it would clear again. It was a good sign for us that the Moravian Year was nevertheless allowed to take

117 Trkanová 1964, 75.
118 Zdenka quotes typical Brno Germanisms: Thronfolger = heir apparent; Frau = wife.
119 i.e. the event planned for the feast of SS Peter and Paul on Monday, 29 June 1914.

place a week later.[120] We all[121] went, even Máŕa's brother, a teacher from Koválovice, came with his wife. We looked forward to the beautiful costumes, the singing and the music as if to something precious and magnificent. Everyone dressed up in the finest clothes they had, after all it was a magnificent hot day. Leoš put on his light-coloured silk suit – all of Brno knew him in it. He'd brought the material for it back from Russia some time when Olga was still healthy.[122] It was true raw silk, called *chesuncha*.[123] From that time on he took a fancy to the material and wore such suits for the rest of his life.[124] I too had white clothes and a panama hat, Máŕa and the people from Koválovice were also dressed up.

The programme began. It was beautiful, but what use was that when suddenly black clouds began to gather. I became frightened. 'Look at those clouds, let's go and take shelter somewhere', I said to my husband. 'Phooey, don't interfere, shut up!' was his response.

And suddenly there was such a storm, a cloud-burst such that I'd hardly ever experienced before. Cries, a wild retreat from the rally grounds, but it was already too late. There was nowhere to shelter, we fell in the slippery mud; we got wet through to the skin, clothes, shoes were ruined, many ladies went away barefoot because their white shoes got stuck deep in the mud; after the storm the place was teeming with bedraggled summer hats. I saved my beautiful panama only by taking it off and throwing it into a covered stand.[125] Once again the show was over. To the ridicule of the Brno Germans the participants of the Moravian Year dispersed in their impossible outfits[126] through Brno. What a waste! My husband and I didn't come off so badly, our clothes were washable, but the people from Koválovice had everything ruined. The wife had to change into Máŕa's clothes and travel home in them. That Brno rally wasn't a happy one.

120 In fact on 12 July 1914 (Šujan 1928, 455).
121 Mrs Janáčková's memory seems to have been faulty. Despite her brief reference to 'Máŕa' a few lines later, it is clear from the servant's account how she (Stejskalová) was left guarding the house and learnt of the outcome only at second hand (Trkanová 1964, 76).
122 i.e. during his extensive Russian tour of 1896.
123 Zdenka called it *čičunča*, but the correct Czech transliteration, *česunča*, was supplied by Stejskalová (Trkanová 1964, 24). This is tussore, a coarse Indian silk, cream or even brown in colour, obtained from the Oriental saturniid silkworm.
124 Janáček's rally outfit was completed with light white shoes and a silk cap (Trkanová 1964, 76). The silk cap was also made from *chesuncha* and Janáček can be seen wearing it in Venice (Plate 18) and Luhačovice (Plate 16).
125 Zdenka gave it to one of her friends in the covered stands (Trkanová 1964, 76). Zdenka set special store by her hats (see Plate 17), and went to Vienna to buy them.
126 Stejskalová (Trkanová 1964, 76) reports that red clothes with floral borders were fashionable – and that the colours ran in the rain.

Despite all these bad omens we all went off for the holidays. We were due to go to Crikvenica only at the beginning of August,[127] meanwhile my husband was in Hukvaldy from 15 July, Máŕa in Koválovice. I alone at home. On 26 July I went early in the morning for the newspaper, I read 'Ultimatum to Serbia'.[128] So war after all. Outside it rained cats and dogs, in the house it was empty, mournful, my instinct foretold unhappy events. Věra Dresslerová ran in, lamenting that her sweetheart would have to go to war. A long, sad day. The next day Máŕa returned, frightened by what was happening. On Sunday I wrote to my husband, telling him to return home.[129] He answered that he wouldn't dream of it, that he wouldn't let his holidays be ruined. In the afternoon of the day that I got his letter, he was there with his cases. He said all the visitors had left Hukvaldy.

Stejskalová gives a more precise reason for Janáček's sudden return: it was expected that civilians would not be able to travel by train, and so there was a possibility that he might not be able to get back to Brno, where he would be needed at the Organ School.[130] And Smetana paints a vivid picture of him arriving 'red-faced and puffing in exasperation, carrying his cases in both hands and with his hat pulled right to the back of his skull, always a sign that the Maestro was in the worst mood.'[131]

That was the end of Crikvenica, but no one worried about that now. Day after day frightening reports circulated. One was particularly disturbing: Russia was going to war against us. Friends among Russophiles met and whispered among themselves; they discussed among themselves what to do now. Suddenly every action was considered high treason. We had fears about Professor Vach, who shortly before had been with the PSMU in Russia.[132] I also had great fears for Leoš. He was chairman of the Russian Circle.[133] He told me

127 See p.117, fn.115.
128 Austria-Hungary sent its ultimatum on 23 July 1914, demanding a reply within forty-eight hours. Serbia accepted most of the Austrian demands within the given time, but the Austro-Hungarian government nevertheless ordered a partial mobilization on 25 July, publicly announced the next day, and declared war on 28 July.
129 If Zdenka remembered the right day this 'Sunday' would have been 2 August, a week after she read about the ultimatum in the paper. Janáček was certainly home by 2 August since he wrote to his niece Věra from Brno on that day (BmJA, B 2322).
130 Trkanová 1964, 77.
131 Smetana 1948, 60.
132 Ferdinand Vach (1860–1939) founded the Pěvecké sdružení moravských učitelů [Moravian Teachers' Choral Society] in 1903. Under Vach the society had undertaken a successful tour of St Petersburg and Kiev in December 1913.
133 See Glossary. One of the members, Albín Kotík, was imprisoned in the Špilberk castle, though later released (Trkanová 1964, 77; Smetana 1948, 64).

to go to Miss Vašková,[134] Bezruč's sister, who was the administrator, and give her a message to destroy all the minutes in which there was any indication of Russophilism and to write new, harmless ones. That was the only precaution he took, otherwise he did nothing to deflect suspicion of Russophilism from himself. He was too proud and uncompromising to do so. He had contacts with Radić,[135] he'd been with him some time past in Hukvaldy, at home he had an extensive correspondence with him and also with many Russians. It didn't even occur to him to read it through and destroy incriminating passages. In my fear for him I then took everything and burnt it. Without his knowledge; he would never have allowed it. He didn't miss it, he never bothered about his correspondence except when he needed something. I feared also that someone would desecrate Olga's grave because of the Russian inscription on the monument. I couldn't go to Leoš with this, so I and the gardener Reichingr masked the inscription with flowers.[136] I waited to see what my husband would say when he noticed it, but he didn't notice during the whole period of the war.

The Russian Circle, whose chief aim was to promote the knowledge of Russian language and culture, had always attracted the attention of the local police. Special permission was needed for its founding (1898), and annual reports had to be submitted to them. The reason was that it was probably seen as a potential platform for pan-Slavonicism, whose aims, if realized, would logically lead to the dismemberment of the Austro-Hungarian Empire. Once war with Russia was declared, the gloves were off and enough minor infringements of permitted activities were found to ban the circle – though this happened surprisingly late, 9 March 1915. Janáček had to watch the police going through the archives (on 14 March 1915).[137] As chairman of the circle since 1909, he was then registered in Viennese police files as 'p.v.' [*politisch verdächtig* – 'politically suspicious'].

Apart from ordering the doctoring of the Russian Circle files, Janáček also took steps to ensure some sort of continuity in the Organ School. Realizing that

---

134 Olga Vašková (1873–1944), schoolteacher, sister of the poet Petr Bezruč (1867–1958), some of whose *Silesian Songs* Janáček set as male-voice choruses (IV/33–6).
135 Stjepan Radić (1871–1928), Croatian politician. With his brother Antun he founded the Croatian Peasant Party (1904), one of whose aims was the federalization of the Austro-Hungarian monarchy. After 1918 he led the struggle for Croatian autonomy within Yugoslavia and was assassinated in parliament. He occasionally wrote for Czech newspapers.
136 'with ivy', according to both Smetana (1948, 62) and Stejskalová (Trkanová 1964, 77). According to Smetana, Janáček 'mutely' consented to this precaution. Quite a lot of ivy and ingenuity would have been required for the operation to cover up both the Russian inscription and also, lower down, Olga's name, written in both Czech and Russian.
137 Vrba 1960, 83–4.

the school would probably lose its state subsidy, he called a meeting of the staff at which he explained that they would all be paid equally from whatever funds he had at his disposal, which in fact meant only the pupils' fees.[138]

General mobilization. Many a family we knew had some member in the army. Even the caretaker Simandl joined up and instead of him my husband appointed his brother-in-law, a small hunchback, Čihánek.[139] They made stores of provisions. We all counted on their being needed for just a few months. I walked into Zádruha[140] and bought what was to be had: flour, rice, coffee, soap. Fears arose that I'd not known all my life, and with them, tension, anxiety, gloomy moods. In September my husband went again to Luhačovice.[141] He wanted me to accompany him. But Máŕa didn't want to remain home alone in these bad times, so I remained at home. That was a mistake. I should have fallen in with his wishes. He always reproached me that I'd left him alone at such a sad time.

Smetana reports that one of Janáček's reasons for getting away from Brno was the 'war-time psychosis' there, partly caused by the army, which had taken over all the Brno schools and the general commotion caused by mobilization. There was also fear of informers. 'In the café Bellevue, in which the Janáček family met regularly on Sunday evenings with a few intimate friends [. . .], Janáček would hush the conversation and suspiciously observe everyone sitting nearby and who hadn't for a while turned the pages of the newspapers they held.'[142]

The Russians were winning, they got nearer, it was said that in Ostrava you could hear Russian cannons. We looked forward to our salvation approaching, but I was nevertheless cautious. I packed up all the china, silver and precious things into trunks, we took it down into the cellar[143] and had strong bars made. My husband got an order from Vienna to send all the collected songs there for safe-keeping.[144] He didn't obey. He told me that he wouldn't hand them over, that they must remain in Moravia. The only thing we did was to buy trunks and

---

138 Smetana 1948, 60–1.
139 Antonín Čihánek (1884–1933). Stejskalová, who had to work closely with the care-takers, reports him as being 'honest and conscientious'. He carried on as caretaker after the Organ School became the Brno Conservatory.
140 The word, originally meaning 'clan', was adopted as the name of a co-operative society which ran a store and a popular cheap restaurant situated in what is today náměstí Svobody no.17.
141 According to the list of Luhačovice visitors, he arrived on 3 September (Štědroň 1939).
142 Smetana 1948, 62–3.
143 i.e. of the Organ School. As Zdenka reported earlier, the house had neither loft nor cellar.
144 i.e. all the materials collected under his leadership as chairman of the Working Committee for Folksong in Moravia and Silesia.

put all the song materials into them and also took them down into the cellar. But the Russians never came.

Inspections began and confiscations of hoarded foodstuffs. Here it was I who said that I wouldn't hand anything over. Mářa and I divided all our provisions[145] into half-kilo packets and hid them in the [Organ School] loft among the beams. Hardships occurred, provisions were rationed,[146] one had to queue up endlessly for them. Mářa would get up at two in the morning to get served as soon as possible. Hardly had the day broken than I'd run off and relieve her. The hardships got worse and worse. The prices of goods soared to dizzy heights, wages didn't change. It was particularly bad at the Organ School. State subsidies stopped, teachers' pay had to be taken only from pupils' fees. And there was little of that, almost all the older students were called up. Only a handful remained. One taught for a pittance. My husband had K 100 a month. At least we had his pension on top of that.[147] It had its good side too in that we didn't have to worry that money would lose its value since we had none. Other people invested it in everything possible: materials, provisions, jewels.

In the early spring of 1915 we went for a few days to Prague. I stayed with Janáčková, my husband's sister-in-law, Leoš in a hotel.[148] I brought bread and Easter cake with me from Brno, at that time nothing could be obtained freely and one couldn't ask for one's hosts to share their tiny ration. I was surprised how jolly it was in Prague: concerts and theatres were full. People came together to forget their worries, to talk to one another. Perhaps it was also because dance parties didn't take place.

Stejskalová has rather more to say about how the Janáčeks coped with food shortages during the war. Bread was not a problem since she would bring flour from her relatives living in the villages of Pořezín and Nové Dvory.[149] They would make the dough themselves, but have it baked by the baker in Rudolfská ulice. Other types of food came from Mářa's relatives, from Hukvaldy (from where, Smetana reports, the Janáčeks bought a whole deer from the forester Vlkovský),[150] and even from Janáček's pupils. In a letter to Gabriela Horvátová Janáček

145 Such as flour, sugar, rice etc. (Trkanová 1964, 78).
146 Also fuel: coal and heating-oil (Trkanová 1964, 78).
147 The pension (from the Teachers' Institute) was of course small since Janáček had retired early, when he was fifty. However, rent on the house (as mortgage repayments) was waived for the duration of the war (Smetana 1948, 68).
148 Janáček wrote to Věra Janáčková on 26 March 1915 (BmJA, B 2325), announcing his and Zdenka's arrival for the Easter weekend on Saturday 3 April. Zdenka stayed with Věra's mother, Joža Janáčková, the widow of Janáček's cousin Augustin Janáček.
149 Trkanová 1964, 78.
150 Smetana 1948, 65.

mentions with approval how a pupil paid his examination fee with a pile of sugar.[151] They were even able to help out Zdenka's relatives in Vienna, who were rather worse off. Fuel was more of a problem, with inadequate supplies of coal for both the house and the Organ School. On the whole it was the two women of the household who bore the brunt of attempting to keep Janáček in the style to which he had become accustomed. Janáček's chief contribution was that he was not a heavy smoker, so that his war-time ration of tobacco could be traded in for foodstuff. He also kept pigeons in the loft to supplement the diet[152] and looked after the hens.

'When I went the rounds of my relatives for provisions they would give me a hen from time to time and we kept them for laying. Altogether there were four, but one got sick and we had to kill her. The rest we had then for several years. The master trained them so that they followed him around like dogs and he named them after the places I'd brought them from or according to their colour: Kovalská [from Koválovice], Slavkovská [from Slavkov] and Bílá [white]. Bílá was the tamest of these, she came pattering right up to the kitchen and talked the whole time. All of them walked freely round the garden during the day, they didn't scratch up anything, they were taught to lay their eggs under the box tree at the path, and the master would go there himself to collect the eggs – that was a joy for him. He would talk with the hens as if with children, they looked at him, answered him with something, and he understood it. Kovalská was the naughtiest and he would then always give her a smack along the wings. When in the evening he sat down in the garden in his armchair with the paper, he'd tap on the table, as the teacher does in class, the hens would rush to him at once, fly on to the table top, and keep him company. After a while, they nodded off, he read beside them, ignoring the fact that from the Organ School and even from the street over the fence it could be seen how he was keeping company with hens.'[153]

In fact despite the shortages, Janáček's health improved in the war. The bad rheumatism which had plagued him all his life seemed to recede and in the end he became so robust that he could take a journey to Prague at night on the platform of a goods wagon without detriment to his health.[154]

As far as clothes were concerned during the war, the Janáčeks fared quite well since they both had reasonable wardrobes which, carefully looked after, lasted them throughout these years. And the replacement caretaker Čihánek, a qualified cobbler, was able to repair the shoes they had. Some time in 1915 Zdenka bought 140 squirrel pelts from a forester. She intended these for herself, but in the end presented them to Janáček that Christmas. He had a fur coat made from them which he then wore to the end of his life. He was very fond of it: because the silk-like quality of the fur made it lighter to wear than a winter coat, and because it was wonderfully warm.[155]

151 8 December 1917 (JA vi, 40).
152 Smetana 1948, 65–6.
153 Trkanová 1964, 78.
154 Smetana 1948, 66.
155 Smetana 1948, 66–7.

My husband had rheumatism and in the holidays [summer 1915] went to have it treated in Bohdaneč. The director of the spa there was Dr Veselý,[156] the husband of Marie Calma; [. . .] they were good friends of ours from the time they lived in Brno. When he returned, we spent several days together at Radhošť.[157] It was so magnificent in those peaceful heights, where we knew nothing of the war and of human misery. And those were, I think, also the last relatively happy days for me: for a long, long time after that I didn't know what it was to have a contented day.

We left for Hukvaldy and lived at my sister-in-law Marie's. Poor thing, she had all of her worldly wealth in Russian bonds and got so hard up in the war that she didn't have anything to live on, she couldn't even pay the interest on her loan for the house.[158] Josefka no longer lived with her husband: he left her his flat in the school and he himself lived in the classroom above. His pupil kept house for him there, a young girl who had hardly left school and whom he later married after the coup d'état.[159] It was agreed that Josefka would cook lunches for us. But on the very first day I got a telegram saying that Mother had had an operation. From the briefness of the information I judged that things were bad, possibly that she was dying. I wanted to go to her at once. Leoš tried to stop me, but I wouldn't be held back and went off the very next day, as soon as I had a connection to Brno. It upset Leoš greatly. He did not want to understand that I had to be with Mother when she was in a bad way. Afterwards Josefka told me that he cried and complained that I had feeling for 'them' but none for him. I didn't understand it: after all, he was well, Josefka was looking after him and he could do without me, whereas I'd be seeing my mother perhaps for the last time. The train connection to Brno was terrible, as it was the whole time during the World War. By the time I got home it seemed as if I'd been battered about. I arrived home, Máŕa was doing the washing. She greeted me strangely. Our little Čertíček didn't bark. I went to find him in the room, I looked at the divan where he used to lie about and then Máŕa let out the lament: Čertíček is no more –

In her account Stejskalová explained that the dog's legs had become infected, and he could neither stand nor walk. She took him to the vet where she learnt that his

156 See Glossary.
157 See Glossary.
158 Stejskalová reported (Trkanová 1964, 79) that the Janáčeks helped her out.
159 i.e. the declaration of Czechoslovak Independence as the First World War came to an end in 1918.

disease was infectious; she had to take him to the abattoir to be put down.[160] Every cloud has a silver lining, however. Smetana reported[161] how the stockpile of second-grade rice stored to keep Čert going during the war was now put to use in supplementing the family's war-time diet. And judging from his Hukvaldy experiences (see p.97 above), Čert and the hens would not have happily co-existed.

So that too. Čert was an old dog, but he was Olga's friend, she told me: keep Čertíček as a memory . . .

But there was no time for laments when my mother was possibly dying. I had to go back to the station to catch the train to Vienna. There they told me:

'My dear lady, there are no more trains today.'

In the war even that was possible. I went home again and, tired to death, slept and slept. The next day I was able to travel to Vienna. Fearfully I rang the bell at my parents' place.

The person who came to open it – was my mother.

'It's good that you're here now. I was waiting so I could go for the operation.'

With old age, she had enlarged [thyroid] glands on her neck and the doctors advised an operation. She wanted to see me before having it, but Father formulated the telegram in an unfortunate way, in such a manner as to suggest that the operation was over. I felt as if a weight had fallen from my heart. The operation was a success. I remained in Vienna and took charge of my parents' household. I wrote about everything to Leoš, it seemed that he'd forgiven my departure although it was too late for me to return to Hukvaldy since in the meantime the holidays were almost over. But it was only an apparent forgiveness – a heavy, very heavy punishment awaited me.

160 Trkanová 1964, 79.
161 Smetana 1948, 65.

7

Jenůfa in Prague

While I was living through all this, the further fate of *Jenůfa* was being decided – and so, too, was mine. Marie Calma-Veselá[1] knew all of *Jenůfa*. Once, during the [summer] holidays of 1915, she was singing the 'Zdrávas královno'[2] from it to herself at home. At that very moment Director Schmoranz[3] from the Prague National Theatre happened to be passing by with the [writer] Šípek-Peška.[4] He stopped under the window and listened. Interested, he then asked what it was. Šípek knew that it was from *Jenůfa* and so one thing led to another until at about Christmas time Kovařovic accepted *Jenůfa* for the National Theatre in Prague.[5] My husband and I were delighted and throughout the entire winter we lived happily and expectantly. When together, we spoke of almost nothing but *Jenůfa*. Leoš promised me that in the summer after the première we'd go together to Luhačovice and how beautiful it would be there. He told me every little detail as soon as he heard anything about the rehearsals for his opera. Nervously, he waited to see how it would be cast, especially the role of the Kostelnička. Then he found out that Mrs Gabriela Horvátová, of whom much was heard, would be singing it[6] though so far he didn't know her personally. He was pleased when Šípek wrote to him[7] that she liked the role. Later she arrived in Brno to sing a guest performance in the Old Theatre.[8] Leoš went to hear her and asked my advice about whether he should visit her. I urged him to do so. So he went to see her in the hotel Slavia, where she was

1 See Glossary.
2 Jenůfa's prayer to the Virgin Mary in Act 2.
3 See p.96, fn.8.
4 Josef Peška (1857–1923), a librettist and theatre enthusiast who wrote under the pseudonym of Karel Šípek. Unaccountably, Mrs Janáčková describes him here as a 'singer'.
5 The long battle for *Jenůfa*'s acceptance at the Prague National Theatre is recounted in *JODA*, JP59–86. The 'open window' story (JP59) is contradicted by Calma-Veselá's own account (JP60).
6 Calma-Veselá suggested in a letter to Janáček as early as 9 December 1915 (*JODA*, JP76) that Horvátová would sing the Kostelnička; for Horvátová see Glossary.
7 On 21 March 1916 (*JODA*, JP91).
8 i.e. the theatre on Veveří ulice (see Glossary: 'Brno Theatre').

staying.[9] He returned somewhat disconcerted and, in answer to my questions whether he'd spoken with Mrs Horvátová, he said with embarrassment: 'Yes, I spoke to her, but you know, she received me in bed.'

Until then my husband wasn't used to the informal ways of the theatre, and with a woman, even when he was passionately courting her, he always respected her modesty and her shyness. Up till now, despite all his flirtations, he was inexperienced in erotic matters and, I'd say, innocent. He was thoroughly nonplussed that the lady had received him in bed. At the time I laughed at it: 'That doesn't matter, so long as she sings the Kostelnička well for you.'

They invited him to Prague for rehearsals.[10] He was flustered, full of uncertainty as to how he'd be understood there. Every day he wrote to me in detail all about it.[11] And Mrs Horvátová was soon the culmination of everything.[12] When he arrived home, he just beamed, he spoke only of her. As if the other performers didn't count for anything. After a few days he went to Prague again[13] and brought back a photograph of Mrs Horvátová as Brünnhilde. New outbursts of enthusiasm, a new trip to Prague. But he continued to write to me daily from Prague. And in the letters he depicted Mrs Horvátová as an angel of virtue, as a charitable soul,[14] wishing to give everything away. I knew only too well from previous occasions that for him this was the beginning of a new infatuation. When he arrived for the last time before the première,[15] he was already completely besotted. I saw that Mrs Horvátová didn't fascinate him merely as an artist but above all as a woman. She invited him to supper with her after the première. He told her that he wouldn't be in Prague alone, but with his wife – that he had a beloved wife. So she invited me too. He informed me of this as if it were the most beautiful thing to be awaiting us in Prague. After that he left on the Monday [22 May 1916]; I was due to follow him on the

9 The visit took place shortly before 28 March 1916, when Janáček wrote to Karel Kovařovic (*JDA*, JP92) about his delight in the way the *Jenůfa* rehearsals were going as described by Mrs Horvátová. For Slavia, see p.109, fn.68.

10 Karel Kovařovic did so in a letter of 28 April 1916 (*JODA*, JP95).

11 The first of Janáček's regular bulletins from Prague to Zdenka about the *Jenůfa* rehearsals (*JODA*, JP96) was written on about 4 May 1916.

12 In his first letter to Zdenka from Prague (*JODA*, JP96) Janáček wrote: 'First and foremost among all the performances is again that of Mrs Horvátová.'

13 He was there by 11 May 1916 (*JODA*, JP98), returning to Brno on 15 May 1916 (*JODA*, JP101).

14 'Then Mrs Horvátová and I visited the sick Maixner and stayed with the poor fellow until 9 o'clock' (letter to Zdenka Janáčková, 11 May 1916; *JODA*, JP98).

15 i.e. on 15 May 1916.

Thursday. In the vestibule at home we said goodbye warmly. He said to me: 'So see you in Prague' and off he went.

Suddenly I was gripped by terrible pain and anxiety. I remained standing in the vestibule. For a moment it was as if I could see into the future. I hid my head in the corner behind the clothes rack and I knew it: Leoš was lost to me.

The première, which had seemed to me one of the most desirable things in the world, was now a horrible nightmare for me. I was frightened by it, I wondered whether I should go to it at all. Máŕa talked me out of this: 'Don't do it, go, the master would get very angry.' And I'd already arranged to travel with Ida Dresslerová[16] and Mrs Váchová, the judge's wife. Besides, my husband wrote very beautifully to me every day. I was also frightened of upsetting him before the première. So we ladies went. Leoš came to meet me and took me to the hotel Imperial. He was pleased that I was there now, but I felt as if turned to stone. He took me to meet Mrs Horvátová right away. My heart was pounding when we entered her apartment. She was expecting us. Her husband wasn't at home, in general they lived somewhat freely and one didn't get in the other's way at all. She caught hold of me, she embraced me and kissed me as if I were an old and beloved friend – she knew how to do things like that. I examined her discreetly but nevertheless thoroughly – I was so curious about her and up to now knew her only from the photograph. She was about forty-four,[17] taller than me, quite well-built, a brunette, with large black eyes, I'd call them 'Junoaugen',[18] a large, sensuous mouth, coarse features, the expression of the face at times almost predatory. Lots of gestures, an exceptionally lively manner; she knew how to speak without stopping. Her behaviour wasn't natural, everything was calculated for effect, but she did it so skilfully that she dazzled the unwary. And my husband, unfortunately, was one of those. It astounded him when she greeted me sweetly with a large bunch of flowers, he was happy when we exchanged pleasantries. Every moment he jumped up and kissed her hand. She told us many things which aimed to demonstrate her interest in *Jenůfa*: she had, she said, invited the director of the Vienna Opera to the première, and he would be sure to accept her invitation. My husband believed it all and was

16 See Glossary: 'Dressler family'.
17 Gabriela Horvátová was thirty-eight at the time.
18 Zdenka uses a German word, but this is not a common expression. It is a reference to the Homeric epithet, the 'ox-eyed Hera'. It suggests that Mrs Horvátová had prominent, if not bulging eyes.

enthusiastic. But we women weighed each other up without any great illusions and found that there was no reason for enthusiasm. It probably became clear to Mrs Horvátová that I wouldn't be such a pushover as my husband because later in the café, where I met her again after the visit, she withdrew her invitation to dinner after the première and determined that we should go instead to the hotel Paříž.[19] Leoš wasn't in the café with us. When my visit to Mrs Horvátová was done, they saw me home and together they went off to Mrs Gabriela Preissová,[20] where they were invited, and then I didn't see my husband until the evening in the Obecní dům.[21] There was tension between us – even in the evening, when we returned to the hotel. I waited for him to say at least a few nice words to me and tell me once again what had gone on in the theatre that day. Nothing. Complete estrangement. I went to bed on the ottoman and wept. Already now I knew for certain how the land lay.

On the day of the première, Friday 26 May, he ran off first thing in the morning. All he said to me was that he couldn't come for me before the première and that we'd meet only afterwards in the hotel Paříž. He had to take Mrs Horvátová home after the performance, he said, and would come with her to the hotel only after that. Feeling lonely, I then walked around Prague the whole morning with Ida Dresslerová and my sister-in-law Joža Janáčková. Fearfully I prepared for the première. Mrs Horvátová, who had provided a seat for me, put some other friends of hers into my box as well, a young couple who were so taken up with themselves that we didn't pay too much attention to one other. At first it made no difference to me: I was too scared about how *Jenůfa* would be received. Only after the first act when the curtain fell and the theatre thundered with warm applause did the weight fall from my heart. I'd so have liked to have had a word with Leoš, to have shown him my pleasure, to have asked him how he was feeling. But he didn't come to see me. I sat alone even in the second interval. I didn't dare go and see him, no one came to see me – I felt terribly isolated. I'd imagined the première so differently.

Waiting for me in front of the theatre after the performance were our Brno friends, who had made a special point of coming for the première. We all went to the hotel Paříž. There I learnt that the

19 Then a comparatively new hotel, near the Obecní dům.
20 Gabriela Preissová (1862–1946), author of the play *Her Stepdaughter* on which *Jenůfa* is based.
21 Janáčková uses here the colloquial term 'Representační dům' [Prestige House] for the Obecní dům [Municipal House] (see Glossary).

Měšťanská beseda[22] had invited my husband for an informal evening party after the première and that he'd refused because Mrs Horvátová wanted to be in the hotel Paříž and that this had displeased the Měšťanská Beseda. If the meeting with my Brno friends cheered me up a bit, this let me down again, so that I was depressed and out of sorts. For a long time we waited for Mrs Horvátová to appear, accompanied by my husband and the conductor Maixner.[23] I went to greet them, I congratulated them – like a stranger. They and my husband sat together at the top of the table, I remained further down among our Brno friends. My husband didn't notice. He probably didn't see me at all that evening. And if he did, what did I mean to him, visibly care-worn and out of sorts, in my black dress, already no longer new, whereas Mrs Horvátová beside him was beaming with her success, with her emerald jewellery and her lively, almost poisonous, mood that day. With difficulty I stopped myself crying. The Brno people saw it all only too well, they were disconcerted – it wasn't a happy time. The school director Mr Mareš,[24] who had also come for the première, came to see me later in Brno and said: 'I was so sorry for you then.'

It was an unbearably long time for me before we got up to go. Mrs Horvátová lived on Václavské náměstí [Wenceslas Square], we were staying near the State Station,[25] so we said goodbye. The conductor Maixner accompanied her, Director Mareš accompanied us. When the latter took his leave from us, my husband at last noticed my pain and began to placate me. It was only Mrs Horvátová to whom he should be grateful for the success of *Jenůfa*, he said. That incensed me. What had her theatrically affected Kostelnička in common with the honest beauty of *Jenůfa*? But I said nothing. With great effort I controlled myself and began to tell him how pleased I was that the première had been such a success. But when we began to speak of those taking part I was careless enough to say what I thought about Mrs Horvátová's voice: that it was no longer up to much, that she shouted too much. Leoš got terribly angry. He immediately stopped talking to me. I was glad that I hadn't also told him my opinion of her acting: she seemed

22 Citizens' Club (see Glossary: 'Beseda'). The Měšťanská beseda was the oldest Czech cultural club, founded in 1845. It became the model for many others established throughout Bohemia and Moravia and an important meeting-place for Czech cultural and political leaders. By 1916, however, its significance was more historical than actual.
23 Vincenc Maixner (1888–1946) joined the National Theatre in 1915 as Kovařovic's assistant and repetiteur and was responsible for much of the preparation of the Prague *Jenůfa*.
24 See Glossary.
25 Since renamed the Masaryk Station [Masarykovo nádráží], it is several blocks away from Václavské náměstí.

to me too theatrical for a woman from Slovácko.[26] This was Tosca, not the Kostelnička.

Early the next morning, Leoš went off to the theatre again. As previously arranged, I went with Ida Dresslerová, my sister-in-law Joža and her daughter Věra[27] to Petřín.[28] There Věra began telling me that the whole of Prague was talking about my husband's courting Mrs Horvátová. She knew things I had no notion of. For instance that Mrs Horvátová was going with Leoš to Luhačovice and that they didn't want me to go too. So much for those promises that in the summer after the première we'd go there together and how nice it would be for us! I had a mind to jump off the observation tower.

When I returned to the hotel, Leoš was there already. He was even angrier than the night before. At once he began to reproach me that he'd been scolded by Mrs Horvátová. He was ill-mannered, she'd said, not to have walked her home at night. He told me that it was all my fault. He threw me a ticket, saying that I'd get a box in the theatre with it, and that we'd see each other only after the performance. With that he went off. Utterly miserable, I went to my sister-in-law Joža for tea that afternoon. Of course they talked again about Mrs Horvátová, and here Joža also confirmed for me what Věra had told me in the morning. In wretched spirits, I went to the theatre and afterwards to dinner with my Brno friends. This time my husband came with us immediately. We returned home on our own; he didn't speak, I didn't either. I cried long into the early hours of the morning. It was Sunday [28 May], we got ready to leave. I packed, then I got a letter from Mrs Horvátová with her photograph apologizing that we wouldn't be seeing one another again.[29] We had lunch on our own, my husband even ordered champagne, but it was too late to make any difference. We travelled home estranged. Mářa, who read all the reviews of *Jenůfa* and was terribly pleased about them, came to meet us at the station with a bunch of roses. She'd rehearsed some special words of welcome. But when she looked at us, she said, she held her breath and didn't utter a word. Taking her aside, I said to her: 'Mářa, something's

26 See Glossary.
27 See Glossary: 'Janáčková, Věra'.
28 Petřín Hill, the largest green space in Prague. It contains an observation tower, a miniature version of the Eiffel Tower, built for the 1891 Jubilee Exhibition.
29 Horvátová's note to Zdenka, dated 28 May 1916 (BmJA, A 4720), asks Zdenka 'to remain a good friend' and regrets that she could not say goodbye, but she did not want to disturb her since Janáček had said that she was feeling poorly. The note, written on her husband's headed notepaper, is signed unusually with her married name, Noltschová.

1 Zdenka at the age of three, with her father, the 'uncommonly good-natured and cheerful' Emilian Schulz (1868).

2 Zdenka Schulzová, engaged to Janáček at fourteen (1879).

Zdenka Janáčková, confident and proud after n years of marriage (1892).

4 Zdenka at sixteen, in her first year of marriage (1881).

5 The Janáčeks' daughter Olga at two.

6 Olga at six.

7 Zdenka with her father, her brother Leo and her daughter Olga; the picture was probably taken durin; the period when Zdenka had returned to live with her parents soon after the birth of Olga.

8 Olga at eight.

9 Olga at fourteen.

Zdenka with her parents Emilian and Anna Schulz and her brother in c1904, taken in Vienna, where Emilian Schulz retired, and where Leo Schulz trained as a lawyer. Zdenka recalls putting this family portrait into her mother's coffin.

11 Olga Janáčková shortly before her departure for Russia (1902). The portrait was made as an advertisement for the studio 'Rafael'. On her death it was displayed in the studio window with a mourning band.

12 Olga's tombstone: her profile was carved in Carrara marble by Professor Vávra after the photograph (Plate 11). Under it, on a black marble plaque, was engraved a verse by the Brno poet Jaroslav Tichý-Rypáček: 'Young and quiet, gentle and good, she fell asleep like a white rose, the beautiful pale flower of spring'.

13 Janáček with the poodle Čert, originally bought to divert the housebound Olga as she lay dying. The photograph was taken in the grounds of the Janáčeks' new house (built 1910) with the Organ School in the background. The garden is newly planted and has not yet acquired its later luxuriance (cf. Plate 20).

14 Zdenka as dutiful widow (1928).

15 Janáček in raffish company in the Moravian spa of Luhačovice (summer 1916). He is seated (*left*) next to Gabriela Horvátová, the Kostelnička in the Prague production of *Jenůfa*, which had opened a few months earlier and had transformed Janáček's fortunes and laid the foundations for his later international success. Half a year later his torrid affair with Mrs Horvátová led to an informal divorce from his wife.

16 Janáček with David Stössel and Kamila Stösslová in Luhačovice (summer 1927). In the spring of that year Janáček's ten-year-old friendship with Kamila had taken on a much more intimate character and was causing concern to his wife.

17 Zdenka (*left*) and her husband's Prague relative Joža Janáčková in 1907. Zdenka shared with Joža not only a love of hats but also her increasing anxiety about Janáček's deepening infatuation with Kamila Stösslová.

18 The Janáčeks as tourists in Venice with Jan Mikota (1925). 'As soon as we emerged from the *pensione*, we didn't know where to look first or what to be most enthusiastic about. Leoš just went on repeating: "I must come here once more."'

9 The Janáčeks in Boskovice the morning after a performance there (14 May 1927) of Janáček's early antata *Amarus*. Behind them stands Janáček's tall and gloomy pupil, Osvald Chlubna. On the left is tanislav Tauber, tenor soloist in *Amarus*; to the right is Mrs Ptáčková (soprano soloist) and František inda (conductor). Mrs Lindová stands between Tauber and Zdenka Janáčková. It was Tauber who later ccompanied Zdenka to Ostrava on hearing the news of her husband's death (see Chapter 10).

20 The Janáčeks at home (1927). Janáček sits at the white table on to which, during the war, his three hens would fly and keep him company (see Chapter 6). Zdenka Janáčková looks on from the vestibule of the house, built in the grounds of Janáček's Organ School (by then the Brno Conservatory). In the foreground the much admired ferns (see Chapter 6).

21 Zdenka Janáčková alone (1930). She is seated in front of the vestibule (cf. Plate 20) but with a new white table. Her miniature pinscher bitch Čipera, bought to keep her company after her father's death in 1923 (see Chapter 8), is waiting for a biscuit.

happened, but don't ask about it now.' She'd already been with us long enough to work out what the matter was.

The height of all my suffering was that Leoš really did want me to be his confidante. He tried to persuade me that there was nothing improper in his relationship with Mrs Horvátová, that it was just a 'merging of souls', as he had instructed to be written also on a wreath with which he presented her during the première of *Jenůfa*. He gave me all her letters to read – but not those which he wrote. She wrote to him daily. At first: 'Highly esteemed Maestro', then 'Dear, beloved, my beloved Maestro', the signature at first 'G.H.' then 'Gabriela', finally 'Jelča'. She always asked to be remembered to me.[30]

Leoš paid for Máňa's journey to Prague to see *Jenůfa*. And he also sent her to Mrs Horvátová.[31] When she returned and told us how she'd spoken with her, she said straight out to my husband: 'But don't think about that lady, she's got lots [of men].'

He said nothing in reply. Now he kept going off to Prague.[32] He also told me that I couldn't go to Luhačovice because he had to devote himself entirely to Mrs Horvátová there. She stipulated, he said, that they should live in the same villa and have rooms next door to one another. So my Prague relatives were well informed. In addition, I heard from many quarters how Mrs Horvátová knew how to play men along. How then could I believe in this 'merging of souls'! Then I got a letter from my brother saying that he'd gone to Halle with Mother, and that I should go and keep house for Father. I read it to my husband. 'Just go, go!'

I saw how glad he was that I'd be away. Only a year ago he wept that I'd left him for my mother. That very day he left again for Prague[33] and told me that from there he'd be going off with Mrs Horvátová to Bohdaneč.[34] The next day I left for Vienna. I was alone with Father, I kept house, I said nothing to him, I just got worried and couldn't sleep

30 Horvátová's surviving letters do indeed reflect the modes of address that Janáčková quotes but they are mostly signed 'Kostelnička'. Many seem to have been written for Janáčková's eyes as well as Janáček's.

31 Horvátová reported to Janáček in her letter of 2 June 1916 (BmJA, B 1178) that Máňa had two seats reserved and in a subsequent letter that day (BmJA, B 1185) that Máňa had been present at the performance that day. On 3 June (BmJA, A 5578) Máňa wrote to Mrs Janáčková describing the success of the performance.

32 He made four trips to Prague during June 1916, all to be present at repeat performances of *Jenůfa*.

33 Probably on 3 July 1916, on which day Janáček sent a card to Zdenka from Prague reporting his safe arrival (BmJA, D 1220).

34 i.e. the spa where Janáček's friend Dr Veselý was now director (see Glossary). From Horvátová's letter of 5 July 1916 (BmJA, B 1179) it is clear Janáček was expected in Bohdaneč on 8 July 1916.

at night. My husband wrote to me how beautifully Mrs Horvátová sang the Kostelnička and what he felt during it. I didn't reply. Mářa wrote to me too: the master had gone off to Prague again. I read it and I shook with pain. My father looked at me and suddenly asked:

'Why aren't you writing to your husband?'

'What's so strange when he's got another woman?'

He wrung his hands: 'Good God, not again?'

I told him everything. He nodded: 'Well, that's what it's like with such a person. You've got what you wanted.'

And again I got a letter from Mářa. 'Madam, the master's gone mad. He's gone off to Prague again. He should be teaching and isn't coming back. The pupils are coming here.[35] What's to be done with them? What should I do? Come home.' I read it to Father.

'There's nothing for it, you must go home.'

Oh, what a journey again! I left the case at the station, and dragged myself home. Mářa was watering the garden. She threw up her hands:

'Ježíšmarjá, what a sight you look!'

'Where's the master?'

'He's home now.'

He was in the garden, he came to meet me.

'What's up?'

'I couldn't stick it out there.'

'Well now, it's good that you've come.'

He led me on to the veranda. I began to cry. I clasped him round the neck, then I knelt before him and begged him for God's sake not to leave me like this, to love me again. He soothed me, he told me that he loved me. But I felt that this was just hollow comfort.

And so it went on. Letters came from Mrs Horvátová as often as three times a day.[36] My husband began to take precautions that they didn't fall into my hands. He looked out for the postman. I did too: I had my doubts about whether Leoš was giving me all the letters to read that he was getting from Prague. One Sunday he got a letter from the postman and I caught sight of it. When he didn't say anything about it afterwards I asked him to show me the letter. He gave it me unwillingly. There were hints that 'something could have happened'. It made me agitated but I mastered myself and returned the letter to him with thanks. He took it and went into his office [in the Organ School].

---

35 It is difficult to place this incident (and thus Janáčková's trip to Vienna). Although July is suggested by the reference to Janáček's trip to Bohdaneč (8 July), the end of term was only a week away. It seems more likely to be during June, when Janáček went to Prague four times.
36 Surviving letters from June and July 1916 came at least twice a day on several occasions.

I began to get dressed for church. And as I did so it occurred to me that I needed the black silk dress now which Leoš promised to buy me as a memento of the Prague première. So I stopped by in his office on my way to church to remind him of his promise. He was sitting writing at the desk. As soon as he saw me, he stared in alarm, jumped up and covered up with his hands what he was writing and cried out: 'No, I won't give it you to read' – although I didn't know at all what he was writing.

From his frightened glance I realized that things were now in a very bad way for me. I wanted to know where I stood. I rushed to the desk but my husband crumpled up the letter and held it firmly. I began to complain: 'So this is the way it is.'

He pushed me out through the door across the passage down the steps and through the garden right into our house, although I was struggling. Desperately I burst into tears – like perhaps any woman who finds herself being deceived by the man whom she loves and who is the only thing on earth left to her. Then he said to me: 'We can't go on like this. You imagine such things, you're ill. The doctor must come here.'

I knelt at his feet and begged him, by the memory of Olga, not to do such things to me, that it wasn't possible for me to bear his infidelity calmly. Whereupon he did the most treacherous and the most sickening thing that he could: because Mářa stood faithfully by me even now and harshly condemned his actions, he sent his confidante, the caretaker's wife Mrs Simandlová,[37] to the Černovice lunatic asylum for the chief doctor Dr Papírník.[38] He arrived that very afternoon. I certainly didn't look well: how many weeks was it that I hadn't slept? I wasn't eating, it distressed me unbearably. Dr Papírník asked me to tell him what the matter was. Sincerely and truthfully I told him everything about the première, about the letters, about Luhačovice. Fine, he said, and now he'd have a word with my husband. He went upstairs to see him in his office and remained there more than an hour. And when he returned, he said to me: 'Madam, your nerves are in a very bad way and you must definitely not go to Luhačovice if Mrs Horvátová is going to be there.'

So here I had my diagnosis and my prescription. Without examination: he didn't even ask me about my physical state, I'd told him only that I wasn't sleeping. For that he gave me Veronal[39] and also

37 See p.108.
38 Alois Papírník (1864–1951), director of the Brno mental institute in the Brno suburb of Černovice.
39 Trade name for barbitone, a barbiturate used as a sedative or hypnotic.

some other pills, telling Máŕa that she must pour cold water over me every morning, and in the evening prepare a lukewarm bath for me. And when my husband came out after him from the office into the house, he said to us both: 'There, there, make it up now and give each other a kiss.'

That was the treatment that medical science had for my pain. Cold water poured over me! And to make me into a madwoman because I was suffering unbearably. Even Máŕa with her simple though healthy common sense saw the superficiality of the doctor's diagnosis. Neither she nor I trusted him and from his advice we chose what suited us: I took lukewarm baths and took Veronal – I wanted to sleep so as to look nice, and not so tortured. And otherwise I put myself into the hands of God and I begged for help from the *Mater Dolorosa* above my bed. My husband continued to go to Prague. Almost every week. I no longer said anything because I saw that he was capable of the very worst things towards me. Another woman would perhaps have dealt with it from the other end and settled matters energetically with Mrs Horvátová, but for one thing that wasn't in my character, and for another I constantly had it in mind that she was singing the Kostelnička and that in her pampered and capricious state of mind she could then drop the role and that I'd have that on my conscience. Where my husband's art was at stake, my pain had to take a back seat.

On one occasion my husband returned from Prague again.[40] It was evening. I was sitting in the bay-window room when he came to see me. He was in a terrible mood, clearly someone had made him angry with me. He began to stride about the room and reproach me that I was his misfortune, that I'd ruined his life, that I was an obstacle to his composition, that I didn't understand him. He abused me terribly. As insinuatingly as he had once been able to entice me and bind me to him, now, just as strongly, almost demonically, he crushed me and tore down my being to its very foundations. I couldn't find a single thought, let alone a word, with which to defend myself. I just cried and cried and he went on at me for two hours until he'd completely convinced me that I was destroying him. It seemed to me that there was only one thing with which, just a little, I could expiate my guilt and show him that I was also capable of making a sacrifice for him. By the time he'd given vent to his anger and gone to bed, I'd made up my mind. I gave orders to Máŕa about what work she had to do in the morning, I plaited my hair and took about twenty Veronal tablets.

40 Perhaps on 9 or 10 July, after his trip to Prague and Bohdaneč.

And on top of that, morphine, which my husband used to take at one time.[41] I told myself that it would be enough for Leoš to be free. Then I went to sleep.[42]

In the morning Máňa was puzzled that I didn't get up for a long time. She came to me, tried to wake me, shook me, began to shout for my husband, who was sleeping next door in the study. He jumped up and ran around the room helplessly and sent her for the doctor. Máňa lashed out at him: that she wasn't going to go for the doctor, that she'd stay with me, that he should get the doctor himself since he'd driven me to it. He went. Doctors came, they found the bottle, they sent Leoš to the chemist's with it. Meanwhile they asked Máňa what had happened, and she didn't hold her tongue. Then the ambulance took me to hospital – my husband later told me that he went with me. In the hospital they pumped out my stomach – he was present, he said it was terrible for him – then I woke up. Leoš was by me. I began to cry: 'Am I still alive? I don't want to be, don't want to be.'

And then I fell into a faint again, only it seemed to me that Dr Rinchenbach,[43] who was also standing at the bedside, said: 'morphine'.

All over Brno they said my suicide attempt was a result of my menopause. That's not true, I'd already stopped having periods roughly in my forty-fifth year, soon after the operation for gallstones – that is five years earlier. I didn't have any difficulties during it, I didn't even know I was undergoing the change of life. Apart from the gallstones I'd always been healthy. My desperate step was caused purely and simply by the breakdown in our marriage. I did it out of love for my husband so that he could be free. At the time divorce wasn't possible without a huge social scandal, it would certainly have got in the way of Leoš's career. I did something that I judged would be the best thing for him and, in the final analysis, for me too because I didn't want to live without him. It wasn't my fault that it didn't succeed.

The next day my brother arrived in Brno. My husband had sent him a telegram: he was embarrassed that they'd write about us in the newspapers and didn't know how to stop it. My brother was

41 It is difficult to know how serious Zdenka's suicide attempt was. By the morning the stomach pump (see below) would not have been much use because the Veronal would have been absorbed. It seems that she took an underdose – a classic 'cry for help'.
42 According to Stejskalová (Trkanová 1964, 154, fn.26), Zdenka's suicide attempt took place on 10 July 1916.
43 Otakar Rinchenbach (1889–1967), worked at St Anna hospital, Old Brno. He later became chief medical officer of Brno.

experienced in such matters and indeed he settled things right away at the police and at the town hall. Then he came to see me in the hospital. He bent over me and kissed me – how I clasped him round the neck! He persuaded me to let my husband do what he wanted, that his glory had gone to his head. He couldn't stay longer with me, he had to return to Vienna. So I lay there again isolated in the third class[44] among curious women and also those who took pity on me. Suddenly Director Mareš appeared at the door. He came to me, took me by the hand and the tears poured down his cheeks. And I said only: 'Mr Director, Mr Director.' He didn't say a single word to me, I also didn't say anything to him; there was no need: he was one of those rare people who understand you even when you don't confide anything to them.

In the hospital something changed within me. As if I'd got tougher and understood my unhappiness in a different way. I saw that what I'd offered as the highest sacrifice my husband took only as an embarrassing, unpleasant incident of which he was guiltless and which on the whole left him unmoved. Not a single word passed between us to the effect that it was all because of Mrs Horvátová, and that it would be necessary somehow to straighten out this intolerable relationship. And so there was nothing but for me to drag the burden of life further, however heavy it was. But it was a great lesson in life for me. I understood how great the suffering and how terrible the forces must be to drive people to suicide. From that time on I've never condemned any suicide case: they are such poor souls.

Dr Papírník visited me too. He started going on at once about what I'd allegedly done. For me he was already past history, I had my own thoughts about him. So I told him only briefly that I'd wanted to give Leoš his freedom. And what would I do now, he enquired. The question seemed to me so inconsiderate and insensitive that I was only able to answer it sarcastically: 'What am I going to do now? My husband promised me a new dress, so I'll buy it and go to the café in it.' To which he said: 'You must stay here a week longer. You mustn't go home until your husband has left.'

But Dr Rinchenbach, who had treated me in hospital, had already said to me beforehand that I could of course go home the next day. Indeed there was no reason why I should stay in hospital where, after

44 At the time of Zdenka's illness there were three grades of patients at St Anna's hospital, distinguished by the amount of nursing they received. Patients of the first class had one-to-one nursing; second-class patients shared a nurse among two, third-class patients a nurse among ten.

all, no one likes being unnecessarily. I was now completely well again. And I felt quite strong enough to take my husband's departure for Luhačovice calmly. When Leoš came to visit me again, I asked him to send a cab for me because I was allowed to return home now. He sent one for me and Máňa with it. But Dr Papírník had arranged that they'd release me only with a declaration signed by my husband. As if I couldn't vouch for myself, as if I wasn't in my right mind. And meanwhile remarks reached my ears from all corners of the hospital, from the patients, from the nurses, even from the porter [–] many of these people knew me from my childhood: it was after all Old Brno[45] – that my husband had gone mad and that he was trying to have me thought mad instead. Understandably I was in a hurry to get away from there.

Hardly had I got home than Dr Papírník was there yet again. And he asked me brusquely why I hadn't stayed in hospital. But I stood up to him energetically: 'Dr Rinchenbach and the other doctors told me that I am completely well but if you want to stay in hospital there, don't let me stop you.'

He was taken aback. But I couldn't resist adding another remark:

'If your wife told you: I love so-and-so, what would you say to her?'

He shrugged his shoulders: 'That she was mad.'

I pointed to my husband: 'Well, there you are then.' He went totally silent and thereafter left me in peace.

From that moment I carefully avoided any sort of scene, I dealt completely calmly with my husband and let him do what he wanted. He was very kind to me and told me every moment not to worry and that between him and Mrs Horvátová there was simply an artistic friendship. I no longer read their letters: my husband didn't give them to me and I didn't say anything about them. But I knew about almost everything: my husband had to talk about it, he had to have someone to tell his exuberant feelings to, and with me, after all, he felt the most comfortable, he could tell me what he wanted, he knew that I wasn't going to tell tales all over Brno. If I didn't want to lose him completely, if I wanted to preserve for myself at least something from those lovely discussions of ours before the Prague première, I had to continue to be his confidante. Need taught Dalibor to play the violin[46] and necessity

45 Zdenka was in the St Anna hospital, Pekařská ulice, Old Brno.
46 The Czech hero Dalibor z Kozojed, imprisoned for his valiant attempt to revenge the death of his friend Zdeněk, was said to have whiled away his time by taking up the violin (somewhat in advance of its invention). The notion is familiar both from Smetana's opera and from this Czech proverb, which suggests one can do almost anything if one has to.

taught me such self-denial that today I am sometimes surprised how I managed.

My husband told me that he'd be in Luhačovice for a fortnight on his own, then Mrs Horvátová would arrive.[47] She would, he said, be too tired to make the journey from Prague to Luhačovice in one go, so could she stay the night in our house?[48] He asked me for it nicely but emphatically. How I had to control myself then in order to give my consent calmly, at least outwardly! But even that wasn't enough for my husband: I had, as graciously as possible, to invite Mrs Horvátová myself in writing. Then he went off.[49] Every day he wrote beautiful letters to me, I also wrote back frequently to him. When Mrs Horvátová informed me that she was accepting my invitation[50] and I let him know this, he suddenly got frightened about it. I myself had a real horror of the visit, but I wrote back to him to be perfectly calm, that I knew what the duty of a host was towards a guest. That was always a matter of course for me and I wouldn't have gone against this under any circumstance.

In this difficult time of war, when things were already in a very bad way, I got together what I could and then I waited for an hour at the station – trains at that time went so irregularly – until Mrs Horvátová arrived. She jumped out of the carriage impetuously, striking in a light-coloured cloak and a green cap which hit the eye at a time when almost every second woman went around either in mourning or with a black band on the sleeve and when the rest of us also avoided cheerful colours out of consideration for them. With a great show of loving, she embraced and kissed me, telling me that she'd been ill so that she'd thought she wouldn't be able to come, but that she couldn't disappoint me in this way. I was correct, coolly welcoming. We went by cab, she told me about herself, about theatre life, and there it suited me to say to her that such an exciting life was no longer the thing for my husband, that he needed calm for his composition. I thought that it would be good in any case if I reminded her of this, but she didn't notice it at all.

Even Mářa did all she could and prepared a good supper for us:

47 Janáček in fact spent only a week in Luhačovice before Mrs Horvátová arrived.
48 This was Janáček's initiative; from Horvátová's letter of 13 July 1916 (BmJA, B 1190), it is clear that she was planning to spend the night of 24 July in Brno at the hotel de l'Europe, though hoping that Zdenka would meet her at the station.
49 Janáček arrived at Luhačovice on 17 July 1916, less than a week after his wife's attempted suicide.
50 Horvátová accepted Janáčková's invitation in a letter of 19 July 1916 (BmJA, A 4725), saying that she was arriving on Monday 24 July on the evening express.

pork with sauerkraut, potatoes, a cake, beer, wine. Considering the times, it was splendid. Mrs Horvátová really enjoyed it. She talked and talked, she talked the whole time, one would say colloquially that she never shut her trap. But in a while I saw that her words should be taken with a pinch of salt, that they weren't always the most truthful. And for my taste her words were at times too 'wild'.

She had to get up early the next morning, I prepared a pack for her and for my husband, we said goodbye and off she went with Mářa, who carried her cases for her. I breathed a sigh of relief: it had gone off well. Afterwards Mářa told me how Mrs Horvátová had begun to dance in front of our house on the pavement, to wave her arms and twitter: 'He's coming to meet me, he's coming to meet me!' Mářa said she'd a good mind to leave her case on the ground and say to her: 'Carry it yourself.' And afterwards at the station, she said, Mrs Horvátová behaved so bizarrely that some of our friends asked Mářa if the lady was from the circus.

Now I began to worry again so much that I couldn't eat or sleep. I knew that they had rooms next to one another. Until she arrived in Luhačovice my husband wrote to me every day, now it began to tail off.[51] If he wrote, it was only about her, how she was looking after him, how she was doing everything for him. But soon he began to complain that people were behaving oddly towards them. In one letter he wrote to me that he met a certain Dr Bartošová.[52] He wanted to introduce her to Mrs Horvátová, but she looked as though she didn't see Mrs Horvátová at all and said to him: and so you're here on your own? You have a very nice wife to leave you here like this. I myself wouldn't be so nice. And off she went. This prompted an angry remark: 'What a poisonous bitch!' I expect he often used to get other people's opinions about his relationship with Mrs Horvátová quite openly because such complaints multiplied in the letters. I even received an anonymous letter from Luhačovice: did I know how my husband and Mrs Horvátová were carrying on with one another? And straight after that a letter from Leoš saying that they had gone off to Velká[53] and that they were oddly received there, that people are scandal-mongers. I wrote back to him: don't think twice about it, I'm also getting

51 Janáčková's recollection is not fully supported by the surviving correspondence. In the first week Janáček wrote her eight letters or cards. After Mrs Horvátová's arrival he continued to write at least daily for two weeks (Horvátová wrote to her frequently too). But after 7 August Janáček wrote only once more before his departure a week later.
52 Janáček described the incident in his letter of 29 July 1916 (BmJA, B 1351). This Dr Bartošová is different from Mrs Josefa Bartošová (see Chapter 5), whom Zdenka knew well.
53 Janáček was at Velká on 5–7 August 1916.

anonymous letters and I'd be in despair if I didn't take comfort that at least you wouldn't bring your mistress into my house. By return of post there was a letter: 'Zdenka, how can you dare to write so offensively? If you have such thoughts Mrs Horvátová can no longer come and see you.'[54]

I took fright. I told myself that like this even our journey to Bohdaneč would fall by the wayside and I didn't want even to imagine Leoš's anger against me. There was nothing for it but to sit down at once and write that I was expecting both of them and to apologize, saying I hadn't meant it like that, and to ask for forgiveness, where I had so much to forgive myself. Well, I got what I wanted. My husband sent a telegram saying that they'd come after all. I was terribly agitated, packing, expecting a guest, trembling at what awaited me this time.

They arrived;[55] at first sight it was clear that they'd become more intimate. They called each other *Ty*.[56] My husband was completely wild with joy that he had her in our house. During supper she forced me to call her *Ty* too. Leoš was delighted with that. We sat for a long while: it was only towards midnight that Máŕa had to get the bath ready for her. My husband went to sleep upstairs in the office [in the Organ School], we remained together in the house. In the morning I went to ask my husband what I should pack for him for Bohdaneč and at the same time I mentioned that I didn't like the *tykání*. He replied: 'I'm proud that she does me this honour.'

We went off, the two of them in an excellent mood, I almost physically ill with grief and trying to control myself. In Pardubice we parted company: Mrs Horvátová went on to Prague, we by coach to Bohdaneč. My husband's good mood was suddenly gone. He sat beside me like a statue. When Marie Calma and Dr Veselý came to meet us at Bohdaneč she was appalled: 'What's the matter with you? I wouldn't have recognized you if you hadn't been with the Maestro.' Suffering had so changed me in a short time. Here everyone knew about it. Šípek-Peška prepared to have a word with my husband, I don't know whether he did so. It had always been useless to try and talk Leoš out of anything that he got into his head.

On 18 August, the day of [Emperor] Franz Josef's birthday, there was a gala performance of *Jenůfa* in Prague. We went to see it. Again of course all on the highest orders of Mrs Horvátová: she invited us to

54 This letter is missing from the surviving Janáček correspondence in BmJA.
55 On 13 August 1916 (letter to Gustav Schmoranz, 10 August 1916; JA vii, 38).
56 See Glossary: 'Ty and Vy'.

lunch, she got us rooms in the hotel Štěpán – two rooms. She said to my husband in front of me: 'Indeed, two rooms will be more pleasant for you than one.'

But in the hotel they told us that there was a shortage of rooms and asked us to make do with one room since we were a married couple. So we stayed together. My husband took me at once to his doctor, Dr Hnátek,[57] a specialist in internal diseases. He examined me and didn't find anything unusual, saying only: 'Madam, you cry a lot.' He didn't ask any more questions, and gave me something to calm me.

Again I was here almost the whole time without my husband. Luckily there were friends from Bohdaneč here. I was to meet them after *Jenůfa*, Leoš was to follow us with Mrs Horvátová. She'd also procured a seat for me in the balcony because my husband had put his box at the disposal of Šípek. During the performance a storm broke and then it rained solidly. When after the performance it was still raining, I said to myself that I wasn't going to walk round Prague on my own in the rain and I went backstage to find my husband to speak to him about it. When I told them who I was, they took me to him at once. It was most unpleasant for him. He had his clothes in Mrs Horvátová's dressing-room. We went there together. He knocked and called out:

'My wife's here, can she come in?'

'Yes.'

She was sitting in a simple shift in front of the mirror and, standing by her, was her repetiteur, the conductor Maixner. I was disconcerted, I blushed, he went red and rushed out. Only Mrs Horvátová wasn't embarrassed. My husband didn't see it, he remained outside. Later at home I told him: 'Good God, I am naive, only now have I seen what goes on in the theatre.'

He didn't demur at all, only saying: 'You shouldn't have gone there.'

At supper in the hotel Paříž I met her husband, Mr Noltsch. Tall, old, perhaps the same age as my husband. The perfect gentleman. He was said not even to live with his wife any more, each got up to his own tricks.

The next day [19 August 1916] it rained. Despite that I went out. When I returned, I met the Rev. Dr Kolísek[58] in the hotel lobby. We knew each other of old, he used to go and visit my husband. He asked

57 Dr Jan Hnátek (1865–1923), from 1903 professor of internal medicine at the Czech university polyclinic in Prague.
58 Alois Kolísek (1868–1938), doctor of theology and enthusiastic promoter of Slovak folksong. Up to 1919 he worked in Moravia and had many contacts with Janáček.

me how I was and I told him openly about my present life. He showed great sympathy to me – but how could anyone help me? In the afternoon we returned to Bohdaneč. With Mrs Horvátová, 'so it would be jollier for us', so she said. It kept on raining, but she resolved that we should go on an expedition into the wood. We dragged ourselves there, wet through, tired, but she didn't give up. My husband tried to control himself as much as he could, I felt sick, but we had to go where she wanted. I'd had enough of this. When we returned and had supper, I said in conversation with Mrs Calma-Veselá that one can get used even to the gallows. My husband didn't notice it, but Mrs Horvátová overheard it, she took umbrage and at once ordered us into another restaurant. There she began to criticize me and complain about me to my husband. He gave me such a telling off! People looked round at us, it was embarrassing. I said that I wanted to go home. So we went, but on the way they held me in an iron grip, both talked at me and chided me. When we got to our room, Leoš began again. He said that he wouldn't be alone with me, that he wanted Mrs Horvátová to sleep with us. He slept on the sofa and she had to sleep beside me. It was a disgusting night. I felt so sick from all this that I threw up.

Hardly had the day broken than Mrs Horvátová went off to her room. My husband went running after her. When they'd returned together again, Leoš began to reproach me that Mářa was saying bad things about Mrs Horvátová, that she didn't greet her and other such nonsense. And both began to nag me into giving Mářa notice. Mářa, my support, the only person on whom I could rely and who devotedly hauled this heavy burden with me, I was meant to send away! I absolutely refused. Great anger. They took themselves off and went to town together. I couldn't eat, I wasn't up to anything at all. In the afternoon, when the three of us were sitting in our room, women from the spa came to ask Mrs Horvátová to sing something for the spa visitors. She refused, she told them that 'yesterday they insulted the Maestro'. She probably overheard something about herself and my husband – it was talked about everywhere now. Leoš also looked offended, he kept the women standing, he didn't invite them to sit down. I didn't know what it was about and was frightened of saying anything myself. Taken aback, the women left and Mrs Horvátová resolved that we would go about no more in this society. They sent me to buy cold meats and we went again to the restaurant where Mrs Horvátová had taken us the day before.

Fortunately we were leaving this unhappy spa the next day [21

August 1916]. We all travelled to Pardubice, from where Mrs Horvátová went to Prague and the two of us went home. It seemed that amid all these unpleasantnesses she was in her element: none of this rubbed off on her and she bid farewell to me so delightfully as if we'd spent the most beautiful days together. When she was already sitting in the train to Prague, my husband jumped in once more after her and I saw how they kissed one another. Motionless, I gazed at it. However, when our express drew in, I thought of Karenina.[59] The wheels turned so invitingly. But immediately I'd remembered that I'd once already wanted to pass through the valley of the shadow of death and that I'd been brought back. And so I calmly sat down in the train opposite my husband. I observed him the whole journey and told him with my eyes: 'I saw it. Why do you torture me so?'

But he looked at the floor the whole time and didn't see me.

Hardly were we in Brno than he sent a telegram to Mrs Horvátová straight from the station. At home Máňa didn't know what to do when she saw the state in which we'd returned. After a few days, which passed peacefully, my husband suddenly rushed in to see me. He said that he couldn't survive without Mrs Horvátová, and asked me to invite her to come to us at once. I sent an invitation. She came immediately. My husband seemed as if he'd gone mad with joy. We sat in my room, she in a dressing gown all unbuttoned; and he virtually gulped down her generous bosom with his eyes. Until she herself said to him – she, who was used to such looks:

'Don't stare so.'

And he passionately: 'But she knows that I adore you.'

They laughed at that. I was in silent torture.

They began to speculate that some of their letters had gone missing. I didn't know anything about this, the caretaker's wife now brought in my husband's post, but Mrs Horvátová looked at me so meaningfully as if to suggest that I was taking the letters. She didn't provoke me: I was innocent, so I could remain calm. So she left it and began to urge my husband to go upstairs with her into the Organ School to see in the office which of their letters were missing. But then my husband remembered himself; he didn't take her into the school after all, telling her that it wasn't possible.

She slept in my husband's study, he with me in my bedroom. In the morning Máňa was all up in arms: she was dusting in the bay-

59 Anna Karenina, the heroine of Tolstoy's novel who commits suicide by leaping under the path of a train.

146   *My Life with Janáček*

window room, Mrs Horvátová was sitting in my husband's study in the rocking-chair, then my husband flew into her room and kissed her tempestuously. She pushed him aside when she caught sight of Máŕa. Then the two of them got dressed and went to complain somewhere that their letters were going missing. They returned crestfallen like wet poodles and didn't talk about it any more. In the evening we all went to the theatre. It was horrible for me to sit like this in the eyes of all Brno: people looked more at us in the box than at the stage.

The next day my husband jumped out of bed and, just as he was, dressed only in his shirt and long johns, he went into the room next door to visit Mrs Horvátová. This the man who before used to be so sensitive in such matters. I told him he should be ashamed of himself. He ran to Mrs Horvátová as if I'd wronged him, she began to shout and attempt to convince me that this was nothing, that if I slept at their place her husband would also make early-morning visits to me in the same way. I thanked her for this kind thought. Then she threw in my face the coarse lie: 'But you've also had other men.' I was quite dumbfounded at this. I didn't know how to answer something like this. And here Leoš himself stood by me: 'Not that, not that, she's innocent.' Mrs Horvátová stopped short and went quiet. I also was silent, I couldn't get over this indecent accusation.

Then they didn't talk with me any more and busied themselves with *The Excursions of Mr Brouček*.[60] But I'd already had enough of everything. They'd turned everything upside down which up to now I'd considered correct and decent; I saw that morally my husband was getting deeper into something which I'd rather he didn't. I resolved that I'd have a word with Mrs Horvátová since there was no sensible talk to be had with him. When she lay down after lunch, I went to her, I told her how many flirtations Leoš had already had, that I'd got over all of them happily, now we were both no longer young, we'd been living together peacefully and pleasantly and that I couldn't take what was going on now. At that time I still didn't know that type of woman and I thought that with plain speaking and pleading I'd soften her. This much I saw clearly, that neither true love nor real artistic enthusiasm tied her to Leoš, that it was all just the caprice of a whimsical woman who was too free in her manners. I didn't know then what became clear to me much later, that one of the greatest

---

60 At the time Janáček was busily finishing and revising his fifth opera *The Excursions of Mr Brouček* I/7 (1908–18). Mrs Horvátová's role in this was as a go-between for Janáček and the Prague literary figures who contributed to the libretto.

thrills of this relationship for her was the very fact of seeing me being tortured, humiliated and desperate. And so my plea fell on deaf ears then, in fact it probably added fuel to the flames.

In the evening we were to have gone to the theatre again. I refused: I told them straight that I wasn't going to act on this side of the footlights. They decided that they wouldn't go on their own. Towards evening they went off somewhere and returned only for dinner. Mářa went for beer, she returned, she put down her bag on the floor and collapsed in front of me. She fainted, she'd been too agitated by what she was seeing and hearing the whole time. The two of them were just then in the garden, I began to call them to help me and I reproached them, complaining that they were to blame for this. They got ready and went off. I revived Mářa; I'd had just about enough of this. Where was I to turn now, for God's sake? I ran to the caretaker and sent a telegram to my brother in Vienna to come at once. This greatly calmed me, I relied on the fact that as a lawyer my brother would find a way out of this. But I shouldn't have gone to sleep peacefully that evening. The two returned and had supper. Mrs Horvátová didn't want to be outdone by Mářa and began to pretend that she also was fainting with agitation. Even an inexperienced person would have seen that this was an act, but my husband didn't realize it at all. He jumped up, lamenting 'Jelča, my Jelča', and when he saw that I was looking on calmly, he cried out at me: 'You beast!'

It was terrible. Never in his life had he said anything like that to me. I stood like a pillar of salt.[61] But Mářa, who was already in bed, now jumped up and rushed in and began to cry out: 'Who's the beast here? Just say that once more!'

He stopped short. In a trice even Mrs Horvátová pulled herself together and everyone went to bed. Though before that, I said to them that my brother was coming and he'd sort things out here. They took fright and went utterly quiet. I remained dressed, waiting for my brother in the night. But he didn't arrive, he didn't get leave. None of us slept. Mrs Horvátová prepared to depart and my husband said that he'd accompany her. I got up early in the morning, I fried schnitzels for them for the journey, I gave her bottled fruit, I returned to her even the sweets which she'd brought me from the confectioners, I fetched the embroidery which my husband had brought me from Luhačovice, and

---

61 The fate of Lot's wife when she looked back, against instructions, on the cities of Sodom and Gomorrah.

threw it in her direction on the table and said: 'That's for you, I don't want anything from him.'

She packed it all up. I went into the kitchen again. When after a while I returned, I saw that she was standing on the desk and from below my husband was handing her her framed photograph. She put it up between the oil paintings of Leoš and me[62] which hung above the desk and said with diabolic derision: 'Angel of Peace'.

My husband laughed enthusiastically at this, while I looked on silently.

Before they went off, Leoš ordered me – clearly pressured by Mrs Horvátová – immediately to move his bed and everything needed for sleeping into his office:

'I won't come here again.'

'But you'll return', I said after my experience of many years. I bade farewell to Mrs Horvátová:

'Excuse the fact that there was an unpleasant scene here. And rest assured that I like you just as much as you like me.'

'What?' – she flew out through the door. Those were the last words that we ever exchanged in this life.

My husband returned in the evening. Scowling, taciturn. He just asked me brusquely whether everything was prepared for him upstairs [in his Organ School office]. It was. Although it was Sunday, Máňa and I had moved his bed and all the other things according to his wishes. He had his supper and went for the first time to his exile – as I'd say – and so it remained until his death. Oh, it was horrible! After thirty-five years of marriage to be so humiliated and yet not to blame. And to have to remember it the whole time, every evening, every morning. When I showed people round our house for the first time, they sometimes tactlessly asked me:

'And do you have only one bed?'

What could I say to them? Either: 'My husband works late into the night. He doesn't want to disturb my sleep.'

Or briefly: 'Yes.'

And as it went on, the worse it got. We didn't go anywhere together: neither to the café, nor to concerts, nor to the theatre, not even for walks. Always him alone, and I – when I really had to go – also alone. I took no pleasure in anything and I dragged my life along like a heavy stone. Leoš was more in Prague than at home. Even at registration [i.e.

62 The oil paintings, separate portraits of Leoš and Zdenka, were executed by Janáček's friend Josef Ladislav Šichan (see p.21). The portrait of Janáček is in his house in Hukvaldy; Zdenka gave the portrait of herself to her brother Leo in Vienna.

at the Organ School] he handed everything over to Professor Tregler[63] and went off to Prostějov, where Mrs Horvátová was singing. I couldn't really understand how anything in the world could make him desert his beloved school. At another time when I was coming back again from the café – I kept up at least some contact with our circle of women friends – and Mářa announced to me that the master had received a telegram, he'd got dressed up and had gone off to Prague at once. Mrs Horvátová was said to be seriously ill. The next day he returned. I got him supper and asked him what the matter was.

'She was seriously ill, but she's well now.'

'Well', I said, 'it couldn't have been that bad if she got better so quickly.'

He began to get angry and shout, but I told him that what he was doing now was madness. A violent scene broke out. He wanted to run away upstairs to the office, he pulled himself out of my grasp when I tried to hold him and locked himself in there. It seemed to me that there was an irrevocable break between us, that he wouldn't come back again. I went after him, Mářa with me, we stood before the door of the office, I begged him in God's name to open up, I even knelt in front of the door, I'd have done anything just to get him to speak to me once more. Eventually he opened the door for me, but he wouldn't speak to me. Crushed, I returned downstairs. A horrible night. He didn't come the following morning. I sent him a note saying that I needed to speak to him. He asked that I should spare him this distress, that he'd send me what was necessary through Dr Rudiš,[64] his lawyer. A terrible day. In the evening I got dressed and went to him. I didn't know myself what I wanted. I just had to see him again. I knocked on the door of the office – at that time it was in the room just next to the stairs on the first floor – but no one answered. I spoke at the door that I was coming to say goodbye to him – nothing. 'So farewell, I'm going' – and I went away.

But he wasn't in the office. He suddenly came out of the door opposite, where Professor Syrůček[65] had his room then. I was so confused that I just said 'Farewell' and began to leave. He invited me to come in and see him in the office. I went. I began to speak without

63 Eduard Tregler (1868–1932), organist and composer. He taught at the Organ School in 1913–14 and 1916–19.
64 Dr Felix Rudiš (1856–1942), Brno lawyer, for many years secretary of the Association for the Promotion of Czech Music in Moravia.
65 Jan Syrůček, professor of piano at the Organ School in 1916–17. He appears to have been a private music teacher with no Brno connections other than in 1916–17. He may have been conscripted in 1917.

thinking, led only by my pain. And right away I hit on what was the most important thing for me – what had upset me again and again, what he forced me to believe but what from the very beginning my instincts told me not to believe: that it wasn't just a matter of artistic friendship between him and Mrs Horvátová. I told him that I knew what Mrs Horvátová had done for him, that their relations were those of two artists, that I meant to suffer all that patiently and wait for him to come back to me again; in one thing alone I wanted to know the truth because I could bear that better than these doubts. Then I went up to him and took him by the hand and looked him straight in the eye:

'Tell me, is she already your wife?'

I didn't say 'mistress' so as not to offend him, so he wouldn't lose his temper again. He opened his eyes wide and burst out at me:

'And what would you say to that?'

'Nothing.'

And he replied quietly with a voice that seemed to catch in his throat: 'So yes, she is.'

But he immediately caught me in his arms and laid me on the bed because my legs gave way beneath me. Then I cried, terribly and long. That was awful pain, worse than later when he died: I felt then as though he'd been returned to me in death, but now I felt that I'd lost him for ever. And I knew that I couldn't exist without him, that it was as if they'd torn me in two. He stood next to me and waited for me to calm down. Eventually I sat down and asked whether their relationship would have consequences.

'Perhaps. I don't know yet.'

I saw how proud he was of it, how much he was longing to have a child. The scandal and all the other consequences – these he wasn't conscious of at all. I sat there wretched. And he added almost joyfully: 'And now I feel relieved. Now I can move back to you below.'

I understood him. By this he wanted to say that he didn't need to pretend any more. He knew that I was too proud to approach him [i.e. in bed] now that he had another woman, just as I knew from experience that I didn't exist for him while he had another relationship – it would be enough for me if I could take care of him, if just now and then he were to say a kindly word in passing. In the flood of joy that he didn't have to lie any more, he was willing to go on living with me although recently he kept on threatening me with a divorce because apparently Dr Papírník said that I was from a mentally unstable family. I'd written to my brother about it just before this scene and I'd asked him again to come and, as a lawyer, advise me on what I should do. Now Leoš began to talk about this also:

'So then, if we've solved this ourselves now, your brother needn't come to us any more. Go downstairs and I'll write to him that it's all fine. Then I'll come to supper.'

I staggered out. Máŕa was waiting in the corridor with Professor Syrůček. She caught hold of me and led me home. I wanted to give an account of myself, but she said quickly:

'Don't speak, I know it all already.'

We got supper ready, my husband came and was very gracious and contented. Then he went upstairs to sleep. I lay awake the whole night.

It's a long time ago now, the pain has ceased, and I can speak about it all because it seems to me as if it wasn't even me who lived through this horror. One is very fortunate that in time the pain does fade away, that new worries pile up, new days arrive and we have to go on. We're like grass; we're cut down, but shoot up again.

The next day we shook down the nuts [from the tree] in the garden: the household had to keep going. But I didn't stick at it, I left the work to Máŕa, I got dressed up and went to see Mrs Váchová. I had to tell someone of my sorrow: she already knew about everything from the première and understood me well. [. . .] And new comfort was waiting for me at the house. My brother had arrived because my husband's letter had been too late to reach him at home. I told him at once that my husband and I had now made up. But before coming to us he'd already gone to Černovice to see Dr Papírník, introducing himself as my brother and a police superintendant and notifying him that he was acting against the law by saying that I was from a mentally unstable family, and that our family would be forced to sue him. Dr Papírník was taken aback and asked for the matter to be patched up and not to be mentioned to anyone. My brother promised him this on condition that there would be an end to such false allegations about our family. Since then Dr Papírník has left me in peace and I thank God that so far I have not needed him nor any of his psychiatric colleagues.

It relieved me that my brother had stood by me in this way and I told him what my husband had confided in me. It didn't surprise him, one could have imagined it, he said. But he didn't want to see my husband at all. So we arranged to meet that afternoon in the café. Then he went off so as not to have to meet my husband. In the afternoon in the café I asked him what my parents were saying about it. He said that they were calm and had sent a message that I'd got what I wanted and must endure it. Later they also wrote to me in this vein. My brother and I then deliberated what I should do now. He told me about the possibility of bringing a charge of adultery against my husband and Mrs Horvátová, which would mean their both going to prison[66] and my husband's losing his position. But both of us dismissed this at once. What good would it have done me? Perhaps only that I'd have been revenged. I didn't have within me a single spark of desire for revenge. So my brother advised the following: be calm, don't shut yourself in, go on seeing your friends, live correctly and don't leave him, whatever's going on. If you were away even for a single night without his permission, he could say according to the law that his wife had left him. See to it that he has no weapons against you.

I accompanied my brother to the station and returned home. I told Leoš everything that my brother and I had said.

From that time we lived beside one another and each did what he wanted. We spoke together, there were no arguments, I didn't reproach him for anything, I didn't want anything from him, I didn't say anything when he went to Prague. He got used to it and gradually he made me his confidante again. I now knew about everything that was going on between him and Mrs Horvátová and sometimes it seemed to me that in this role I was indispensable for him. This at least –. He now gave me very little money: he needed it all for Prague. Once I spoke about it with Kovařovic: 'What's the use of my performing *Jenůfa*?', he said. 'He [Janáček] travels here and uses up with her what he gets from the royalties.'

It was November, All Souls' Day. He was preparing to go to Prague. I said to him gently: 'Any message for Olga?'[67] He began assuring me that he had to go to Prague.

Another time a telegram arrived. Telegrams flew the whole time from Mrs Horvátová. This one had come unstuck, things being so slack in the war. I told myself that at the very least I too had as much right as any postman, and I read the telegram. It went: 'All lost through excitement.'

I saw what the clever Mrs Horvátová meant by this and that she was leading my husband a merry dance. Well, I learnt to do that too. I

66 This is an exaggeration. At the time adultery was punishable under the Austrian penal code of 1852 (repealed in Czechoslovakia only in 1951) and imprisonment would have been appropriate only in the gravest instances. However this law was enforced only if the husband was the injured party.
67 All Souls' Day is on 2 November, but if Zdenka was going to the cemetery, she would probably have gone on All Souls' Eve, a traditional candle-lit event when families visited the graves of the dead.

hadn't forgotten the cruel lesson he taught me for lack of sympathy over the health of his beloved. I resolved now to do better. I gave him the telegram as if I didn't know anything. He sat down to lunch and began to read: then he jumped up, buried his head in his hands and ran around the room as if demented. I ran quickly to him: 'Tell me, what's the matter?'

He went on running: 'All's lost, all's lost.'

I looked stunned and implored him: 'That's terrible, that's terrible, I beg you, tell me, perhaps it will relieve you.'

He was so helpless, he suspected neither her nor my little tricks, he was glad to find sympathy and burst out: 'She's had a miscarriage.'

I threw up my hands. I began to lament, I pitied him and when he said that he had to go to Prague at once, I willingly prepared everything for his journey. While he ran off somewhere before his departure, I calmly went off to the café because I had my own opinion about this miscarriage just as I had about its beginning. I wasn't wrong. When I returned, Mářa announced joyfully that the master hadn't gone off anywhere. Apparently he'd sent a telegram saying that he was coming and by return of post there was a reply here: 'Everything fine again now, don't come.'

My husband apparently told everything to Mářa and added: 'I'm glad that I don't have to go, I'm so tired.'

Then for a long time he was nice to me for my 'sympathy' over this 'mishap'. Before Christmas he told me that he was going to Prague because Mrs Horvátová was again going to be the mother of his child, but he'd also like to celebrate Christmas Eve with me. So I should do the fish the day before Christmas Eve,[68] that we'd celebrate it together. I refused. I was invited with Mářa to the Dresslers for the 24th. But he wouldn't have it any other way, so Christmas Eve was celebrated a day earlier at our house. As a present he gave me K 100, although I didn't want to take it. He promised that he'd write to me and went off. We then celebrated Christmas Eve very nicely at the Dresslers. Naturally Leoš was also talked about. His cousin got very angry about him: he said that through this foolish relationship he would shorten his life by ten years.

On Christmas Day I got a letter from my husband. A terrible one. Someone had written an anonymous letter to Mr Noltsch[69] from Brno. God knows what was in it if it upset even the old *roué*, hardly morally

---

68 See Glossary: 'Christmas Eve'.
69 i.e. Gabriela Horvátová's husband.

scrupulous himself. But my husband thought that I was the writer. He wrote to me: 'Zdenka, who was that beast?'

I lost my temper at such suspicion, and I sat down and wrote a reply: 'Leo, I'm not the beast, so I'm returning you the letter.'

The caretaker's wife wrote the address for me so that he wouldn't perhaps return the letter if he recognized my handwriting. Then he didn't write to me any more although he was in Prague during the entire [Christmas] holidays. He simply sent a telegram saying when he was coming back. We waited, but he stayed on a whole day longer. He didn't greet us, he didn't say a word, frowning, terrible. I stood for a while helplessly, then it was I who began talking. Most unhappily. That if it has to be like this the whole time, and if he has to insult me continually, it would indeed be better for us to separate. Of course I didn't mean it the way I said it. But he latched on to this at once. All right, if I thought so. And at once he wrote a form of words for me saying that I consent to a divorce and suggested that we appoint Dr Rudiš as a solicitor. I began to quibble:

'Oh no, I won't sign anything, until I consult someone.'

'But Rudiš will advise you.'

'We won't have just one solicitor, will we, I won't sign.'

But now he insisted on this and set off at once to Dr Rudiš. No sooner had he returned than he asked me if I also had a solicitor. I didn't feel like doing anything, but he got at me more and more insistently until I said that I'd go. I got dressed, he stood at the piano and waited. I went up to him: 'Listen, you're forcing me. I don't suppose any woman has got divorced like this. I don't want it, and you're sending me away. Into the cold, into misery, into the war.'

He stood like a statue, unfeelingly, evil.

So I went. Máŕa, weeping, accompanied me across the garden. Pupils coming out of the Organ School asked her:

'What's the matter with the mistress?'

'Don't ask, don't ask', she wept, and, instead, ran home.

I didn't know where to go. At Dr Hanf's[70] I had a woman-solicitor acquaintance, so I went there. She was the only one there in the office. She copied out my marriage certificate and told me to come again in the afternoon when Dr Hanf would be there. I went to see the Dresslers. They wrung their hands. Dr Dressler decided that in the evening he'd come to us and have a word with my husband. When I got home I gave Leoš the marriage certificate as proof that I'd been at

70 Dr Ludvík Hanf (1878–1938), a Brno lawyer.

the solicitors, and he was quite happy. In the afternoon Dr Hanf told me not to be in too much of a hurry, that he'd have a word with Dr Rudiš about it. That such an old couple ought not to get divorced at this stage. Of course I agreed with him. But just in case it came to a divorce I told him my conditions: I asked for my husband's state pension and that it must be stated that I was not at fault in the divorce. I should explain that at the time there was a law that in the case of her husband's death a divorced woman would receive his pension only when she wasn't to blame for the divorce. I had to think of that too. I had nothing and it was now too late for me to start learning some sort of job.

Leoš came to dinner that day as if nothing was amiss. When he was sitting down to eat, Dr Dressler arrived. He said only: 'I've come.' My husband made a tremendous leap to the clothes rack, calling out: 'Don't say anything, don't say anything', he grabbed his greatcoat and hat and rushed out. Dressler looked after him: 'Well, what an extraordinary business, but of course he's crazy, isn't he. Who would want to get mixed up in this?' He turned on his heels and went off too.

Máŕa and I remained staring at one another. When we recovered, I sent her upstairs into the office – I assumed that my husband had escaped there – to tell him to come home now, that Dr Dressler had already gone. Leoš returned, sat down to supper and continued to eat with an excellent appetite.

Again there was peace for a few days. I ran the household as before, he composed downstairs in his study, we talked with one another, we just never mentioned Mrs Horvátová. I kept on thinking about what I'd live on now. I wanted to take Máŕa with me and did my sums as to whether the pension would be enough for both of us. But after a week Leoš began again: when did Dr Hanf say he'd call me? I fobbed him off, but because he kept going on about it, I went there. I said that he should do something because my husband couldn't wait any longer. He informed me that he'd spoken with Dr Rudiš and they'd said to one another that it was nonsense for an old couple to divorce for such a thing. That it could be done differently.

'We will write a sort of contract saying that you're getting divorced privately. You, madam, will undertake to keep the peace, you won't stop his doing anything, and will continue to run a collective household. He will promise to behave decently towards you. Only in the case that the two of you don't observe this, would it go to a court divorce and he'd then pay you his pension. You'll both sign this document and it will be kept with one of us. Do you agree?'

I gladly agreed to this strange 'divorce' because it gave me the chance to go on being with Leoš. Dr Hanf asked me further not to say anything to my husband, only that 'they're working on it now'. I gave him this message, he was happy with it and there was peace again in our home. Then after some time he said to me that he'd invited both solicitors to our house for a discussion about the divorce. They decided among themselves, however, that this discussion wouldn't be at our house, but at Dr Hanf's office. Soon afterwards they invited us there. But my husband took fright that he had to go to my solicitor. He decided that he wouldn't go and said to me also: 'I'm not going anywhere, get Rudiš to go there instead of me.'

So I went to Dr Hanf on my own. Dr Rudiš brought a letter from Leoš in which he apologized that he was poorly. I told both of the lawyers that he was in perfect health. Whereupon Dr Rudiš said that my husband was doing nothing but foolish things and that he'd had a serious word with him already. I explained to them why it was, that Mrs Horvátová was going to have a baby and that he was hugely looking forward to being a father. Rudiš laughed: 'Gábinka,[71] Gábinka, so well known all over the Czech homeland, is she expecting a baby?' I saw that he thought exactly the same about it as I did.

Dr Hanf then read through the 'divorce settlement'. Dr Rudiš agreed with everything. They pointed out to me that I must observe the conditions, especially as far as keeping domestic peace was concerned, I promised this and signed immediately. Dr Hanf doubted that my husband would sign too: after all, the contract had no legal basis: both lawyers had rigged it up to steer my husband away from a divorce which would have been a scandal, and the ruin of us both. But Dr Rudiš knew his client better: indeed after a few days Leoš victoriously announced that he'd signed the 'divorce'.[72] He was content, he'd got his way, and believed that in the eyes of the law he now had complete freedom and that I'd no right to criticize him for marital infidelity since he was 'officially' divorced. It didn't even occur to him to study the laws about it: he never ever observed the law in anything, he made them up for himself.[73]

---

71 A diminutive of Gabriela.
72 The agreement between Leoš and Zdenka Janáček is dated 19 January 1917 (in the typescript) and is signed by them both. A translation is printed as Appendix 2.
73 The agreement between the two is a signed contract which allows either party to institute divorce proceedings if its conditions are not met. It is not an 'official' document if by 'official' Zdenka means ratified by a court of law, but since it makes provisions for her maintenance should the agreement fail it is further along the line than Zdenka perhaps imagined. It is a misrepresentation to say it had 'no legal basis'.

From that time there was peace in our house. It was a point of honour for me to observe precisely the conditions of the agreement that I'd signed. I learnt to control myself so that I no longer considered him my husband and stifled my feeling towards him so much that I don't even know whether I loved him then. I began to look on our relationship from a strictly rational basis, and reason told me to be content that my social position was unshaken, that in this terrible time of war I had a secure home and a crust of bread. My parents also looked at it in the same way. Among outsiders, especially women, I met with understanding and sympathy. I learnt that they called me 'that martyr'. I know that many of them would gladly have helped me, I recognized it from their eyes, in their voices – but what could anyone have done? I was much strengthened by Mrs Adéla Koudelová,[74] an exceptionally fine, good-hearted, pious lady – and for all that so unhappy in her family life: her husband had died, and one son after another was dying. We knew each other already from a very long way back, mostly from Vesna to which she was indeed a mother.[75] In about February 1917 I visited her once. Gently she made reference to my suffering and with the great strength of a deep faith and religious conviction she advised me to turn to God. It was hard. From Olga's death I'd come to hate God, believing in him but not believing that he ever wanted to help me in my suffering. I prayed only to the Virgin Mary. There are such times in a human soul. But Mrs Koudelová converted me. She herself was in the Marian Association attached to the Dominicans and she advised me to go there, saying that the women have sermons for themselves. I went. I soon realized that almost all women who went there had some profound sorrow. Next to me a beautiful young brunette was sitting. I learnt that her name was Marie Zahradníková,[76] that she'd been in Brno for fifteen years and that one of her friends had brought her here. Her husband had died, a teacher at the Brno Technical University, and she couldn't forget him. Also her nerves were in a poor state. We talked about all this together and each pitied the other. Indeed we women found comfort here. Before Easter I'd decided to go again to confession – it was the first time since the last rites for my Olga. It was hard, but there was an intelligent confessor at the Dominicans who had a gift for understanding such things. He conversed very wisely with me. Mrs Zahradníková came at the same time as me. From that time we became very close.

74 See Glossary.
75 See Glossary. Mrs Koudelová was chairman of the Vesna Society in Brno.
76 See Glossary.

My husband went to Prague for Easter [1917],[77] he was preparing
to go there for the Whitsun holidays too, but when they were almost
upon us he proclaimed that he was staying at home because Mrs
Horvátová wasn't going to be in Prague. And I don't know why, but I
got the impression that Mrs Horvátová had already grown tired of the
relationship. I'd waited the whole time to see when the promised child
would be born. But nothing: Mrs Horvátová went on singing and my
husband made no reference to it. And he'd surely not have resisted
boasting about his fatherhood. When it had gone on too far, I became
convinced that she may well again have suggested to him something
about a miscarriage. Such a thing was likely: he still believed
everything she said.

For the summer holidays he was going off to Luhačovice. I asked
him if she'd be there too. To this he answered only laconically: 'Well,
perhaps.'

I told him that I'd like to go to Hukvaldy to stay with Josefka for a
break. He was pleased that it was to her that I'd be going. After his
departure[78] I bottled the fruit from our garden as I always did, and also
began making preparations for the journey. We didn't write to one
another. Just once he sent me a message through a former pupil not to
worry about provisions, because he'd made an 'acquaintance in flour'
in Luhačovice. From the same messenger I also learnt that Mrs
Horvátová was not in Luhačovice. That was news! My husband in
Luhačovice alone and taking care of provisions for our household! I
felt that cracks were showing in this passionate, stormy relationship
from which I'd suffered so much. And what happened next convinced
me more and more that I wasn't mistaken. Leoš sent me a card: 'If
you're going to Hukvaldy, go via Frenštát and bring my coat, I'm
going to Radhošť.'[79] I thought to myself that he'd nevertheless go with
Mrs Horvátová. But a few days later he wrote to me that it was
unnecessary for me to go via Frenštát. And two days before my
departure for Hukvaldy, he suddenly sent a telegram: 'I'm coming
home.'[80] The very day I wanted to leave. It made me angry, I was
already prepared for the journey, I'd had a carriage ordered for the

---

77 Janáček wrote to Universal Edition on 2 April (Hilmar 1988, 37–8) that he was going to
Prague the next day. He was still there until at least Easter Monday (9 April), when he wrote
a congratulatory note to Theodor Schütz (BmJA, B 1779).
78 Janáček arrived in Luhačovice on 3 July 1917.
79 Undated card (BmJA, A 4964) in which Janáček proposed to meet Zdenka on 25 July.
For Radhošť see Glossary. Janáček would have needed warmer clothing for the chillier
temperatures on the mountain.
80 Neither the second letter nor the telegram survive.

station and I'd like to have gone off. But on the other hand I was frightened of irritating him. I went to consult Director Mareš. He advised me to stay home. So I cancelled the carriage, I baked cakes, and began bottling the gherkins. As early as ten in the morning a carriage clattered up in front of the garden, Leoš leapt out of it beaming, and at once began telling me merrily that he'd travelled first thing by the early morning express, and that in Luhačovice he'd met a young married couple. 'They really love one another, you know.'

He pulled out a photograph and gave it to me. A young woman, brunette, evidently a second edition of Mrs Horvátová, except much younger, about twenty-five years old, in a *dirndl* or some sort of folk costume – at that time many women wore these sorts of fantasies on national costumes; they were meant to show the intensely patriotic feeling of the wearer. My instinct clearly told me: 'Mrs Horvátová has fallen off his shovel, now this one's taking over.' But my reason objected that I was wrong, that this lady was surely too young. And furthermore my husband continually related how much the couple loved one another, how delightful they were, until suddenly he blurted out: 'You know, I've invited them, they're coming on Saturday [4 August 1917].' I was surprised by Leoš's liveliness, his kindliness to me, and because he was again inviting guests to visit us.

'But I'd wanted to go away.'

'Oh no, you can't, you must be here, I've told her about you, she wants to meet you.'

Janáček's meeting with Kamila Stösslová was a fateful juncture in his life. Although the friendship remained tantalizingly formal for almost a decade, the vast quantity of letters he wrote her almost from the day he met her[81] are testimony to his emotional involvement, an involvement that spilt over into his compositions and which was more and more to take over his life.

How could I go when such things were happening? I thought hard how I'd entertain these two: at this time there was already a terrible shortage of provisions everywhere. I had my work cut out, but on Saturday, when my husband went to meet the guests at the station, I was decently prepared. I received them on the veranda. I was surprised to see two decidedly Jewish types. Especially Mr Stössel, although he was in soldier's uniform, looked very much like a red-haired Polish Jew. Of course I didn't let on at all but I was most surprised at Leoš. The wife apologized profusely that she was putting me out, but my

81 See *IL*.

husband apparently wouldn't have it any other way and definitely
wanted the two of us to get to know one another. I thought she was
quite nice: young, cheerful, one could have a really good talk with her,
she was always laughing. She was of medium height, dark, curly-
haired like a Gypsy woman, with huge eyes, black and almost
protruding – 'Junoaugen' as with Mrs Horvátová – with heavy
eyebrows, a sensuous mouth. The voice was unpleasant, shrill,
strident. Her husband was sturdy, much taller than Leoš, with reddish
blond hair, but with a pleasing appearance and very nice manners. She
was called Kamila, he David. He dealt in antiques. My husband had
suggested that I sell him my china, but I refused. Both promised the
whole time that they'd look out for provisions for us, Mr Stössel was
in the army in Přerov and knew how to come by them. His wife lived
there too, they rented a house there, they had one little son with them,
the second was with the wife's parents in Písek.[82] One thing was
certain: that they brought activity and laughter into our sad quietness.
We had tea in the garden, Leoš beamed, and busily waited on her, Mr
Stössel was overjoyed at his wife's success. She began to pick apricots.
She stood on the ladder, Leoš looked at her enthusiastically from
below, not caring that people from the opposite windows were looking
on curiously to see what was going on at our place. They slept the
night downstairs with me, in the morning they went to see friends and
arrived back only at teatime. She again saw to it that there was lots of
commotion and fuss until, late in the evening, someone from the
military hospital next door told her off for carrying on like that at
night. Only then did she quieten down. I had to show them my china.
Mr Stössel made it clear that it wasn't worth much until I said to him
that it wasn't for sale since the pieces were family heirlooms. She,
however, was always enthusiastic, she liked many things at our place
and Leoš would most gladly have given her the lot if they hadn't been
mine. When I saw that, and the fact that she was in ecstasies about one
old folk plate, I gave it to her. Straightaway she promised me a
morning jacket in return.

When in the evening my husband went upstairs [into the Organ
School] to sleep, the three of us remained sitting around and chatting.
She soon turned the conversation to Mrs Horvátová. She knew about
everything; Leoš, she said, had confided everything in her, and
apparently also complained about my not having understood his

82 Přerov is in Moravia, 82 km north-east of Brno; Písek, where the couple moved in April
1919, is in southern Bohemia.

friendship. In reply Mrs Stösslová had told him it was difficult for her to make a judgement when she didn't know me. That was the reason why he'd invited her to see me. So that was it, then: my husband had made this young person, whom he'd just met, the judge in our affairs. Fine, I went along with that too. I told her how I saw it. She made it abundantly clear that she was sorry for me, she showed friendly concern, she was full of understanding, so much so that Máŕa and I later said to one another that it was probably good my husband brought her to us, because she understood me and could have a good effect on him. That she really did have a big influence on Leoš was something I found out very soon. Her husband left for Přerov on Monday [6 August]; she, however, was persuaded by my husband to stay longer with us, until I left for Hukvaldy, because we'd be going the same way as far as Přerov. It wasn't pleasant for me, but I had to appear to welcome this proposal. And then on Monday morning when, to fill time, Mrs Stösslová was looking over the photographs hanging in my husband's study and came across the unhappy picture of Mrs Horvátová that she herself had christened 'Angel of Peace', I said to her:

'You can see for yourself, I think, how I feel when I have to look at this here for days on end.'

'Wait a moment, I'll fix it.'

She went straight into the garden to my husband, spoke with him for a moment, rushed back and laughed: 'He gave me the picture because it's not important to him any more.'

Together we took down the picture of Mrs Horvátová and Mrs Stösslová took it back with her to Přerov. What I, our friends and lawyers couldn't manage was achieved in a trice by this clever, cheerful, nice little Jewess. In this way she very much won me over. After that I rather liked her. When later I travelled with her in the train, we had quite a lot of time for chatting and so I got to know her well and her circumstances. She was a Czech Jew, her father[83] had been first a butcher in Písek, then he traded in horses. Mr Stössel was domiciled in Lwów through his father,[84] but his mother lived in Strážnice, so he spoke Czech, though worse than his wife. After the coup d'état [declaration of Czechoslovak Independence in 1918] he was to have been deported from the Republic as a foreign subject,

83 Adolf Neumann (1864–1942).
84 David Stössel's father Marcus Stössel (1851–99) came from what is now Lv'iv, Ukraine. At the time it was Lemberg in Austrian Galicia; from 1918 to 1939, as Lwów, it was part of Poland.

but my husband saw to it that he wasn't expelled.[85] In the war they lived a 'Tschacherl'[86] life, he lent money to officers, which is why he had a good reputation. Although clever, his wife wasn't particularly intelligent. She told me she hadn't liked going to school and didn't like learning. That was certainly true because her letters were full of grammatical mistakes. In music she was totally ignorant, knowing almost nothing about composers. She called Leoš's pieces 'those notes of yours', and hadn't heard of Wagner. In literature it wasn't any better. Once she wrote to Leoš: 'Send me something to read that's not too long, a love story with a happy ending.'[87] She gained my husband's favour through her cheerfulness, laughter, temperament, Gypsy-like appearance and buxom body, perhaps also because she reminded him of Mrs Horvátová, although she'd none of that woman's demonic qualities or artfulness. She was natural, sometimes almost uninhibited. One couldn't exactly say that she won my husband over, for she didn't try to. He himself had begun to send her bouquets and letters in Luhačovice:[88] it seems that it was more Mr Stössel with his fine business flair who realized the value of this attachment of a well-known composer. She herself was completely unimpressed by my husband's fame, and also by his person: sometimes she laid into him quite sharply and at other times he seemed almost ridiculous in her eyes. On that journey we became very friendly. I felt I'd no option when I saw how desperately Leoš wanted this friendship. I said to myself that she could be a good support for me against Mrs Horvátová. In Přerov we said goodbye to one another warmly. Her husband came to meet her at the station, and brought me the promised morning jacket. I continued to Hukvaldy. Josefka was very nice to me. She no longer stuck up for Leoš, they'd got angry with one another. He had wanted to go to her the previous Easter with Mrs Horvátová, but Josefka had refused. She herself already knew what marital infidelity felt like and what it's like when you have to be around the other woman the whole time. After a fortnight I prepared to return home. Leoš wrote to me to look in on Mrs Stösslová in Přerov, saying that she'd give me roast goose. But she wasn't there. Soon afterwards she invited both of us

85 In his letter to Kamila Stösslová of 8 March 1928 (*Hž/IL*, no.605), Janáček describes writing a reference for David Stössel in support of his application not to be repatriated.
86 Here Mrs Janáčková uses the demeaning diminutive of a Viennese dialect word with intimations of under-the-counter deals.
87 Janáček attempted to send her something along these lines (see his letter to her of 7 January 1918, *Hž/IL*, no.37).
88 See *Hž/IL*, nos.1–2.

to Přerov.[89] At Dýma in Brno my husband bought her a little knitted silver bag as a present,[90] like those much in fashion at the time. We were royally entertained at their place, they had a larder crammed full, some Italian woman cooked for them. When Leoš produced his present for Mrs Kamila, they wouldn't accept it and refused it so persistently that we had to take the bag home again. On the whole they did us many more favours at first than we did them. Mr Stössel sent flour to us via soldiers, his wife corresponded in a friendly fashion with me, and irreproachably with my husband. I didn't get jealous of her: I felt confidently that it was indeed just friendship. Even Mrs Horvátová knew about this friendship of Leoš's. After my husband's death I read in their letters of that period: 'that Kamila of yours'.[91]

The relationship between me and Leoš improved from that time. Just once more I felt the torment of jealousy: in the autumn of 1917 Mrs Horvátová sang again in Brno. I was visiting Director Mareš and on the way I met Mrs Zahradníková. Just as we were going past the Old Theatre, Leoš rode by in a carriage with Mrs Horvátová. He jumped out and helped her alight. I couldn't move, I couldn't tear my eyes away. As I gazed at the two of them all the wrong which I was forced to suffer on her account returned to me and drained my strength away. Mrs Zahradníková caught me and just went on speaking to me:

'For God's sake, I beg you, pull yourself together.'

At home I spoke about it to my husband. He replied: 'It was cruel for you, but I didn't see you.'

What a strange person! How rich in feeling, yet sympathy and forgiveness were things he didn't know. He could love so much, he knew how to be so full of love! [. . .][92] And yet the same person who could take supper in a friendly fashion with the hens, could cruelly and without feeling kick aside someone that he knew loved him above her own life. He knew how to inflict wounds that wouldn't heal.

Leoš remained at home for Christmas Eve [1917], saying that he'd

89 This visit took place on 8 September 1917 (Hž/IL, no.365).
90 A small shop selling pipes and tobacco (*dým* = smoke) and evidently a few other goods. Its location near the station suggests that the bag may have been a last-minute idea.
91 Janáček began telling Horvátová about the Stössel family's misfortunes on 7 January 1918 (JA vi, 53–4). None of Horvátová's letters survive from this period but it is clear from Janáček's letters that his new enthusiasm had not gone down well. Four days later he was moved to comment: 'The Stössels are nice people and you shouldn't wrong them' (11 January 1918; JA vi, 56).
92 As an example Zdenka describes Janáček's treatment of the hens. See the more detailed account of this by Stejskalová on p.124 above.

go to Prague only on Christmas Day. I was pleased and did all I could to make him enjoy being at home. As a present he gave me an unusually large amount, a whole K 1000. I was surprised at it and at first didn't want to take it. Also because I didn't have a present for him myself: I was afraid that he'd throw it back at me. I said this to him, but he replied: 'Why wouldn't I accept it?'

Then I plucked up my courage and said warmly: 'Besides, the biggest present for me is that you stayed at home for me on Christmas Eve.'

He went blood-red and tears came into his eyes. And the next day – he went off to Mrs Horvátová. He didn't stay long. Formerly he'd even stay the night there, now she sent him to the hotel Karel IV. That probably didn't amuse him.

At that time a great new success was in store for *Jenůfa.* It was due to be given in Vienna in February 1918. It was said that Jeritza[93] had pushed it through with the young Emperor Karl because she wanted to sing Jenůfa. On the other hand, another version alleged that the court sponsor of *Jenůfa* was the Empress Zita, a good musician (her favourite instrument was the organ on which she was said to play very well) on account of the 'Gebet zur Maria'.[94] Again I had the jitters about how *Jenůfa* would be received in Vienna, and personal fear came into it too. For my husband said to me: 'I want you to be at the première, but I also want Mrs Horvátová to be there.'

To have to meet her at the première of *Jenůfa* in Vienna! Again to suffer some new evil! In these circumstances I didn't know what to do other than to ask my husband for Mrs Stösslová to come too. I counted on her being my protector. My husband consented and I immediately wrote her a letter of invitation extending also to her husband. They promised me they'd come. In the New Year my husband began to travel to rehearsals in Vienna. He returned hugely pleased with Jeritza. Once he brought me chocolates from her. Some tycoon invited her and my husband to the Sacher House[95] and she gave him the sweets for me there. At each rehearsal he returned ever more joyfully and more kindly to me. Except when we made plans for our stay in Vienna, and he said to me: 'It would be good if you stayed at

93 Maria Jeritza (1887–1982), soprano. Born in Brno as Marie Jezlizka, Jeritza joined the Vienna Hofoper in 1912, and sang regularly in Vienna for the next twenty years, creating Jenůfa at the Viennese première as well as several Strauss roles. She was also a favourite at the Metropolitan Opera and sang the first Jenůfa there in 1924.
94 i.e. Jenůfa's prayer to the Virgin Mary in Act 2.
95 i.e. the hotel Sacher, Albertinaplatz, Vienna, renowned for its Sachertorte.

your parents and I in the hotel Post. I couldn't devote myself to you if she's going to be there'. That hurt me: 'You know that it would be a bitter pill now' – but I swallowed it.

I feared Mrs Horvátová unnecessarily. On the day of the première she had to sing in Prague and therefore was due to come and listen only to the dress rehearsal. But hardly was Leoš in Vienna – he went there a few days before the première – than he wrote to me saying that he needed some of his photographs and asking me to bring them with me, Mrs Horvátová wasn't coming to Vienna at all: 'So come at once.'

Of course I went at once. I put up at my parents' and went to see my husband. He greeted me almost warmly. We then went around almost always together. It was so strange that he spoke German here the whole time, he who couldn't bear to hear a single word of German at home. The next day one of the Viennese-Czech societies put on *The Bartered Bride* and invited my husband. We went there and were very warmly received. We much liked being among the Viennese Czechs, we felt at home.

On the morning of the première the Stössels arrived and also stayed in the hotel Post. Lots of acquaintances, both Leoš's and mine, also arrived, among them Director Mareš and Max Brod.[96] In the evening I sat in a box with J.B. Foerster[97] and with the Stössels all dressed up. If I was fearful at how *Jenůfa* would be received in Prague, here I was almost shaking with worry over it. The court, the Austrian aristocracy, the elegant audience, a select musical intelligentsia, it dazzled me and got me all churned up inside. The first bars sounded – God how they sounded! After all, there were nearly a hundred musicians sitting in the orchestra. The curtain went up, I heard around me only a sort of 'Ahhh!', so beautiful it was. A Slovácko village sparkled before us and behind it into a great distance fields shimmered. So much sun everywhere, altogether the lighting was splendid. Jeritza shone, with her silvery voice, deeply felt acting and beautiful fair-haired appearance. She was the best Jenůfa I ever saw and heard. The Slovácko folk costume suited her magnificently. It was a real one, all the soloists had genuine folk costumes, the chorus painted ones, everything correct to the last detail. People from the Viennese opera had gone at the time to study [folk costumes] in Slovácko. It was clear to me after the very first act that in this guise and in this performance *Jenůfa* had to triumph in Vienna. The success was enormous. After the second act Leoš was

called on stage several times, and he had to take a bow, Director
Hertzka[98] with his wife and Gabriela Preissová[99] came to my box to
see me – well, we both took great pleasure in it and our friends with us.
Only one thing made me sorry: that no one from my family shared in
this glory. My parents were now too old, but my brother would have
liked to come with me into the box. My husband didn't invite him
however, and I didn't dare ask him about it.

The next day we all travelled home. I and my husband on our own. I
remember that we were hungry in the train and how glad we were
when some gentleman offered us smoked meats. Otherwise it was a
very nice journey. Between Leoš and myself things had cleared up
again a good deal during those days. Director Mareš noticed this at
once after the première and told me how pleased he was about it.

Mrs Horvátová was meant to go with my husband to a subsequent
performance. He already had tickets for her and everything prepared,
but suddenly she sent a telegram saying that she wasn't coming. It
surprised me how calmly Leoš took this. He invited my friend, Mrs
Váchová, and she went to Vienna with him. It was already very
striking that three times Mrs Horvátová had cried off attending the
Viennese *Jenůfa*. My friends said to me that she wanted to sing the
Kostelnička at the première and did all she could to bring this about
and when she didn't succeed, she got angry. It definitely wasn't the
same now as before between her and Leoš.

In the holidays [summer 1918] my husband and I were in Hukvaldy:
I stayed with Josefka and he with the Sládeks. I don't know what I did
wrong, but on that occasion my sister-in-law was nasty to me the
whole time. I did all the work with her, but she kept on reproaching me
that she had too much to do, she bossed me around whenever she
could. In the end Leoš stood up for me energetically: he told her that
he could see well how much I was helping her so what else did she
want from me? I can't tell you how much that pleased me, coming
from him. And when we went home, he willingly carried sacks of
vegetables from Hukvaldy with me, for there was already a great
shortage of vegetables in Brno. Straight after our return Máŕa went
foraging again in the Českomoravská vysočina. Leoš showed a new
kindness to me: he volunteered that he'd come and sleep downstairs in
the house, so that I wouldn't be alone. As if on purpose my brother
arrived that very day; I'd got some flour for him. Fearfully I went to

98 Dr Emil Hertzka (1869–1932), head of the Viennese firm Universal Edition which
published *Jenůfa* and Janáček's later works.
99 See p.130, fn.20.

tell my husband. He didn't say a word about it but nevertheless I cautiously didn't offer a bed for the night to my brother, he had to go into a hotel. He came to us only the next morning. My God, he was hungry! We had plum dumplings, I can't tell you how many he ate, poor thing. He and my husband spoke coldly, but decently. My brother began to say how the Emperor Karl was probably going to have himself crowned as Czech king.[100] My husband was so quiet you could have heard a pin drop. Through Herben[101] he was initiated into what was happening in Bohemia and abroad. Although otherwise he told me everything, in this matter he knew how to keep as silent as the grave, he never betrayed even by a glance what he knew. Even in my dreams it never occurred to me that we could have such excellent leaders and a whole army beyond our borders.[102] To me it seemed that even Karl's coronation was a splendid success in Czech affairs.

At the beginning of the season [autumn 1918] Mrs Horvátová was due to sing again in Brno: a messenger came to us saying that she was staying in the hotel de l'Europe.[103] My husband took the news soberly and went to the rehearsal to see her. I set off to meet Máŕa, who was due to arrive from one of her foraging expeditions. She brought flour, eggs, butter to the Zábrdovice station[104] – all things which were then strictly requisitioned in Brno, but slipped through quite easily in the small Zábrdovice station. We dragged them home breathlessly but pleased as Punch that we'd added something to our impoverished larder. In the evening my husband came and said: 'She hasn't anything with her to eat, please boil some eggs for her and put a piece of bread in with them.'

Máŕa was all anger when, for the hated Mrs Horvátová, she had to cook the eggs for which she'd struggled so much. I didn't lend a hand in this: I was sorry for Máŕa and regretted the eggs. My husband took them, a piece of bread with them, a spoon, and salt and carried it all to

100 In different circumstances this might have been considered a great advance in Czech political liberation. The previous emperor, Franz Josef I, steadfastly refused a Czech coronation, thus symbolically downgrading the status of Bohemia and Moravia within his multi-ethnic empire (there were coronations in Vienna and Budapest only).
101 See Glossary.
102 A reference to politicians in exile such as T.G. Masaryk, who spent the war years outside the country lobbying for an independent Czech (and Slovak) republic, and the voluntary army of Czechs, the Czech Legion, which fought abroad for the realization of such aims.
103 Also known as the hotel Europa, later Evropa, an Art Nouveau building on the corner of Janská and Masarykova.
104 A station, now demolished, on the Brno–Tišnov line just before the terminus at the main Brno station.

the Old Theatre. In the evening he came home soon after the performance. The next morning he went to see Mrs Horvátová in the hotel, but in a short while he returned and told me that she had had to leave that very night for Prague – that she'd received a telegram. But Máŕa already had a different account. From pupils at the Organ School. Some of them had gathered after the performance and followed Leoš to see, she said, whether our old man was going to sleep with Horvátová. They went right to the hotel, they saw how the two said goodbye and my husband went home. They thought that this was just for show, that he'd return again, and they went on waiting. But after a while Mrs Horvátová emerged with her cases, got into a cab, and rode off to the station. So Máŕa and I said to one another that Leoš had again been deceived, otherwise he wouldn't have gone in vain early in the morning to the hotel. I'd have given I don't know what to find out how it now stood between them. But he suddenly turned silent about it, as if she didn't even exist in this world. Soon he went off somewhere and during his absence he got a letter from her. I couldn't stop myself, I had to see what she was writing to him. It was in fact Leoš's letter to her. He wrote that Sylva [Šebková], the sweetheart of the conductor Maixner, had said that Mrs Horvátová had been unfaithful to him with Maixner, and that he could see this for himself if he came to the station at the time she indicated. He had gone there and had seen them both going into Maixner's flat. Sylva had apparently gone on to say to him that Maixner was preparing to box his ears – so he had taken himself off to Maixner's flat to have his ears boxed. There was apparently a scene there, and Maixner had told him that Mrs Horvátová was and would continue to be his (Maixner's) mistress. Leoš prefaced all this with the greeting 'Jelča'[105] and ended: 'You can see that it can't be the same between us any more. Don't worry, I won't harm you in Brno. Difficult to know how to sign myself. The Author.'

This letter was returned to him and she added a couple of lines, derisively inscribing it to 'The Author'. She described her successes and explained that she'd been summoned by telegram from Brno to Prague. The other things about which Leoš had written to her in the letter didn't merit even a mention. I took great pleasure that Leoš had finally seen for himself what sort of woman Mrs Horvátová was. I kept the letter.[106] I said to myself that when it came to it, I'd a right to it

---

105 A diminutive of 'Gabriela'.
106 But also probably destroyed it: it has not survived in the Janáček Archive.

after all that I'd endured. My husband didn't look for it and never found out that I'd intercepted it. Soon after that they stopped writing completely,[107] and the relationship for which I'd suffered so much was at an end.

107 Apart from a brief note in 1928 congratulating Mrs Horvátová on the twenty-fifth anniversary of her début in the National Theatre, Janáček's last surviving letter to her is dated 23 June 1918 (JA vi, 90). It is short and to the point and suggests that much of the heat had gone out of the relationship.

8

Coup d'état. The death of my parents

And suddenly 28 October was here. We suspected something, confused prophecies of peace began to appear, the newspapers were full of hints but we didn't imagine it would be like this. Máŕa brought us the first rumour. In the morning she kneaded the bread and took it to the baker in Rudolfská ulice. She raced back beaming: 'Oh my! – Austria has collapsed! It's the end of the war, the soldiers are tearing the [Austrian] eagles from their caps, everyone's pinning on a [Czech] tricolour.'

As soon as Leoš heard this, he grabbed his coat and dashed into the town. I waited impatiently for him the whole morning, I was terribly curious to learn what was going on. He came back blissfully happy and spoke more than he ate. Straight after midday I too ran into the town. So many impressions! I met Mrs Váchová, the judge's wife, crying with joy. I saw Dr Hynek Bulín[1] making a speech to the people from a car telling them to maintain order. I hunted for a tricolour but it was impossible to get one. In a few hours all the shops had sold out. Eventually Mrs Heindlová,[2] a good friend of mine and the proprietor of a china shop in Rudolfská ulice, from that moment renamed Česká, gave me half of hers. I remembered that I had an appointment on the corner of the Great Square[3] with Mrs Zahradníková.[4] It was a wonder that we found one another in that ant-heap of people. [. . .]

When we all got home again that evening, the place was full of happy anticipation. It seemed to us that heaven on earth had come. There would be no war, we wouldn't be hungry, Máŕa and I laughed – at that time everyone thought of food above all. Leoš now came out with everything that he had learnt from Jan Herben. And already he had his own idea: to turn the Organ School into a conservatory. He talked about it constantly, he thought about it and began to

1 See p.109, fn.65; Bulín was one of the leaders in raising Czech national consciousness in Brno before independence in the early days afterwards.
2 Marie Heindlová (?1875–1955).
3 Now náměstí Svobody [Freedom Square], one of the two main squares in Brno.
4 See Glossary.

negotiate with influential people. He was amazingly happy, he was always running off to town. Again we got a bit closer to one another. We went together to concerts, for walks; we met each other halfway. However we didn't live together as a married couple. Despite this I was calm: I now knew for certain that it was all over with Mrs Horvátová, Mrs Stösslová didn't cause me concern, it was then indeed just friendship. Everywhere around us was full of joyous work for the new state, my husband had such an excellent plan in his head – it was beautiful.

But it was not given to me to take pleasure in this for long. It was said that there was famine now in Austria, especially in Vienna. I kept on thinking of my family. They couldn't move from Vienna: for one thing my brother would have lost his good position – he was then a police superintendent – but, above all, Mama was by then already very ill, so that there could be no thought of moving. It was now almost halfway through December – perhaps the 13th. In those gloomy winter days I saw them before me the whole time until eventually I decided that I'd go and see how they were getting on. I wanted to take them a few provisions – it was allowed by then. I put potatoes, bread and a few *buchty*[5] into my 'rucksack' – during the war this became a common expression. I left at six in the morning, reaching Vienna only towards midnight – we'd waited such a long time in Břeclav.[6] It was raining cats and dogs, I was so overloaded that I was bent almost double. Luckily I caught the last tram. I reached my parents' flat, I looked up at the windows. I was puzzled that there was a light on since no one knew that I was coming. I rang at the gate. The caretaker, who knew me, looked at me compassionately and told me: 'Frau Mama ist schwer krank.'[7]

My legs gave way beneath me, I could barely stagger up to the second storey. My brother came to open up for me. I didn't recognize him, he was so decrepit and thin. I almost didn't recognize my father. They were amazed: 'You here already! Mama is in a very bad way.'

It transpired that they had sent me a telegram, but I hadn't received anything: I came thanks only to my instinct. I went into the room. Cold. A candle flickered feebly – at night gas lighting wasn't allowed. And Mama lay there terribly ill. She turned only her eyes towards me and said weakly: 'Zdenka, ich werde nie mehr gesund.'[8]

5 See p.4, fn.23.
6 The last town on the Czech border on the Brno–Vienna line.
7 'Your mother is very ill.'
8 'Zdenka, I'm never going to get well again.'

My brother and Papa walked helplessly around her. They told me that the maid had contracted the Spanish influenza which was raging so terribly at the end of the war, and that she'd died in hospital. Mama had caught it from her and was by now beyond help. She now had pneumonia as well. I bent over her. She was hungry, she wanted a little coffee. From the kitchen Papa brought some impossibly nasty liquid which the two poor helpless things had concocted themselves. It was enough to make one weep. I offered her at least some of the *buchty* I'd brought.

'Ja, ja, ja', she responded eagerly when I asked her whether she felt like eating it.

And so, mortally ill, with pneumonia, she was eating *buchty* and coffee in that cold, unheated room. I felt terrible just seeing all that. Tired to death, I then curled up on the divan in her room and just wanted to sleep.

In the morning [Saturday 14 December] a rude awakening. I saw from Mama that it was indeed the end. And around her it looked awful: dirt, disorder – male housekeeping. There was a pot on the cooker with peas, they tried to cook them, but they didn't manage to since they didn't know that they had to soak them first. They didn't know how to do anything. Well now, in this I could help them: I squared up to the work, I ordered my brother to find a daily help, I took everything firmly in hand. But I couldn't give Mama her health back. She had a doctor, but he said that it was all hopeless and no longer visited. I gave her compresses at least. I wrote to my husband saying that Mama was in a bad way so he mustn't get cross if I nursed her until her death. He wrote back at once, saying I should just stay. I saw that it wouldn't be long: she was visibly going downhill. On Sunday she was a bit better, she began to eat, but immediately brought it all up. On Monday, at my brother's request, she had the last rites. Her body began to stop functioning, but her spirit still remained untouched by the illness. She continued to take an interest in everything and to make her own caustic comments. When she received extreme unction, she drew my attention to the fat priest: 'Du, Zdenka, schau, der Pfarrer is aber nicht unternährt!'[9]

Every day a young woman from the provisions office to which my parents belonged came to ask after her health. A nice, quiet, pretty girl – if not exactly young any more. Mama was very glad to see her, she told me about her, how she helped them with the rations, she called her

9 'Look, Zdenka, the priest isn't undernourished, is he!'

simply 'Fräulein Josefina' and introduced her to me with the words: 'Das ist mein Schutzengel.'[10]

She knew that she was going to die. She recited from Schiller's *Wallenstein*:

> Ich denke einen langen Schlaf zu tun
> Denn dieser letzten Tage Qual war gross.[11]

Just as Olga once did, she too wanted to look nice in her coffin. She wanted light-coloured clothes, fresh flowers and reminded me several times: 'Zdenka, nicht auf die Zähne vergessen.'[12]

On Monday night [16 December] she began to be restless, she clutched at the bedspread and continually repeated: 'Das ist schreck-lich, das ist schrecklich.'[13]

And again she clasped me to her and gazed at me deeply with her dark, big eyes. When we could no longer look at her suffering, my brother got dressed and went to get our former GP, who had just then returned from the war. He came, he gave comfort, he tapped at her chest, he gave an injection. She fell asleep after that and didn't wake up again. She remained alive the whole night, the whole [of the next] day until midnight. She died between Tuesday and Wednesday 18 December 1918. She breathed continually with the same tempo as the dying Olga did. I already had it in my ears and in my blood. I lay on the divan, suddenly I heard a different tempo. I jumped up, I went to her, she'd breathed her last. Just like that time. So I'd lived through it for a second time.

'My Mama, my dear Mama!' She was a good wife, she was a good mother to me. The way she brought me up and her principles made me a faithful and honourable wife, not departing by a whisker from what she'd instilled in me at home. It was she who had cultivated within me the feeling for duty, economy and modest personal requirements. Perhaps I'd also inherited something of her nobility and also a certain pride. I know she had her faults too: she was obstinate and domineering, but which of us doesn't have our faults? [. . .]

She wished to look nice in her coffin – I dressed her up. A light-coloured suit, a white silk headscarf on her greying hair, fresh flowers. Among them we put with her into her grave the picture where the four

---

10 'This is my guardian angel.'
11 'I'm thinking of taking a long sleep because the pain of these last few days was great' (from Wallenstein's final speech in *Wallensteins Tod*, Act 5 Scene 5, lines 3678–9).
12 'Zdenka, don't forget about my teeth.'
13 'It's terrible, simply terrible.'

of us were photographed together [see Plate 10]. And I didn't forget about the teeth. As soon as she'd breathed her last, I put her false teeth into her mouth. They had to give me strong wine afterwards to recover from it, but I did what Mama wished.

I sent a telegram to my husband. 'I feel for you' – he answered. He didn't come to the funeral.

With mourning it was simple in those hard times: I took Mama's black suit and somewhere bought a mourning hat. [. . .]

After the funeral we had a [family] conference and decided that my brother and my father would continue to remain in the old flat and that the daily help would cook for them. On Sunday [22 December] I travelled home.

It was a terrible journey. The trains were full to bursting just with soldiers, I was glad to be sitting on my case near the toilet. Soldiers passed back and forth, they had become completely coarsened by the war, wild, inconsiderate, in dirty, smelly rags. And the journey was endless. We travelled from two in the afternoon until midnight. At the station no one was waiting for me, Mářa had come to meet the afternoon train and thought that I'd no longer be coming home that day. The trams were no longer running at that late hour. An officer was going to our part of town and attached himself to me. I was glad that I didn't have to walk alone.

On the Tuesday two days later it was Christmas Eve and I didn't have anything prepared. Straight after that journey, on Monday, I got up terribly early in the morning and the whole day[14] I cooked and baked so it would be as it was in other years and Leoš would not feel hard done by. He pitied me when he came home in the evening and saw me all worn out. On the morning before Christmas I was preparing to go into town to buy him some sort of present. I got dressed; suddenly I got huge pains as if from gallstones. I cried out, my husband rushed up and he and Mářa laid me down and called the doctor. He gave me an injection and ordered me to lie down. What a nice Christmas Eve that was for us! Mářa had to do everything herself, I continued to be sick so that towards evening we had to call Dr Jirka[15] again. Leoš was very good to me, he looked after me and showed great sympathy towards me. On Christmas Day things got even worse for

14 The Czech text has 'týden' (week) in error for 'den' (day): Zdenka arrived back two days before Christmas Eve.
15 Dr Otakar Jirka (1881–1953), a well-known Brno doctor (Dr Jirka is mentioned by Stejskalová (Trkanová 1964, 73) as treating Janáček in 1913). Janáčková, however, sometimes writes 'Jirků', which is another possible surname.

me. Instead of a hot-water bottle I placed an electric blanket against me and thoroughly burnt myself. So I said to myself that it would be better if I went to hospital. Dr Jirka called out the senior consultant Dr Bakeš[16] to me and he had me taken to St Anna's. I then went home at New Year, they didn't want to operate on me. Leoš was very tender towards me the whole time; he travelled with me to the hospital and visited me there every day. Afterwards I was confined to bed at home for a long time. My burn opened up. No sooner was I able to walk than I thought that I should go and see [my family] in Vienna, as I'd promised. But meanwhile they had closed the border, I couldn't travel, and there were even difficulties with writing.

In February 1919 another painful blow. Lorka[17] died in Švábenice. I much regretted it; because of her good and refined nature she had always been the one I liked most of all my husband's family. On the way from the funeral in Švábenice we stopped off in Přerov at the Stössels,[18] Leoš insisted on it. We were very graciously received, at that time it was a still unclouded friendly relationship. We returned home in the evening.

Life ran on with its worries and its hustle and bustle. With my husband everything now revolved around turning the Organ School into a conservatory. For my part I worried about those two in Vienna. From letters I knew that there was great poverty and disorder there, the daily help was a thief, and Papa didn't get on with my brother. Separately, each sent me desperate letters. And there was no way I could get there. Not until May was I able to obtain a passport for myself.[19] I set off immediately. Although I wrote and told them when they should expect me, no one was at home. I stood at the door, I rang, suddenly a neighbour came out, a dentist, and said: 'Gnädige Frau, nehmen Sie sich den Herrn Schulrat zu sich nach Brünn.'[20]

I was taken aback, I wanted to ask him what was going on when my father came. As soon as he saw me, he stopped on the stairs, wrung his hands, and begged in an old man's voice: 'Zdenčička, please, take me home, I can't stand it here.'

We went in. That flat! Mama would have been appalled at what had become of it now. Piles of dirty cups in the kitchen, God knows when

16 Dr Jaroslav Bakeš (1871–1930), surgeon at St Anna's from 1906, from 1922 at the former military hospital at Žlutý kopec, where he operated on Zdenka's goitre in 1927 (see p.208).
17 See Glossary: 'Janáčková, Eleonora'. She died on 12 February 1919.
18 This visit took place on 15 February 1919 (see *Hž*, nos.107–8).
19 Necessary now for crossing the new state border between Czechoslovakia and Austria.
20 'Madam, take the school director back to Brno to live with you.'

they last washed the dishes. I asked about the daily help – he said they didn't have one at all. I got changed and began to create some order. As I did so Papa complained about my brother. I got ready to give him a real ticking off when he came home from the office. Except that when my brother also began to tell me about the situation, I had to admit that he too had a case. How, for instance, could I judge between them when my brother complained: 'Yes, I come home, I'm hungry, and he doesn't want to give me bread.'

And Father's response: 'He knows well enough that all bread is rationed.' For lunch they went to the soup kitchen, I'm not surprised that they were hungry the whole time. Everywhere a woman's hand was lacking. And it could have been there if only my brother had wanted. When he went off to the office again, my father told me that Fräulein Josefina,[21] whom I'd met at my mother's death-bed, was my brother's sweetheart going back to his student days. As long ago as seventeen years ago he had had trouble on her account with Mama, who was against this friendship with a penniless girl, although she'd never even seen her. It seemed that at that time my brother had obeyed her and forgotten his former love. It had been a mystery to us that he'd never wanted to get married, although among the would-be brides that would have wanted him there was even a millionairess. At home we all imagined that he was a great hater of women. Only when the talk sometimes touched on Josefina he stuck up for her, saying she was 'ein braves Mädel'.[22] None of us suspected that he still loved her and that he was in touch with her. When during the war she got into the provisions section and began to have dealings with my parents, so that she even came to their flat, neither she nor Leo let slip that they knew each other intimately. Mama, who hadn't a good word to say about the old Josefina, fell heartily in love with the new one. Despite this, my brother wasn't brave enough to own up to it all at home, and Josefina, on the other hand, was too discreet to exert pressure on him. She was a splendid girl. Her surname was Mašínová [*recte* Maschin], her father was a shoemaker, an old Bible-reader,[23] a patriot, a self-aware Czech who used to talk enthusiastically about Palacký[24] and read Czech newspapers every day. Her mother too was Czech. And what was odd:

21 Josefina Maschin (1887–1960).
22 'a good, solid girl'.
23 *písmák*, an uneducated man of humble stock who loved reading, especially the Bible (*Písma* = Holy Scripture).
24 František Palacký (1798–1876), the leading Czech historian of the nineteenth century and a prominent figure in the Czech national revival.

the daughter couldn't speak Czech and the son already felt himself completely German, a convinced socialist. He's now in Russia. Josefina, like her sister, was a trained dressmaker. She was refined, undemanding, self-sacrificing, loving. After Mama's death she looked after Father in every way she could.

When I learnt all this, it seemed strange that my brother was keeping it secret and that he didn't get married. After all the only obstacle had been the pride of my mother, who couldn't bear her Leo to marry a penniless, uneducated girl. My father and I, on the contrary, would have wished it with all our hearts. When I'd thought it all through I took Leo to task and advised him to marry Josefina. He didn't want to. God knows what his excuse was, I think that he couldn't even find one sensible reason. I couldn't make it out. As a result I had a head full of worries when I prepared to go home again. I had to tell Father the painful truth that he couldn't stay at our house, that I myself 'didn't know the hour or the day';[25] although things were now better between my husband and myself. I promised him only that I'd find him accommodation with a family friend in Brno, so that he could be near me. That was also my first concern when I got home.[26] My friend Mrs Žaludová, who after the death of her husband lived in Komárov,[27] had a nice room in which she was willing to put Father up. I was pleased that he'd be in good hands and with an old friend of his, and I made ready to go to Vienna to tell him. But on the eve of my departure, the Stössels arrived at our home.[28] My husband was terribly pleased at this, I couldn't leave. They stayed the night at our house, they remained also a second day, only on the third day did Mr Stössel go off. I couldn't stay any longer, I set off, and Mrs Stösslová stayed alone with my husband. I wasn't surprised by this, I'd already got used to worse things, besides which at this time I didn't lay any claim to my husband; also I knew unmistakably that it was a purely friendly relationship. On my return Máŕa told me how one day she listened through the open door to a snippet of their conversation: the young wife was boasting to Leoš how everyone told her how beautiful she was and how everyone was in love with her. She couldn't get off the subject and Leoš, who at first had listened enthusiastically, began to

25 Probably an allusion to St Mark, 13: 31–2: 'Heaven and earth shall pass away: but my words shall not pass away. But of that day and that hour knoweth no man.'
26 She arrived back in Brno on 16 May 1919 (*Hž*, no.117).
27 Originally a village to the south of Brno, incorporated in 1919.
28 From Janáček's remark in his letter to Mrs Stösslová of 16 May 1919 (*Hž*, no.117) 'Just come to Brno and make yourself at home at our house' it would seem that the Stössels had invited themselves to stay, presumably before his next letter (3 June 1919; *Hž*, no.118).

reply tersely and crossly, and eventually made it clear that he found it stupid. My interest, however, was taken up with more serious things than the conversations of my husband with Mrs Stösslová: I'd made up my mind that Leo and Josefina must get married. Father also wanted it. I had a word with Josefina, and that nice girl who had been his friend for seventeen years said with an innocent expression: 'Der Leo hat gegen mich keine Pflicht, er ist ganz frei.'[29]

I tried all the more now to get my brother to marry her. Eventually I succeeded. Father was due to travel with me to Brno as soon as he'd put his affairs in Vienna in order. I left for home contentedly. But after a day or so I got a letter from him making excuses for not coming to Brno because the young couple had begged him to remain with them after the wedding. I wasn't angry: he'd be among his own family all the time, and I couldn't offer him that in Brno. When I and my husband went for a walk to the Špilberk[30] on the last Sunday [before he went off to Luhačovice],[31] it seemed the right moment for me to tell him what troubles I'd had with my brother and my father. He heard me out courteously, but nothing more. I saw from this that the barrier between him and my family was still insurmountable and that I couldn't count on any amicable resolution. Hardly had Leoš left for the holidays than I got another letter from Father. Full of woe. Apparently Leo had said that he didn't want to get married and Father said he didn't want to stay in this chaos any longer. He had everything packed up, he said. I clutched my head and raced off to Komárov. Luckily, because of Leoš's departure, I hadn't got round to telling my friend Mrs Žaludová that Papa wasn't coming to Brno. Now I simply gave instructions to have everything ready for him, and went off to Vienna to fetch him. Before I arrived there everything had been sorted out, they were preparing for the wedding, only this time Father didn't relent and was already getting ready to go to Brno. So I took him off. Again it was a foul journey and Papa was old for such an expedition. In Břeclav we missed the train and had to spend the whole night at the station. The people round us lay down on the ground, Father sat on the chair, I sat next to him on the case. I wrote to Máŕa to meet us, she in turn didn't get the letter. We went on our own by tram to Lužánky.[32] We couldn't manage the cases, so I went

29 'Leo has no obligation towards me, he is completely free.'
30 See p.2, fn.11; the Špilberk was a fifteen-minute walk from the Janáčeks' house.
31 Janáček started his annual holiday in Luhačovice on 6 July 1919. The Sunday before was 29 June.
32 i.e. the nearest tram stop at the time, an eight-minute walk from the house.

home with one, Father kept an eye on the other at Lužánky. Just to
make matters worse, Máŕa wasn't home. It was a job before we got
everything home. And then we still had to have a bath – we were
impossibly dirty from the whole thing. When Papa eventually lay
down, he sighed deeply: 'Oh, it's so good to be home again', and he
fell happily asleep. The next day I took him to Komárov. They
welcomed him warmly as one of the family. The next day he came
running back to us. I was frightened that he didn't like it there, that
he wanted to go away again. But he told me, completely overjoyed:
'I've come to tell you how happy I am.'

While my husband was on holiday[33] it was fine: we visited one
another, we went on walks together, we got along with one another
beautifully. We were also together at our house on the last day before
Leoš's arrival. I was cooking, Father was taking a walk in the garden.
Suddenly through the open window of the veranda I heard him
sobbing. I ran out to him. With his white head lying on the top of our
round table – the very one where Leoš had had friendly conversations
with the hens – he was crying piteously like a child.

'What's the matter, Papáček?'

'Ah, today's the last day that I'm here. From now on I'm not allowed
to come to you.'

'But I did tell you in Vienna how things were at our place.'

'Is your husband really so bad?'

'Look here, Father, how could I ask him for something like that
when I'm glad simply that I can live with him in some sort of fashion?'
He nodded his head helplessly and calmed down.

The next day Leoš made a very long face when I told him that
Father was in Brno. I apologized that I couldn't help it, that Papa was
a free agent and could do what he wanted. He said nothing more.

Father had a very unpleasant incident with the move. The cases in
which he sent all his clothes by rail arrived completely ransacked. It
wasn't at all unusual at that time of general demoralization caused by
the war. Stealing on the railways was rife and it was useless to demand
compensation: either one got nothing at all, or the lost items were
valued at their prewar price, so that the trifle was hardly worth the
effort of embarking on the complicated official route for compensation. We estimated then that Papa had at least Kč 10,000 stolen:
however, he was insured and he got Kč 5000 in compensation. So he
then had nothing to put on except what we had brought together on

---

33 Janáček was in Luhačovice until 27 July 1919.

the very first day in the hand-luggage. It was a great blow for a pensioner at a time when materials were made either from nettle fibres[34] or from paper, and for a price several times higher than good woollen material during peacetime. Pensions had still not been adjusted then and were being paid at prewar levels.

Another unpleasantness of the move was that my brother resented my father's departure. He didn't write to us at all until in August he sent a telegram – certainly thanks to Josefina – that they'd had the wedding, that they were going on their honeymoon trip to Luhačovice and that they would drop by at our house. Because my husband was away again[35] I invited them to stay with us, but out of pride my brother didn't accept this because my husband hadn't invited him. When they returned from Luhačovice they visited Father in Komárov. And hardly had they met than the two men fell out with each other again. My brother reproached my father for giving me things which he'd taken to Brno, while all the time they were lost on the railways. So these two parted out of sorts, whereas I and my new sister-in-law got on famously together.

Father lived in Komárov for about two years, then I found him a room nearer us, on Falkensteinerova [now Gorkého] with the post-office superintendent [Josef] Vyroubal. He was happy in Brno. He'd got used now to the fact that he could come to our house only when Leoš wasn't at home. Pensions had been adjusted so that he could now live decently. I always went to see him in the morning when I went shopping, Máňa and I looked after his laundry. Every week I took him with me to the Akademická kavárna[36] where we had our women's circle of friends. Apart from Mrs Zahradníková there were still a few of my longtime friends who all soon became very fond of Father. He was the only man among us. He got so used to the café that he then went there every day. His sight began to get weaker, he couldn't read, I had to tell him about everything new in the world. Things were then brightening up everywhere after the privation of wartime, it seemed that humankind would eventually become wiser and devote its strength to more sensible and more elevated things.

Meanwhile my husband's longed-for plan had succeeded. With the help of Moravian politicians and the musical profession a conservatory had been established.[37] At first it was run by a board of trustees,

34 Nettle stalks were used in the region during the First World War as a textile replacement.
35 Janáček was in Hukvaldy from 10 to 20 August 1919.
36 The Academic Café, a corner café on Falkensteinerova 11, closed in the 1990s.
37 The Private Brno Conservatory of Music, established in September 1919.

my husband was director, the composer Jan Kunc the secretary,[38] the teaching staff taken partly from the Organ School, partly from the Music School of the Philharmonic Society of the Brno Beseda. A number of excellent new teachers also came, whom the war had driven from their good posts abroad. There were plenty of students in all sections, lots of activity, work, enthusiasm. After a year, when the conservatory had proved itself, it became part of the state education system. But my husband was not appointed director again after nationalization. He became professor of the master school of composition.[39] It hurt him, he felt that with this 'elevation' he'd been sacked from his work in the conservatory and suspected that an intrigue lay behind it. Later it turned out that he wasn't wrong.

From the very beginning I was in very close contact with the conservatory: I knew about everything that was going on there, I became close friends with many of the teachers, I became fond of many of the pupils. In particular I used to like my husband's youngest pupil very much, the little boy Ruda Firkušný,[40] who used to go to lessons accompanied by his mother. It gave me real pleasure at the pupils' performances when I could see how hard these young people tried and how they were growing artistically; among them I felt like one of the family.

Time ran on. Not much changed at our place. After two years Leo and Josefina came to visit Brno again at Christmas [1922]. At first they stayed at my father's. Then my husband went off to Hukvaldy[41] and I invited the young people to stay with us. Everything went off very well, New Year's Eve in particular was a great success at our house. We stayed at home, we drank tea, wine; it was such a warm family affair. None of us dreamt that this would be Father's last Christmas. The whole winter he was completely healthy. On 25 January [1923] he had a birthday, we celebrated it in the Akademická kavárna. The ladies brought him bunches of flowers, they congratulated him, I ordered liqueurs, Father was touched and so overjoyed that at the end he even made a speech. Winter passed, on the last day of April we were at the café again, Papa chatted with us as usual, but when we wanted

38 See Glossary.
39 The Brno Conservatory was nationalized in 1920, and Janáček's pupil Jan Kunc named as director. Janáček for his part was appointed professor of composition in the master school (i.e. postgraduate division) of the Prague Conservatory. Although he gave a few public lectures in Prague, his teaching was done in Brno, for which purpose he retained his office in the Brno Conservatory.
40 The pianist Rudolf Firkušný (1912–96), after 1948 resident in America.
41 Janáček was in Hukvaldy by 28 December 1922 (see *Hž/IL*, no.214).

to leave, he could barely stand. He was scarcely able to move: I took him home and put him to bed. He didn't want the doctor. I ran home but returned again – he was sitting outside although he had a temperature. When he was no better the next day, I took no notice of what he said and had Dr Rinchenbach to see him. He diagnosed pneumonia. It was cured, Papa walked again. Sometimes right up to Koliště into the Zemanova kavárna.[42] At the end of June, however, the pneumonia recurred. It took a very serious turn. I wanted to have Father taken to hospital to the Milosrdní bratři,[43] but he implored me to leave him at home. So I engaged a nurse for him. Some time after 1 July he was in a very bad way and he said to me then: 'I am at peace and harmony with everyone except your husband. I'd like to speak to him.' I passed on the message to Leoš.

'Is it already so bad then?'

'Yes, quite bad.'

'Well, then, when I get back from Hukvaldy.'

I said this to Father. He waited. My husband returned from Hukvaldy[44] but he didn't go to see Father. Father's condition deteriorated again. He had terrible attacks, he choked, feeling relief only when the blood spurted out. And he repeated the whole time: 'Your husband, your husband.'

I didn't want to stir from Father, so Mrs Vyroubalová rushed off for Leoš. He came at once. When he saw now what had become of Father, he turned away, he ran to the window and wept. Father called to him. They embraced. In fits and starts Father told him that he'd always followed his successes with joy although they had not been on good terms. They parted reconciled.

Then it got a bit better again, the patient developed an appetite, I prepared eggs in wine for him, he even drank beer. He moved over from the bed to the easy chair, he had himself shaved, but this was all an illusion. The last two nights I didn't stir from him again, it was so bad. My husband was at Hukvaldy again[45] and I didn't want to summon my brother, who had been twice during my father's illness

42 A few blocks away from the Janáčeks' house; Zemanova kavárna [Zeman's café], a strikingly modern building by the architect Adolf Loos, was demolished in the 1960s to make way for the new Janáček Theatre. It was reconstructed (1996) in a location nearby.
43 The Milosrdní bratři [Hospitallers of St John of God] had their monastery on Vídeňská ulice.
44 *recte* Štrbské Pleso, Slovakia, where he read Čapek's play *The Makropulos Affair*. According to his letter from there (BmJA, A 6645), Janáček was planning to return to Brno in the early hours between 18 and 19 July 1923.
45 Janáček was there at least by 24 July 1923, when he sent a card to Zdenka (BmJA, A 3836).

and was not now well himself. So again I bore it all myself. The nurse urged that Father should be given the last rites. I too had already mentioned it to him earlier, but he didn't want it, so I stopped talking to him about it. But now he obeyed the nurse. On Saturday 28 July in the morning he had the last rites given to him. I wasn't present, it was too hard – I was going through this now for the third time. From that moment Papa didn't say a word to anyone. When I came to see him he seemed serious, almost not of this world. I asked him anxiously if he knew that I was near him. He simply nodded his head, I felt that he'd consciously bade farewell to everything temporal and that even I wasn't excepted from this. From then on I sat next to him silently. In the afternoon he suddenly sat up and got another attack. I supported him from behind, the nurse wiped away the blood from the front. I looked at him, his eyes bulged and he struggled terribly. Death devoured him, I called out: 'He's dying', and I ran from the room, not even knowing why myself. Mrs Vyroubalová and her servant caught hold of me and didn't allow me back again. As it was, the end came in a few minutes. When I returned, Father was lying dead on the bed without pillows. It remained for me simply to cover him with kisses, which he could no longer feel. [. . .]

I wrote to my husband in Hukvaldy that Father had died. I didn't tell him when the funeral would be, I thought that if he wanted to, there would be plenty of time for him to come. Mr Vyroubal told my brother what had happened. Father was buried on Tuesday 31 July [1923] at the Central Cemetery, in Vladíček's grave. The little boy had lain in a child's grave for eleven years, then we bought a large grave, we exhumed the little coffin and buried him again. When twenty years had elapsed I urged my husband to buy the site again but he didn't want to, resenting the outlay. So Father bought that grave for himself for Kč 300. The memorial stone which stands there now I later had erected myself. He always used to say: 'Will you visit my grave?' I go, I've been going faithfully every week now for fifteen years.

My brother and sister-in-law came for the funeral on Monday evening and stayed with me. On Wednesday morning [1 August] I got an express letter from my husband[46] in which he sent his condolences and informed me that he was arriving on Wednesday afternoon, asking me to get everything ready because he was going off again immediately to a music festival in Salzburg.[47] It galvanized us into

46 This letter has not survived.
47 Janáček was going to the First ISCM Festival in Salzburg, where his Violin Sonata VII/7 had been selected for performance on 5 August 1923.

action. My brother and sister-in-law began to pack at once and went off by the noon train. I prepared my husband's things. There was even more running around once he arrived. He had to be off again in two days, he wanted new cases, there were plenty of errands and shopping trips. I couldn't even talk with him about Father's death. Nor did he request such a talk. And so again I carried my grief alone, alone too I saw to the whole estate: the death certificate, the notary, moving out. When after his return from Salzburg my husband went off again to Luhačovice,[48] my brother arrived for his share of what Father had left. Then we both took it to Vienna. I stayed with them only a few days. I felt very low there, although my brother and sister-in-law did all they could to make my stay pleasant. But they still lived in the old flat and it all reminded me of the time when my parents were still there. In Brno it was better: here there was a continual flow of interests and duties, I had friends and acquaintances here.

And after a time another being arrived who wanted my love and who also returned my love. I was in great need of this: there was no longer Papa here, who would pet me, although I was now old; he'd embrace me and stroke me like a child and would say to me tenderly: 'Little girl, little girl!'

I felt that I was simply burning for this, to be warmly and selflessly loved by some being whom I could take into my arms and stroke, who would look at me with devoted eyes. No such human being was to be found – it was a dog who became attached to me. Čipera.[49] A miniature pinscher bitch, light-brown with a beautiful little head and doe-like eyes.[50] I brought her home not long after Father's death: she was then a small puppy. I didn't have her ears docked, nor her tail. Perhaps in the eyes of dog fanciers it was a mistake, but I looked on it as an unnecessary maiming. Just think of all that Čipinka could say merely with those two ears! How beautifully she knew how to prick them up and cleverly waggle them when she was waiting for something nice, and with what charm she tilted her little head with one cornet-shaped ear pointed and the second hanging down when she

48 On 16 August 1923.
49 'Čipera' denotes a smart, agile, nimble person or thing (the adjective 'čiperný' is frequently used of spry old people). It is not a common name for a dog. Zdenka uses a number of diminutives: 'Čipinka', 'Čiperka', 'Čipa'.
50 The breed was virtually unknown outside Germany before 1900 (the Deutscher Pinscherklub was established in 1895). It became popular between the two wars in Czechoslovakia as a *ratlík* (Zdenka's term) and also in America, where the Miniature Pinscher Club of America was established in 1929. See Plate 21 for a photograph of Čipera and Zdenka.

was observing something, or was considering something in her doggy manner. She was clean and an outstanding guard dog. She barked furiously the moment anyone touched the gate into our garden. God forbid that a visitor should touch anything there. I was always surprised at the way she could recognize good-hearted people. When people like that came to us, she made friends with them at once, remembering them long afterwards. When they opened the garden gate, she barked joyfully and when they went in she'd jump up high at them, like a deer. Then Mářa would rush off for a little bit of biscuit and surreptitiously slip it into the hand of the visitor so that Čipa would leave them in peace. And there were yet other people who, though they came to us for years, who had never done her any harm, but had always been nice to her, always caused her to growl untrustingly. In time I learnt to rely a great deal on her in this: she never made a mistake, though sometimes I discovered the truth about those people only after a long while.

Of her own accord she didn't long for motherhood and never had a litter. Perhaps because of this she kept her 'slim line' all her life. And perhaps also because of this she had an incredibly sweet tooth – I acknowledge, of course, that I and Mářa were not blameless in this. She was our darling and we both spoilt her equally badly. When she took it into her head to sleep with me in bed, she got her own way; we could never refuse her whimpering and begging. She had a way with people. She also won over our strict master and he fell warmly in love with her.[51] They had breakfast together, she lay down beside him when he composed. At first she couldn't abide the piano being played, but she got used to it in time. Only military music she detested, when she heard it, she howled unbearably. She was such a stay-at-home body, she didn't like going for walks, she was happiest 'cooking' with us at the stove and waiting until something good would accidentally fall. She soon worked out that I always brought her a lump of sugar when I returned from the café. As if she had a clock in her head, she was calm until seven in the evening, when I went off. But afterwards she didn't give Mářa a moment's peace until she went with her into the garden to look out so that she wouldn't miss her sugar lump. It sometimes happened that a guest stayed late into the night at our house. Then she was very ill-mannered: she took up a position in front of them and,

51 Some of Janáček's notes on Čipera have survived (BmJA, S 63). They span five years, from 1923 to June 1928, and consist of observations of Čipera in various situations, sometimes including the notated speech melodies of Janáček and Mářa Stejskalová, and of Čipera's responses.

through her whimpering and with her eyes, she indicated to them clearly and positively that it was high time they went. In the summer her kingdom was the garden, where she walked about and basked the whole day. She brought into our sad, depressed quietude a little merriment, playfulness, liveliness, everything for which we all longed, and which fate always smothered as soon as it began to spring to life. With her around one was able to live a little more easily.

9

Seventieth birthday. Reconciliation

On 3 July 1924 Leoš was seventy. He'd reached this age in more or less good health (there were only some signs of a hardening of the arteries) and in mental freshness which his admirers described as 'eternal youth' and which in the end fooled him too. But I knew best of all that it wasn't true, that there was a mismatch, that his body could no longer cope with the stormy tempo to which his spirit drove it. To him old age seemed a misfortune: he didn't want even to hear that he was seventy already. Whenever I wanted to begin consulting him about how to celebrate that notable day he would brush it aside, shaking his gleaming snow-white head and would burst out: 'Please don't talk about it!'

Before the summer holidays arrived and he set off to Hukvaldy, the Foerster choral society[1] prepared a little serenade for him. Professor Ferdinand Vach and his wife knew about it and came to visit us in advance. The society sang in the courtyard of the conservatory, our guests and I listened from the veranda, Leoš went to the garden gate. I was so moved that I barely took in what he was saying when he offered his thanks. Suddenly I heard him saying with a raised, almost defiant voice: 'Ten years from today I'll be standing here again.' It struck me to the core. You shouldn't have said that, I thought to myself, it's a challenge to fate.

On the day of his birthday he fled from the congratulations to Hukvaldy. Before he left we celebrated at home. I roasted a goose, I gave him flowers and a Valašské Meziříčí tapestry[2] with toadstools, Máňa gave him an exquisite little cup for black coffee. He took pleasure in the gifts but complained that he was now seventy.

On 3 July the doors at our house were in constant motion. Visit after visit, heaps of flowers. I received everything with thanks and just kept on repeating that, unfortunately, my husband wasn't at home. He meanwhile spent the day peacefully at Hukvaldy with Josefka. There they didn't trouble him with any celebration. From Hukvaldy he

---

1 Brněnský pěvecký sbor Foerster [Brno Choral Society Foerster], founded by Karel Vach, the son of Ferdinand Vach, in 1920.
2 i.e. from the town of Valašské Meziříčí in Valašsko.

looked in on Luhačovice.[3] Then some time in September or October
we set off together for Hukvaldy[4] again to pick fruit – from our own
garden around our own house, which Leoš had bought in 1922 from
his sister-in-law Marie.[5] Towards the end of the war she was so badly
off that she had nothing to live on and had to move in with her sister in
Gleiwitz in Prussian Silesia.[6] Josefka looked after the cottage for her,
living in the attic room there. After the coup d'état, when there was a
great shortage of housing, they hired out the ground floor to some
official so that Marie at least received rent from it. But it wasn't
enough for her to live on, she didn't intend to return, so she offered the
cottage for sale to Leoš. He agreed on the one hand so that Josefka
would have somewhere to live, and on the other because he wanted to
have somewhere of his own in Hukvaldy. It greatly surprised me when
he told me that he paid Kč 40,000 for the cottage; I had no idea that he
had so much money.[7] Not long afterwards he came home one day and
announced to me merrily: 'Well now, I have my own forest at
Hukvaldy.'[8] He loved that property of his at Hukvaldy, especially the
forest, although later he'd sometimes get angry: 'My forest! What on
earth do I get out of it? All Hukvaldy is making use of it at my expense
and all I do is pay for it.' However, we used to get a fair amount of use
out of the garden: we'd make *povidla*[9] at Hukvaldy for consumption
throughout the year and apple wine[10] from the apples: at the time we
drank lots of it at our place.

   With the new season the celebrations of my husband's seventieth
birthday began at the Brno theatre. The head of opera, František
Neumann, staged three of my husband's operas: *Jenůfa*, *Káťa
Kabanová* and *The Cunning Little Vixen*. The outside of our box
was always completely festooned with flowers. My husband would
much rather have run away from it, but I was proud to be beside him

3 Janáček was in Luhačovice from 15 to 30 August 1924.
4 The Janáčeks were in Hukvaldy from 13 to 27 September 1924 (see *Hž*, nos.256 and 258).
5 In 1905 František and his wife (with whom Olga Janáčková had stayed during her fateful
visit to St Petersburg in 1902, see Chapter 5) moved back to Hukvaldy, acquiring the
property which František left to Marie at his death in 1908. Janáček's purchase of the house
from Marie was completed on 31 December 1921 (Procházka 1948, 147–8).
6 Now Gliwice, Poland.
7 He probably did not; Procházka (1948, 147–8), summarizing documents of the deeds of
sale drawn up by the notary Rudolf Štursa in Místek, gives Kč 6000 as the price, made up
of a deposit of Kč 1000 and Kč 5000 on signature.
8 Janáček bought land, including part of the Hukvaldy forest, on 10 May 1924 and a
further portion on 21 April 1925 (Procházka 1948, 150–1).
9 A thick fruit preserve usually of plums, baked in the oven rather than boiled. To those who
have not acquired the taste it seems rather sour but is a sure cure for constipation.
10 This is rather stronger than English cider.

and it was a gala event for me. I remembered our beginnings, all we'd been through; I was delighted that his life's work had been crowned with such success and I asked myself whether I'd always been a help to him in this. I told myself that to the best of my feeble powers and abilities I'd always stood faithfully by his side, including those times when he didn't even want it.

January 1925 brought us the most unexpected and most beautiful thing that could have happened. Leoš was in Hukvaldy from before the New Year.[11] When he was due to return, I said to myself that I'd go and meet him. He was due to arrive in the afternoon [of 3 January] so I had my hands full with work all morning. I couldn't even read the newspaper. In the middle of all this a messenger from the dean's office of the Philosophy Faculty[12] of Masaryk University arrived with a letter. I signed for it and put it aside. When later I greeted my husband at the station, I noticed his animated face. He kept on looking at me knowingly, and suddenly said: 'Well, you see. I left as Janáček, I return as a doctor.'

I opened my eyes wide at him.

'Well, haven't you read the papers? I learnt about it on the journey from *Lidové noviny*. It's there in the daily reports.'

What a surprise that was! I told him about that letter from the university. We raced home and no sooner had Leoš got inside than he tore open the letter. They'd invited him to the dean's office. He went there the very next day and returned beaming: he'd been unanimously voted honorary doctor by the whole body of professors. His joy! The first honorary doctorate of Masaryk University! What recognition from the highest Moravian intellectuals! The graduation was to be a gala affair and was set for 28 January [1925]. There was a rehearsal for it just as in the theatre. My husband was terribly nervous; he kept repeating: 'If only it was all over.'

The day before the graduation he got a dry cough, such a strange one, going on and on without stopping – it was probably his heart. It frightened me. And with guests gathering at our house, the hustle and bustle, final preparations, I was almost in a daze. I sent Leoš upstairs to sleep and got through it all on my own, so that he could calm down. In the morning Professor Souček[13] took us by car to the Philosophy

---

11 He sent a card to Zdenka on 28 December 1924 (BmJA, A 4993), saying that he had arrived safely. He returned to Brno on 3 January 1925.
12 The equivalent of an arts or humanities faculty in Britain.
13 Stanislav Souček (1870–1935), professor of Czech language and literature at Masaryk University.

Faculty. Leoš went to the dean's office, I into the Great Hall. I was trembling with nerves. The Great Hall was full to overflowing with representatives of the authorities, schools, musical associations, there was even a deputation from the Old Brno monastery, crowds of students at the back. Finally it began. With ceremonious dignity the gentlemen from the university entered in long dark gowns and sat down in their places. Leoš, pale, behind them – to me he looked like a criminal. Exceptionally, in view of his age, they allowed him to sit down. Fanfares, a festive chorus, then the dean of the Philosophy Faculty, Professor Arne Novák,[14] began to speak. An outstanding speaker with a beautiful sonorous voice, he made the point that in Leoš were joined the scholar, the collector and the creative artist going his own, new and individual way. Although it was all indeed just as he said, nonetheless it was novel for me, I now seemed to be seeing my husband from a quite different angle from the one I was used to. Then the rector of the university, Professor Edward Babák,[15] greeted my husband and asked the proposer, Professor Antonín Beer,[16] to perform the act of graduation. Professor Beer spoke Latin and Leoš answered him – 'Spondeo ac polliceor'[17] – and then he began to speak in Czech. It was him all over. Sharp, punchy in expression, he cried when he remembered his parents; every inch an artist, a real musician, even when he spoke about his composition from a scholarly point of view. He ended by acclaiming the republic and President Masaryk. What he said was so different from the speeches of the other gentlemen. It had a wholly distinctive and unusual form – as if he were made of different stuff from them. And only when I got home, when I recovered from my stupefaction and joy, I remembered that he hadn't coughed once, that once again I'd been unnecessarily anxious.

We were then invited when Professor Arne Novák gave his dean's party; and a week after that we in turn invited all the participants to 'U Polenků'.[18] Also with us here was our longtime adviser and friend Director Mareš. It was a very cordial atmosphere and established ties of warm friendship between us and Masaryk University.

This was a joyous time – full of things which invigorated us and reconciled us to everything bad that had gone before. Things brightened up at home. We were now like two good friends. We went

---

14 Arne Novák (1880–1939), professor of Czech literature at Masaryk University.
15 Edward Babák (1873–1926), professor of physiology at Masaryk University.
16 Antonín Beer (1881–1950), professor of German language at Masaryk University.
17 'I promise and vow.'
18 A restaurant at Česká ulice 29.

everywhere together, we consulted each other. When Leoš was composing downstairs in the study[19] and something went well for him, he'd call out to me: 'Zdenka, come here', and I'd rush to him and listen, and tell him what I thought about it. Sometimes he'd play such beautiful melodies: I'd like to have heard them once more later on in the work, but he often did nothing with them and instead had yet another idea. I used to ask him: 'Why don't you stay with it just a little longer? Why don't you develop it?' And he'd smile: 'As if you understood! I for one wouldn't like it like that.'

I was content with the present state of our relationship, I didn't want anything more. I'd reconciled myself to the thought that I was here for my husband's comfort, I knew that I was financially secure. Although he didn't give me much and I continually had to scrimp and save, I was certain that he had money and that he'd give me it if I really needed it. And that was all I ever wanted. He began to be attentive and generous to me: at Christmas he gave me a whole Kč 1000 because I didn't want a present. When he was in Prague he always brought me back some little gift: perfume, sweets, gloves. What pleased me more about these presents was that he thought of me. As a result of all this, I began to revive – I'd almost say I was blooming. Once again I could dress nicely, it pleased me, I was delighted when something suited me. With surprise and delight I observed that he noticed this too. And after a while even Máňa said to me with a conspiratorial grin: 'That master of ours, he's looking at you again.'

I found it pleasant, something like that always flatters a woman. But I didn't draw any conclusion from it. Leoš continued to have complete freedom and I didn't take any interest in how he lived outside the home. I knew only that the affair with Mrs Horvátová had long since come to an end and that his relationship with Mrs Stösslová was mere friendship. She and I had already stopped writing to one another,[20] we had little contact with one another, neither of the Stössels even came to Leoš's graduation.

In the spring of 1925 we got ready for the musical festival in Prague. They were planning to give *The Cunning Little Vixen* at the National Theatre.[21] Leoš went off a few days earlier,[22] I arrived after him. In the

19 i.e. in the house, rather than upstairs in his office in the conservatory.
20 Stösslová's letters to Janáčková, quite frequent in the beginning, stopped in July 1922. Another nine letters were written in 1926 and 1927. None of Janáčková's letters to Stösslová survive.
21 The orchestral section of the Third ISCM Festival was held in Prague, 15–20 May 1925, and included the Prague première of Janáček's *The Cunning Little Vixen* I/9.
22 On 11 May (see *IL*, p.68).

hotel he received a letter from Mrs Stösslová. She wrote that she couldn't come to the première, from which I realized that he'd invited her.

The account that emerges from Janáček's letters is as follows: Janáček wrote several times to Mrs Stösslová inviting her to the première. He heard nothing and, on the assumption that no news was good news, set off to meet her at the station on Monday 18 May as he had suggested, only to find David Stössel with a message that Mrs Stösslová was ill. Zdenka found herself having to sign Janáček's letter of regret.[23]

In the evening we went to the concert [*recte* performance], afterwards somewhere with friends. I was cheerful, I felt that I was well dressed and that I looked pretty. Dr Felber[24] from Vienna paid me the compliment that I'd grown younger. It gratified me that now even other people noticed it. I thoroughly enjoyed myself and took no notice of Leoš. We returned home in a good mood, arriving at the hotel at about one in the morning. I began to undress: I had a low-cut gown of black silk and a long floral jacket over it. As I was taking it off and stood only in the gown Leoš suddenly jumped up to me unexpectedly and wanted to kiss me in the hollow of my neck. It came out of the blue, I wasn't prepared for it; I was too unused to expressions of love. I pushed him aside and said indignantly: 'How dare you!'

He didn't answer me and went out. I got undressed quickly and jumped into bed. I was upset and offended that after all that had happened he could approach me in such a way: without excuse, without permission, as if I were a thing with which he could do what he wanted when he liked. I huddled to the very edge of the bed and made out as if I were sleeping. He returned, undressed, lay down, put out the light. For a moment, silence. Then he said tenderly: 'Zdenka, come to me.'

Again I lashed out: 'What an idea! How dare you! You've wronged me so!'

'I've wronged you, I've wronged you terribly. But you must have seen for a long time now that I'd like to make amends. In Brno I was frightened for I know that you're an innocent and proud woman. Here it's easier for me.'

'No, I've worked hard for this calm. Let us just continue to live beside one another. I can't forget things. I see you continually with Horvátová.'

23 *IL*, pp.68–9.
24 Erwin Felber (1885–1964), critic and writer on music.

'Zdenči, can't you see that I'm returning to you for I've realized that you're the kindest of all the women I know. I love you again as before. Zdenčička, we can still be happy, believe me.'

'But surely you have Stösslová!'

'What an idea! We're just friends. She'll be pleased when I tell her that things are well between us.'

And he went on asking, promising, urging more and more passionately. I thought about it. What should I do? Refuse and then reproach myself for it? Who knows what he'd then do out of spite. And perhaps we could indeed live out these few last years in a happy accord. It would be nice. And correct. So then, let me not be an obstacle to this.

Without any flare of desire, without joy, in tears – I made my peace with him. It was difficult. After all those disgusting things with Mrs Horvátová it seemed degrading to me.

In the morning I was awoken by his kisses. He was happy, he was sparklingly tender, he said things which for such a long, long time I'd been unused to hearing and which nevertheless now sounded unutterably sweet to me. He was charming as before, he captivated me. [. . .] But after all those unclean experiences with Mrs Horvátová I felt a bitterness: 'Nine years, for nine years you left me aside, you kicked me out of the way.'

'Nine years, nine years', he repeated thoughtfully, 'what a waste!'

But those were only moments; at other times I was captivated by his youthful ardour, his dazzling blandishments, his passionate eloquence, so that everything else lost its importance for me. Even the Prague première of *The Cunning Little Vixen* didn't excite me as much as earlier premières of Leoš's works. Neither of us was taken with the performance. In Brno it was much more effective because it was more natural. I couldn't agree with Pujman's production at all,[25] nor even with the musical interpretation: all the bloom which had gone into it through my husband's passionate sensibility seemed to me to have been wiped off. When later we'd got back to Brno it was with some apprehension that we went to hear the very next performance of *The Cunning Little Vixen*.[26] After the performance, Leoš heaved a sigh of relief, we looked at one another and said to each other: it's beautiful after all.

25 Ferdinand Pujman (1889–1961), house producer at the Prague National Theatre from 1921. Janáček was particularly incensed at Pujman's interpretation of the end of the opera with the Forester 'convulsed in death throes' (*JODA*, LB63).
26 On 2 July 1925; Janáček wrote the next day to Max Brod saying how much he preferred the Brno version (JA ix, 187).

That time I returned from Prague happy. We went by car through Václavské náměstí to the station. At the Noltschs' house, where Mrs Horvátová lived, my loathing of her flared up again within me, but at the same time so did the joyful knowledge that she couldn't harm me any more. I looked in her windows and felt something like victory. Half questioningly I turned to Leoš: 'So it was I who won after all.' He nodded seriously and genuinely: 'Yes, it was you.'

It was a glorious trip home. Everything had become rejuvenated, joyful. Mářa stared at us uncomprehendingly. When in the evening Leoš went off upstairs to sleep as usual, I told her what had happened in Prague. She was overjoyed. Suddenly there was quite another atmosphere in the house. Cheerfulness, brightness, intimacy. We greeted each other affectionately, we took our leave with kisses when he had to go off somewhere. We spent our holidays separately again: I at Hukvaldy with Josefka, he in Luhačovice, but he often made the journey to see me and in between we used to write to one another.[27] Even Josefka noticed the change and was pleased when I told her that we'd made up.

Janáček's making up with his wife on the evening of the Prague première of *The Cunning Little Vixen* emerges in Zdenka's telling as the culmination of a long rapprochement. This may well be, but it is also clear that Janáček acted partly out of pique at Mrs Stösslová's failure to turn up to see the opera. His hurt is evident in his letters to her that followed; he even declined an invitation to visit her in Písek after the festival and in his letters to her wrote more than once that he and Zdenka had made up.[28]

In September 1925 we travelled together to the musical festival in Venice.[29] On the journey we stopped off in Písek.[30] He begged me so much to travel with him, and I was pleased that he wanted to have me there with him. Only after his death did it become clear from Mrs Stösslová's letters why he needed me there. Which is to say that even then rumours had begun flying around Písek and my visit was meant to demonstrate that there was nothing in it and that I knew about everything. [Later it transpired that] my husband had also wanted Mrs

27 Janáček was in Luhačovice from 3 to 24 June 1925 (Štědroň 1939 has 4 June, but Janáček wrote from Luhačovice to Stösslová on 3 June; *Hž/IL*, no.318). From the addresses of his postcards to Zdenka it is clear that she was in Hukvaldy at this time. Janáček himself was in Hukvaldy from 9 July to 7 August, by which time Zdenka was back in Brno (see letter to Brod from Hukvaldy, 9 July 1925; JA ix, 187–8; and letter to Zdenka announcing his return, 4 August 1925; BmJA, A 5004).
28 See *IL*, pp.68–72.
29 This was the separate, chamber section of the Third ISCM Festival (see p.191, fn.21).
30 The Janáčeks stayed overnight in Písek from 31 August to 1 September 1925.

Stösslová to travel to Italy with us; she refused in a letter to him.[31] So that everything which had made me so happy was based on a delusion: to my husband I was just a puppet which he pulled this way and that according to need. But at the time I knew nothing about all this and was pleased that at last we were travelling somewhere. All my life I'd longed in vain for us to do lots of travelling. I used to argue with Leoš about it, but he feared both the difficulties of travelling and the expense. And now I was about to see Italy, that most bewitching of all my desires.

We stayed a day in Písek, then we travelled to České Budějovice and sat next to Dr Hipman[32] and Dr Štěpán[33] in the Prague express. Leoš was hugely delighted by this meeting and assumed that we'd be travelling happily together with them all the way to Venice. But it turned out – great traveller that he was – that he'd booked another route in Brno, via Ljubljana and Trieste, whereas they were going direct via Tarvisio.[34] They were there in Venice a whole day before us. My husband fumed when we found ourselves on our own again. He was so maddened by anger that he wanted to return home. He threw the tickets to the ground. He didn't speak. In Trieste all the hotels were full, everywhere only Italian was spoken. We couldn't get a room anywhere and we couldn't speak Italian. Eventually after much negotiation a chambermaid from the hotel found us a private room. Terrible – it looked like a den of thieves. But it was clean; it turned out that it was with Slovenes and that they knew Czech from soldiers in the war. This placated us. And also we were by now so worn out that we didn't look at anything much; we didn't even eat, we simply turned in. We were just getting to sleep when a large Italian barrel organ launched into *Aida* in the courtyard. It thundered like an organ in church. With a start Leoš turned over angrily and hissed 'The devil take *Aida*, I want to sleep', and then spoke no more.

The next day we looked round Trieste. There was little time for us to take our fill of all that beauty: [. . .] it was soon midday when we had to continue our journey. In Venice Mikota the secretary of Hudební

31 Janáček in fact invited both the Stössels to Venice in his letter to Mrs Stösslová of 10 August 1925 (*Hž*, no.340). From his subsequent letters (17 August, 26 August; *Hž*, nos.341–2) it is clear that Mrs Stösslová did not bother to reply. No letter of refusal has survived. Zdenka need not have felt too aggrieved over the matter; in an earlier letter to Mrs Stösslová he wrote: 'If Zdenka wants to go to Venice, then I shall go there' (27 July 1925; *Hž*, no.336).
32 Silvestr Hipman (1893–1974), composer and official in the Umělecká beseda.
33 Václav Štěpán (1889–1944), pianist and writer on music.
34 Italian town on the border with Austria.

matice Umělecké besedy[35] was waiting for us and took us to the
pensione near S Maria della Salute.[36] We were very grateful to him for
taking care of us in this very strange city, whose language we didn't
understand. When he left, my husband told me that they'd agreed he'd
come for us again in the evening and take us to the festival concert. We
had a bit of a rest, then we got dressed and waited. No one came. The
next day it transpired that he and my husband had misunderstood one
another. And we'd looked forward to ordering supper through him;
now we were left in the lurch. We were hungry and thirsty. Leoš
already began to lose his temper asking again why we'd come, so I
went downstairs in the *pensione* to ask them to give us something to
eat. But no one there understood German, let alone Czech. So I did as
in the old anecdotes: I went into the kitchen, I pointed to the tea pot
and when I'd seen from their faces that they understood, I went
contentedly upstairs. I looked forward, by this means, at least to a
replacement for supper, thinking that with the tea they would certainly
serve pastries, open sandwiches or perhaps bread and butter. But in a
moment they brought us up – just tea. My joy was over. So from the
cases I unearthed some biscuits which I'd taken with me from home[37]
and served them with the hot water. It wasn't much use to us and so we
went to sleep hungry the second day running. But on the other hand –
the next morning! As soon as we emerged from the *pensione*, we didn't
know where to look first or what to be most enthusiastic about. Leoš
just went on repeating: 'I must come here once more.'

[. . .] In the Teatro La Fenice they gave my husband's first quartet,
that passionately emotional piece written under the impact of Tolstoy's
Kreutzer Sonata. It's said that it arose as a consequence of our marital
disagreements. That's not true: Leoš wrote it after the death of Olga at
a time when we were getting on well with one another. At the time
everybody was talking about this work by Tolstoy and it made a deep
impression on everyone, and so it's not surprising that it should have
inspired my husband too, just as *Taras Bulba*[38] did. The quartet is not
based on the experiences of our married life. Here in Venice I too was
surprised by its originality and everyone liked it very much.

---

35 Jan Mikota (1903–78), then secretary of the ISCM's Czech Section. This fell under the
aegis of Hudební matice Umělecké besedy, the music publishing house of the Umělecká
beseda. Mikota is shown with the Janáčeks in Plate 18.
36 At the east end of the Grand Canal.
37 Maybe she did, but Janáček was under the impression that they were eating Mrs
Stösslová's *buchty*, presumably given them in Písek for the journey (see *Hž/IL*, no.348).
38 Janáček's 'Rhapsody for orchestra' *Taras Bulba* VI/15, completed in 1918, was inspired
by the novel by Nikolay Gogol.

Janáček wrote his First String Quartet VII/8 in the autumn of 1923, but it allegedly incorporates material from his lost Piano Trio X/22 written in 1908: both works carry the subtitle 'after Tolstoy's *Kreutzer Sonata*'. That a work based on Tolstoy's novella might reflect the Janáčeks' marital problems is an obvious inference, given the subject matter of the Tolstoy (about an unhappily married couple), but as Zdenka stresses – and significantly repeats – it was a subject to which Janáček had been attracted artistically many years before the marriage disintegrated in 1916–17.

Zdenka's account then goes on to describe the regatta, held on Sunday 6 September 1925, with the Janáčeks sitting in their booked seats on the steps of S Maria della Salute. She also mentions a 'very nice Englishman' who travelled with them to the concerts from the *pensione*. Ten years on she had forgotten his name.

I'd have been so glad to have had a look at somewhere else in Italy, we talked about Padua, but my husband didn't have the nerve to travel on his own, because, he said, we didn't know Italian. So we returned home. Early in the morning, about five o'clock and while it was still quite dark (it was already September), a gondola came for us and while the city was still sleeping it took us silently along the canal to the station. [. . .] We travelled via Tarvisio, Dr Štěpán with us. This was in turn a different type of beauty, the splendid variety of natural scenery which we saw from the windows of the restaurant car [. . .]. Then came Vienna–Brno. Again the old tracks of everyday life.

This trip had an unpleasant sequel for us. The second day after our return my husband got pains around his midriff. He went to the doctor, who told him that it was from his kidneys and that he should take a hot bath. But it didn't seem like kidneys to either of us; we thought rather that it was fatigue after the journey. But when even after a proper rest it didn't get any better and my husband couldn't bear to have clothes on him, I conducted an inspection. Around his waist he had a wreath of large white blisters. I already knew something like that as shingles. I told Leoš. He took himself off to the doctor.

'Doctor, it's not my kidneys, it's shingles.'
'Who told you?'
'My wife.'
'Show me. Well, it's true.'

He got ointment, I smeared it on him at home and bound it up with an iodine gauze. It was a wonder he didn't go mad with the pain, he put on his clothes and rushed off to Dr Trýb.[39] The latter knew at once

---

39 Dr Antonín Trýb (1884–1960), from 1921 professor of skin and venereal diseases at Masaryk University in Brno. Three years later Trýb wrote the text for Janáček's chorus to celebrate the laying of the foundation stone for Masaryk University, IV/45.

that it was fish poisoning[40] – in Venice my husband had eaten tuna in oil – he put a new ointment on it and said that the iodine gauze was like poison for it. So at home another bath and I smeared him afresh. He went about for a long while with blisters, he endured a great deal before they dried up: around his hips he had a sort of whitewash belt from the ointment. This made me think a bit and I said to myself that the body can no longer cope with such irritating fare; I began to be very cautious in my choice of food for him.

It was already well into autumn [1925] by the time we got round to our usual Hukvaldy trip. After our return, life continued pleasantly. My husband travelled a lot to Prague, sometimes I went with him. Everywhere there were plenty of concerts of my husband's pieces. I have an amusing memory of one of them in the winter in the Brno Besední dům. At the time, Ilona Kurzová[41] played the remarkable Concertino [VII/11]; my husband, who always liked her very much, was delighted by her performance. After that followed the wind sextet *Mládí* [VII/10].[42] The clarinettist Krtička[43] had an accident: it was really cold at the time – I remember how in the interval the ladies congregated round the heater and warmed their hands – and when he transferred his instrument from the cold into the heated hall, one of the keys got damaged somehow so that it didn't give out a sound. And it was unfortunately just that note which was the most prominent in my husband's piece. The unfortunate clarinettist noticed the defect only on stage during the performance. He really couldn't do anything other than what he did: he played his part calmly omitting the non-sounding note. Apart from a few musical experts, no one would have noticed anything, after all very few knew how to get their bearings in Leoš's pieces at the very first performance. But as we sat next to one another in the front row, my husband began to fidget in his seat after a few bars, scratching his head and tut-tutting: '*Ježišmarja*,[44] what is that fellow there doing to me!'

He got more and more angry; now all the people in the vicinity were looking at us. I sat there on tenterhooks. No sooner had they finished

---

40 With the localized symptoms it is in fact more likely to have been shingles rather than fish poisoning, which would have had more generalized manifestations.
41 Ilona Kurzová-Štěpánová (1899–1975), a leading pianist, who gave the première of Janáček's Concertino (Brno, 26 February 1926).
42 Zdenka has conflated the première of the Concertino (16 February 1926) with that of *Mládí* (21 October 1924). It was at the latter that the incident she goes on to relate took place (see Svatava Přibáňová's preface to the Complete Critical Edition, SKV E/6).
43 Stanislav Krtička (1887–1969), from 1919 chief clarinettist at the Brno Theatre.
44 *Ježíšmarjá* ('Jesus Mary'); a common expletive, written in the manuscript without *čárky* [length signs] on the vowels to suggest Janáček's distinctive short-vowel dialect.

playing, than he shot out of his seat and pushed his way to the green room. I didn't hear how he tore a strip off that unfortunate player because a group of acquaintances gathered round me asking what had happened to the Maestro. I know only that before long he was back again, he ran up the steps to the stage and, bursting with indignation, proclaimed: 'Dear audience, that wasn't my composition. Mr Krtička made out as if he was playing and he wasn't.'

And again, new concerts in Prague. We travelled there together, from where my husband left for a day in Písek to see the Stössels.[45] On his return he negotiated with the Ministry of Foreign Affairs for a trip to England. Putting it into operation was chiefly the work of Mrs Rosa Newmarch,[46] a great promoter of my husband's works in England. I greatly respected that wise and highly educated woman and I know that she was fond of me too. Whenever she was in Brno she always visited us. She and I spoke German together, but we nevertheless couldn't make ourselves understood without an interpreter.[47] At that time she wanted me to go to England too but it didn't work out: it was a sort of official trip, with my husband being paid for by the Ministry of Foreign Affairs.

Leoš got enormous pleasure out of his trip to England. At first I was worried about him: partly because of his great age and general helplessness on his travels, partly because he didn't speak English. But I calmed down about it when I learnt that [Jan] Mikota, the secretary of Hudební matice, who spoke English perfectly, would be going with him. So my only worry was about warm clothing: for the journey I gave him a sweater and a new English overcoat. When I burst into tears during our parting, tears welled up in his eyes too. During that journey he was very attentive to me. As soon as he got to Prague he wrote to me, he sent a wire from Děčín, also one from London as soon as he arrived there.[48] Just at that time there was a transport strike.[49] It wasn't possible to get anywhere, he travelled all the time in the

45 Janáček visited the Stössels briefly on 19 February 1926 before attending concerts in Prague on the following two days.
46 Rosa Newmarch (1857–1940), English writer on music; after 1918 she devoted attention to the music of Czechoslovakia, in particular that of Janáček, whom she met for the first time in April 1922 (see Fischmann 1986, 49) and with whom she corresponded.
47 Since German was Zdenka's mother tongue this statement appears to be an indictment of Mrs Newmarch's German.
48 Janáček charted his progress to Zdenka mostly by postcard: from Prague (27 April 1926; BmJA, A 3941), from the Czechoslovak border town of Děčín (28 April; BmJA, A 3940) and a telegram from London (30 April; BmJA, B 994).
49 i.e. the General Strike, which broke out on 1 May 1926 and was still going after Janáček left.

embassy car. They even moved him from the hotel to the embassy to avoid difficulties with travelling. He wrote to me about everything[50] and, full of joy and excitement, I read how respected he was in London, all the places where he was invited to tea and receptions, and that he was with Countess Lützow,[51] and also that he wasn't pleased with the English performance of his pieces. He told me that they played his quartet 'like icemen'[52] and that he was very out of sorts when he heard his Concertino in their rendition. In particular the pianist[53] didn't suit him at all. He wired to Prague for Ilona Kurzová. By some oversight however, the telegram didn't get there in time, she didn't turn up and so my husband didn't permit them to give his Concertino. He also wrote to me that they wanted to take him by plane to Paris. In the end, however, he travelled by boat to Holland[54] and then home from there. He wired me from Prague saying when he was arriving.[55] I went to meet him joyfully, but I waited for him in vain. So I set off the next day somewhat uncertainly for the noon express: and on that he indeed returned. We were both overjoyed when we were together again. At home he caught me impetuously in his arms and went on kissing me so that I found it all too much. And he kept on talking about it: he had things to say all the time about that very beautiful trip. He was much taken by Holland, he kept repeating how nice the people there were and how beautiful the women. He also told me why he'd been delayed for a day. He wanted to buy some pieces of amber for me and travelled to Písek for Mr Stössel to choose them for him.[56] In the happiness that I had him home again and in my joy at his success, it didn't even occur

50 Janáček sent Zdenka a further three cards and five letters during his one-week stay in London.
51 Anna z Bornmannů, widow of Francis, Count Lützow of Dreylützen and Seedorf (1849–1916), a Czechophile Austrian diplomat, who had settled in London and who published books in English on Czech literature and history. Janáček recorded his invitation to 'lunč' with Countess Lützow on 5 May 1926 in a card to Zdenka (BmJA, A 3995).
52 *jako ledoví muži.* A reference to the lack of warmth in the English style of performance; on 3 May 1926 (BmJA, A 3877) he wrote to Zdenka that they (the Woodhouse Quartet) were playing the quartet 'correctly but coldly'. The concert, which included *Mládí* VII/10 and the Violin Sonata VII/7 in addition to the String Quartet, took place at the Wigmore Hall on 6 May 1926.
53 Fanny Davies (1861–1934), a much respected though by then elderly pupil of Clara Schumann.
54 Janáček sent Zdenka a card from Vlissingen (Flushing) on 8 May 1926 (BmJA, A 3871).
55 Janáček sent a telegram on 11 May 1926 (BmJA, B 995) saying that he would be arriving on the 12th.
56 Janáček was in Písek on 11–12 May 1926. Another reason for his late return was a reception organized at Hudební matice on 12 May to celebrate his English tour. He sent Zdenka a postcard from the event, signed by some of the guests (BmJA, A 6988).

to me that there were beginning to be rather too many trips to Písek.

Zdenka was being a little unfair. Janáček began going to Písek in 1924. In 1925 he made three trips (the last in Zdenka's company on the way to Venice) and two in 1926.[57] The increase in trips to Písek occurred only in 1927, after Zdenka sent him there herself to get him out of the way during her house-painting (see Chapter 10).

But this trip too couldn't pass by without causing a breakdown in his health. Once, soon after his return, he was getting dressed. He came to see me, saying: 'What are these cuffs you've given me?' and that he couldn't get them on. I was astonished at this, since they were cuffs which he'd worn for ages. I inspected them: they were fine. I looked at his hands; they were completely swollen so that they almost shone and were distinctly bluish. Again it was from food. He never paid attention to himself abroad, he ate too much meat. He told me that somewhere he'd helped himself to something which looked like goose blood and attacked it with gusto. Only after a while he realized that it was caviar, but since he now had it in front of him, he ate it up. I wrung my hands. I remembered the rash after his trip to Venice and said to myself that my careful choice of food for him wasn't in vain.

And again a new trip – to Berlin for the première of *Káťa Kabanová*. Fritz Zweig[58] conducted it in the theatre in Charlottenburg.[59] Leoš was determined I should go too and I accompanied him with pleasure. It was getting on for the end of May. There in Berlin I saw what it was to be a famous composer. Hardly had we arrived – I remember that it was on a Friday [29 May] – than we were showered with attention in the hotel. It was brought about by the enquiry of our ambassador, Dr Kamil Krofta,[60] whether we'd yet arrived in Berlin. The latter also came straightaway to see us in person, he invited us to Sunday lunch at the embassy, he informed us that there'd be a reception after the première and he put the embassy car at our disposal. We were delighted by his attentions. That very evening the conductor Zweig came to consult Leoš. The next day there was a dress rehearsal for *Káťa Kabanová*. It was really like a performance: there was clapping just like at a première. What a fuss around my husband! After the

57 See *IL*, 'Diary of Meetings', pp.365–7.
58 German conductor (1893–1984).
59 This was the large theatre (seating 2300), which had opened in the Berlin suburb of Charlottenburg in 1912. In 1925 it was taken over by the city as the Städtische Oper and placed under the directorship of Bruno Walter, and so began its most famous era.
60 Dr Kamil Krofta (1876–1945), Czech historian and diplomat. He was professor of Austrian history at Charles University in Prague from 1911. From 1920 he worked in the Czechoslovak diplomatic service (as ambassador to Germany in 1925–7), later becoming Czechoslovak Minister of Foreign Affairs.

rehearsal there was a photo call, painters sketched him – really everything was on a grand scale. The evening, on the other hand, was nice and intimate among the Berlin Czechs who had arranged a celebration of, I think, Palacký.[61] Dr Herben[62] made a very beautiful speech there. He also accompanied us on Sunday morning on a car trip to Sans Souci.[63] A delightful little palace; we spent several hours there walking along the terraces of the garden. Then we drove to lunch at the embassy. There weren't many of us: Dr Krofta, his daughter, Dr Herben and his son, a consulate official, several officials from the embassy and the wife of one of them. We were entertained royally: ham omelette, venison, compote, iced dessert, black coffee, liqueurs. In the afternoon we went to the zoo. On the way a Czech couple who had been at the evening party the day before attached themselves to us. Very pleasant people. They then accompanied us all the way to the hotel and told us interesting things about the conditions of Czechs in Berlin.

Monday [31 May 1926] there was the première. In the morning we drove again to the theatre – my husband wanted to talk to Zweig again – after that we wandered around Berlin on foot. Everything here seemed to me so enormous that it oppressed me; especially in the Siegesallee I had this unpleasant feeling. We were both apprehensive when in the afternoon we got ready for the theatre. Before the première we spoke with the director and the intendant of the theatre. The latter stared at me and asked me: 'Haben Sie Angst?'[64] That was probably because I was, by all accounts, quite green with fear.

We sat in the front row of the orchestral stalls. The huge theatre was packed: the whole of our embassy, the consulate, the rest an entirely élite audience, splendid instruments in the orchestra, above them the very best cast, magnificent sets, in the intervals huge applause, calls for the composer, the next day beautiful reviews – well, both of us were thoroughly delighted. After the performance there was a reception with dazzling society: Schoenberg, Schreker, Kleiber,[65] almost every

61 František Palacký (1798–1876), the leading Czech historian of the nineteenth century. The Berlin Czechs may have been commemorating the fiftieth anniversary of his death, which fell on 26 May 1926.
62 See Glossary.
63 Frederick the Great's summer palace near Potsdam.
64 'Are you afraid?'
65 The conductor Erich Kleiber (1890–1956) had conducted the Berlin première of *Jenůfa* at the Deutsche Staatsoper in 1924. Arnold Schoenberg (1874–1951) and Franz Schreker (1878–1934) were both teaching in Berlin at the time, Schoenberg as head of the composition master class at the Prussian Academy of Arts and Schreker as director at the Hochschule für Musik.

outstanding Berlin artist. Kleiber and Zweig began to vie with one another to secure the première of my husband's opera *The Makropulos Affair* for himself. Zweig wanted Leoš to sign a contract with the Charlottenburg theatre there and then. But afterwards it all fell through.[66] We stayed until two in the morning. I was overjoyed and could have happily lived such a life all the time.

The next day we wandered round Berlin again. At a kiosk my husband bought fat cigars which they called 'Jenufa'. He was sorry when he learnt that he was allowed to take only four of them over the border. So he begged the kiosk-holder at least for the cigar box. At the man's astonished glance he explained to him that he was the composer of the opera after which the cigars were named. He spoke German everywhere there; it's not true what was later said about him that he ostentatiously spoke Czech everywhere. I remember that he even made speeches in German when they gave *Jenůfa* in Berlin for the first time.[67]

We lived through glorious days there and were sorry that they were over so soon when we said goodbye at the station to the ambassador Dr Krofta and the conductor Zweig. As a final touch I got a beautiful bouquet, and the train now took us and Dr Herben to Prague. [. . .] After our usual autumn trip to Hukvaldy, Leoš didn't feel well. He didn't say anything to me and went to consult Dr Jirka.[68] When he returned home, he said to me with a laugh: 'You could have finished me off.'

I knew immediately what he was referring to. He was too impulsive in our conjugal relations, but his old body was not equal to his youthful ardour, it was too much of a strain on his heart, his breath came forced. So much so that I would be fearful and would beg him to control himself. But such talk was useless. Now, however, he had it confirmed by the doctor.

You see,' I told him, 'you didn't want to listen to me. Now it has to stop.'

He accepted this and from that moment we began to live like two good old friends. I was content, after all it was for his health and thus also for his works. And I thought, foolishly, that he'd look at it like that too.

---

66 The Berlin rivalry for the première of *The Makropulos Affair* was in fact more between Klemperer (at the Kroll Oper) and Kleiber (at the Staatsoper). The Staatsoper production was fully cast but fell through in the autumn of 1927 (see Simeone 1993).
67 Berlin, Deutsche Staatsoper, 17 March 1924. Zdenka could know about the German speeches only at second hand since she did not go to Berlin with Janáček then.
68 See p.174, fn.15.

Leoš's death

It was perhaps in October 1926 that they gave *Jenůfa* at the Prague German theatre. Leoš very much wanted the Stössels to be at the première.[1] I wasn't particularly keen to travel, but he kept on urging me to go so much that I became aware that it was very important to him that I meet Mrs Stösslová again. For when she at first replied to his invitation, saying that they wouldn't be going, he said to me: 'So now, there's no need for you to make the journey. I'll go on my own.' But then the day before his departure he ran up beaming all over: 'The Stössels are travelling to Prague after all. Get ready quickly to come too.'

He went incognito, not wanting the theatre to know that he'd be at the performance. Hardly had we put up at the hotel, however, than there was a telephone call enquiring whether the Maestro was there. He told them to say no. Then we went together to Hudební matice, where he had some dealings and from where he phoned the Stössels. I don't know which of them answered the phone, but the sudden change that came over his face the moment he heard the voice greatly surprised me: an other-worldly, dreamy expression such as I'd never seen him with before. He agreed with them that we'd meet up in the Obecní dům café. We waited for them there for ages, and it was almost time for the theatre before they appeared. Leoš's face lit up so much that it hurt me. We greeted each other, talked for a while, then Leoš suggested that it was high time to go to the performance. Mrs Stösslová refused: 'But I already know *Jenůfa*. I'd rather go to something that I don't know, and then we'll meet up in the restaurant.'

My husband and I were left dumbfounded. After Leoš's death Mrs Stösslová told me that he gazed at her in such a way that she was frightened of going to the theatre. So we went on our own, he out of sorts, I not myself because I felt that once again something wasn't quite

---

1 The première, under Alexander Zemlinsky, was at the Neues Deutsches Theater in Prague on 23 October 1926. Janáček had been invited, as he wrote to Mrs Stösslová on 29 October (*Hž*, no.411), but he did not go. By his next letter to her (31 October; *Hž*, no.412), he had heard how good Zemlinsky's interpretation was and decided to attend the performance on Friday 5 November 1926.

right. In the theatre we met the director of the [Brno] Conservatory Jan Kunc[2] and bought tickets together. Leoš's incognito didn't work: he was recognized and called for. He had to go on stage and then sat in the director's box. I caught sight of Mrs Horvátová in another box: she clapped enthusiastically. The performance was of a high standard and restored my low spirits. I was cheerful again when we met the Stössels in the Obecní dům once more. My husband proposed where we'd meet the following morning but again she put it off. Not until lunch time did we have them as our guests. They'd just fitted out a picture gallery in Karlín.[3] Leoš was very pleased to accept their invitation to go and have a look. While Mr Stössel showed me everything, Leoš walked round with his wife. Then he came to me: 'So now, I've just bought a picture.' It was a reproduction of Balestrieri's *Beethoven Sonata*.[4] Mr Stössel said reproachfully: 'But you shouldn't have.' And she, merrily: 'Well, just for luck. He's our first customer.'

They went off on Saturday evening [6 November 1926], Leoš having tried in vain to persuade them to stay longer. We remained until Sunday evening. I returned home a little alarmed, but nothing further happened to cause disquiet. It was only just before Christmas that an ugly shadow again passed fleetingly over. It was the time of the Brno première of *The Makropulos Affair*.[5] It was a great success: libretto and music united in a work of genius which in places left the spectator shattered. It seemed to me that the work surprised Leoš himself, rising above even his expectations. In the interval friends came to the box to give their congratulations. When Professor Kurzová[6] spoke enthusiastically about the new opera, Leoš suddenly blurted out so loud that the whole box heard it: 'And I wrote it, I tell you, with such a stupid woman [in mind].'[7]

Everybody froze; I rather wanted the ground to swallow me up. With her exceptional tact Professor Kurzová tried to turn the remark

2 See Glossary.
3 David Stössel's antiques shop 'Galerie Vera' opened in Karlín, a suburb of Prague, in January 1927. The Janáčeks' visit seems to have been a preview.
4 Lionello Balestrieri (1872–1958), Neapolitan painter, chiefly of scenes with an artistic subject matter.
5 Brno, National Theatre, 18 December 1926.
6 Růžena Kurzová (1880–1938), at the time professor of piano at Brno Conservatory (1919–28). She was the mother of Ilona Kurzová (see p.198, fn.41).
7 If this is an uncharitable reference to Mrs Stösslová, as Zdenka seems to be suggesting, then it perhaps reflects Janáček's current exasperation with Kamila (over the German theatre *Jenůfa* incident). The conception of Elina Makropulos as emotionally unresponsive certainly shows a certain similarity with Stösslová's attitude at the time. Some weeks later he wrote to her: 'So come and see that "icy one" in Prague; perhaps you will see your photograph' (*JODA*, VM62).

into a joke but Leoš didn't go along with it. What was I to do? Run away? And have everybody ask me what had happened? I remained and glossed over the matter as if nothing had happened. So general calm was preserved, and again things were fine between us.

Until I myself made the mistake which I'll always regret, although I tell myself that perhaps even without it all those things which were to come would have happened anyway. When before Easter 1927 we got ready for spring cleaning and I gave our house a critical inspection, I saw that it had to be painted. I arranged for a painter to come on the Tuesday after the Easter holiday. Máŕa said to me: 'There'll be lots of fuss again. When the master is at home, one can't do anything.'

It was true. During spring cleaning Leoš really got in the way everywhere and wasn't prepared to lessen his huge demands. It was always better – for him too – when he was out of the house. And then the unfortunate thought occurred to me to pack him off to Písek for that period, thinking that he'd like to go there. Indeed, he agreed to it the moment I put it to him. He went off on Easter Sunday [17 April] and stayed there for a few days.[8] Mrs Stösslová wrote to me that they were having a good time there and that it was only me that they were missing, and he himself added a few lines to this.[9] I felt sorry. But there was so much work to do – and just then I was coming to a decision about a very serious matter: an operation. Since my forty-fifth year or so I'd noticed that my neck was swelling. Not even iodine helped. This mattered to me: I had to go out frequently in society; fashion dictated a plunging neckline, it was so unpleasant. And what upset me most of all was that my husband took it so badly. Many times in company when I'd forgotten to cover up my defect he hissed at me quietly: 'Your neck.'

At that time my friend Mrs Korcová[10] had earnestly advised me to be operated on by the excellent Brno surgeon, later senior consultant at the hospital on the Žlutý kopec,[11] Dr Novotný.[12] My head was full of it, not knowing whether to take her advice or not. Hardly had Leoš returned from Písek than I told him what I had in mind. I hoped that he would advise me, but he didn't comment. I went to see Dr Novotný. He didn't want to operate, saying that it would be too dangerous, and

8 Until 23 April (*IL*, p.366).
9 Zdenka omits to say that Janáček sent a postcard on 18 April (BmJA, A 5036) recording his safe arrival, signed by 'Leoš, Stössel and Kamila' and on 21 April 1927 a letter (*IL*, pp.102–3) describing his time there.
10 Žofie Korcová (1874–1961), widow of the literary critic and Brno teacher Jan Korc.
11 'Yellow Hill', a suburb of Brno.
12 Dr Antonín Novotný (1890–1961).

advised iodine spas. I came home with this news. Leoš was evidently pleased that I wouldn't be going for an operation and immediately wrote off himself for brochures about iodine spas. I might well have gone off there, but something happened that turned everything at our house upside down again.

I went upstairs to tidy in my husband's office. He wasn't there, but once again, he'd carelessly left the cabinet open. I wanted to close it but caught sight of a few letters scattered about there. I wanted to tidy them up. And as I picked them up, I saw the signature 'Your [*Tvá*] Kamila'. It was as if someone had thrust a knife into me. I grabbed the letter and read. 'What you [*Vy*] ask of me cannot be', Mrs Stösslová wrote to my husband. And at the end 'So then – Your [*Tvá*] Kamila – that at least has already come true for you.'[13]

That at least. I knew my husband too well to imagine that it would be enough for him, and that far from being satisfied he'd go on with his vehement attack – that he wouldn't give up until he'd got everything. I pocketed the letter and, depressed, went downstairs. Máŕa at once realized that something had happened and I didn't try to hide it from her. We were both dispirited. Leoš came home. He went first into his office. After a while he rushed downstairs in a rage: 'Give me back the letter you stole from me.'

'I won't return that letter to you. You shouldn't have left the cabinet open. As your wife I have the right to keep it. You wouldn't return such a letter to me either.' He didn't say a word. Then I reminded him what he'd said to me in Prague after the première of *The Cunning Little Vixen*, I reproached him for trying to attract me to him again then and asked him why he'd taken my hard-won peace from me, why he'd lied to me that he loved me and would continue to love me. To which he answered offhandedly: 'It only occurred to me when I lay next to you.'

We didn't speak further about it. But within me all had changed. [. . .] I realized all the futility of my life, right up to the end I'd have to struggle with my husband's infidelities; not even my love was a cure for them, not even that I tried to understand him and that I'd always stood faithfully beside him, not even old age – nothing. [. . .] And when I realized this, everything lost its value for me. As before, there was the seductive thought of escaping from this life. Not by

13 Zdenka was upset by the use of the informal and familiar form *Tvá*, but in fact this form is used only once, almost in quotation marks, whereas in the remaining lines that Zdenka quotes Mrs Stösslová addresses Janáček formally with the *Vy* form (see Glossary: 'Ty and Vy'). The letter has not survived.

suicide – I'd never repeat that – but as chance would have it there was within reach the possibility of an inconspicuous and respectable death: the risky removal of that unfortunate goitre. By the morning I'd made up my mind. I went to see my brother-in-law Dressler to ask him to have a word with Dr Novotný. He was glad to do it for me: the operation didn't seem dangerous to him, in fact he advised me to go ahead with it. But in the end Dr Novotný didn't want to operate on me. He said I should go to the senior consultant, Dr Bakeš. I decided to go. Leoš was getting ready to leave for Hukvaldy. Then I remembered that I might again need written confirmation of his consent to my operation. I asked him for it and he wrote it out for me at once. We talked no more about it: he didn't care about anything and at the beginning of June[14] he went off. I wrote my will and gave orders to Máňa about what to do during my absence. Now all that remained for me was to get even with Mrs Stösslová for her deceitful friendship. I packed up the brooch which she'd given me when we were still writing to one another – again a parallel with Mrs Horvátová (she'd also given me a brooch) – and wrote a letter to go with it: 'Mrs Stösslová, Although I don't know how to very well, I'm writing to you in Czech' (beforehand, I used to write to her in German) 'so that you will understand it better. I have read your letter with the signature "Tvá Kamila" and have it in my possession. This has convinced me that you have pretended to be my friend. No married woman writes to a married man like that. I don't want to see you ever again. I am returning the brooch to you. I wore it seldom, and unwillingly.'

I sent it off and went to Dr Bakeš for an examination. He decided on an operation. [. . .]

Zdenka then provides a blow-by-blow account of the operation for the removal of her goitre, which took place under a local anaesthetic on Friday 17 June.

On Thursday [23 June] I'd already had the stitches removed when I received a telegram and at the same time a letter from Leoš.[15] In the telegram he congratulated me on the successful outcome of the operation. In the letter he wrote: 'Dear Zdenka, I thought you'd do something like that. You went like a heroine. Go on being one and ask Stösslová to forgive you for insulting her.' So that was my first greeting from home. I didn't even get cross. I just showed it to my female cousin

14 Janáček left Brno for Hukvaldy on 5 June 1927 (Janáček sent Kamila a card on the way from Kyjov; *Hž*, no.455).
15 Neither has survived.

from Třebíč, who came to visit me: 'So see what I get straight after my operation.'

In the afternoon Máŕa came. 'Madam, the master has written that he's coming home and going straight off again to the festival in Frankfurt.'[16] He'd written nothing to me about it. In the morning the doctor told me that he'd let me go home on Friday. That would have meant arriving in the middle of all that fuss over my husband's arrival and departure. I told myself that it would be better for me if I stayed in hospital. So I asked the senior consultant if I could leave on Saturday afternoon. He agreed. I gave orders to Máŕa about what to pack and what to prepare and stayed on without further ado. On Friday morning I was walking in the park when a nurse called me: 'Mrs Janáčková, I have joyful news for you. Your husband is in Brno and has phoned that he'll visit you this afternoon.'

The usual fear of my husband's arrival placed a heavy hand upon me again. In low spirits I organized matters connected with my departure from the hospital: I went to the office to pay, I thanked Dr Bakeš. Then I sat down at the open door of the room. [. . .] I heard Leoš's footsteps. He offered his hand to me: 'What have you gone and done!'

'What have I done? My neck is all right now. How many times have you drawn my attention to it with saying: "Your neck".'

'Do you need money?'

'No. I paid for it with the money which father left me.'

We remained sitting in the corridor. Nobody disturbed us there. Suddenly he asked me: 'Tell me whether you think that I have an intimate relationship with Stösslová?'

'No.'

He heaved a sigh of relief: 'Well, that's good then'. He added that on Saturday morning he was travelling to Frankfurt, and then we said goodbye. [. . .]

I waited for a long time to see whether my husband would write from Frankfurt. But it was only after several days that Ilona Kurzová wrote to me from there and he just added a sentence.[17] Then I learnt

16 The Fifth ISCM Festival in Frankfurt, at which Janáček's Concertino for Piano was played on 30 June 1927 by Ilona Kurzová.
17 Janáček wrote a postcard to Zdenka on 30 June 1927 (BmJA, A 3713), two days after reaching Frankfurt. He announced his safe arrival, he looked forward to the concert that evening and gave Zdenka an approximate date (5–6 July) of his return to Brno. Ilona Kurzová added her signature. The next day Janáček and Ilona Kurzová were two of the five signatories of a joint postcard to Zdenka telling her of the success of the concert (BmJA, A 3726).

that he hadn't travelled directly to Frankfurt, as he'd told me in the hospital, but from Prague he'd gone again to Písek, where he stayed two days before travelling to the festival.[18] He returned cold, reserved. He told me that he was going off to Luhačovice, that Mrs Stösslová would also be there. I was frightened that she'd come to us beforehand, that everything would repeat itself as with Mrs Horvátová. But Máňa reassured me: the master had apparently told her that Mrs Stösslová was already in Luhačovice. He spoke little to me and now completely avoided any talk about Luhačovice. He knew that in the hospital they'd recommended a stay in the mountains to me, but he didn't say a single word about my going somewhere with him. Suddenly, total unconcern, again Luhačovice, the hospital – everything just like ten years ago. The old wound, having healed only on the surface, ached again. He went off. He didn't write to me. That disturbed me even more. Eventually I wrote to him that he was cruel, that I was frightened that there was something the matter with him, and asked him to send me a wire saying whether he was well. He sent a telegram and he also wrote the next day. He apologized and made excuses. From then on he sent me news of himself.

The sequence of events as described by Zdenka is not corroborated by the picture that emerges from Janáček's letters and cards to her.[19] He arrived in Luhačovice on 16 August and wrote to her immediately that day, describing the result of his medical examination. He wrote a postcard on 20 August and from 22 August he wrote to her most days until his departure. The telegram survives (BmJA, A 5029), but was sent a week into his stay, on 23 August. The letters of 22, 25 and 27 August all make some attempt to pacify her. Perhaps they succeeded; by 29 August the tone is cheerful and he described day-to-day trivia such as another visit to the doctor and a 'delightful black dog' that spa visitors were playing with; by 31 August he was speculating what food Zdenka would be welcoming him back with ('a young hare or a goose?').

Once he boasted to me that he'd bought magnificent original paintings from Mr Stössel which were very valuable and which he'd certainly sell at a most advantageous price to a big gallery.[20] Since I knew my husband's business talents, I took this report of an 'advantageous purchase' with a pinch of salt. The Stössels were then in financial straits, Leoš was well-off, I suspect that their plans for him were of a

18 Janáček spent two days in Písek (5–6 July 1927; see *IL*, p.366), thus after rather than before the Frankfurt festival.
19 All in BmJA.
20 The paintings were two long panels by František Dvořák (1862–1927) entitled *Laškující amorci* [Dallying Cherubs]. According to the original owner, they had been exhibited in Munich, an assertion later found to be false (*Hž*, no.491).

completely commercial nature. He was in Luhačovice for three weeks, it was a hard time for me which became more bearable only when I learnt that Mrs Stösslová had left.[21] Leoš and I had arranged that straight after his return we'd leave for Hukvaldy and that we'd stop off in Radhošt'[22] on the way. So when he was due to return, I prepared everything for our departure. But instead of this he wrote to me that although he was coming home he would be leaving again immediately for Písek, where the pupils of Professor Ševčík[23] were giving his First Quartet and wanted the composer to be present. Only then would we go to Hukvaldy. The postponement annoyed me, although once again I said nothing to him when he arrived. Only Máŕa told him: 'Doctor, the mistress said that if that trip to Hukvaldy would have to be put off for a long time, she'd rather not go at all – that it wasn't worth it.' He said nothing in response, but nevertheless returned early from Písek.

Janáček mentions arrangements for the trip to Radhošt' in his letter to Zdenka of 27 August 1927.[24] The next day he wrote again saying that the Lipkin-Bennett Quartet from Philadelphia, then studying with Ševčík, wanted to play his quartet in America and asked him to listen to it in Písek on 9 September. He asked them to put off the concert by a month. If they could not postpone it, he would travel to Písek for a rehearsal on 8 September.[25] By the time he wrote to Kamila Stösslová on 1 September the plan had crystallized into his going to Písek for rehearsals on the 8th and the 9th, but not staying for the concert on the 11th.[26] He seems to have stuck to this plan, since he wrote to her from Brno on 11 September.[27]

We went off [on 12 September].[28] It was rotten weather, we'd have done better to have travelled straight to Hukvaldy. But my husband had already written from home to the painter Ondrúšek[29] at Bystřice pod Hostýnem suggesting that he and his wife accompany us to Radhošt'. Painfully, I suspected from this that he didn't want to be alone with me. Although he waited for us in Bystřice, Ondrúšek excused himself from going with us, saying that he wasn't ready since

21 Mrs Stösslová left on 28 August; Janáček's remaining days in Luhačovice (until 2 September) were spent writing her mournful letters about how empty the place was without her (*Hž/IL*, nos.474–81).
22 See Glossary.
23 Otakar Ševčík (1852–1934), internationally known violin teacher. In 1906 he retired to Písek, where he attracted a colony of outstanding young violinists.
24 BmJA, A 5031.
25 BmJA, A 5032.
26 *Hž/IL*, no.481.
27 *Hž/IL*, no.484.
28 The date of departure is given in Janáček's letter to Zdenka of 9 September 1927 (BmJA, A 5037).
29 František Ondrúšek (1861–1932). After a successful career as a portraitist in Germany, Ondrúšek retired to live in his native Bystřice pod Hostýnem in Moravia in 1920.

he'd only just got the letter, and that his wife certainly wouldn't go. But my husband tried so long to talk him round that Ondrúšek decided that he'd follow us on the next train to Frenštát. From Radhošť he'd then travel with us to Hukvaldy to give his opinion on the new original paintings which Leoš assumed that Mr Stössel had already sent to Hukvaldy. Ondrúšek went home to get himself ready and we continued by train to Frenštát. We reached our destination at noon and had to wait until evening for Ondrúšek. So I suggested that we travel to Kunčice because there was an excellent restaurant there. After lunch it stopped raining and we went for a walk. Then it all came back: we'd been here once with Olga, on her last expedition from Hukvaldy. We went to the hotel where we'd stopped off with her then, but in its place there was now a workers' convalescent home. I said to myself how quickly everything changes on this earth. At this moment Leoš began talking about Mrs Stösslová. How jolly it was with her, he said, describing how they'd walked together around Luhačovice and laughed that people would think God knows what about them while in reality there was nothing at all. 'And you know, I don't need a woman at all any more, those things have quite passed me by.'

Why was he telling me this? I knew very well that his infatuation wasn't yet at that stage and in the hospital I'd told him that I didn't consider his relationship was an intimate one. So it had a different drift and I guessed what it was: he wanted to make it clear to me that he didn't need me. I got so angry that it made me sick when we returned by car to Frenštát. All the calm which I'd faked in the train, all the put-on cheerfulness was gone. A little glass of gin in Frenštát revived me at least enough for me to welcome Ondrúšek and continue on our way by car to Radhošť. We stayed in Tanečnice. It would have been so beautiful there if I hadn't had such worries. But instead I talked in my sleep, and when Leoš woke me, I began crying. He tried to pacify me, saying that Mrs Stösslová had wanted to write to me. I replied that I wouldn't accept a letter from her. And I didn't sleep again all night long. We stayed a few days. We went on lots of walks, I in front, Leoš and Ondrúšek behind me. Ondrúšek was very attentive and kind to me: he'd been in Luhačovice previously and had worked out what was upsetting me again. And yet another feeling ruined what would have been a nice stay: the suspicion that I'd never see Radhošť again, so that I walked around everywhere as if I were saying goodbye. I looked back at Radhošť for a long time when once again we went by car down to Frenštát. The coachman from the Hukvaldy brewery was waiting for us and drove us to our house.[30] Ondrúšek, however, didn't stay with us, he lodged at the castle with Archbishop Prečan,[31] with whom he'd been a fellow student. His trip to look at the paintings was all in vain – they weren't yet in Hukvaldy. But when we talked about them among ourselves, he told me that by all accounts Leoš's purchase probably wouldn't prove to be so marvellous after all.[32] Leoš and I were reserved with one other, and this troubled me. When even Josefka noticed it, I told her what the matter was again. She said, without any sign of sympathy: 'Heigh-ho, these old gentlemen, they get up to such tricks.'

Leoš went around completely out of sorts. He wanted a change the whole time, he couldn't stick to one place. He had permission to hire the estate coach and on this occasion he made great use of it: we rode around a lot. On one occasion we went to Místek. We kept on recalling the early days there, we said to ourselves that only the two of us were left from the whole of that company, we thought of 'The Frýdek Madonna'[33] from Leoš's [piano] work, *On the Overgrown Path* [VIII/ 17], then Leoš decided that we'd visit his former pupil Kolařík,[34] who was choir director here. Poor thing, he took great pleasure in our company, he plied us with wine, but then became melancholy, complaining that he wasn't well. We had a nice chat, we parted from him affectionately, and drove home. Two days later, my husband was opening the post and remained sitting rigidly as if he'd received a sudden blow: 'Kolařík is dead.' He died the very night that we visited him[35] – he'd had a heart attack. I wanted us to go to the funeral, but my husband feared that it would upset him too much. He always avoided funerals. For a long time afterwards we couldn't get over it.

[. . .][36] Even when we were in Hukvaldy my husband didn't stay at home, we always went for walks, mostly in our forest. How many

---

30 This was Janáček's usual arrangement for getting to and from the station.

31 Dr Leopold Prečan (1866–1947), from 1923 Archbishop of Olomouc.

32 Ondrúšek had no inhibitions about conveying his view to Janáček either, as the latter noted in a letter to Kamila Stösslová (26 September 1927; *Hž*, no.493). When Janáček appealed to the Prague collector Otto Kretschmer he heard that the painter František Dvořák had 'no significance in Czech painting' (*ibid*). Readers may judge the quality of the pictures for themselves from the reproduction of *Dallying Cherubs* in *IL*, Plate 37.

33 Like Buda and Pest, Frýdek and Místek have become one, bisected by a river. Although in the case of Frýdek-Místek the union took place only later, it would have been perfectly natural in 1927 to think of Frýdek when one was over the river in Místek.

34 František Kolařík (1867–1927) studied at the Brno Organ School in 1882–5. He was organist and choir director in Místek from 1886 until his death. He often accompanied Janáček on his folksong field trips in the area.

35 Kolařík died on 20 September 1927.

36 Description of visits to Příbor, Štramberk and to see Dr Hrstka's collection of Moravian folk ceramics and embroidery omitted.

times we sat on the bench where Leoš later caught his death! You go
for a long time through the forest, you walk uphill the whole time and
you get quite tired, but it's well worth it. A little path suddenly opens
out, a young maple rustles here above the simple wooden bench and,
when you sit down on it, a vista of part of the magnificent Lašsko[37] lies
before you: there are waves upon waves of hills, forest after forest
murmurs, one forest is crowned with an old castle, while further
down, in Podoboří and Podlesí, it's white with cottages. [. . .]

But even in this tranquillity, in this beauty I didn't find peace of mind
during these holidays: here more than anywhere else I was anxious
and sad. Leoš sat next to me well wrapped up in his coat – up there on
the hill it's very windy, so for that reason I always used to take our
coats with me even when it was really beautiful weather – he didn't
talk, but he was peaceful while I was full of anxiety, full of forebodings
which I was unable to account for.

As at other times we picked the apples, we made wine from them,
and then we prepared to leave. My husband was due to travel to
Berlin, where Klemperer was conducting his Military Sinfonietta.[38]
Before leaving I also went to say goodbye to Mrs Rakowitschová.[39]
When I caught sight of her old bitter memories swept over me, but
because it was now a matter of indifference to me I spoke openly with
her as had never been the custom before.

'Mrs Rakowitschová, I've come to say goodbye to you. I doubt that
I'll ever come to Hukvaldy with my husband again.'

'Why?'

I told her that he had a new relationship again and that I suspected it
would end badly between us. And then I suddenly turned the
conversation directly to what had once so bothered me: 'Come on,
tell me – we're both old now and it was all over long ago – what sort of
relationship did you have with him?'

She was taken aback, but then she said to me: 'I can assure you that
there was nothing bad in it. Here and there a little kiss, but we didn't
do bad things together. I'm glad that I can tell you.'

At home Josefka was curious about what we'd said to one another. I

37 Janáček's native region; see also Glossary: 'Lachian/Valachian'.
38 Like her husband, Janáčková refers to the work by the title given on the manuscript and
at the first Brno performance. The published title – the standard title today – omits 'Military'.
Otto Klemperer conducted the Berlin State Orchestra at the highly successful Berlin première
on 29 September 1927 at the Kroll Oper.
39 See pp.52–3.

told her. She was appalled; she said how I could ask such a thing.

In Brno there was lots of work to do. I spent all my time working so that I wouldn't keep on brooding on my woes. Leoš went off to Berlin, he wrote to me coldly from there,[40] then he returned, and began to go to Písek more and more frequently.[41] With all my strength I made myself keep calm so there'd be no scenes at our house. I was terrified of Christmas. I thought that he'd go off again and leave me. When he told me that he'd be staying at home, I was overjoyed. At once I began to prepare for the most beautiful Christmas holidays. I bought him a grey silk scarf and some other little trifle and he for his part gave me Kč 1000 and brought me a spray for perfume which I'd wanted. To make sure he'd really enjoy it, Máňa and I took great trouble over the dinner. He used to like having roe in the fish soup and then carp in aspic: we always garnished it so decoratively that Leoš used to say it was a pity to eat it. We'd have fried fish with celeriac salad, then apple strudel, then various sweet biscuits – we used to cook as many as fifteen different varieties – fruit, beer, wine. In recent times we'd cooked even more carefully than before. I knew that Mrs Stösslová couldn't compete with me here at all. Leoš, who was used to his food being well prepared, well presented and at the same time quite light, was taken aback several times by her cooking and even said so to me at home. So I tried to attract him to me at least in this respect. And on that Christmas Eve I succeeded. He got himself into a good mood, he was kind and I was too. On the grand piano we always used to have a tiny artificial tree beneath which lay the presents. This time we stood for a long time in front of it and reminisced – Leoš spoke about my parents when they were still alive. I was moved by it and it brought me closer to him again. We parted in friendly good humour to go to sleep.

But the very next day it all went wrong for me. A package came from Písek – by express post. There were sweets in it – probably for me – and some sort of bright red tie.[42] The package gave me the cold shivers. But my husband joyfully began opening it and immediately boasted to me about what he'd got. I reminded him that once upon a time I'd also given him expensive and carefully chosen ties and that he'd always pooh-poohed them and that he never liked getting

40 Janáček went to Berlin on 28 September. His postcard from Berlin on his second day (BmJA, A 5038), the day of the première of the Sinfonietta, is full of news and is not noticeably cold in tone.

41 From October to December 1927 Janáček spent three to four days in Písek each month (see *IL*, 'Diary of Meetings', p.366).

42 The package indeed arrived on Christmas Day, as is corroborated by Janáček's letter of thanks to Kamila (*Hž/IL*, no.545).

practical presents from me. I didn't accept the sweets and later, after the holidays, Leoš took them off to Hukvaldy. The package disturbed me dreadfully, but I controlled myself. And that was good. At least the semblance of Christmas peace was maintained, neither of us uttered a bad word, we went off for walks together, to the café, even New Year's Eve was nice. At first Leoš wanted to go to the Zemský dům,[43] but then we said to ourselves that we'd rather stay at home. After a good supper with beer and wine I mentioned before it ended that at ten the next day we'd have pig's chin – which he loved eating. After midnight we wished each other a Happy New Year and went to bed.

The saying goes: as at New Year so the whole year. That 1 January 1928 was truly a correct forecast of the whole of that unhappy year: it was the worst New Year of my life. At about eight o'clock Leoš came down for breakfast as usual. Mářa was at church, I served him coffee myself. He was irritated in some way. At first he didn't talk, then he blurted out: 'I'm going off to Prague for a meeting of the folksong committee. And then I'll go to Písek.'

Písek again, first thing in the morning on New Year's Day! After a pause I asked dejectedly: 'And must you stop off in Písek every time you go to Prague?'

He banged his fist on the table making the plates jump. I thought that he was going to throw them all at my head. Angrily he shouted: 'All you ever do the whole time is suspect me!' And now it all rained down on me: that I didn't understand him, that only at the Stössels did he feel happy and that at our place it was miserable, that he could have stayed there the whole holiday period but out of consideration for me he'd stayed at home and now what did he get for his pains? I started weeping. He began to get dressed. He calmed down. Then he called to me: 'Bring me that new tie that I got from Stösslová.'

I felt that something nasty was on the way again, but I went and got the tie. He knotted it in front of the mirror in my bedroom: it was garishly red and clashed violently with his pure white head of hair but he was wholly and blissfully taken with it. Then he picked up the tie-pin which I'd given him once: 'And now that tie-pin from you. You see, the tie from Stösslová and the tie-pin from you.'

Well, he really succeeded with the symbolism. This was how he'd have wished it: both her and me, the two of us at once, I housekeeper

43 Regional House, built in 1924–5 on the corner of Kounicova ulice (the Janáčeks' street) and Žerotinovo náměstí. There was a French restaurant there (now the reading room of the University Library) where Janáček proposed taking Mrs Stösslová in his letter of 6 May 1927 (*Hž/IL*, no.441).

and confidante, she mistress and 'muse'. My heart ached with disgust, but I kept quiet since that was the most effective defence. Máňa meanwhile had returned and I began to get ready for church. He came from his study to see me:

'And when are we going to eat that pig's chin?'

'I've lost my appetite for it.'

'If you don't want it, I don't either.' And again he fulminated that I was ruining his New Year. I felt desperate. I shouted to Máňa: 'I'm going, but I don't know if I'm coming back.' I ran outside.

I stood on the street and didn't know what to do. Some acquaintances passed me by and with a smile wished me a Happy New Year; and I implored them: 'For God's sake don't wish me happiness and contentment, I'm desperate.'

My legs carried me to St Tomáš's,[44] but I couldn't pray, although I calmed down a bit. I began to think about it all sensibly. I told myself that it would be best if I returned home and said to my husband: 'All right, you continually reproach me for being unnecessarily suspicious, that your relationship is purely platonic. So I'll go with you to Písek, there everything will be aired and sorted out and everything will be all right again.'

With that decision I came home. But my husband wasn't there. I went into the kitchen. At that moment someone rang the bell. My friend Mrs Korcová had come to wish me a Happy New Year. Máňa went to open the door for her and asked her not to come to us that day, that it wasn't the right mood for it. But she wouldn't be put off and came to see me anyway. At that moment Leoš returned. I didn't want to delay my decision and went immediately to see him in his study and told him what I'd made up my mind to do while in church. He looked at me with alarm and blurted out: 'They'd throw you out.'

'So now: I knew that you wouldn't agree because what you're trying to tell me isn't the truth.'

But now the storm broke. It was terrible. Mrs Korcová ran off. She said later that she was trembling the whole day. No one had any appetite for lunch or tea, each of us went around in a daze; the whole day was a write-off. When it began getting dark, Leoš sat down at the piano. I thought it over for a while and plucked up courage, then I sat down next to him: 'Look here, must there really be such hell all the time?'

44 Built by the Augustinians in the fourteenth century, it has served as a parish church since 1784 and was Zdenka's nearest church.

He started crying. Again he reproached me that I'd spoilt New Year for him. I was resolved that nothing would make me argue with him any more, that I wouldn't react to any reproaches, and that I'd calm him down at any price. So I knelt down to him, I tried to talk him round and asked his forgiveness. He sat motionless. But nevertheless he too began to calm down, so that he even asked me for supper. We ate it, it made me feel faint. I went to sit down in the study in the armchair, wanting to rest there in the dark. Suddenly it seemed as if the ceiling was falling down on me. I wanted to shout, but only a moan came out. Leoš rushed up, he put the light on, I saw that he was frightened that something might happen to me. He sat down next to me and said: 'It can't go on like this, we must make an end of it.' He wanted to remain downstairs with me during the night, but I refused. Even he needed his rest. Bruised, exhausted, depressed, we parted on that ill day, our last New Year's Day together.

On 6 January he went off to Prague and from there to Písek. On 12 January he was home again.[45] He sat down to breakfast and was reading his favourite *Lidové noviny*.[46] Suddenly the paper rustled in his hand:

'Těsnohlídek is dead', he burst out agitatedly.

'That's not possible! Only if he did it himself.'

'Yes, he shot himself.'

That gentle, dear poet, whose verse in *Lidové noviny* we read with such pleasure, a good person, who so loved nature and the unnoticed poor,[47] who had introduced into our country that beautiful custom of Christmas trees in town squares, for my husband and myself he was above all the author of the text of *The Cunning Little Vixen*. Leoš was much taken with it when it came out in *Lidové noviny* as a serialized novel with Lolek's pictures,

---

45 Janáček went to Prague on 6 January to meet Gustav Holst, who was then in Prague (the meeting was postponed to the next day) and then to Písek on Sunday 8 January. He returned to Prague early on Monday morning in time for a meeting of the Folksong Commission. He was back in Brno on 11 January.

46 [People's Paper]. Daily Brno newspaper founded in 1893 as the organ of the liberal Lidová strana [People's Party].

47 Rudolf Těsnohlídek (1882–1928) was well known as feuilletonist and law reporter in *Lidové noviny*. In the latter capacity he acquired an unrivalled knowledge of characters on the edge of Brno society. His love of nature is evident in his best-known work today, his novel *Liška Bystrouška* [The vixen Bystrouška], the basis for Janáček's seventh opera, *The Cunning Little Vixen* I/9. He shot himself in the editorial office of *Lidové noviny* on 12 January 1928.

from which it really originated.[48] With great zest he'd turned the tale into an opera. He wrote the libretto with Těsnohlídek's novel in front of him, composing the music at the same time. He often used to talk to me about it. He said that he liked the idea that animals could do and say things on stage that people wouldn't be allowed to. He had in mind chiefly Bystrouška's[49] behaviour.

In addition, Bystrouška had also brought us close to the Těsnohlídeks. We often sat with them in the café. I liked them both, she[50] always elegant, slim, a chatty, pleasant companion. As my husband told me about Těsnohlídek's death, I thought a great deal about how she'd take it. I was terribly upset when later my husband returned from the post with the news that she too was dead. With seeming calm she'd accepted the news of her husband's death; then she saw to it that she was left at home alone and gassed herself. I went to the funeral on my own, my husband having already set off for Hukvaldy.[51] Seeing those two coffins side by side gave one a real shock. There were no funeral services, they took them from the Arts and Crafts Museum building[52] to the náměstí Svobody, where they loaded them into cars and took them off to Pardubice for cremation.[53] I was moved almost unbearably when Těsnohlídek's old father made the sign of the cross over the car as the door was being closed. I could hardly make my way home, I couldn't think of anything else. I wrote to Leoš in Hukvaldy, describing what effect the funeral had had on me and that I wouldn't want to outlive his own death, that I wanted to share that with him too. He didn't answer me. I was in a strange mental state: our disagreements and the Těsnohlídek tragedy heightened my sensitivity towards every piece of news about a broken marriage. One day or other I read in *Národní politika* that a man had killed his wife out of jealousy. Again it upset me as if it were something extremely momentous and when, as every day, I sent *Lidové noviny* to Leoš in Hukvaldy, I enclosed this news item with it. By return I had an indignant letter demanding why I sent such things to him and asking

48 Dr Bohumil Markalous, an editor on *Lidové noviny*, acquired some 200 sketches by the painter Stanislav Lolek depicting the adventures of a clever vixen, who constantly outwitted the local forester. Těsnohlídek was instructed to provide a text to accompany them. The result was serialized in *Lidové noviny* from 7 April to 23 June 1920.
49 Bystrouška ['Sharp Ears'], the animal heroine of Janáček's opera *The Cunning Little Vixen*.
50 Olga Těsnohlídková, née Vasická (1893–1928), was his third wife.
51 On 14 January 1928 (Janáček wrote a note to Kamila from Kojetín, on the way; *Hž/IL*, no.562).
52 Now the Moravská Galerie, Husová třída.
53 There was no provision for cremation in Brno until 1930.

me for an explanation.[54] But meanwhile I'd calmed down again so that I could explain to him that I'd not meant anything by it, that I was just too upset by the funeral. My letter, however, did not reach him in Hukvaldy; by then he was in Prague for the première of *Káťa Kabanová*.[55] He sent me a letter from there saying that the change of surroundings had had a good effect on him, that I too needed it and that therefore next time I should go to Prague with him.

I've no idea what had had such a good effect on him there; on the contrary, I learnt that he had an unpleasant incident there. The Stössels also arrived for the première. Before it, my husband met his niece Věra in a café. She warned him against the Stössels, of whom she'd heard from a reliable source that all they wanted was to exploit my husband financially and that they'd boasted that they would inherit from him. Leoš was taken aback but he parted with Věra amicably. The next day, however, he arrived at her flat with Mr Stössel, who indignantly asked Věra to name the gentleman to him, saying that he'd sue him. Leoš's niece didn't take fright, she proclaimed that she'd reveal the name only in court. Mr Stössel went off with this affair unsettled, but my husband stayed on. Angrily he laid into Věra and then went off in a rage. From that moment he didn't want to know his niece. Both described the incident to me in letters.[56] The result of this well-meant warning was that Leoš now travelled to Písek every fortnight.[57]

Now he found another pretext for his visits: he said that Mrs Stösslová inspired him in his composition. He said he was happy only with them, only there did he feel at home; Mrs Stösslová's old mother was said to love him like a son.[58] But I was certain, given his mood when he returned home, that they were setting him against me while he was there, that Mrs Stösslová now hated me. I also hated her: for her false friendship, for luring my husband away, for depriving me of my peace. I was convinced that their affectionate feelings were not

54 The 'indignant letter' was written from Prague on 20 January 1928 (BmJA, A 5048) complaining that he was getting anonymous newspaper cuttings from the papers and asking whether the sender was his wife. Janáček wrote a similar letter the next day (BmJA, A 5050) saying that it was having a terrible effect on him.
55 The première was of the first German production of the work in Prague, at the Neues Deutsches Theater, on 21 January 1928.
56 Neither letter has survived, but Janáček commented on the incident several times in his letters to Kamila (e.g. 29 January 1928, *Hž/IL*, no.571; 19 February 1928, *Hž/IL*, no.589). In the latter letter he describes discussing it with Zdenka 'in peace, and in quietness, and reprovingly'.
57 Janáček made two trips to Písek in February 1928, three in March, one in April (though he also met Kamila in Prague that month), one in June, and none in May or July.
58 Mrs Jetty [Henrietta] Neumannová was born in 1865 or 1866 and was thus at least eleven years younger than Janáček.

based on real love for Leoš, that they would have mocked him if he'd been poor and unrecognized. Had I not witnessed so many times how that lady really regarded my husband's art? She seemed to me to be even more dangerous than Mrs Horvátová: the former was a whimsical, fickle actress, while here was a clever businesswoman.[59] And I had no idea how far she wanted to take this play-acting with my husband.

And Leoš wouldn't listen to reason. Blindly he rushed into it, as if he was dazed. Eternal youth, free and passionate love, tempestuous desire for life's pleasures danced its phantom dance before him and he wanted to grasp it with his elderly hands. I couldn't avoid seeing that he was rushing headlong to disaster, my instinct now shouted aloud. I knew him too well to be talked into something about his lady-friend and muse. The powerful genius of his art didn't need a woman for it to work, it was inherited and to an even larger extent God-given. Without her it would have crystallized in some other way and perhaps to even greater things. However much he wanted to hide it from himself and excuse himself in his own eyes, I knew for certain that it was only his ageing manhood which drove him all the time to Písek. I was ashamed of it. I wanted him to be morally above this. And – I also wanted to have him only to myself. Those were desperate times for me. I even used to get palpitations from it all.

On 22 February he set off for Prague to attend rehearsals for *The Makropulos Affair*. He wanted me to join him on 1 March. The fact that he'd invited me didn't prevent his going off to Písek from 25 to 27 February. When I learnt about it I no longer wanted to go to Prague. I thought that he was inviting me there only out of pity. And that was something I didn't want to accept. But then he wrote to me again, and even sent a telegram; Mářa kept on at me trying to persuade me to go, so I went. He came to meet me; he was pleased that I'd fallen in with his wishes. But he made the point that I didn't look well.

The première was a success. The evening after was also a success, which we spent with the whole company in the hotel Šroubek.[60] I got into a good mood and began to tell myself that I saw everything too blackly, that it would be put right again as so many times before. I cheered up. The next day on a walk through Prague I bumped into Mrs Horvátová. She looked on me angrily, I responded with a smile.

59 Mrs Stösslová was not a businesswoman, nor do her surviving letters suggest any interest or talent in business matters.
60 The hotel, in Václavské náměstí, included a well-known restaurant, the Café Europa.

That brighter moment was too precious for me – and indeed it didn't last long either. At noon Mr Stössel phoned Leoš, suggesting they meet in a café. Leoš invited me too, but I refused. He returned home beaming, with a new tie-pin in his tie from Mrs Stösslová. My good mood vanished. I remembered the scene on New Year's Day, his 'the tie from Stösslová and the tie-pin from you'. Now that he also had a tie-pin from her, my one could be pensioned off. But it was necessary to preserve decorum. In the evening there was a concert at the Smetana Hall, the pianist Hollman played my husband's Capriccio excellently.[61] On 3 March we travelled home; it would never have occurred to anyone that this would be our last trip together to Prague.

On 7 March Mr Stössel arrived in Brno. He needed my husband to pull a few strings. He was a foreign national from Lwów and on the basis of some new edict he was now going to have to return there. It goes without saying that Leoš did everything possible to help him to become a citizen of our state.[62]

The day afterwards, on the other hand, there was a pleasant event: Mrs Horvátová sent me a letter. I didn't open it and sent it back in another envelope. I told my husband about it at midday. He was surprised: 'What does that woman want from you?'

'She's surely telling me that you've got another lady love.'

'That's possible', he agreed. But he didn't praise me for sending the letter back unopened.

On 22 March he went to Prague again and from there, naturally, to Písek. He returned completely ill,[63] but a fortnight later he travelled there again.[64]

Everybody now knew about Leoš's new passion. They laughed at it, they pitied me, they slandered us, they informed me about what was going on in Písek. I heard on the grapevine that Mrs Stösslová was saying that we had a large estate, that I was preparing two rooms for

61 Janáček's Capriccio for piano left hand and chamber ensemble VII/12 was written at the request of Otakar Hollman (1894–1967), who gave the première in Prague on 2 March 1928.

62 Zdenka does not mention her own attempt to do the opposite, by suggesting, in her letter to Joža Janáčková of 8 March 1928, that Joža's daughter Věra might try and prevent Stössel's application going through (BmJA, A 6429).

63 Janáček arrived in Písek on the evening of 23 March 1928 and left for Brno on the morning of 25 March. There is no evidence that he was ill on his return; Zdenka possibly confused this with Janáček's trip to Písek in 8–12 December 1927, when he arrived back with a bad cold.

64 Janáček's next trip to Písek was only in June 1928, but he did meet Mrs Stösslová in between in Prague, 7–10 April.

her so that she could spend the summer there with her family.[65] I learnt that their financial circumstances were worse and worse all the time, something I'd thought for some while when I saw how my husband kept on lending them money.[66] He didn't brag of it to me, but I couldn't help noticing it.

At the beginning of April the *Glagolitic Mass* was being given in Prague in the Obecní dům.[67] A strange celebration of God. When my husband was composing it he used to say to me: 'Now I'll write a cheerful mass for the people.'

I didn't know what to say about it when I heard it for the first time. Certainly it wasn't the way in which I addressed God. My husband's relationship to God was not at all clear to me; he never stood in the way of my religious duties, but he never took part in them himself. However, he had required that our children should pray. He never observed Friday fasting, saying that he'd fasted quite enough as a chorister, but he observed the fast on Christmas Eve and Good Friday. I never saw him pray. We never spoke together about religious things: I was frightened that again I'd touch a dissonant chord. In this case it would have been especially difficult for me.

At that time in Prague the Brno Philharmonic Beseda sang the *Glagolitic Mass* under the direction of Professor Kvapil.[68] I didn't go because Leoš invited the Stössels. But I learnt about everything that had happened there when the ladies from the Beseda returned. During the concert the Stössels apparently sat with my husband in a box. Opposite them President Masaryk and Dr Alice Masaryková.[69] The ladies from the Beseda said they were ashamed that my husband flaunted his new affair so openly and provocatively, and that only I should have been with him in the box. Although the artistic success of the concert was great, Leoš returned home depressed. I didn't have to press him much for him to tell me what had happened to him. He said

65 This rumour sounds like an elaboration of the fact that in May 1928 Janáček extended his Hukvaldy cottage by adding a first-storey room in place of the loft; the extra room was indeed intended for Mrs Stösslová's visit.

66 If Zdenka had evidence for this allegation she did not supply it. Janáček sent presents to Mrs Stösslová and bought objects from the Stössels (such as pictures and carpets) which he did not need, but there is nothing in his extensive correspondence with her that suggests that he made an outright loan to her or her husband.

67 The Prague première of the *Glagolitic Mass* III/9 was in the Smetana Hall on 8 April 1928.

68 Jaroslav Kvapil (1892–1958), a graduate of Janáček's Organ School, was choirmaster of the Brno Beseda from 1919 to 1947.

69 President T.G. Masaryk (1850–1937), first president of the Czechoslovak Republic. After the death of his wife his daughter Alice (1879–1966) often accompanied him on official engagements.

that the President got up immediately after the concert and left, as if ignoring the composer. And Leoš had expected that the President would have had him summoned into his box to talk with him. This distressed him very much at the time.

After the performance he arrived home from Prague on his very name-day, on 11 April.[70] I didn't know whether he'd be back that day at all and so I hadn't made any preparations. And when I saw him so out of sorts, I didn't even dare wish him well. He told me that the day before he'd been to Karlštejn with the Stössels. But after his death I realized from the diary which he kept that he'd been there with her alone, and that he then went off with her to Zdice, which he mentions among the outpourings of love for her.[71] Although he hadn't told me the truth, I somehow suspected it. I also got the feeling that he was now burning with love even more than when he went off. More terrible and more certain was the premonition that it would all end badly. I now clutched at anything which I thought might just perhaps open Leoš's eyes. So, despite all my experience of never getting useful advice or a helping hand from her, I also wrote to Josefka. I begged her to persuade Leoš that the Písek couple were only making a show of love towards him in order to exploit him financially. In reply she told me not to write such things to her, that old gentlemen must do extravagant things like this, that I must reconcile myself to it, and that during my husband's next visit to Hukvaldy she'd give him the letter to read. I couldn't understand that his own sister could have so little prudence and take the fate of her brother so lightly.

For me it was now certain that Leoš's relationship with Mrs Stösslová was fateful for us. This was no longer a suspicion, it was the result of continually mulling over and exploring all the circumstances from every angle. It was an improper relationship: Mrs Stösslová was after all someone else's wife and the mother of two lads. With my husband's intransigence and passionate nature it would be sure to disrupt the household there. What would happen to the children? And there was something else: even if you disregarded the difference in race, Mrs

70 The name-day for Lev or Leo is celebrated on 10 November (18 February in the East), after Leo the Great (pope 440–61). In the Czech lands 11 April is usually the (male) name-day of Stanislav.
71 Zdenka was right to believe that Janáček had been alone with Mrs Stösslová on a visit to Karlštejn (see p.25, fn.5). From Janáček's fond recollections (*Hž/IL*, nos.627–8) it is evident that David Stössel was not with them. But Zdenka may have got the wrong idea about Zdice, which is merely a town on the Prague–Plzeň railway line where Janáček needed to change to get to Písek on 6 April (a visit later abandoned; Janáček met up with the Stössels in Prague the next day).

Stösslová didn't exactly have the best reputation in Písek and Leoš was compromising himself very much with her: his age, his reputation, his honorary doctorate, all bound him to a life of propriety; that he ignored this couldn't go unpunished for long. And this was the main thing: he was heedless of the inviolable laws of nature, he was convinced that his 'eternal youth', about which the reviews reassured him more and more [. . .], gave him the right to love a woman almost forty years his junior. Perhaps it would have been possible if Mrs Stösslová had been a refined and sophisticated woman but she was impetuous, selfish, reckless, instinctive, too unintelligent to realize her responsibility towards Leoš's love. It's true that she was refusing it, but cleverly, just enough to inflame him all the more. Once I said all this to my husband. He sat in the armchair and simply nodded his white head vigorously as if he were agreeing: yes, yes, it's so. And his passion became all the more vehement.

I took it very ill of Josefka that she didn't see all this and thought that I was doing it out of sheer jealousy. I took it ill that she even came to like Mrs Stösslová and received her graciously at our house in Hukvaldy.[72] Hadn't she found out for herself just where too great a disparity of age in love can lead? She surely couldn't help seeing that it was more than friendship: for some time Leoš had no longer been hiding the fact that he wanted to make Mrs Stösslová his wife. They'd exchanged rings that looked very much like wedding rings,[73] and he called her 'Janáčková' in letters.[74] He'd stopped making the excuse that she was his source of inspiration and no longer concealed that it was an erotic relationship. And especially at Hukvaldy[75] he'd made no bones about it. But I think that it was quite a pleasant thought for Josefka that I was suffering through this, otherwise she'd have destroyed the letter and wouldn't have threatened me with the fact that she'd give it to Leoš to read. I got a terrible fright from this, fearing that it would be another day of reckoning if not a complete break between my husband and myself. There was only one way of averting it and one that I made use of: I at once told Leoš everything

---

72 Zdenka anticipates: Mrs Stösslová's visit to Hukvaldy was in August 1928.

73 This was hardly an 'exchange' of rings. Janáček wore a ring supplied by Mrs Stösslová at his own request (in 1919); nine years later he presented Mrs Stösslová with a ring on his visit to Písek in January 1928 (see *IL*, Glossary: 'ring'). The symbolic status of this action is reinforced by his very last composition written into the Album for Kamila Stösslová entitled *Golden Ring* (Janáček 1996, 49–50).

74 Janáček did so twice, when discussing the dedication of the Second String Quartet (25 May 1928, *Hž/IL*, no.664; 29 May 1928, *Hž/IL*, no.667). At the time when Zdenka dictated her memoirs these letters were still with Mrs Stösslová so she can only be reporting what either her husband or Kamila told her.

75 i.e. where Josefka was.

myself. I managed to do so in such a way that he wasn't even very angry.[76] Josefka later carried out her threat, but it didn't get her anywhere, he told that he already knew about it all.

He began to be very stingy because Písek cost him lots of money. Once he said to me that whenever he went into the Živnobanka,[77] they immediately produced the green [withdrawal] slip for him without asking, because they knew that he would only be withdrawing money. At the end of April he went off again[78] and returned completely infatuated, he could neither look me in the eyes, nor would he tell me what had happened to him. I just got the impression that lots of money was at stake.[79] Meanwhile Máŕa and I made ends meet as best we could but he continued to believe that he was giving us too much. He kept on looking for pretexts for going to see the Stössels. At the end of June he told me that he had to go there to take his leave of old Mrs Neumannová, the mother of Mrs Stösslová, who, he said, was dying of cancer. It was so painful when I compared this attentiveness with the way he behaved when my own parents were dying. He stayed there for four days, from 21 to 25 June,[80] and when he returned he told me that the old lady had gone for treatment to Jáchymov,[81] and that he'd been on an expedition with the Stössels to Zvíkov and that they'd been very cheerful.

On 1 July he went off to Luhačovice. When after three weeks he returned he looked in very bad shape.[82] I looked anxiously at him slowly shuffling around our garden. At one point I told him this. He answered that he'd taken the mud baths in Luhačovice at temperatures of up to 39°. I told him that he ought not to do that, that it would weaken his heart too much. At another time I couldn't resist saying to

76 In a postscript dated '19 May, morning' to his letter of 18–19 May 1928 (*Hž/IL*, no.659) Janáček wrote to Kamila: 'Two months ago Z. wrote a letter to my sister full of false statements. When she knew that I was going to Hukvaldy – she told me about the letter. My sister of course answered her appropriately. That was the exchange of views today! It's all over.'
77 A colloquial form of 'Živnostenská banka' [Trade Finance Bank], where Janáček had an account.
78 Janáček was in Písek on 23–5 April 1928, after a meeting of the Folksong Commission in Prague.
79 According to Janáček's letter to Kamila on his return (25 April 1928; *Hž/IL*, no.639), she had, seemingly for the first time, told him that she loved him. There is no support in his correspondence for any financial transactions at this period; however, two months later Janáček made his will in which Mrs Stösslová was one of the main beneficiaries.
80 Janáček was in fact in Písek for only two days, 23–4 June 1928.
81 Mrs Neumannová's cancer was diagnosed on 2 June 1928; she moved around several sanatoria until early July, when she was taken in at Jáchymov (see *IL*, p.358).
82 Stejskalová recorded in her diary that Janáček had lost seven kilos (Trkanová 1964, 166, fn.18).

him that he treated his health too frivolously. And I don't know how it came into my mind to add: 'One day you'll get pneumonia and then that will be the end of you.'

He nodded his head and said quietly: 'Yes, yes.'

It was on the path in our garden and a fortnight later it came true.

One day he informed me, all excited, that Mrs Neumannová had died and that he was now going off with Mrs Stösslová to Hukvaldy so she could recuperate.[83] That was a body blow. I knew that it was the beginning of the end, only I couldn't think what sort of end. I'd have cried out in pain at the thought that she'd now be living for some weeks with Leoš in our little house in Hukvaldy – aloud I asked him when I should get the cases ready. He answered: on 30 July, only he didn't yet know whether her husband and son would also be going with her. So, on my birthday.

The remaining few days passed between us in peace. I left all my pain for the nights, when I didn't sleep and thought what would happen next. On 29 July he set off cheerfully to the station to meet her. We had lunch together for the last time. We had veal, potatoes and salad. I was praised that I knew how to prepare roast veal excellently. Oh God, what good did that do me! He wore his new light-coloured silk suit, he put on a cap and went off cheerfully. I didn't sit idly by, I didn't weep, I went to make jam because it was high time that something was done with the apricots in our garden. It had to be, work and duty called and I wanted to be equal to them until the very last moment. But my thoughts were with Leoš all the time. I knew that he'd taken his guests to the Exhibition of Contemporary Culture.[84] Towards evening it began to spot with rain, I was worried that his new clothes would get wet and shrink. Towards nine a car stopped outside our garden, I heard his voice saying goodbye. He wanted to go up to sleep [in the Organ School] at once, but I called out to him and asked him if he wouldn't come into the house. He came. To the question whether he'd got wet, he answered no, that they'd taken a car. His clothes were crumpled. I suggested that he change out of them, that we would have them ironed by the morning. He consented. But he evidently wasn't in a good mood and Máŕa and I immediately told each other why. Mrs Stösslová hadn't come alone, but with her husband.[85]

---

83 Mrs Neumannová died on 17 July. Mrs Stösslová wrote to Janáček about it only on 21 July (the funeral was on 20 July). In the same brief letter (*IL*, p.336) she announced her arrival in Brno a week later: 'I want peace and I'll find it only in your presence.'
84 See below, p.229.
85 She had also brought her younger son, Otto, then twelve years old.

The last day. He was due to leave before noon. Máŕa flatly refused to carry his cases to the station, saying that she couldn't vouch for herself if she met Mrs Stösslová. I suggested to Leoš that he take a taxi. We all waited on the veranda for it. Seemingly peacefully. Leoš suddenly stepped up to me: 'You've got a birthday today?'

'Yes.'

'You forgot my birthday this year.'

'I didn't, but I thought you wouldn't care for my wishes.'

He gave me his hand: 'I wish you the very best.'

He didn't realize at all what heart-rending mockery that was. I clutched the table and held on to it with all my strength. I couldn't speak. At that moment the car came rumbling up. Máŕa grabbed the cases and rushed out, Čipera after her. We were alone. He gave me his hand again and wanted to kiss me – while the other woman was waiting for him at the station.

I turned my head away: 'Must it be so?'[86]

'It can be and it must be.'

He kissed me vigorously and left.

Čipera barked outside. I was frightened that she might dash under the car. I ran after her and called her. Leoš was still in the garden. He caught me by the arm. But I saw that I could no longer hold out from crying, so I broke away and raced home. The car hooted and went off.[87] He was gone. He was gone for the rest of my life.

Day after day I waited for a letter. Eventually a week later a letter and a postcard came at the same time. The letter was from England from Mrs Newmarch[88] with a visiting card on which my husband had written: 'Be good enough to get me a translation.' And on the postcard: 'We've arrived safely. Cheerfulness in the house, as it should be. The money arrived. Leoš.' The last sentence concerned the Kč 33,000 royalties which my husband had been expecting from Universal Edition in Vienna for some time. It was all one to me since I realized that there wouldn't be much for me from that money anyway. After all, when he left he had given me Kč 600 for the whole month for the two of us.

From that two women can live very well, he said to me then, and I

86 Unconsciously or not, Zdenka was quoting the words Beethoven attached to the slow introduction of his final string quartet op.135, 'Muss es sein?' Janáček's reply was more elaborate than Beethoven's positive 'Es muss sein!'
87 In Stejskalová's reminiscence of the same incident (Trkanová 1964, 117) the car had trouble starting and a group of people began gathering round it.
88 This was presumably in response to Janáček's letter to Rosa Newmarch of 2 June 1928 (Fischmann 1986, 157); Mrs Newmarch's letter, however, has not survived in BmJA.

was too proud to explain to him that keeping up a household like ours cost much more than that. But that 'cheerfulness in the home, as it should be' stung me. What that sentence didn't say! It was a reproach that my household was sad and that I didn't know how to be cheerful; it was an explanation why he was running away from me; it was praise for Mrs Stösslová, who a week after the death of her mother could wander round Hukvaldy in a red *dirndl*[89] and sing merry little songs to Leoš's accompaniment; and it was informing me how useless I was and how joyful it was without me. I couldn't answer it. Besides, there was no need: it was the last card which Leoš wrote in his life.[90]

In order to dull my pain I let myself be talked into going, on Friday 10 August, with my friend [Marie] Zahradníková[91] to the Exhibition of Contemporary Culture. For this, with much ceremony and at great expense, the Brno Exhibition Site had been built at Bauer's Ramp in Pisárky.[92] It was a wonderful thing for Brno, spacious grounds with pavilions in the most modern style, a coloured fountain, a high tower, old trees transplanted here with great art and at huge cost, examples from all branches of human knowledge and art – everything outwardly splendid but put up in a hurry, without real foundations. Here Brno overestimated its resources: the years of economic crisis came, there was no longer the money for expensive projects, grass has grown on the exhibition site, the pavilions have fallen into disrepair. But at the time it was magnificent, crowds of people, foreigners from every corner of Europe, lots of entertainments. The day we went, there was a huge concert in the evening and we found ourselves in high society. I pretended to be cheerful and I drank lots of wine. I returned home late, at 1.30 a.m. And meanwhile that afternoon they'd taken Leoš off, mortally ill, to the sanatorium in Ostrava.

Saturday passed in the usual work, on Sunday morning I went again to my friend and we agreed we'd go again that afternoon to the exhibition. Then I went to church. I got home, took my things off, when at that moment I received a telegram: 'The Maestro seriously ill, come immediately, Dr Klein's sanatorium. Kamila.'

89 Zdenka's mention of a *dirndl* stresses both that Mrs Stösslová was not wearing mourning and that she was wearing a type of folk costume more associated with Austria (specifically the Tyrol) than with Moravia or Bohemia. Stösslová's *dirndl* appears to be one of her summer 1927 outfits (see *IL*, Plates 5 and 12).
90 Janáček wrote at least two more notes, one on 9 August 1928 to the local doctor in Hukvaldy asking him to visit (printed in Procházka 1948, 170) and one on 11 August 1928 from the Ostrava sanatorium to the Swiss writer William Ritter (see p.242), postponing their meeting (printed in Knaus 1988).
91 See Glossary.
92 See p.79, fn.69.

After the first terrible shock, I ran off to town to find out when the next train to Ostrava was. On the way I met Director Tauber,[93] the well-known tenor from the Moravian Teachers' Choir. I told him what had happened and that I wanted to ask my cousin Dressler to travel with me. Then I rushed to the Brumovský travel agency in Zámečnická ulice and from there to the Dresslers. I'd only just told them why I'd come when someone rang the bell. I went to answer it myself. Director Tauber stood at the door. He was taken aback when he saw me. To my agitated question as to what had happened, he said, equally disturbed, that he had to speak to Dr Dressler. My legs gave way. I called my cousin and then went into the second room to see his wife:

'Ida, my husband is dead.'

'How can you think that?'

'But I know it. You'll see I'm not mistaken.'

Again someone rang. I rushed outside. It was Mrs Brumovská. She got into a complete panic when she saw me. That was enough. I grasped her hand: 'My husband is dead.' She nodded her head. With legs like lead I went to see Tauber and Dressler: 'I already know, you don't have to tell me.'

They stood like statues. I fell on the divan and buried my head in my hands: 'What now?'

We had to act fast. I asked Dressler: 'Will you come with me?'

He couldn't. Tauber said: 'A car is already waiting downstairs.'

I turned to him and with clasped hands begged him to travel with me. He agreed. We went downstairs. A car from the undertaker's, Charitas, was waiting. It had happened like this: after I'd parted with Director Tauber, he'd met an employee of this undertaker who told him that my husband was dead and that they'd already prepared a car to take me to Ostrava. That was why Tauber was looking for me to tell me gently. I was without my wits and without support, and glad that someone was doing the thinking for me. So I did everything that the Charitas employee suggested, and I was grateful to him. He advised me to take with me my husband's black suit and underwear, saying that they'd bring the coffin straight after us; he recommended that we leave at 1 p.m.

Afterwards they dragged me through the newspapers demanding to

93 Stanislav Tauber (1878–1959), concert tenor, the chief solo tenor of the Moravian Teachers' Choral Society and celebrated soloist in many Janáček choral works (he can be seen in Plate 19, in a group after the performance of *Amarus* III/6). He was headmaster of a boys' school at the time of Zdenka's memoirs, hence her form of address 'Director Tauber'. He described the events of the next couple of days in his memoirs (Tauber 1949, 102–4).

know why I'd assigned the funeral to Charitas and not to the city undertaker. The man who wrote it simply couldn't imagine how I felt and that I'd grasped every helping hand extended to me. I'd never wish him to go through anything similar.

The car took us home. Máˇra was waiting in the courtyard. She bowed and without speaking kissed my hand. Then [Jaroslav] Lederer, the caretaker of the Conservatory, clasped my hand. He'd come because Charitas had announced the death of my husband to the Conservatory. And Máˇra meanwhile had received the telegram from Dr Klein. [. . .]

Quickly on, on, to get ready for the journey. I packed everything according to the instructions and we left at 1 p.m. When Director Tauber and I sat down in the car he said: 'And now we must be brave.'

He recalled his last meeting with my husband. Then we began to consider the death announcement. In the face of death I couldn't play the role of the beloved wife when the reality was so terribly different. So I asked Tauber that Leoš's brother Josef[94] put out the announce- ment in his name. At first Tauber tried to talk me out of it, but later in Ostrava when he saw how things were, he no longer insisted.

It was a beautiful summer afternoon; they were celebrating harvest- home in the villages through which we travelled. Music and whoops of joy drifted into the car, but throughout the journey we were thinking and talking about that unexpected death. Towards five o'clock we arrived at the sanatorium. We were greeted by a chambermaid and the doctor treating Leoš.

'Where's my husband?'

'Already in the mortuary at the cemetery.'

So I wasn't even to see him on his [death-]bed. They led me into the salon and the doctor told me about the course of Leoš's illness and his death. He died of heart failure while suffering from pneumonia. The doctor told me that the lady who'd accompanied him had brought him from Hukvaldy in what was by then a completely hopeless state. It was Friday evening. He had a temperature of 40° but he was walking and completely conscious. They called in the chief consultant of the Ostrava hospital to the sanatorium; he x-rayed him and proclaimed that there was no hope, that the heart wouldn't stand it. Mrs Stösslová remained in the sanatorium and also had herself examined and x- rayed at my husband's expense. I asked why I hadn't been called in time before the end. The doctor answered that they'd wanted to

94 Josef Janáček (1858–1941), Janáček's oldest surviving brother.

summon me by telegram but Leoš apparently got very angry and forbade it. Similarly he also gave orders that his stay in the sanatorium should be kept from the public. The doctor said that he was a little better on Saturday, but in the night his condition worsened considerably. He grew weak, he asked for paper to write on. They gave him some and in a shaky hand he tried to write a codicil to his will. But his consciousness was already growing dim, the codicil was confused and unsigned, so the court didn't accept its validity later when dealing with the estate. I no longer remember the exact version, but he wrote something like this: 'To Zdenka Janáčková the interest on Kč 100,000 until death, to Mrs Stösslová the interest on Kč 100,000 until death.'[95] He asked for a new piece of paper and wrote again: 'The keys, the keys, the keys. Mrs Stösslová has the keys.' He wanted to sign it, but he said: 'I can't do any more.'

The doctor comforted him: 'You can sign when you feel better.'

I think that he didn't believe in this comfort, that he already knew how things stood. My view is confirmed by the fact that he refused an injection to stimulate him: 'Let me die, nothing will help me now.'

The doctor spent the whole night with him. Alone. Mrs Stösslová slept in her room. In the morning he wanted nevertheless to give him an injection, but while he was preparing it he looked round and saw how Leoš had inclined his head to one side. It was the end. Then they immediately sent me a telegram. He said that Mrs Stösslová took all my husband's things and moved out into a hotel.

So now I knew roughly how it had all happened. And I told myself that it all needn't have happened if it had been me in the place of that frivolous, thoughtless Mrs Stösslová, who had every quality other than what was needed to nurse a sick man. She now seemed terrible to me: it was through her voluptuous looks that Leoš had been lured to his death. And now it was necessary to go to her because she had all Leoš's things and I needed the keys to his Brno writing-desk, where he kept all his official documents. It was a terrible thought that I'd now have to speak to her, but it had to be. We went by car to her hotel,[96] Director Tauber and the Charitas employee coming with me. We didn't have to look long, she was standing in the vestibule. Director

---

95 Janáček wrote five codicils to his will; this was the last (containing much the same provisions as the fourth) and because unsigned, was declared invalid by the courts. Zdenka misremembered its provisions. Apart from granting Kamila the royalties on four works (see p.235, fn.103), it gave Kamila a lifetime interest in Kč 200,000 which had been split between Zdenka and Kamila in Janáček's earlier provisions (see Procházková 1996, 60–6).
96 The hotel Imperiál, according to Tauber's account (1949, 103).

Tauber wanted to spare me and went to her himself. But she ran up to me, grasping me by the right shoulder and asked: 'Are you angry with me?'

I pushed her aside after this senseless question: 'Be off with you, you've stolen and destroyed my husband.'

She began to exclaim plaintively: 'I'm not to blame, there was nothing going on between us.'

'Shut up, now is not the moment to say such things and I'm not asking about them. Where did my husband wish to be buried?'

She said that she didn't know anything, that he hadn't said anything. I turned to the Charitas employee and gave orders for my husband to be taken to Brno. Then I had to go on dealing with her.

'They said you have all my husband's things and his keys. Give them to me.'

'I won't give them to you, he gave them to me, and I must be present during everything.'

'Mrs Stösslová, I am his legal wife and I have the right to what I'm asking. Give me the keys to the Brno writing-desk.'

She refused. I asked Director Tauber: 'Mr Director, please deal with her, I can't do so any more.'

Both men went out with her into the street and I waited quite a long time in the vestibule. Eventually Director Tauber returned and asked me if I was now strong enough to go on dealing with her, that she wanted it. I had to find the strength. She invited me to go into her room with her.[97] There she swore to me by the love for her husband and the happiness of her children that she hadn't had a relationship with my husband and that he hadn't even kissed her hand.[98]

I reproached her that she knew how much I loved Leoš, that since my children had died I had no one else on this earth apart from him, that she knew what a gloomy life I'd led, that nevertheless she'd taken him from me without mercy.

'I loved him so much and now he's gone', I let out a moan.

Suddenly she opened her bag and began to take out keys, my husband's gold watch and chain and a completely empty purse. That made me wonder where the Kč 33,000 which my husband had

97 Tauber's account (1949, 103) of the Stösslová–Janáčková confrontation differs somewhat from Zdenka's. Since their altercation in the vestibule was arousing attention he suggested to the ladies that they continued in Stösslová's room and when she then still refused to hand over Janáček's effects, he took her out on to the street, and threatened her with the police. She then showed him the album with Janáček's codicil to his will (p.235).

98 This was something of a white lie. Janáček first kissed Kamila on 19 August 1927, an event thereafter celebrated in his letters to her as 'Friday–feast-day' (see *IL*, p.349).

received from Universal Edition could be. The money didn't mean anything to me at all, but I didn't want to leave it to *that* woman. 'My husband wrote to me that he received lots of money at Hukvaldy. Where is it?'

She replied that they'd taken Kč 15,000 with them to Ostrava and of that she'd given 4000 to the sanatorium.

'And where's the 11,000?'

'The Maestro gave it to me to buy something for myself.'

'Do you have a witness?'

She didn't answer.

Then we changed the topic of conversation. But she kept on asking me to go to Hukvaldy with her, saying that the rest of the money would certainly be there. I decided to go – after all, what else did I have to do in Ostrava until the Charitas employee had finished with everything? I handed him the underwear and suit for Leoš's change of clothes for the coffin and, accompanied by Director Tauber, we set off.

On the journey she began to speak to me again. Among other things she said: 'Be glad that he's dead now, at least you'll have peace. I'm also glad now that there'll be an end to all this.'

I had a bag open on my lap. Suddenly she threw something into it.

'What's that?'

'Just a ring with his name that he gave me. What should I do with it?'

'What should I do with it?'

But I kept the ring for myself. It strikingly resembles a wedding ring, it has narrow grooves and diagonally against it in high relief is the name 'Leoš'. My secretary has it now, similarly the Balestrieri print[99] because I couldn't bear to have these things about me at home.

We got to Hukvaldy almost in the dark. I knew that Mrs Stösslová was hand in glove with Josefka, therefore I asked her to tell my sister-in-law herself what had happened. The servant[100] took me into the dining-room. In a trice Mrs Stösslová came with the keys to the writing-desk. Together we unlocked it and in a drawer I found the keys to the Brno writing-desk and a purse with Kč 7000. So in a fortnight they'd gone through some Kč 11,000. At that moment my sister-in-law came into the room sobbing.[101] I reproached her for not making me aware of Leoš's illness. She said he hadn't wanted it. And she asked

99 See above, p.205.
100 Otylie Krsková (1904–1987), in service with Josefa Dohnalová.
101 According to Stejskalová, it was only at this point that Josefka learnt that her brother was dead (Trkanová 1964, 121).

what I'd do now, whether I'd move to Hukvaldy. Up till now it hadn't even occurred to me to think about it, but somehow it flowed from my inner self so that I told her 'no'. I like Hukvaldy, but my roots are in Brno, I have lived there all my life, all my dear ones are buried there, I have my friends there, I have our little house there – it would be hard for me to move away from Brno. But my sister-in-law looked at it differently. She said sarcastically: 'Well now, since there aren't concerts and cafés here, you wouldn't enjoy yourself.' I was angry that she could say such stupid things at a time like that.

While Mrs Stösslová packed her things up, I asked my sister-in-law not to move anything until I came again, we said goodbye and returned to Ostrava. We got there about 10 p.m. The Charitas employee was waiting for me at the hotel. They now had everything ready and were preparing to take Leoš to Brno. He said that they would stop in front of the hotel so that I could have a look. This was the hardest moment of the whole day when I went down the stairs. A crowd was already standing there. I went through the crowd, they opened up the back of the car and showed me the coffin. I placed my hand on it – that was all I could do. When they left, I returned to my room and despite terrible tiredness I stayed awake the whole night.

Director Tauber and I were due to leave early the next morning. I got up towards five o'clock and went to see Mrs Stösslová, who was meant to be getting my husband's things ready for me. Once again I reproached her for what she'd done, for dragging an old man around after her like a youngster. She told me that she'd always liked me and that we could be good friends again now. She took her album[102] and showed me one page. In it Leoš had left her the proceeds from the royalties for *Káťa Kabanová* and *From the House of the Dead*. I was so agitated that I thought that it was for *The Diary of a Young Man who Disappeared*.[103] She didn't let me go on reading, she snatched the album away and said: 'What you give me is your affair.'

So then, business deals over Leoš's corpse. I owed her an answer. I asked her what she was going to do now. She said that she was going

102 This is the Album for Kamila, published in facsimile and Czech transcription (Procházková 1994) and English translation (Procházková 1996), a book in which Janáček wrote words and music celebrating his visits to Písek and his thoughts about Kamila from 2 October 1927 until 10 August 1928, two days before he died. It contains the fourth codicil to his will dated 5 August 1928 (see p.232, fn.95).

103 In fact the allocation of royalties was more extensive than Zdenka remembered. The final page of the codicil written into the album goes as follows: 'The royalties from *Káťa Kabanová*, *The Diary of One who Disappeared*, *From the House of the Dead* and from our Quartet (no.2) belong to you' (Procházková 1996, 47).

to Písek. I replied: 'You're doing the right thing.' And so we parted.

The car had broken down, we had to wait until eight o'clock before we could leave. In Brno we stopped first at the undertaker's, where I completed negotiations over the funeral. It was to be on Wednesday [15 August] and, as they told me, at the town's expense. At home Máŕa announced to me that in a short while the director of the theatre [František] Neumann was coming to discuss the funeral with me. He arrived even before I had time to change. Poor thing, when he was making his condolences he didn't suspect that within six months he'd follow my husband – fifty years old in full strength, continually active, agile as a military man, energetic – that within days he'd be overcome by flu. He came now on unpleasant business. Although the town of Brno wanted to take charge of Leoš's funeral, it didn't want to assign it to an outside undertaker when it had its own. I, however, had already signed a contract in Ostrava with Charitas from which it didn't want to withdraw. While I was still talking with Neumann, the people from Charitas came. A long discussion followed which didn't lead any-where. Only on Tuesday afternoon was it decided that the town would pay Charitas for what it had done already and would take over the rest itself. Charitas was accused of greed, but I remember it only with kind thoughts and must be thankful to it for relieving me tactfully and caringly at the first and hardest moment when I was alone and helpless.

They took Leoš to the chapel of St Marie in the Old Brno monastery. I set off there on Monday afternoon to have a look at him because I hadn't yet seen his face since his death. By chance Mr Sedláček, the flautist from the theatre who had copied music for my husband,[104] came to see us at that very moment and so he accompanied me there. The two of us were alone in the chapel. Through the glass lid of the coffin I fixed my gaze on Leoš. His face was glowering, distorted, angry. Olga and Mama had smiled in their coffins, my father had had reconciled calm on his face, but as I gazed at Leoš I couldn't help thinking: you didn't like dying, you fought with death. I couldn't say goodbye to him by embracing him and making the sign of the cross: between us lay the glass barrier. I kissed that at least. I thought that I'd choke with grief, without tears, without words.

Then I dragged myself back through town, for I had to buy something to complete my mourning outfit. At home many mourners

104 Václav Sedláček (1879–1944) played flute in the Brno Theatre orchestra (1910–35). Janáček employed him as his chief copyist and amanuensis from 1916 until his death.

were already waiting for me. I had to talk to them, send telegrams to relatives, do something about a funeral wreath. In all this I was alone and dead tired. I slept a deep sleep that night. On Tuesday morning my niece Věra arrived from Prague. She made life much easier for me, she helped me a lot. In the morning I went again to see Leoš with my friend Mrs Heindlová.[105] I took him a bouquet of white roses. He was still unchanged. And as I stood watching him, suddenly tears poured from my eyes. I can't begin to describe what a relief that was. I cried and cried without stopping and the incurable tension within me began to give way. What a precious gift tears are.

They told me that his Reverence the Abbot Bařina[106] wanted to speak to me about the funeral ceremony in the church. They took me to him weeping through the church, where there were now lots of people around Leoš's coffin. His Reverence told me that he'd conduct the funeral consecration himself: 'He lived here, he worked here, we'll accompany him from here.'

I thanked him as if in a trance. Then I went home. Věra was already waiting for me. She also wanted to look at her uncle. Although I'd just come from there, I turned round and went again with her. I couldn't do otherwise, I had to see Leoš again. In the chapel my niece looked through the glass cover and said to me: 'Auntie, don't look now, Uncle's changing, blood is running from his mouth.' I obeyed her. My image of Leoš has not been distorted through the decomposition of death like my image of Olga.

A gentleman came up to me. 'Is that the composer Janáček?'

'Yes, it's my husband.'

He was startled, he drew back, but it seemed suddenly as if Leoš no longer belonged to me, but to the public. I said farewell to the coffin and then didn't go to the chapel again until the funeral ceremony.

In the afternoon I negotiated with the employees of the town's undertaker: eventually we concluded that the funeral would be on Wednesday morning, as had been previously arranged. I went to sleep with the heavy thought of what awaited me the next day. 15 August, my Olga's birthday. Early in the morning I got up and dressed in mourning. No sooner was I ready than my brother-in-law Josef came with the son of our former landlords in Hukvaldy, Sládek.[107] At 7.30 a car came for us and we drove to the Old Brno monastery. The Chapel of St Marie was beautifully decorated with flowers and the abbot

105 See p.170.
106 See p.91.
107 See Glossary: 'Sládeks'.

conducted the ceremonial consecration assisted by the whole monastery. Afterwards they told me that there were many people there,
that the catafalque was magnificently decorated, but I didn't take in
anything of that. After the ceremony they laid the coffin on the hearse
and we accompanied it by car to the Town Theatre.[108] Then I went
home to be host to the mourners. At ten there was the funeral at the
theatre. The opera director František Neumann was waiting for me in
the entrance and led me up the stairs to the coffin, which stood on a
high catafalque in the foyer. I saw only the masses of flowers and
lights. They put me in an armchair and at once the theatre orchestra
under Neumann began to play the final scene from *The Cunning Little
Vixen* where the Forester – sung by Arnold Flögl[109] – reminisces. As
soon as I heard the first few bars it was if a strong stream of light shone
through that eerie indistinctness which had enveloped me from that
Sunday. Music was necessary for me to grasp fully what had
happened, so that I could feel in its full intensity that Leoš, who had
written this work so packed with life, was now lying dead. In that
theatre, where we had experienced so much, in front of which he used
to wait for me like a lover, and where he had had so many joyful
successes. And now there was an end to it all. That moment of clear
realization was so terribly painful. I sprang to my feet, I didn't know
how to express all that I'd just felt other than with the cry
'Bystrouška'.

I began to fall. Mářa, who had walked everywhere that day in my
steps like a faithful dog, caught me. I didn't take in anything more, I
knew nothing of the funeral speeches, of Dvořák's Requiem which the
Beseda Philharmonic Society apparently sang most beautifully: I was
like a machine without a memory and without consciousness. I
remember that someone from Prague expressed condolences, but what
I did during all this, I don't know. I revived a little when Dr Dressler
led me out on to the street, where we lined up for the procession
behind the hearse and when the sorrowful sounds of the French horns
behind us from the terrace of the theatre grew fainter. At the station we
got into cars and drove from there to the Central Cemetery. Now I
could think again. They told me that they were burying my husband in
a grave of honour, but I didn't know where it would be. I thought it
would be where the mayors and councillors of the city of Brno are
buried. But at the cemetery we went further and further past that

108 See Glossary: 'Brno Theatre'.
109 Arnold Flögl (1885–1950) was a member of the Brno Opera (1924–30). As bass soloist
there he created the role of the Forester at the première of *The Cunning Little Vixen*.

group and I quietly lamented: 'Where are they taking him from me, where are they taking him from me?'

We went past the grave where Papa and Vladíček lie, we turned the corner round Olga's grave. Yes, nothing was left to me now other than graves; now my life itself had become just a grave. Eventually we stopped at the wall beside the place where Radovan sleeps, that good-looking only son of Professor Arne Novák.[110] It is just a few graves away from Olga. I thought to myself that it would have been better if my husband were to lie in the family grave next to his daughter since it was already in the same row. But the funeral ceremony was already in progress. It was conducted by Father Albín Zelníček, for many years professor of religion at the Organ School and then at the conservatory.[111] In an overwrought state Director Neumann said farewell to Leoš, the national anthems[112] sounded and clods of earth began to fall on the grave. My cousin Dressler led me away.

And now I had to put grief aside. It was my duty to look after the hospitality for the many mourners and relatives from out of town for whom I'd ordered lunch in the Besední dům. I had to go among them, thank them for their sympathy, talk to them. A rumour reached me immediately that Mrs Stösslová had also been at the funeral. What did it matter to me now? That weight which oppressed me remained the same whatever happened. I couldn't bear staying long in the Besední dům and I went home. There Dr Brod and Dr Krampus from Universal Edition were waiting for me to express their sympathy for me once again. Apart from that, Dr Krampus came on Universal Edition business. It was abhorrent that on the day of my husband's funeral I should have to take over his business affairs about which I certainly knew a lot but which he'd never allowed me to look after. Now all at once I had to be up to it. The gentlemen left, my brother-in-law [Josef Janáček] also left, as did my female cousin.[113] I remained alone with Věra. Towards evening the composer Chlubna arrived. My husband's pupil, tall, thin, always serious, even gloomy, he suited my mood well that day.[114] It had always been possible to speak sincerely and openly

110 See p.190, fn.14.
111 Father Albín Zelníček (1877–1942). He taught religion at Brno schools; at the Organ School and Brno Conservatory he taught liturgical studies.
112 During the Czechoslovak Republic the Czech national anthem was followed immediately by the Slovak anthem.
113 Thea Kostínková, from Pardubice.
114 Osvald Chlubna (1893–1971) studied with Janáček at the Brno Organ School in 1914–15. Janáček entrusted him with the orchestration of the final act of his first opera, *Šárka* I/1; after Janáček's death he reorchestrated *From the House of the Dead* I/11. His height and his gloomy demeanour are evident in Plate 19.

with him, and today I needed this especially. I confided in him that I didn't like the place where my husband was buried, that I'd have preferred him to be in the family grave if his grave wasn't going to be down below, among the other graves of honour. He tried to change my mind, but I stuck to my own view until under the influence of the whole of that horrible day I burst into tears. It was already evening when Mr Chlubna left. I could hardly keep upright for tiredness. Máňa led me to my bed.

After the requiem mass [at the monastery] in Old Brno my niece [Věra Janáčková] and I went the next day to the cemetery. I was surprised that the grave wasn't covered with earth but only with planks. A cemetery official told me that Leoš would be transferred below [to the graves of honour] because the mayor didn't like this place. I responded: 'I'm so pleased, I didn't like it either, I didn't want to leave him here.'

I went straight to the cemetery office and spoke by phone with Mayor Tomeš.[115] He invited me to visit him at the Town Hall. I stopped off at his office directly on the way back from the cemetery. He told me that the exhumation of my husband's body would take place within the next few days.

On Friday 17 August in the morning we met at Leoš's present grave, the mayor and his wife, Director Neumann and some acquaintances. Mrs Tomešová placed a bunch of flowers on the transferred coffin, I a bouquet of red roses; the coffin was lowered into the new grave, they covered it with soil, and so, after six days of restless journeying, Leoš's body found peace after death.

I had to travel to Hukvaldy for the score of *From the House of the Dead*. My husband had had it with him there and Universal Edition had asked me for it. When after the funeral I mentioned this to Mayor Tomeš he offered me a city car and as company he gave me Mr Robert Smetana,[116] who was then in the music archive of the museum. And another of my husband's pupils, the composer Pavel Haas,[117] attached himself to us.[118] When we entered the Hukvaldy house and I saw my husband's writing-desk and harmonium again, a

115 Karel Tomeš (1877–1945), Mayor of Brno in the period 1926–35.
116 Robert Smetana (1904–88), later professor of music at Olomouc University. He was a musicology student under Vladimír Helfert at the time and had worked in the music archive of the Moravian Museum since 1924. See also Introduction, p.xvi.
117 Pavel Haas (1899–1944); he studied at the Brno Conservatory (1919–21) and graduated from Janáček's Master School in Composition in 1922.
118 According to Stejskalová's account of the same incident Zdenka's cousin from Pardubice, Thea Kostínková, was also one of the party (Trkanová 1964, 124).

terrible fit of grief came over me. I threw off my mourning hat,[119] which was weighing heavily upon me, I plunged into desperate weeping and wailing, and I sharply criticized Josefka, who was here with us, that she and Mrs Stösslová had nursed my husband badly, that they should have written when he fell ill, that I'd have saved him. She defended herself by saying that Leoš didn't want it. But to this day I'm convinced that he'd have got better if I'd been with him. When I'd calmed down I found the score of *From the House of the Dead*. A new sorrow lay in wait for me in the writing-desk: photographs of the Stössel family with Leoš. Everything was falling on me here, and I endeavoured to settle my affairs as soon as possible. It was necessary to take away my husband's clothes and underwear, because everything was growing mouldy with the damp since no one was airing them or taking care of them. For this reason I also took with me all the ribbons from the wreaths which Leoš had received on various occasions. Mr Smetana advised me to have Leoš's portrait photographed in Brno.[120] We took it down; I told my sister-in-law that I was taking it to Brno only temporarily and that I'd bring it back here again. On the writing-desk lay a letter without an address. I asked her what it was: she replied that Leoš had written it last thing before leaving for the sanatorium,[121] but she didn't know to whom. I took it with me as well to seek advice in Brno about whom it might belong to.

After a few days my sister-in-law in Valašské Meziříčí[122] wrote to me: 'Please, what have you done to Dr Hrstka that he writes so ill of you in the newspapers?' I was surprised to think that Dr Hrstka could write ill of me, that nice Dr Hrstka from Štramberk,[123] Leoš's friend, whom I also knew well, and whom I'd never wronged in any way. I searched to find the newspaper it was in until I came across the *Moravsko-slezský týdeník* of 21 September 1928, where I found an article in the *Besídka* section entitled 'In the steps of Maestro Leoš Janáček'.[124] In it Dr Hrstka described how in the company of

119 Shown in Plate 14.
120 This is the oil painting by Šichan, made at the time of Janáček's wedding (see p.148, fn.62).
121 In fact the letter was written in the sanatorium, the day before he died, see p.229, fn.90.
122 Anna Janáčková [née Schiedecková] (1861–1952), widow of Janáček's older brother Karel (1844–1919).
123 Dr Alois Hrstka (1864–1931), the local doctor in Štramberk.
124 Zdenka's search was indeed out of the way, the entertainment supplement (*Besídka*) of a regional newspaper, the 'Moravian-Silesian weekly'.

William Ritter[125] he visited Hukvaldy after Leoš's death, how Josefka welcomed them in our house and complained sadly that I and two gentlemen had taken away everything from Hukvaldy: pictures off the wall, wreaths and palms which he'd brought here from all over the world, even a letter which Leoš had instructed her to give to Mr Ritter as soon as he arrived in Hukvaldy. Mr Ritter was very surprised that we could have taken a letter which didn't belong to us, but what pained me most in that article was that they said that Leoš had wished to be buried in Hukvaldy and would never have allowed himself to be taken back to Brno. It was very, very painful to read these unjust reproaches from someone to whom I'd been sincerely inclined. I was not surprised at Josefka, who had always behaved to me like this, and in this way had now got her own back for what I'd said to her during my last visit. [. . .]

Josefka likewise had said nothing to me about knowing that the letter was in fact intended for Mr Ritter. Mr Ritter then visited me in Brno; he mentioned the letter and I gladly handed it over to him. If he'd maybe had a poor opinion of me in the light of my sister-in-law's information, I think that he changed it after this visit when we spoke sincerely to one another. The proof of this is the beautiful letter which he later sent me from Switzerland.[126] When Dr Hrstka's article came out, Mr Ritter had already had his letter.

Finally there was the question of the wicked rebuke that Leoš had always wanted to remain in Hukvaldy in life and in death. As far as I know, he never talked about it to me or to anyone else. He loved life too much to think about what should happen to him after his death. He even avoided funerals wherever he could. Only once did he say in passing that he should be burnt, but I had the impression, since he never did anything further about it, that this was only one of those fleeting notions of which he used to have ever so many. He really didn't think of death: after all he spoke at his seventieth birthday so confidently and convincingly: 'Ten years from today I'll be standing here again.' There was nothing in writing on which I could have acted after his death; nor did Mrs Stösslová know anything. So I had him buried here where he lived and worked, in the earth where his teacher Křížkovský lies,[127] as do his children Vladíček and Olinka. I confess

125 William Ritter (1867–1955), French-speaking Swiss critic, novelist and writer on music. He offered Janáček two librettos in 1924, kept in regular touch with him thereafter, spending time with him in Luhačovice in July 1928.
126 Undated letter to Zdenka (BmJA, D 1364).
127 See p.27.

that I wanted to have him here, near me, so that I could visit him frequently and tend his grave when I could no longer do anything else for him. But if he'd ever expressed a wish to be laid to rest in Hukvaldy, I'd have carried out his will, although it would have been difficult for me. Both Josefka and Dr Hrstka are long since dead and gone, but the thorns with which they pricked me in that *Moravsko-slezský týdeník* article prick me still today, although I know that what they said was unjust.

I can't describe the suffering I lived through at the time. Everywhere I went I met sympathetic or curious eyes: in all of them was written that they knew how my husband met his end. The good condemned it, the bad laughed. And I'd always wished him to be [perceived as] highly elevated and pure. I wanted the future at least to forget about it. When the Moravian Quartet were due to play his Second String Quartet [VII/13] dedicated to Mrs Stösslová and called 'Intimate Letters', I tried as hard as I could to prevent the work from carrying this title. I didn't succeed. For a long time I didn't go to concerts where I'd hear that passionate rearing up of Leoš's longing for another woman – a longing which destroyed him. By now I was entirely certain that my instinct didn't deceive me when it suggested to me, long before the end, that Leoš's relationship with Mrs Stösslová would be fateful for us.

People didn't keep silent and they told me what had gone on in the last days of my husband's life at Hukvaldy. How Mrs Stösslová lived with my husband in our house and had the son in a hotel,[128] while Mr Stössel went on business trips. How a fortnight after the death of her mother she went around Hukvaldy in a red *dirndl*, how she and Leoš were merry together, how she sang and he accompanied her on the piano, how Josefka looked on affably at this and proclaimed that it was all pure friendship. They told me how the illness came about. Mrs Stösslová's son arrived to see her. All three went for a walk in our wood. Leoš in his light-coloured silk clothes. Nobody of course gave a thought to the thing that used to be my first care: to take an overcoat for him. It was muggy. They reached our bench and while the lad ran around in the forest, the two of them sat on the bench. They didn't take any notice of the boy and meanwhile he got lost. When they remembered him, my husband rushed off to find him. I can imagine how youthfully he started running round the forest. People said that it

128 Otto Stössel recalls sleeping in the same room with his mother rather than in a hotel (personal communication).

was quite a long time before he found the boy.[129] He got covered in sweat, got tired, then he sat again on the bench and on top of all that he even took off his coat as well. This was where the disaster lay. Even before they walked down to the village beneath the castle he felt shooting pains. Why wasn't I there! I'd have put him to bed at once, I'd have given him compresses. It didn't even occur to Mrs Stösslová. She wasn't from the line of careful Marthas. And also she didn't fear for him as I did. And he certainly exerted himself as long as he could in her presence until the very last moment. He thought that his life force and his will to live would get him over this sort of chill, he didn't want to show himself to be old and sick, in need of care. Why didn't they send for me! Ridiculous male pride: in this way he would have acknowledged that the reality bore out my view, that it isn't possible to be eternally youthful, that to old age belong resignation and careful-ness. How could he have admitted this to his 'silly woman' [i.e. Zdenka], how could he have entrusted his powerless body to her experienced hands? He preferred to leave without saying goodbye, hard and uncompromising as throughout his whole life.

It was terribly hard to learn all this piecemeal from strangers, and then to put it together bit by bit and think about it during the long, desperate nights. From time to time moments of such grief and sadness came over me that I had to cry out aloud, otherwise perhaps I would have choked. That loneliness without his voice, without his playing the piano was frightful. But a hundred times worse was being uncertain why he hadn't wanted to see me before his death and the knowledge that I'd never find this out. One time I said to myself: he was fond of you, he wanted to spare you the sight of his dying. Another time: he hated you so much that he never wanted to see you again. And yet another time: he was frightened what would happen if you met Mrs Stösslová in such circumstances. Then further: pride and vanity didn't allow him to summon you, in this way he'd have had to acknowledge defeat. But these are only conjectures. I will never know the real truth. One thing I know for certain: that it thwarted my idea of departing together with him as I'd always imagined and as I'd furthermore written to him after the death of the Těsnohlídeks. Could I come near him for eternity when he didn't want to see me here on earth? It was cruel, very cruel of him to leave me in this way.

129 Accounts differ of how Janáček caught the chill that led to his death. Otto Stössel, who was twelve at the time, has always maintained that Janáček did not search for him and that he found his own way back.

Glossary of names, places and concepts

archbishop's estate The Archbishop of Olomouc (originally a Prince-Bishop and until 1848 a feudal landowner) owned the Hukvaldy domain continuously from the sixteenth century until the 1950s. By Janáček's time the estate included a new manor house to replace the castle (burnt down in the 1760s) and a walled-off game reserve with park and stud-farm.

Beseda A friendly conversation, neighbourly gathering for a chat. From this primary meaning several subsidiary meanings developed in the nineteenth century, notably that of a social organization, e.g. the Beseda brněnská [Brno Beseda], for which the Besední dům was built and a type of dance (see p.31, fn.29).

Besední dům Building erected in Brno 1873 for the Czechs' cultural gatherings and other entertainments. See 'Beseda' above.

Brno Theatre Zdenka records going as a child to see an operetta in the temporary Interimstheater (see p.7). The performance would have been in German, and this building, in what is now Moravské náměstí, was replaced after eleven years by the Stadttheater (opened 14 November 1882), an opulent and well-equipped theatre built on the former ramparts ('Na hradbách'). The Schulz family had a single season ticket; Zdenka recalls taking turns with her mother to use it (p.44).

The Czech population of Brno was not so lucky in its theatre provision. From 1874 touring companies performed in the Besední dům (see above); it was there that Zdenka probably saw Gounod's *Faust* in 1880 (p.31). On 6 December 1884 the Czech Provisional Theatre opened in an adapted building on Veveří ulice. It was only after Czechoslovak Independence that the Czechs had access to the German theatre. Thus Janáček's *Jenůfa* was given its première in the Veveří theatre in 1904, but *Káťa Kabanová* and later operas were given in the German theatre, now known as the National Theatre, but often referred to as the Town Theatre. The theatre on Veveří ulice (later known as the 'Old Theatre') remained in use as a drama theatre until its demolition in 1952; the former German theatre is still in service as a drama theatre, renamed the Mahen Theatre.

Brod, Max (1884–1968) German-speaking writer and critic, born in Prague. He was the friend and biographer of Kafka and, following the Prague première of *Jenůfa* in 1916, a staunch friend and supporter of Janáček, most of whose opera librettos he translated into German.

Calma-Veselá, Marie [Hurychová, Marie] (1881–1966) Writer (under the name of Marie Calma) and singer, married to Dr František Veselý, director of the spa at Luhačovice, where Janáček met her in 1908. Both were crucial in the campaign to get *Jenůfa* produced at the Prague National Theatre.

Christmas Eve The Czechs have retained the Catholic celebration of Christmas on Christmas Eve. Since this is a fast day in Catholic countries, fish (usually carp in this region) is served at the main meal. Another familiar feature of Christmas food in the region are the sweet biscuits baked in many different varieties by each family.

Dohnalová [née Janáčková], **Josefa** [Josefka; Pepka] (**Adolfína**) (1842–1931) One of Janáček's older sisters. She worked in the Hukvaldy school as a domestic-science teacher from 1876. In 1892, at the age of fifty, she married a local teacher, Jindřich Dohnal (1868–1938), and moved with him to Hulváky, near Ostrava, returning to Hukvaldy in 1901, when Jindřich became headmaster of the local school. The marriage did not work out (she was twenty-six years older than he was), and the couple were divorced in 1919. She was close to her brother and took his side in the family quarrel over Mrs Stösslová. She kept house for him in his Hukvaldy cottage and lived there until her death.

Dressler family Dr Karel Dressler (1864–1943) was a cousin (once removed) of Janáček's, the grandson of his aunt Johanka, who married the farmer Jan Dressler in Abrechtičky. He was a medical doctor and treated Olga during her final illness. His wife was Ida Dresslerová (1876–1929), née Janotová. Their three daughters included Věra Dresslerová (1897–1921).

Heindlová, Marie (d 1955) Owner of a glass and porcelain shop on Česká ulice, and friend of Zdenka Janáčková.

Herben, Dr Jan (1854–1936) Writer, journalist and politician.

Horvátová, Gabriela [married name Noltschová] (1877–1967) Singer. A Croat by birth, she sang in Zagreb and in German opera houses before being engaged in 1903 by the Prague National Theatre, where she became one of the theatre's most useful and versatile singers and was assigned roles which ranged from mezzo (Carmen, Kundry) to dramatic soprano (Tosca, Libuše, Brünnhilde). A high point in her career was her portrayal of the Kostelnička in *Jenůfa* in 1916. She retired in 1930. Janáčková describes her husband's passionate affair with her, and its impact on his married life, in Chapter 7. The advent of Kamila Stösslová was responsible for his waning interest in Mrs Horvátová.

Hudební matice Music publishing organization, founded in Prague in 1871, under the aegis of the Czech cultural club, the Umělecká beseda. Hudební matice published the second edition of *Jenůfa* and thereafter many of Janáček's later non-operatic works.

Hukvaldy A village in northern Moravia, Janáček's birthplace. Janáček, who left home at eleven, revisited his home village frequently from the 1880s: on his honeymoon, for folksong-collecting expeditions, and on holidays with his wife and daughter. In 1921 he bought a small house there from his sister-in-law Marie Janáčková and installed his sister Josefa Dohnalová there as housekeeper. Thereafter he went several times a year. Zdenka usually joined him in the summer and autumn or went there on her own.

Janáček, František (Josef) (1856–1908) One of Janáček's younger brothers. He worked as a mechanical engineer in Gleiwitz, Prussian Silesia (now Gliwice, Poland) and in 1883 married Marie Koziczińska there. From 1895 he worked in St Petersburg, where Janáček visited him the next year, and where Olga Janáčková paid her ill-fated visit in 1902. František himself fell ill; he was operated on in 1905 and then purchased a cottage in Hukvaldy, where he lived until his death. His widow returned to Gliwice, selling the cottage to Janáček in 1921.

Janáčková [née Grulichová], **Amálie** (1819–84) Janáček's mother. In 1838 she married the teacher Jiří Janáček, with whom she had thirteen children. Leoš was the ninth, born six years after his father was appointed schoolmaster in Hukvaldy in 1848. Leoš was sent to Brno as a chorister at the Augustinian Monastery in 1865. After his father's death a year later his mother went to stay with relatives in Příbor; in the 1870s she went to Brno to keep house for Leoš and some time after his marriage in 1881 she moved in with her daughter Eleonora. In the summer of 1884 she returned to Hukvaldy a few months before she died of cancer.

Janáčková, Eleonora [Lorka] **(Amálie)** (1840–1919) Janáček's second oldest sibling, a needlework teacher in Švábenice near Vyškov (see p.48).

Janáčková, Josefa *See* Josefa (Adolfína) Dohnalová.

Janáčková [née Procházková], **Josefa** [Joža] (1865–1937) The widow of Janáček's cousin Augustin Janáček (1851–1900). She lived in Prague with her daughter Věra (see next entry).

Janáčková, Věra (1891–1967) Janáček's 'niece' (*recte* first cousin once removed), the daughter of his cousin Augustin Janáček. Janáček got to know Věra, who lived in Prague with her widowed mother Josefa Janáčková, initially during her brief period of boarding school in Brno, and later during Janáček's trips to Prague. She met Kamila Stösslová in 1918, early on in the relationship with Janáček, and did her best to upset it, remaining outspokenly critical at the time of Janáček's death.

Josefka *See* Josefa (Adolfína) Dohnalová.

Koudelová, Adéla (1858–1946) For many years chair of the women's educational society Vesna (see below). She was the wife of the lawyer and member of the Austrian parliament Dr Josef Koudela (1845–1913), ennobled by the Austrian administration in 1908.

Kovařovic, Karel (1862–1920) Composer, conductor and head of opera at the National Theatre in Prague (1900–1920). Kovařovic's attitude to Janáček had been soured by a sarcastic notice that Janáček, in his capacity as music critic, wrote about the Brno première of Kovařovic's opera *The Bridegrooms* in 1887. He refused to accept *Jenůfa* for production at the Prague National Theatre in 1903 and persisted in this view until finally persuaded by Janáček's friends in late 1915.

Kunc, Jan (1883–1976) Composer, critic and administrator. He graduated from Janáček's Organ School in Brno in 1903 and studied further at the Prague Conservatory (1905–6). He became the administrator (1920–3) and director (1923–45) of the Brno Conservatory (the former Organ School).

Lorka *See* Eleonora Janáčková.

Lachian/Valachian Lašsko and Valašsko are adjacent ethnographic regions in Moravia but were not differentiated until the folklorist František Bartoš did so in his *Dialektologie moravská* (1886–95). Before then a Lach (a man from Lašsko) would have called himself either 'Moravian' or 'Valachian'. A good example of the change in usage is Janáček's retitling of his *Valašské tance* [Valachian Dances], published as such in 1890, to *Lašské tance* [Lachian Dances], published as such in 1928. (See *JW*, pp.187–8.)

Luhačovice Spa resort in Moravia. In 1902 the spa was acquired from its owner Count Otto Serényi and it rapidly developed into a fashionable Czech-speaking resort, largely on account of the efforts of its first director, Dr František Veselý. In 1902 it attracted 2024 registered summer visitors; by 1926 the number was 9559, mostly from Czechoslovakia. Janáček was among the best-known and most faithful of the visitors, spending several weeks there almost every summer from 1903 until his death. It was in Luhačovice that he met Kamila Stösslová and her family in 1917.

Lužánky Brno's largest park. Originally the garden of a Jesuit monastery, the park was given by Emperor Josef II to the citizens of Brno in 1786, from which time it was known as the Lužánky. A hall and pavilion, now part of a leisure centre, was built in 1853–5 and from about this time a garden restaurant and café were opened during the summer months with open-air concerts and other entertainments. In Janáček's day it was a well-known place for social outings. The Sunday morning concerts of the Organ School were given in the Lužánky hall in 1911–14.

Machová, Eliška (1858–1926) Schoolteacher, co-founder of the girls' schools run by Vesna in Brno and of the Útulna, the women's shelter in Brno.

Mareš, František (1862–1941) Schoolteacher, from 1888 director of Vesna schools in Brno. In 1900 he became the first chairman of the Club of the Friends of Art. He came into contact with Janáček in both capacities and seems to have been a sympathetic friend to Mrs Janáčková.

Money Janáček died a comparatively rich man. A few days before his death his annual royalty payment came through from Universal Edition in Vienna: Kč 31,000 (Czechoslovak crowns), equivalent in 1928–9 to double a year's salary for a professional person in Czechoslovakia. A teacher, for instance, got Kč 1100 a month, a high-grade civil servant Kč 1750. Zdenka was right to describe birthday presents of Kč 1000 in her later years as generous, though she felt Kč 600 for a month's housekeeping in August 1928 was not.

   The Czechoslovak *koruna* or crown (Kč) was established in 1919 after Czechoslovakia broke away from the former Austro-Hungarian Empire at the end of the First World War. The official parity of Kč 24.02 to £1 (the prewar parity of the Austrian Kroner) was soon eroded by inflation so that by 1921 the *koruna* stood at over Kč 400 to £1. By 1923, however, the *koruna* had stabilized at Kč 160 to £1. Janáček's final royalty payment of Kč 31,000 was worth almost £2000, over double the annual salary of a general practitioner in England at the time.

From 1892 to 1918 the currency in Bohemia and Moravia was the Austrian Kroner (K), *koruna* in Czech. This replaced the currency introduced by the Habsburg empire in 1811, the Gulden, known in Czech as the *zlatník* (zl.) or informally as a *zlatý*. Conversion in 1892 took place at the rate of 1 zl. = K 2 (the respective parities with the pound were approximately 10 zl. and K 24). The ducats that Zdenka refers to in Chapter 2 were gold coins (as opposed to the silver *zlatník*). Their value fluctuated but 20 ducats would have been roughly the equivalent of 100 zl., i.e. £10.

Zdenka does not mention how much she got for housekeeping at the beginning of her marriage, but we know that Janáček paid 25 zl. a month for Olga's upkeep in the early 1880s. In 1894 Mářa Stejskalová received a monthly salary of 6 zl. with free accommodation and food, except for supper, for which she was paid 2 zl. a day. Vladimír's wet-nurse got 12 zl. a month and full board.

Neumann, František (1874–1929) Conductor and composer. He became music director of the newly reconstituted Czech opera in Brno after the First World War and in this capacity gave the premières of *Káťa Kabanová*, *The Cunning Little Vixen* and *The Makropulos Affair*.

Obecní dům [Municipal House] Building (1905–11) in náměstí Republiky, containing the Smetanova síň [Smetana Hall], the home of the Czech Philharmonic, and a restaurant which Janáček began frequenting from the days of the *Jenůfa* rehearsals in 1916. The first Prague performances of some of Janáček's works took place in the Smetana Hall.

Písek Town in southern Bohemia in which Kamila Stösslová's parents lived; Kamila and her family moved there in 1919. Janáček began visiting Kamila Stösslová in Písek in 1924. The frequency of his visits increased in 1927 and especially in 1928 (see *IL*, 'Diary of Meetings', pp.365–7). The train journey from Brno to Písek was long (almost eight hours, with only one trip a day) and Janáček generally tried to combine his visits to Písek with trips to Prague, from where it was much more accessible.

Radhošť Mountain (1129 m) in the Beskydy hills, south of Frenštát. Well known for its view and the folk legends attached to it, it was graced by the complex of wooden buildings designed by Dušan Jurkovič in a striking combination of Jugendstil and Slovácko folk style. These included the hotel Tanečnice [Dancer], where the Janáčeks stayed in 1927.

Rakowitschová, Mrs **Františka** [née Jungová] (1864–1950) The second daughter of Josef and Marie Jung of Hukvaldy. In 1885 she married Rheinhold Rakowitsch, employed as a forestry official on the estate of the Archbishop of Olomouc in Hukvaldy. For an account of Janáček's interest in her see pp.52–3.

Ruprecht, Father **František** (1841–1903) Professor of religion at the Teachers' Institute. He was an active figure in Czech Brno, especially in the Beseda Brněnská (see Helfert 1939, 272). He officiated at the marriage of Leoš and Zdenka Janáček.

Russian Circle A group in Brno founded by Janáček in 1898, after his return from

Russia, dedicated to the promotion of Russian language and culture. It was closed down in 1915 during the First World War.

Sládeks Family in Hukvaldy. Vincenc Sládek (1865–1944) was a gamekeeper and married to Antonie (1863–1941). The Janáčeks often stayed with them during their visits to Hukvaldy and knew them affectionately as the 'Sládečeks'. Their son, also Vincenc (1895–1929), attended Janáček's funeral.

Slovácko [Moravian Slovakia] Ethnographic region in Moravia bordering on Slovakia, with distinctive dialect, folk music and folk crafts. Janáček's third opera, *Jenůfa*, is set there.

Smetana Hall *See* Obecní dům.

Stejskalová, Marie [Máňa] (1873–1968) The Janáčeks' servant from 1894 until Zdenka Janáčková's death in 1938. Her arrival is described in Chapter 5, and thereafter she remains important in the narrative. Her reminiscences, a useful source of information about Janáček's daily life (but see Introduction), were published in 1959.

Stössel, David (1889–1982) Husband of Kamila Stösslová. His father had moved from Lwów (then Austrian Galicia) to Strážnice in Moravia and Janáček intervened to prevent his repatriation to Poland (see p.222). A businessman, he dealt in antiques and pictures, which he sold in a shop he opened in the Karlín district of Prague in January 1927 (see p.205). After his wife's death and shortly before the Second World War, he pawned the letters Janáček wrote to her and other Janáček documents and emigrated to Switzerland.

Stösslová [née Neumannová], **Kamila** (1891–1935) Wife of David Stössel. She came from near Písek, Bohemia and moved to Moravia with her husband David after their marriage on 5 May 1912. They had two sons, Rudolf (1913–78) and Otto (1916–). Janáček met the Stössels on holiday in Luhačovice in 1916 (see p.159) and this initiated a friendship between him and Kamila which lasted until his death and which was the inspiration for many of his later compositions. At first the relationship was welcomed by Zdenka Janáčková as a means of detaching him from Gabriela Horvátová, and in the early years she corresponded with Kamila and had the couple to stay, though such visits ceased after the Stössels moved to Písek in April 1919. Janáček began to visit the Stössels there in 1924, but it was only in April 1927 that the friendship took a more intimate turn. Janáček began to address Kamila in the familiar form 'Ty'; he visited more frequently and began writing to her daily. Janáček's obsession with Kamila led to a marked deterioration of his relationship with his wife.

Town Theatre *See* Brno Theatre.

Ty and Vy *Ty* is the intimate form of 'you' (singular), used among family and close friends. This form of address is known as *tykání*. The corresponding possessive pronoun ('your') in its feminine form is *Tvá* and it was one occurrence of this word in a letter from Kamila Stösslová to Janáček that particularly upset Zdenka (see p.207). *Vy* is the formal form of 'you' (singular and plural).

Útulna [shelter] The Útulna ženská v Brně [The Women's Shelter in Brno] was founded on 12 September 1899 by Eliška Machová (see above) as a shelter for needy young women from the country seeking work in Brno, though it soon began taking in orphans and abandoned children. In 1900 it was renamed the Moravská ústřední útulna ženská v Brné [The Moravian Central Women's Shelter in Brno]. The Janáčeks were involved from the start – Zdenka was on the committee as treasurer – and helped in fund-raising exercises. Zdenka appeared as Libuše in a *tableau vivant*; Janáček wrote three Slavonic dances (VI/11–13) for the Slovanská Beseda organized to mark the opening (10 January 1900) for which Zdenka organized the costumes and rehearsed the Lachian *Požehnaný* (VI/11) (see pp.67–8). The next year Janáček's *Our Father* (IV/29) was written and performed for another fund-raising concert. After Mrs Machová's departure for Prague in 1902, Marie Steyskalová (1862–1928) became director. It was under her, a decade later, that the Brno Útulna founded a special children's home in the Croatian coastal resort of Crikvenica, a circumstance which led to the Janáčeks' holidaying there in 1912. The Útulna continued to exist until it was closed down by the Communist administration in 1950–1.

Váchová, Vítězslava [Viktoria] (1876–1957) Friend of Zdenka Janáčková. She was the wife of Dr Jindřich Vácha (1872–1954), chief judge at the highest court of law in Brno.

Valašsko *See* Lachian/Valachian.

Veselý, Dr František (1862–1923) Medical doctor, the creator of the public spa at Luhačovice. He was chairman of the Club of the Friends of Art and a leading force, with his wife Marie Calma-Veselá, in the campaign to get *Jenůfa* produced at the Prague National Theatre. In 1915 the Veselýs moved to the Bohemian spa of Bohdaneč, where Dr Veselý became chief medical officer.

Vesna Founded in 1870 as a choral society, it later became an educational establishment for girls. In 1886 Eliška Machová, the general secretary, founded a girls' school of which František Mareš became director in 1888. By the turn of the century the society had evolved into a series of schools, providing instruction for girls both at an academic and at a practical level (Olga Janáčková learnt sewing there; Máŕa Stejskalová attended school there for a year). Many of the Janáčeks' friends held important positions in Vesna. Apart from František Mareš and Eliška Machová they included their landlord Julie Kusá-Fantová (one-time chairman of the Vesna committee), Adéla Koudelová and Josef Němec.

Vyroubal, Josef (1866–1945) A post-office superintendent, later a post-office executive. He lived with his wife Marie and daughter Otilie at Falkensteinerova ulice no.29, where they provided a home for Zdenka's father, Emilian Schulz, for the last two years of his life (see p.180).

Zahradníková, Marie (1875–1956) Friend of Zdenka Janáčková. She was the widow of the director of the Brno Technical University. Zdenka met Mrs Zahradníková at the Marian Association, where Zdenka was seeking religious consolation after the breakdown of her marriage in 1917 and thereafter they remained close friends.

Žaludová [nee Kossauerová, later Motyčková], **Cyrilla** (1865–?1921) She was the daughter of a mill-owner Jindřich Kossauer in Želišice near Brno, and was herself born at the Královský mlýn [King's Mill] in Komárov, near Brno. She married Janáček's friend Berthold Žalud on 8 August 1882 at St Jiljí in Komárov; Janáček and his father-in-law Emilian Schulz were witnesses. The couple lived in Old Brno and Cyrilla soon became 'like a sister' to Zdenka. When the Janáčeks separated Mrs Žaludová cleaned for Janáček and provided neutral territory for Janáček's visits to see Olga. After the death of her husband on 19 July 1886 Mrs Žaludová moved in with her brother, now renting the Královský mlýn in Komárov, where Zdenka often visited her. In 1898 she married Jan Motyčka (1867–1928) and with him eventually took over the mill. From September 1919 she provided a home in Komárov for Emilian Schulz. He presumably moved with them in 1920 to Brno, Falkensteinerova ulice no.9. The next year Schulz lodged with the Vyroubal family in the same street.

Appendices

APPENDIX I
Olga's final illness

Zdenka's description of Olga Janáčková's illness is a classic one of the evolution of chronic rheumatic heart disease. The earlier pages tell us that Olga had rheumatic fever affecting her joints and her heart (on p.57 it is described as affecting the pericardium – the outer membrane lining the surface of the heart – and on p.62 Zdenka speaks of chronic heart disease). The later pages detail the insidious progress of heart disease leading to heart failure, congestion of the lungs, and then waterlogging of the abdomen and legs.

From a medical point of view this condition is best appreciated from descriptions in the most famous medical textbook of the times (and for that matter, of all times), William Osler's *The Principles and Practice of Medicine*. Born in Ontario in 1849, Osler was successively professor of medicine at McGill (Montreal), Pennsylvania, Johns Hopkins Hospital (Baltimore), and Oxford, where he was Regius Professor and honoured with a knighthood. He died in 1919.

Young adults are most often affected by rheumatic fever, Osler points out, and the most frequent complication is endocarditis (inflammation of the inner lining of the chambers of the heart). The heart valves, which separate the chambers of the heart from each other, are particularly affected (and most frequently the mitral valve, which separates the left atrium from the left ventricle – respectively, the upper and lower chambers of the left side of the heart). 'In many cases,' Osler writes, 'the curtains [valves] are so welded together and the whole valvular region so thickened that the orifice is reduced to a mere chink. [. . .] Failure of compensation brings in its train the group of symptoms [. . .]: rapid and irregular action of the heart, shortness of breath, cough [. . .]. The liver may be greatly enlarged and in the late state ascites [fluid in the abdominal cavity] is not uncommon, particularly in children.' And Osler comments earlier in this section that with 'judicious treatment the compensation may be restored and all the serious symptoms pass away'. Later he goes on to say that: 'Patients may have recurring attacks of this kind, but ultimately the condition is beyond repair and the patient either dies of a general dropsy, or there is progressive dilatation [enlargement] of the heart, and death from asystole [cessation of the heartbeat]'. This description, from the first (1892) edition of Osler's classic textbook, emphasizes that the initial effect of disease of the mitral valve is to throw a strain on the left atrium, which becomes enlarged, and then to cause congestion of the lungs (the 'bronchial catarrh' in Zdenka's account), and ultimately the rest of the heart and the body itself. At that time the origin of the process leading to rheumatic fever was unknown; today we realize that it is due to an unusual reaction by the body to infection by the germ called streptococcus (usually a severe sore throat). Nowadays, full-blown rheumatic fever is still seen in the developing world, but in the developed world such an infection is usually nipped in the bud by treatment with antibiotics. If rheumatic fever does occur, then it can be treated with large doses of aspirin or steroids, while if rheumatic heart disease supervenes and the valves become fused or loose, then they can be split into their component parts by a surgical operation or replaced altogether with a graft or an artificial valve.

STEPHEN LOCK

Leoš Janáček's and Zdenka Janáčková's divorce settlement

Minutes of the negotiations between Mr Leoš *Janáček*, musical composer in Brno and Mrs Zdenka *Janáčková*, née Schulzová, wife of the same, in the presence of their representatives Dr Felix Rudiš and Dr Ludvík Hanf, solicitors in Brno, as follows:

Without meanwhile entering into formal divorce proceedings in court and without thereby abandoning the grounds on which it would be possible, if needs be, to seek a court divorce, the married couple Leoš and Zdenka *Janáčkovi* have agreed to regulate their future marital state in such a way as would have arisen from the realization of a voluntary divorce *complying with the consequences of such a divorce*.

The *Janáčeks* will continue to run a *domestic household* together as before, at the same time both will do their best to preserve domestic calm and peace and not upset the feelings of the other by harsh treatment.

If as time goes on it transpires that the essential domestic peace is fundamentally and continually disturbed by the behaviour of either of the parties and thus the running of a household in the same way as before seems to be impossible, or if either of the parties directly or through others seriously threatens by word or deed the social standing of the second party or defames it publicly or in front of strangers, an application for a *voluntary legal divorce* by the party thus threatened or affected would be instigated for which the following conditions affecting property were agreed:

For the support of Mrs Zdenka *Janáčková* Mr Leoš *Janáček* undertakes, in the case of a court divorce, to pay out or, rather, leave his whole pension which on the basis of the Pension Decree of 25 September 1904 (no.16583) he receives as a music teacher at the Imperial and Royal Czech Institution for Teacher Training in Brno with its subsequent rises as requested and which yields at present K 227 a month.

Since a divorce in court would furthermore be without fault on the part of Mrs Zdenka *Janáčková* and in the case of a divorce her support after the death of Mr Leoš *Janáček* also must be secured according to his intentions, it was agreed that from Mr Leoš Janáček's estate and namely from the royalties from his operas which would accrue to his estate an annuity should be paid to Mrs Zdenka *Janáčková* for life which together with the pension she would receive as the widow of a music teacher, would equal the earnings, guaranteed according to these proceedings to Mrs *Janáčková*, i.e. the pension of Mr Leoš *Janáček* ceded to her.

Also regarding these proceedings Mr Leoš *Janáček* will give, in the case of a voluntary divorce in court, to Mrs Zdenka *Janáčková* at her request a binding undertaking, fully consistent with the law, whereby the above-mentioned claim of Mrs *Janáčková* is assigned with regard to his estate and heirs in an unambiguous manner.

In Brno 19 January 1917
[signed] Zdenka Janáčková
Leoš Janáček

Bibliography

Items are arranged alphabetically by author, then chronologically under that author. Czech diacritics are ignored in alphabetization.

ABBREVIATIONS

ed.   editor, edited by

Eng.   English

Hž   Svatava Přibáňová, ed.: *Hádanka života: dopisy Leoše Janáčka Kamile Stösslové* [The riddle of life: the letters of Leoš Janáček to Kamila Stösslová] (Opus musicum, Brno, 1990)

IB   Jakob Knaus, ed.: *'Intime Briefe' 1879/80 aus Leipzig und Wien* (Leoš Janáček-Gesellschaft, Zürich, 1985)

IL   John Tyrrell, trans. and ed.: *Intimate Letters: Leoš Janáček to Kamila Stösslová* (Faber and Faber, London, 1994)

JA   Janáčkův archiv, first series, general ed. Vladimír Helfert (i) and Jan Racek (ii–ix)

    iv *Korespondence Leoše Janáčka s Artušem Rektorem*, ed. Artuš Rektorys (Hudební matice Umělecké besedy, Prague, enlarged 2/1949)

    vi *Korespondence Leoše Janáčka s Gabrielou Horvátovou*, ed. Artuš Rektorys (Hudební matice, Prague, 1950)

    vii *Korespondence Leoše Janáčka s Karlem Kovařovičem a ředitelstvím Národního divadla* [Janáček's correspondence with Kovařovic and the management of the National Theatre], ed. Artuš Rektorys (Hudební matice, Prague, 1950)

    viii *Korespondence Leoše Janáčka s Marií Calmou a MUDr Františkem Veselým*, ed. Jan Racek and Artuš Rektorys (Hudební nakladatelství, Orbis, Prague, 1953)

    ix *Korespondence Leoše Janáčka s Maxem Brodem*, ed. Jan Racek and Artuš Rektorys (Státní nakladatelství krásné literatury, hudby a umění, Prague, 1953)

JODA   John Tyrrell: *Janáček's Operas: a Documentary Account* (Faber and Faber, London, 1992)

JW   Nigel Simeone, John Tyrrell and Alena Němcová: *Janáček's Works: a Catalogue of the Music and Writings of Leoš Janáček* (Oxford University Press, Oxford, 1997)

OM   *Opus musicum*

trans.   translation, translated by

Altman, Karel: *Krčemné Brno: o hostincích, kavárnách a hotelech ale také o hospodách, výčepech a putýkách v moravské metropoli* [Victualler's Brno: on taverns, cafés and hotels but also on pubs, bars and dives in the Moravian, capital] (Snip & Co, and Doplněk, Brno, 1993)

Baedeker, Karl: *Austria, together with Budapest, Prague, Karlsbad, Marienbad: Handbook for Travellers* (Karl Baedeker, Leipzig; Allen & Unwin, London, 1929)

Bauerová, Anna: *Tisíc jmen v kalendáři* [A thousand names in the calendar] (Šulc a spol., Prague, 1992)

Bednaříková, Marie and others: *Dějiny university v Brně* [The history of the university in Brno] (Universita J.E. Purkyně v Brně, Brno, 1969)

Bulín, Hynek: *Besední dům v Brně 1872–1922* (Brno, Slavnostní výbor, [1922])

Černušák, Gracian, Štědroň, Bohumír and Nováček, Zdenko, eds.: *Československý hudební slovník osob a institucí* [The Czechoslovak music dictionary of people and institutions] (Státní hudební vydavatelství, Prague, 1963–5)

Cmunt, Eduard and others: *Almanach lázní Československé republiky* [Almanac of spas of the Czechoslovak Republic] (Balneologický ústav Karlovy university v Praze, Prague, 1949)

Dřímal, Jaroslav and Peša, Václav, eds.: *Dějiny města Brna* [The history of Brno], ii (Národní výbor města Brna/Blok, Brno, 1973)

Drlíková, Eva: 'Fedora Bartošová: básnířka nebo žena literárních vloh?' [Fedora Bartošová: poet or woman of literary gifts?], *OM*, xxiii (1991), 323–6

Dufková, Eugenie and Srba, Bořivoj, eds.: *Postavy brněnského jeviště* [Figures of the Brno stage], i–iii (Státní divadlo v Brně, Brno, 1979–94)

Eichler, Karel: *Životopis a skladby Pavla Křížkovského* [The biography and compositions of Pavel Křížkovský] (Brno, Knihtiskárna benediktinů raj-hradských, 1904)

Fischmann, Zdenka E., ed: *Janáček–Newmarch Correspondence* (Kabel Publishers, Rockville, Maryland, 1986)

Flodrová, Milena: *Brněnské hřbitovy* [Brno cemeteries] (Brno, Rovnost, 1992)

Flodrová, Milena, Galasovská, Blažena and Vodička, Jaroslav: *Seznam ulic města Brna s vývojem jejich pojmenování* [Catalogue of streets of the town of Brno with the evolution of their naming] (Muzejní a vlastivědná společnost, Brno, enlarged 2/1984); for continuation see Zřídkaveselý 1996

A Handbook for Travellers in South Germany and Austria, i (John Murray, London, 15/1890)

Helfert, Vladimír: *Leoš Janáček*, i (Oldřich Pazdírek, Brno, 1939)

Herain, Karel: *Plan of the Capital Prague . . . A Guide through Prague . . . Index of Streets* (Orbis, Prague, 1926)

Hilmar, Ernst, ed: *Leoš Janáček: Briefe an die Universal Edition* (Hans Schneider, Tutzing, 1988)

Janáček, Leoš: *O lidové písni a lidové hudbě* [On folksong and folk music], ed. Jiří Vysloužil (Státní nakladatelství krásné literary, hudby a umění, Prague, 1955)

Jurkovič, Dušan: *Pustevna na Radhošti* [The 'Pustevna' on Radhošť] (A. Píša, Brno, 1900)

Knaus, Jakob: 'Poslední dopis' [The last letter], *OM*, xx (1988), no.9, pp.xxv–vii

Kožík, František: *Po zarostlém chodníčku* [On the overgrown path] (Československý spisovatel, Prague, 1967, 3/Velehrad, Prague, 1983)

Kožíšek, Alois V.: *Brno, hlavní město Moravy* [Brno, the capital of Moravia] (Zemský cizinecký svaz v Brně, Brno, 1926)

Kožíšek, Alois V., ed.: *Brno: město a okolí* [Brno: town and surroundings] (Národohospodářská propagace Československa, Brno, 1928)

Kubíček, Jaromír and others: *Literatura o Brně z let 1801–1979: soupis publikací a článků* [Literature about Brno 1801–1979: list of publications and articles] (Státní vědecká knihovna etc., Brno, 1980)

Kundera, Ludvík: *Janáčkova varhanická škola* [Janáček's Organ School] (Velehrad, Olomouc, 1948)

Kyas, Vojtěch: 'Janáček se neměl o koho opřít?' [Did Janáček have no one to rely on?], *OM*, xxv (1993), 33–42

Kyas, Vojtěch: *Slavné hudební osobnosti v Brně/Berühmte Musikpersönlichkeiten in Brünn (1859–1914)* (Opus musicum, Brno, 1995)

Lázňovský, Bohuslav: *Průvodce po československé republice* [A guide to the Czechoslovak Republic] (Orbis, Prague, 1926)

Macek, Petr: 'Leoš Janáček a František Ondrúšek: přátelství skladatele a malíře' [Leoš Janáček and František Ondrúšek: the friendship of composer and painter], *OM*, xx (1988), 52–6

Masarykův slovník naučný [The Masaryk encyclopedia] (Československý kompas, Prague, 1924–36)

Míka, Zdeněk, ed.: *Dějiny Prahy v datech* [The history of Prague in dates] (Panorama, Prague, 1989)

Mrázek, Ivan: *Kamenná tvář Brna* [The stone face of Brno] (Moravské zemské muzeum, Brno, 1993)

Ottův slovník naučný [Otto's encyclopedia] (J. Otto, Prague, 1888–1909)

Prachář, Augustin: *Velké Brno* [Greater Brno] (Ústřední spolek učitelského na Moravě, Brno, 1925)

Přibáňová, Svatava: 'Nové prameny k rodokmenu Leoše Janáčka' [New sources for Leoš Janáček's family tree], *Časopis Moravského muzea: vědy společenské*, lxix (1984), 129–37 [Přibáňová 1984a]

Přibáňová, Svatava: *Opery Leoše Janáčka doma a v zahraničí* [The operas of Leoš Janáček at home and abroad], *Program* [Státního divadla v Brně] (1984, special no.) [Přibáňová 1984b]

Přibáňová, Svatava, ed.: *Dopisy strýci/Dopisy matky* [Letters to his uncle/Letters from his mother], published as supplement to Vincenc Janáček: *Životopis Jiříka Janáčka* [The autobiography of Vincenc Janáček], ed. Jiří Sehnal (Opus musicum, Brno, 1985)

Procházka, Jaroslav: *Lašské kořeny života i díla Leoše Janáčka* [The Lašsko roots of the life and work of Leoš Janáček] (Okresní a místní rada osvětová ve Frýdku–Místku, Frýdek–Místek, 1948)

Procházka, Vladimír, ed.: *Národní divadlo a jeho předchůdci: slovník umělců divadel Vlastenského, Stavovského, Prozatímního a Národního* [The National Theatre and its forerunners: a dictionary of artists at the Patriotic, Estates, Provisional and National Theatres] (Academia, Prague, 1988)

Procházková, Jarmila, ed.: *Leoš Janáček: Památník pro Kamila Stösslovou* (Moravské zemské muzeum, Brno, 1994; Eng. trans., Moravské zemské muzeum, Brno, 1996, as *Leoš Janáček: Album for Kamila Stösslová*)

Procházková, Jarmila and Volný, Bohumír: *Narozen na Hukvaldech* (Moravské zemské muzeum, Brno, 1994; Eng. trans., Moravské zemské muzeum, Brno, 1995, as *Born in Hukvaldy*)

Racek, Jan, ed.: *Leoš Janáček: Fejetony z Lidových novin* [Feuilletons from *Lidové noviny*] (Krajské nakladatelství, Brno, 1958)

Sajner, Josef: 'Patografická studie o Leoši Janáčkovi' [A pathological study of Leoš Janáček], *OM*, xiv (1982), 233–5

Sáňka, Hugo, ed.: *Šedesát let českého gymnasia v Brně 1867–1927* [Sixty years of the Czech Gymnasium in Brno 1867–1927] (Výbor pro oslavu šedesátiletí, Brno, [1927])

Simeone, Nigel: 'Zamyšlené uvedení Janáčkovy Věci Makropulos v Berlíně roku 1928' [The proposed Berlin production of Janáček's *The Makropulos Affair* in 1928], *OM*, xxv (1993), 245–8

Sirovátka, Oldřich and others: *Město pod Špilberkem: o lidové kultuře, tradicích a životě lidí v Brně a okolí* [The town under the Spielberg: on folk culture, traditions and the life of the people in Brno and in the surrounding area] (Ústav pro etnografii a folkloristiku AVČR, Brno, 1993)

Slavnostní promoce Leoše Janáčka čestného doktora fil. fakulty Masarykovy university v Brně 28.I.1925 [The graduation of Leoš Janáček as an honorary doctor of the Philosophy Faculty of Masaryk University in Brno, 28 January 1925] (Ol. Pazdírek, Brno, 1925)

Smetana, Robert: 'Z posledních dnů' [From the last days], *Hudební rozhledy*, iv (1928), nos.4–8 [unpaginated]

Smetana, Robert: 'Domek za konservatoří' [The house behind the conservatory], *Lidové noviny* (3 June 1933)

Smetana, Robert: 'Leoš Janáček na Hukvaldech' [Leoš Janáček at Hukvaldy], *Lidové noviny* (12 August 1933)

Smetana, Robert: *Vyprávění o Leoši Janáčkovi* [Stories about Leoš Janáček] (Velehrad, Olomouc, 1948)

Štědroň, Bohumír: 'Leoš Janáček a Luhačovice', *Vyroční zpráva Městské spořitelny v Luhačovicích za rok 1938* (Luhačovice, 1939)

Štědroň, Bohumír: 'K Janáčkově opeře Osud' [Janáček's opera *Fate*], *Živá hudba*, i (1959), 159–83

Štědroň, Miloš, Frimlová, Lea and Geist, Zdeněk, eds.: *Besední dům: architektura, společnost, kultura* [The Meeting House: architecture, society, culture] (Státní filharmonie Brno and Moravské zemské muzeum, Brno, 1995)

Straková, Theodora: 'Setkání Leoše Janáčka s Gabrielou Preissovou' [The meeting of Leoš Janáček with Gabriela Preissová], *Časopis Moravského musea*, xliii (1958), 145–63

Šujan, František: *Dějepis Brna* [The history of Brno] (Musejní spolek, Brno, enlarged 2/1928)

Tauber, Stanislav: *Můj hudební svět* [My musical world] (Vladimír Hapala, Brno, 1949)

Trkanová, Marie: *U Janáčků: podle vyprávění Marie Stejskalové* [At the Janáčeks: as told by Marie Stejskalová] (Panton, Prague, 1959, 2/1964)

Tyrrell, John: *Czech Opera* (Cambridge University Press, Cambridge, 1988)

Vašek, Adolf. E.: *Po stopách dra Leoše Janáčka* [In the tracks of Dr Leoš Janáček] (Brněnské knižní nakladatelství, Brno, 1930)

Veselý, Adolf, ed.: *Leoš Janáček: pohled do života a díla* [Leoš Janáček: a view of the life and works] (Fr. Borový, Prague, 1924); annotated edition by Theodora Straková in *OM*, xx (1988), 225–47

Vogel, Jaroslav: *Leoš Janáček: Leben und Werk* (Artia, Prague, 1958; Czech original, Státní hudební vydavatelství, Prague, 1963; Eng. trans. abridged, Paul Hamlyn, London, 1962, reprinted Supraphon, 1997; fuller second edition, Orbis, London, 1981, as *Leoš Janáček: a Biography*)

Vrba, Přemysl: 'Ruský kroužek v Brně a Leoš Janáček' [The Russian circle in Brno and Leoš Janáček], *Slezský sborník*, lviii (1960), 71–85

Zřídkaveselý, František: *Nové a změněné názvy ulic v městě Brně 1984–1996* [New and changed names of streets in the town of Brno 1984–96] (Muzejní a vlastivědná společnost, Brno, 1996)

Index

Institutions are indexed under their respective towns or cities.

Index

273

Vladimír (son), 53
religious faith: confirmation, 20; church-
   going, 135, 217, 229; duties, 223; goes
   to confession, 83–4, 157; regains faith,
   157; wishes to pray to miraculous
   Madonna, 73
suicide attempt, 136–7
tries to ban subtitle 'Intimate Letters', 243
trips away (without Janáček): Bad Ischl,
   102; Hukvaldy, 108, 158, 161, 162,
   194, 234, 240; Komárov, 48; Ostrava,
   230; Prague, 128–9, 191; Vienna, 96,
   97, 99, 102, 108, 113, 115, 125, 126,
   132–4, 165, 171, 175, 177, 178, 184,
   221; see also under Janáček family
trips back to Brno (without Janáček), 96,
   97, 103, 115, 134, 174, 177, 178, 236;
   see also under Janáček family
works in garden, 109
see also Janáček family; Schulz family
Jandová, Marie, 52
Janský Vrch, 2
'Jenufa' cigars, 203
Jeritza, Maria, 108, 164–5
Jirka, Dr Jaroslav, 174–5, 203
Johannisberk, 2
Josefka, see Dohnalová, Josefa
Joža, see Janáčková, Josefa
Jungová, Marie, 52

Kallus, Rudolf, 97
Kaluschka [née Axman], Grandmother, 25,
   26, 30, 40, 107; description, 5, 17;
   disapproves of Zdenka's speaking
   Czech, 17; gifts to Zdenka, 19;
   relations with Janáček, 10, 11, 17;
   unable to speak Czech, 17, 19
Kaluschka, Gustav, 1, 26, 40
Kaluschka, Julius, 5, 6, 15, 21
Kalusová, Eliška, 87, 91
Kalusová, Mařenka, 87, 92
Karawanken mountains, 113
Karl, Emperor, 164, 167
Karlovy Vary, 115
Karlštejn, 25, 224
Kleiber, Erich, 202–3
Klement, Karl, 6, 14
Klement family, 14
Klemperer, Otto, 203, 214
Klenka, Dr Eduard, 30
Klíč, Otakar and Jaroslav, 95, 107
Koláčná, Antonie, 114, 116
Kolařík, František, 213
Kolín, 15, 26, 40
Kolísek, Rev. Dr Alois, 143
Komárov, 47, 48, 177, 178, 179, 180, 252
Korcová, Žofie, 206, 217

Kostínková, Thea, 239
Koudelová, Miss, 32
Koudelová, Adéla, 157, 247, 251
Koválovice, 119, 120, 124
Kovařovic, Karel, 96, 127, 152, 247
Královka [Královský mlýn], 47, 252
Krampus, Dr, 239
Krátký, Father Augustin, 37, 83
Křížkovský, Father Pavel, 27, 28, 242
Krk, 112, 113
Krofta, Dr Kamil, 201, 202, 203
Kroměříž, 1, 2, 115; archbishop's park, 1;
   German Realschule, 1
Krsková, Otylie, 234
Krtička, Stanislav, 198–9
Kuhlová, Marie, 57
Kunc, Jan, 109, 181, 205, 247
Kunčice, 212
Kuncová, Mrs, 109
Kupari, 112
Kurzová, Professor Růžena, 205–6
Kurzová-Štěpánová, Ilona, 198, 200, 209
Kusá(-Fantová), Julie, 30, 32, 103, 251
Kusý, Dr Wolfgang, 30
Kutná Hora, 26
Kvapil, Jaroslav, 223

Lašsko, 214, 248
Lederer, Jaroslav, 231
Lehner, Father Ferdinand, 24
Leipzig, 11, 13, 15; Conservatory, 11, 13
Lev, Josef, 25
Lhotský, Josef, 3
Lidové noviny (newspaper), 189, 218, 219
Lipkin-Bennett Quartet, 211
Ljubljana, 113, 195
Lock, Stephen, xix, 255–6
Lolek, Stanislav, 218
London, 199, 200
Lorka, see Janáčková, Eleonora
Lützow, Countess, 200
Luhačovice, 47, 48, 97, 98, 103, 111, 114,
   122, 127, 132, 133, 135, 139, 140,
   141, 147, 158, 159, 162, 178, 179,
   180, 184, 188, 194, 210, 211, 212,
   226, 245, 248, 250
Lwów, 161, 222, 250

Machová, Eliška, 32, 67, 68, 111, 248, 251
Maixner, Dr Emerich, 80
Maixner, Vincenc, 131, 143, 168
Máli, Fräulein (pastrycook), 18
Mářa, see Stejskalová, Marie
Mareš, František, 68, 92–3, 131, 138, 159,
   163, 165, 166, 190, 248, 251
Marie (girlfriend of Janáček's), 47–8
Marie (Zdenka's great-aunt), 5